PATERNOSTER THEOLOGICAL MONOGRAPHS

'The Eyes of Your Heart':

Literary and Theological Trajectories of Imagining Biblically

PATERNOSTER THEOLOGICAL MONOGRAPHS

A full listing of titles in this series and Paternoster Biblical Monographs appears at the end of this book

PATERNOSTER THEOLOGICAL MONOGRAPHS

'The Eyes of Your Heart':

Literary and Theological Trajectories of Imagining Biblically

Alison Searle

Foreword by Luke Ferretter

WIPF & STOCK · Eugene, Oregon

Wipf and Stock Publishers
199 W 8th Ave, Suite 3
Eugene, OR 97401

"The Eyes of Your Heart"
Literary and Theological Trajectories of Imagining Biblically
By Searle, Alison
Copyright©2008 Paternoster
ISBN 13: 978-1-60608-602-5
Publication date 4/10/2009
Previously published by Paternoster, 2008

This Edition reprinted by Wipf and Stock Publishers
by arrangement with Paternoster

PATERNOSTER THEOLOGICAL MONOGRAPHS

Series Preface

In the West the churches may be declining, but theology—serious, academic (mostly doctoral level) and mainstream orthodox in evaluative commitment—shows no sign of withering on the vine. This series of *Paternoster Theological Monographs* extends the expertise of the Press especially to first-time authors whose work stands broadly within the parameters created by fidelity to Scripture and has satisfied the critical scrutiny of respected assessors in the academy. Such theology may come in several distinct intellectual disciplines—historical, dogmatic, pastoral, apologetic, missional, aesthetic and no doubt others also. The series will be particularly hospitable to promising constructive theology within an evangelical frame, for it is of this that the church's need seems to be greatest. Quality writing will be published across the confessions—Anabaptist, Episcopalian, Reformed, Arminian and Orthodox—across the ages—patristic, medieval, reformation, modern and counter-modern—and across the continents. The aim of the series is theology written in the twofold conviction that the church needs theology and theology needs the church—which in reality means theology done for the glory of God.

Series Editors

† David F. Wright, Emeritus Professor of Patristic and Reformed Christianity, University of Edinburgh, Scotland, UK

Trevor A. Hart, Head of School and Principal of St Mary's College School of Divinity, University of St Andrews, Scotland, UK

Anthony N.S. Lane, Professor of Historical Theology and Director of Research, London School of Theology, UK

Anthony C. Thiselton, Emeritus Professor of Christian Theology, University of Nottingham, Research Professor in Christian Theology, University College Chester, and Canon Theologian of Leicester Cathedral and Southwell Minster, UK

Kevin J. Vanhoozer, Research Professor of Systematic Theology, Trinity Evangelical Divinity School, Deerfield, Illinois, USA

For Nathan, Ian and Pam

Contents

Foreword by Luke Ferretter	xiii
Acknowledgements	xv
Abbreviations	xvii
Chapter 1 Introduction	1
Mapping the Terrain	2
Historical Context	2
Theological Context	3
Defining a 'Biblical' View	5
Theologians on the Imagination	11
Logos, Language and Literary Criticism	16
The Holy Spirit and Artistic Inspiration	17
Biblical Perspectives on the Imagination	22
A Brief Synopsis	28
Chapter 2 Towards a Biblical View of the Imagination	31
Defining 'Imagination': Biblical Word Study	32
Problems of Definition and the 'Heart'	36
Imagination Defined	40
The Literary Form of Scripture	45
The Biblical Metanarrative	45
Pluriform Structure and Language	47
Eschatology of Hope	48
Imagination and Faith	49
Inspiration and Creativity	50
Conclusion	57

Chapter 3 A Creative Imagination? John Bunyan and the Pilgrim's Unexpected Progress — 59
Biblical Aesthetics and *The Pilgrim's Progress* — 60
A Biblical Understanding of the Creative Imagination — 71

Chapter 4 The Eye of Faith: Imagination in Relation, the *Letters of Samuel Rutherford* — 80
Biblical Aesthetics and the *Letters of Samuel Rutherford* — 81
The Role of the Realistic Imagination in Communication and Relationships — 94

Chapter 5 The Moral Imagination: Narrative, Character and Hermeneutics in Jane Austen's *Pride and Prejudice* — 107
Biblical Narrative and the Moral Imagination — 113
Literary Form, Moral Imagination and Hermeneutics in *Pride and Prejudice* — 125
Implications for a Biblical Understanding of the Moral Imagination — 138

Chapter 6 An Idolatrous Imagination? Biblical Theology and Romanticism in Charlotte Brontë's *Jane Eyre* — 141
Idolatry — 144
Biblical Balance: The Mediating Imagination — 156
Eschatology and Transcendence — 165

Chapter 7 Intimations of Transcendence: C. S. Lewis and the Eschatological Imagination — 169
Paul Ricoeur on Metaphor and 'Poetic' Language — 170
Lewis on Myth, Metaphor and Joy — 172
Narrative, Metaphor and Imagination in *Till We Have Faces* — 178
Lewis on the Imagination that 'Tastes and Sees' — 187

Chapter 8 Conclusion — 193
'Through a mirror in a riddle': The Visual/Verbal Imagination — 194
'The play's the thing wherein I'll catch the conscience of the king' — 203
Imagining Biblically — 205

Bibliography   **211**

Index   **227**

Foreword

The last thirty years of literary criticism have been characterized by the 'theory revolution'. A dizzying and exciting plethora of philosophical, psychological, sociological and above all political texts and ideas have been brought to bear on the interpretation and even construction of literary and cultural texts of all kinds. In amongst this array of approaches, a discourse that has at best been forgotten, and more frequently despised and denigrated, is that of Christian theology. The more traditional and orthodox the theology, the less it has a place at the contemporary table of literary interpretation. Even in these more recent years of the 'return to religion' in critical theory, this remains true. Searle changes that. This book boldly and unashamedly reads the literary canon as well as the canon of critical theory in the light of Calvinist, evangelical theology. Searle quotes substantial passages from the *Institutes of the Christian Religion* in the early pages of the book, bringing to bear in a truly refreshing way the details of Calvin's thought upon contemporary culture and its critical traditions, without distorting or dismissing those traditions. Alister McGrath speaks of the 'sheer intellectual excitement' of the study of Christian theology.[1] It is this excitement that motivates Searle, and that she communicates on every page to her readers. She quotes Edward Mendelson, who speaks of thinking in 'a different direction' than relentlessly forward, as the still contemporary ideology of progress demands. For Mendelson, however, this direction was backward, a 'return to the resources of the Scriptures and the Christian tradition' in order to understand the contemporary world.[2] Searle, whose thought is informed by Gadamer, amongst many others, knows that this neither possible nor desirable. Her direction is simply different, simply new. It is, in Gadamer's sense, traditional, an understanding of the thought of the past in the light of that of the present and vice versa. In this age of contemporary neo-orthodoxies, nothing could be more welcome or more genuinely needed.

The subject of Searle's study is what she calls 'imagining Biblically'. This phrase means many things, and her study is an exploration of the ways in which

---

[1] Alister McGrath, *Christian Theology: An Introduction*, 4th ed. (Oxford and Malden, MA: Blackwell, 2006), xxi.
[2] See p. 5.

the Biblical texts and modern literary concepts of the imagination inform one another. There are a plethora of these relationships. Searle modestly makes no claim to have exhausted all the resources of her interdisciplinary inquiry, but this book is a formidable step in that direction. Indeed, one of the ways in which Searle's text reflects that of the Bible itself is in its sheer polyvalence, the sheer number of things and kinds of thing that she says within the covers of one book. Readers will find those claims and arguments that attract and persuade them the most. Some will find the detailed lexical study of the Biblical words that can or have been translated in terms of the concept of the imagination particularly valuable. Others will be especially persuaded by Searle's close readings of literary texts, from Bunyan to Brontë. Still others will find her thorough surveys and analyses of the theology and philosophy of the imagination most useful. And these are just a few examples from the many approaches that Searle undertakes in order fully to mine the resources of the meanings of the Biblical text for the theory of the imagination. She writes with equal fluency about typology, eschatology, and teleology. She draws with equal insight upon the thought of Augustine, Jonathan Edwards and Paul Ricoeur. She several times makes the point that her study of the Bible and the imagination is of use to readers who do not share her theological beliefs about the nature of the Bible, and she is right. The many relationships between one of the most fundamental texts and one of the most fundamental concepts of Western literary history are explored here for the benefit of all literary scholars and theologians, whatever their beliefs about the Bible itself.

In Chapter 6, on Charlotte Brontë, Searle argues that Brontë's 'feminism' is 'primarily biblical'.[3] This phrase seems to me rich with potential meanings. One of the values of the chapter on Brontë is that Searle mines from Brontë's work a theory of the imagination that is both Biblical and specifically feminine. She does something similar in her analyses of Samuel Rutherford's correspondents in Chapter 4. Whilst this is little more than a subtext of the present book, it seems to me that Searle has a great deal to tell us about the relationships between evangelical and feminine experience. One can only speculate on the directions her future work will take. What is certain is that the present book is as close to an exhaustive survey of the many relationships between the Biblical texts and the theory of the imagination as we have at present. It will be many years before this ceases to be the most authoritative work in the field.

Luke Ferretter
Baylor University
November 2008

---

[3] See p. 145.

Acknowledgements

I would like to thank many individuals who have given generously of their time and expertise in the course of researching and writing this book. My PhD supervisors, Professor Barry Spurr in the early stages, and Professor Luke Ferretter throughout, read and commented on various drafts of the manuscript. I have very much appreciated their criticism and support. Drs Noel Weeks, Ian O'Harae and Susannah Macready gave generously of their time and theological expertise to comment incisively on the work in progress, as did Dr Margaret Turnbull.

My research was supported by an Australian Postgraduate Award, a Supplementary Scholarship from the College of Humanities and Social Sciences at the University of Sydney and various other grants administered by the University, which I acknowledge with gratitude. These also enabled me to undertake a period of research overseas and I benefited from conversations with Professors John Beer, Jeremy Begbie, David Jasper, Roger Lundin, Alan Jacobs and Kevin Vanhoozer. I am deeply indebted to these scholars for their willingness to discuss literature, biblical studies and the imagination, enabling the development of ideas central to the argument that follows; this is not to suggest that they would endorse all (or any) of the conclusions of this study. I would also like to thank Professors Elisabeth Jay and Roger Lundin and Dr Liam Semler for the stimulating encouragement and critique they provided when examining my PhD thesis.

Earlier versions of sections of several chapters have been published in the journals *Literature and Aesthetics*, *Renascence*, *The Dalhousie Review*, *Christianity and Literature* and a collection of essays, *Oral and Written Narratives and Cultural Identities: Interdisciplinary Approaches*, eds., F. C. Fagundes and I. M. F. Blayer (New York: Peter Lang, 2007). I am grateful to the editors of these publications for permission to use the material here. I would like to thank Dr Anthony Cross of Paternoster for his assistance in preparing the manuscript for publication.

The dedication acknowledges my greatest debt: to Nathan, Ian and Pam.

Alison Searle
Cambridge
November 2008

Abbreviations

ASV American Standard Version

ESV English Standard Version

KJV King James Version

NIV New International Version

NASB New American Standard Bible

RSV Revised Standard Version

Unless otherwise noted, the English Standard Version has been used for all scriptural citations. The King James Version is used in the chapter sections focused upon John Bunyan, Samuel Rutherford, Jane Austen and Charlotte Brontë, as this is the translation that they used and quote from in their writings. I have used the English Standard Version throughout Chapter 7; as C. S. Lewis used a variety of translations, there is no need to quote the King James Version.

Chapter 1

Introduction

In recent decades, much attention has been paid to literary aspects of the Bible, the influence of the Bible on literature, the role of the imagination in theology, together with the need to maintain a closer relationship between the disciplines of literature and theology. Surprisingly, little work has been done on what the Bible itself has to say concerning the imagination and the implications that this has for literature and life. This study explores the concept of what it means to 'imagine biblically': that is, I consider the trajectories opened by an analysis of the biblical text as a literary and religious document and the contribution this makes to an understanding of the imagination. The Bible is, of course, a seminal text in both literary studies and theology in the Western tradition: a fresh examination of the perspectives it offers on so vital and comprehensive a function of human nature as the imagination provides the opportunity to rearticulate and engage with influential aspects of literature and criticism latent within this tradition, which have been suppressed or ignored, to the impoverishment of contemporary dialogue. It holds the potential to reconfigure the ways in which we think about issues like inspiration, faith, creativity, imitation, empathy, moral criticism, and the structure of literary works.

The key terms of this study, the Bible and the imagination, have been the subject of intense debate and broad-ranging discussion, which is often shaped by the parameters of the discipline within which they are being considered, or the individual concerns of the person developing an argument. This is further complicated by the fact that both the biblical text and imagination are implicated in the essentially theological questions about hermeneutics, epistemology and ontology, that have emerged from contemporary literary theory, and brought the human sciences to a place of intellectual crisis.[1] In this Introduction, I will briefly examine some of the ways in which the relationship between the Bible and imagination has been configured, by both theologians and literary critics (the conjunction linking this pairing masks a complex array of potential relationships). The survey is necessarily selective, framed in order to foreground aspects of the biblical text and imagination that are most pertinent to the particular concerns of this study. In the process, I will outline the Evangelical hermeneutic which shapes my reading of the biblical text,

---

[1] This point is made seminally and incisively by Hans Georg Gadamer in *Truth and Method*, 2nd ed. (London: Sheed and Ward, 1975), 241-5.

concluding the argument with a brief overview of the direction that will be pursued in the following chapters.

Mapping the Terrain

Historical Context

Stephen Prickett, in a detailed historical account, traces the separation and consequent inoculation of biblical hermeneutics from literary criticism during the eighteenth and nineteenth centuries.[2] In many respects, the story he tells forms the institutional and cultural context for this consideration of what it means to imagine in terms of the trajectories opened by the biblical text. He considers specifically the 'tenuous but amazingly persistent debate over the past three hundred years on the relationship of poetry to religious language.'[3] In the process, he effectively uncovers the gradual, but decisive rejection of a literalist interpretation of the authority of the Word of God, as understood through an Enlightenment framework, by many of the intellectual elite, particularly proponents of the new Higher Criticism, Romantics in England such as Samuel Taylor Coleridge, and later novelists or poets including George Eliot, Thomas Hardy and Matthew Arnold. Generalising broadly, in Britain a circle of influential critics rejected the old model of biblical authority as divine revelation, effectively instituting a new hermeneutic that reestablished its influence on aesthetic grounds, which invoked the internal acquiescence and submission of the reader. This, simultaneously, became the model and inspiration for a new type of literature and criticism, modulating the broader outline of gradual secularisation proposed by M. H. Abrams under the phrase 'natural supernaturalism.'[4] In Germany, however, there was no such fusion of literary and theological studies. Whilst theology as a discipline was not construed in the same repressive and empiricist terms as it had been in Britain, it was, nevertheless, cut off from its association with literary criticism, enabling the 'poetic' to become an ill-defined category that eventually embraced the whole of the Bible, Shakespeare, and Wagner, as well as other art forms, leaving no effective basis for detailed differentiation and analysis.

Although a recognition of this clear disciplinary segregation, an understanding of its consequences, and an attempt to rectify its deficiencies have become something of a critical commonplace in both disciplines over recent decades, due to the ground-breaking work of scholars such as Prickett,

---

[2] Stephen Prickett, *Words and the Word: Language, Poetics and Biblical Interpretation* (Cambridge: Cambridge University Press, 1986).
[3] Prickett, *Words and the Word*, 3.
[4] M. H. Abrams, *Natural Supernaturalism: Tradition and Revolution in Romantic Literature* (New York: W. W. Norton, 1971).

David Jasper, and T. R. Wright, the contours of the discussion often remain shaped by Enlightenment assumptions concerning the objective nature and authority of biblical criticism, and the implicitly Romantic notion that if the Bible is to have any effective authority for a contemporary reader, it will lie in its aesthetic qualities, as individually appropriated by readers or reading communities. Prickett problematises the cruder implications of such segregation in his critique of the presuppositions lurking within the manifestos of various Bible translators, but an acceptance of the scientific authority of biblical criticism and the necessity for a more subjective, basically Coleridgean, notion of hermeneutics underlies the structure of his entire argument. It is here, despite the indebtedness of Romantic literary theory to the aesthetic qualities of the Bible, that the essential thrust of Abrams's argument retains legitimacy, because the effective locus of authority and initiative has shifted from the revealed, objective Word of a Divine Other, to the subjective apprehension and creative, transforming consciousness of the human subject. The 'closed systems of hermeneutics' characteristic of empiricism that claim 'to possess the Word' are overcome finally not through the action of the Spirit of God, as a theological account would traditionally have rendered it, nor due to its inspired status as the Word of God, but rather by a sensitive openness on the part of those 'capable of being translated by it.'[5]

Prickett itemises the various complications that this division between theology and literary criticism has raised in both disciplines, explicitly noting that the only possibility of resolution lies in a reintegration of their key concerns: 'the German Higher Criticism, nineteenth-century English poetic theory, French twentieth-century discussions of the relationship of author to text, and the American Sapir-Whorf hypothesis in linguistics all have common origins in eighteenth-century debates over poetry and hermeneutics.'[6] It becomes obvious that 'problems that first surfaced in biblical studies have been, and in many cases still are, paradigmatic of wider hermeneutic, epistemological, and linguistic problems.'[7] Given this situation, it is inevitable that exploring the trajectories opened by the biblical text insofar as they inform the concept of imagination will involve forays into numerous disciplines and areas of theological contention. However, this study is conducted on the premise that returning to the roots of literary criticism in biblical studies can open new and productive ways of thinking about the imagination.

Theological Context

In order more specifically to understand the role of the imagination in the historical developments that Prickett traces, and the methodology that underlies

---

[5] Prickett, *Words and the Word*, 242.
[6] Prickett, *Words and the Word*, 3.
[7] Prickett, *Words and the Word*, 2-3.

the biblical perspective deployed here, it is necessary to turn to a complementary, but different analysis of our contemporary 'culture of interpretation' by Roger Lundin. Like Prickett, Lundin starts with the present, though with the more overt intention of taking 'an account of contemporary culture by exploring the historical background to some of its central beliefs and by considering the ethical and theological implications of those beliefs.'[8] It is this explicitly theological dimension that distinguishes his account from that of Prickett. In Lundin's work both the Enlightenment and the Romantic movement are seen to share a

> distinct perspective upon the place of the self in nature and society. Both emphasized the self as an entity in isolation, equipped in its solitude with a panoply of powers. In the Enlightenment...faith was centered upon rationality as the instrument of power, while in romanticism it was the intuition or imagination that promised to deliver humans from their bondage to ignorance and injustice.[9]

The postmodern response to the failure of 'rationality and the imagination' to 'supply certain access to the truth' is, in the oft-quoted words of Jean-François Lyotard, an 'incredulity toward metanarratives,' and the celebration of a solipsistic or therapeutic narcissism, which enables the dethroned (post)modern subject to create its own reality, shaped by and accountable to nothing other than the desires of the heart. It is the alternative approach, implicit to a degree in Prickett, which Lundin enumerates, that forms an essential presupposition of this study: one 'may turn – or return...to the Bible, to the church, and to tradition for the truth.'[10]

Lundin traces the problematic shift from modernism to postmodernism, noting that while the latter shares the scepticism of the biblical text about the power of the self to apprehend truth, it nevertheless holds to a 'romantic understanding of the self.' The imagination is no longer a means by which one 'discovers' the objective reality of the external world, nor in Kantian terms does it 'create' an inner world that corresponds to objects beyond the self. Rather, it is the function through which the postmodernist standing 'alone in nature, defying demands upon the self and searching for that which will satisfy...no longer harbors hopes of discovering truth or secure principles. Instead, driven by the ideals of therapy and consumption, it seeks, by whatever means will work, to provide satisfactions for the unencumbered self.' Morality is no longer regulated by authoritative guidelines or principles; it becomes an issue of personal preference. Ultimately 'there is no goal for the actions of the

---

[8] Roger Lundin, *The Culture of Interpretation: Christian Faith and the Postmodern World* (Grand Rapids: Eerdmans, 1993), 2.
[9] Lundin, *The Culture of Interpretation*, 5.
[10] Lundin, *The Culture of Interpretation*, 4-6.

Introduction

self save the fulfillment of its desires.'[11]

These conclusions are a theological assessment of the epistemological, cultural and ethical implications of the Enlightenment project for the self and the imagination. Theorists of the imagination, whether theologians or literary critics, often attempt a kind of median position between Romantic confidence in the self and the relativist anarchism of the postmodern imagination, concerned particularly with the implications for traditional understandings of objective truth. These have much to offer and some will be explored shortly. However, their presuppositions are inherently problematic from a methodological perspective, and while this study will draw upon their rich insights, it differs fundamentally on the point of departure. It is not a matter of moving beyond the modern or indeed the postmodern 'as the idiom of progress would suggest.'[12] The next step is 'one that moves in a different direction...a return to the resources of the Scriptures and the Christian tradition for the purpose of formulating creative responses to the impasses and needs of the contemporary world.'[13] Below I outline the hermeneutic that informs my reading of the biblical text as I explore the concept of what it means to imagine biblically. It also acts as the reference point from which I assess the various attempts of theologians and literary critics to consider the imagination theologically later in this Introduction. In the process of considering this literature, I shall also indicate points that I intend to develop in subsequent chapters.

Defining a 'Biblical' View

This study considers what the biblical text as a whole, read within the context of the hermeneutical tradition assumed, has to say concerning the imagination and specifically its points of intersection with literary studies. The approach taken in this study can be briefly described as 'Calvinist' or 'Evangelical.' It is still a lively tradition, with a thoroughly engaged supporting scholarship. Additionally, in historical terms, it represents the approach of a broad cross-section of readers within Western culture to the text, thus providing a useful contextualisation for authors like John Bunyan, Samuel Rutherford, Jane Austen and Charlotte Brontë, who shared its primary assumptions.[14] In this

---

[11] Lundin, *The Culture of Interpretation*, 5-6, 53-4, 75. The emphasis on 'therapy' in Lundin's analysis is more relevant to American than Continental European varieties of postmodern theory.

[12] Edward Mendelson cited by Lundin, *The Culture of Interpretation*, 184.

[13] Lundin, *The Culture of Interpretation*, 183-4.

[14] C. S. Lewis is the only exception amongst the authors considered in this book. For a detailed analysis of his view of Scripture see Michael J. Christensen, *C. S. Lewis on Scripture: His Thoughts on the Nature of Biblical Inspiration, the Role of Revelation and the Question of Inerrancy* (London: Hodder and Stoughton, 1980).

section I outline the basic premises that undergird and frame the reading of the biblical text in the chapters that follow.

The biblical text was recognised by the early Church Fathers generally to be the verbally inspired and authoritative Word of God.[15] During the sixteenth-century Reformation this was emphasised freshly under the popular slogan *sola scriptura* and embraced by almost all the different Protestant groups. The essence of their position is usefully summarised in John Calvin's *Institutes of the Christian Religion* (1559), Bk 1, Sections 6-9. Calvin states that the autographs of Scripture are inerrant;[16] their authority consists in the fact that they are the very Word of God, not in the value attributed to them by the church.[17] They are essential to a true knowledge of God, as creation, while it speaks clearly and comprehensively of God as Creator, is insufficient to lead individuals to the truth.

> For as the aged, or those whose sight is defective, when any book however fair, is set before them, though they perceive that there is something written are scarcely able to make out two consecutive words, but, when aided by glasses, begin to read distinctly, so Scripture, gathering together the impressions of Deity, which, till then, lay confused in our minds, dissipates the darkness, and shows us the true God clearly. God therefore bestows a gift of singular value, when, for the instruction of the Church, he employs not dumb teachers merely, but opens his own sacred mouth; when he not only proclaims that some God must be worshipped, but at the same time declares that He is the God to whom worship is due; when he not only teaches his elect to have respect to God, but manifests himself as the God to whom this respect should be paid.[18]

Human beings in a fallen condition are unable rightly to perceive God, the world and their relation to it, without the Scriptures.[19] But, while the Scriptures contain adequate testimony in themselves to the fact that they are the Word of God: 'Scripture bears upon the face of it as clear evidence of its truth, as white and black do of their colour, sweet and bitter of their taste;'[20] this is only affirmed by the reader, when they know the inner confirming work of the Holy Spirit.[21] Thus, Calvin asserts, while there are proofs that can be given to natural reason that the biblical text is the Word of God,[22] no one will be persuaded of this, due to the radical fallenness of human nature, unless granted divine

---

[15] Clark H. Pinnock, *The Scriptural Principle* (San Francisco: Harper & Row, 1984), x.
[16] John Murray, *Calvin on Scripture and Divine Sovereignty* (Philadelphia: Presbyterian and Reformed Publishing, 1960), 11-31.
[17] John Calvin, *Institutes of the Christian Religion*, Vol. 1, trans. Henry Beveridge (Edinburgh: Calvin Translation Society, 1845), 1.7.1-4.
[18] Calvin, *Institutes of the Christian Religion*, 1.6.1.
[19] Calvin, *Institutes of the Christian Religion*, 1.6.1-4.
[20] Calvin, *Institutes of the Christian Religion*, 1.7.2.
[21] Calvin, *Institutes of the Christian Religion*, 1.7.1-5.
[22] Calvin, *Institutes of the Christian Religion*, 1.8.1-13.

Introduction

assistance.

> Let it therefore be held as fixed, that those who are inwardly taught by the Holy Spirit acquiesce implicitly in Scripture; that Scripture carrying its own evidence along with it, deigns not to submit to proofs and arguments, but owes the full conviction with which we ought to receive it to the testimony of the Spirit. Enlightened by him, we no longer believe, either on our own judgement or that of others, that the Scriptures are from God; but, in a way superior to human judgement, feel perfectly assured – as much so as if we beheld the divine image visibly impressed on it – that it came to us, by the instrumentality of men, from the very mouth of God. We ask not for proofs or probabilities on which to rest our judgement, but we subject our intellect and judgement to it as too transcendent for us to estimate.[23]

Calvin's confidence in the authority and inerrancy of the Word of God underlies the literary work of almost every author who will be examined in the course of this book. It is therefore critically relevant to examine this traditional doctrine in order to provide an historical context, but it is also pertinent to the formulation of a concept of the imagination defined in terms of the trajectories opened up by the biblical text, as its theological presuppositions are incorporated in the hermeneutic approach to Scripture utilised at the level of theoretical analysis. There has been a consistent tradition of scholarship developing and elaborating this faith commitment to the unity and authority of the Bible in the face of consistent challenges offered by other disciplines such as the natural sciences, historical-critical scholarship, and more recently, philosophy and literary theory. It is impossible to provide more than a cursory survey of the relevant literature here. The classic statement of the doctrine, 'that the Bible is, in its *autographa*, the infallible Word of God',[24] in the modernist era was provided by Princeton theologian, Benjamin Warfield, in a series of articles that have been collected in *The Inspiration and Authority of the Bible*. He traces its history as a fundamental conviction of the Christian church;[25] comprehensively elaborates how Scripture testifies to itself as the Word of God;[26] demonstrates the ways in which it is the revelation of God;[27] outlines that it is an essential premise for all clear thinking and doctrinal propositions, and sustainable, despite the higher criticism emerging in the nineteenth-century.[28]

In philosophical terms, Warfield's defence of the doctrine has been extended

---

[23] Calvin, *Institutes of the Christian Religion*, 1.7.5.
[24] B. B. Warfield, *The Inspiration and Authority of the Bible* (Philadelphia: Presbyterian and Reformed Publishing, 1948), 3.
[25] Warfield, *The Inspiration and Authority of the Bible*, 105-28.
[26] Warfield, *The Inspiration and Authority of the Bible*, 131-66, 245-407.
[27] Warfield, *The Inspiration and Authority of the Bible*, 71-102.
[28] Warfield, *The Inspiration and Authority of the Bible*, 169-226.

and supplemented by Cornelius Van Til, in a lengthy introduction to Warfield's articles and other subsequent publications.[29] Similarly, John Murray has concisely examined Calvin's doctrine of Scripture and extended its insights through dialogue with the neo-orthodox approach of Karl Barth.[30] Other issues, such as the possibility of a unified interpretation of canonical Scripture, and its historical authority, have been analysed in the wake of a recent engagement between biblical scholarship and literary studies. F. F. Bruce has discussed the critical material surrounding issues of the canon, concluding that:

> Today indeed there has been a tendency...to emphasize the differences among the New Testament writers to a point where their common and fundamental witness to Jesus as Lord has been overlooked. But this unity of witness is a unity in diversity, and it is the province of exegesis to bring out the diversity within the comprehensive unity.[31]

The approach taken towards the biblical text necessarily incorporates a view of God, human beings, the world; the way in which communication occurs; epistemology; hermeneutics; essentially an entire worldview.[32] Thus, to refer back to Bruce, whether or not the biblical canon is seen as a unified whole, forming authoritative Scripture, or alternatively if it is understood to be an eclectic collection of disparate texts that need to be deconstructed, has significant implications for the concept of imagination developed on the basis of this text as a literary and religious document. This moves one into the realm of hermeneutics, the issues are no longer so much: 'Is this what the original text really said?' or even, 'What does it mean for these words to be the Word of God?,' as 'What is a text?', 'How does it mean?', 'What is the relationship between interpretation and truth?' and so on. There is a close link here between the disciplines of biblical criticism and literary studies. As Prickett noted, the questions first asked in the discipline of biblical criticism are now being asked of all texts. This raises issues of philosophical and theological import.

Recent developments in 'postmodern' literary theory have posed a serious challenge to determinate meaning. Deconstructionism particularly, in its various permutations, with its radical philosophy of language and implicit theological claims, has prompted a rich and variegated response from some literary critics and theologians who have attempted to address the concerns it raises from a broadly biblical perspective. Valentine Cunningham has offered a witty and persuasive response to postmodern theorists, reiterating the

---

[29] "Introduction," 3-71, Warfield, *The Inspiration and Authority of the Bible*. For example, Cornelius Van Til, *The Protestant Doctrine of Scripture* (Phildalephia: den Dulk Christian Foundation, 1967).
[30] Murray, *Calvin on Scripture and Divine Sovereignty*.
[31] F. F. Bruce, *The Canon of Scripture* (Downers Grove: InterVarsity Press, 1988), 333.
[32] J. I. Packer, *Honouring the Written Word of God: The Collected Shorter Writings of J. I. Packer, Volume 3* (Carlisle: Paternoster Press, 1999), 3.

Introduction

importance of textual contexts, the inextricable connections between word and world, and the importance of a tactful close-reading of texts in the aftermath of an abundance of theorising.[33] Luke Ferretter, in the process of outlining a Christian literary theory rooted in Scripture, addresses the complex range of issues raised by Marxism, psychoanalysis and poststructuralism from a biblical perspective.[34]

Kevin J. Vanhoozer engages with the challenge to determinate meaning posed by modernism and postmodernism alike from the context of theological hermeneutics. He analyses the arguments put forward by Jacques Derrida, Stanley Fish and others, drawing upon their insights, but noting that a degree of arrogance is implicit in the august and definitive claim that one cannot deduce meaning from a text. He counters the issues posed by deconstructive literary theory, or the 'hermeneutics of suspicion', with an Augustinian approach, drawn primarily from *On Christian Doctrine*.[35] This recognises the philosophical and theological depths which deconstruction sounds, situating matters of textuality, reading, power and knowledge within a broader relational context, and urging for a substitution of suspicion with faith, when dealing with texts and people.

> I defend the belief that we can come to know something other than ourselves when we peer into the mirror of the text....Augustine['s]...writings provide considerable guidance in the endeavour to formulate the theology that funds a Christian morality of literary knowledge....[L]anguage...is the preeminent instrument for cultivating personal relationships, between one human and another and between humanity and God. As such, language is a kind of semantic sacrament, a means of communicating through verbal signs...."The knowledge is superior to the sign simply because it is the end towards which the latter is the means"....Readers who treat the text as a mirror onto which they project their own devices and desires fail to distinguish author from reader and so fall prey to interpretive idolatry. Finally, with regard to the morality of literary understanding,

---

[33] Valentine Cunningham, *In the Reading Gaol: Postmodernity, Texts and History* (Oxford: Blackwell, 1994); *Reading After Theory* (Oxford: Blackwell, 2002). He further examines overlaps between postmodern readings, negative theology and the appropriation of Scripture by believers in "The Best Canons in the Best Order? Canons, Apocryphas and (Post)Modern Reading," *Literature and Theology* 14.1 (2000), 69-80. For an exploration of Christian unreason that engages with Derrida see John Schad, *Queer Fish: Christian Unreason from Darwin to Derrida* (Brighton: Sussex Academic Press, 2004).

[34] Luke Ferretter, *Towards a Christian Literary Theory* (London: Palgrave Macmillan, 2003).

[35] This study is obviously indebted to Augustine's theology, particularly his discussion of language and desire; constraints of subject-matter and space prevent me from exploring this in more detail. For a recent analysis of these aspects of his theology see Elena Lombardi, *The Syntax of Desire: Language and Love in Augustine, the Modistae, Dante* (Toronto: University of Toronto Press, 2007).

Augustine advocates what is for him the prime hermeneutical virtue, namely, charity....Life together is largely a matter of interpretation....The Golden Rule, for hermeneutics and ethics alike, is to treat significant others—texts, persons, God—with love and respect.[36]

This hermeneutic is the one that I seek to adopt in approaching the biblical text and the literary texts of the various authors considered in order to develop the concept of what it means to imagine, defined in terms of the literary and theological trajectories opened by the biblical text. It is framed by a relational understanding of language, which entails an ethical dimension to the acts of reading, writing, and interpretation.

The strictly theological dimension of these processes in the context of contemporary pluralism is discussed by Don Carson in *The Gagging of God: Christianity Confronts Pluralism*,[37] which begins by analysing the revolution in epistemology, theology and literary criticism that has undermined the claims of traditional 'metanarratives' in postmodern Western culture. Carson responds with an articulation of the biblical plotline, focused on the person of Jesus Christ. This understanding of the scriptural canon as a narrative unity, forming a persuasive metanarrative, is the interpretative framework within which this study will be conducted, structuring the reading of the biblical text when exploring various dimensions of the imagination.

The ethical aspects of interpretation and the concept of hermeneutic responsibility, articulated in broad theological terms by Vanhoozer, are brought more directly into the sphere of imagination, fictional texts and literary criticism, by Roger Lundin and his collaborators in *Disciplining Hermeneutics: Interpretation in Christian Perspective*.[38] These critics utilise speech act theory

---

[36] Kevin J. Vanhoozer, *Is There a Meaning in This Text? The Bible, the Reader and the Morality of Literary Knowledge* (Leicester: Apollos, 1998), 31-2. This can be compared productively with Kevin Mill's exploration of Paul's New Testament epistles and his elaboration of 'the work of faith, hope and love in language...showing how they disrupt the assumptions and mores of contemporary modes of interpretation.' Kevin Mills, *Justifying Language: Paul and Contemporary Literary Theory* (Houndmills: Macmillan, 1995), 177 and passim.

[37] D. A. Carson, *The Gagging of God: Christianity Confronts Pluralism* (Grand Rapids: Zondervan, 1996).

[38] Roger Lundin, ed, *Disciplining Hermeneutics: Interpretation in Christian Perspective* (Leicester: Apollos, 1997). See also the hermenutic approach outlined by Richard B. Hayes in *The Conversion of the Imagination: Paul as Interpreter of Israel's Scripture* (Cambridge: Eerdmans, 2005). Johannes Nissen elaborates further on the perspectives delineated by Vanhoozer and Hays, integrating an exploration of hermeneutic approaches to Scripture with a consideration of the analogical imagination and the development of biblical ethics. Johannes Nissen, "Bible and Ethics: Moral Formation and Analogical Imagination," *Theology and Literature: Rethinking Reader Responsibility*, eds. Gaye Williams Ortiz and Clara A. B. Joseph (Houndmills: Palgrave Macmillan, 2006), 81-100.

as a means of substantialising ethics as a crucial dimension of interpretation. They also offer a way in which the implications of the biblical text (necessarily as interpreted) can be used to understand the imagination, particularly as it relates to literary studies. Similarly, the metaphor of performance has recently been adopted in the field of theological hermeneutics in order to elucidate the process of interpreting and applying Scripture and the relationship between the biblical text and doctrine.[39] This metaphor has also been deployed productively to explore the relationship between theology and the arts in ways that have important ramifications for my attempt to develop a concept of imagining biblically deduced from Scripture.[40]

In brief then, I am drawing on the Evangelical tradition of an inerrant and authoritative view of the biblical text, understood in terms of its own articulated hermeneutic to be the Word of God. This entails reading the canon as a holistic text, providing a comprehensive worldview expressed in narrative terms, which will frame all aspects of the following discussion and condition the particular interpretation of specific passages. As mentioned earlier, this view of Scripture is shared by all but one of the authors I am considering, so it provides a viable theoretical framework for dialogue between the biblical and literary texts under consideration, as I explore aspects of what it means to imagine biblically. While this tradition is foreign to many contemporary literary critics, the Bible and its study form the historical context for contemporary literary studies and the whole burgeoning discipline of hermeneutics. It is therefore suggestive and fruitful to return to the foundational text of Western literary culture and see what light such an analysis sheds on the imagination.

Theologians on the Imagination

In an amusing variation on the popular argument of historical and political 'suppression' as a grounds for bringing in a voice or perspective not acknowledged in contemporary scholarship, theologian Helmut Thielicke notes: 'it seldom seems to have occurred to anyone to investigate the element of suppression in the principle of self-resting finitude and the irrelevance of the transcendent.' Is it possible that the ultimately suppressed 'other' of contemporary society, thought and scholarship, is in fact God himself? Such a possibility, if entertained seriously, does not simply entail a diplomatic readjustment of competing voices in the polyphony of the academy, as given the nature of the Person thus rigidly suppressed, 'dominant schools of thought in...different fields [would be] dramatically flawed in a foundational sense.'[41]

---

[39] Kevin J. Vanhoozer, *The Drama of Doctrine: A Canonical Linguistic Approach to Christian Theology* (Louisville: Westminster John Knox, 2005).
[40] Trevor A. Hart and Steven R. Guthrie, eds., *Faithful Performances: Enacting Christian Tradition* (Aldershot: Ashgate, 2007).
[41] Helmut Thielicke cited by Lundin, *The Culture of Interpretation*, 177-8.

That is why the methodology of this study must be conceived as a step in another direction, returning, rather than moving beyond. The pertinence and repercussion of these issues upon the project in hand can be demonstrated by considering a rather extreme example.

Geoffrey Kaufman, in *The Theological Imagination*, asserts that it is impossible to begin with Scripture if one desires properly to understand God, as the Bible itself is seen to be implicated in the perpetration of various politically incorrect crimes he finds objectionable. He argues that individuals are responsible imaginatively to construct an alternative that better suits the human condition, itself the criterion by which it was initially established that the biblical idea of God was false.[42] He exemplifies a tendency to privilege imagination at the expense of any authoritative biblical revelation, which finds subtler modifications in the work of David Bryant, Kathleen Fischer, Paul Avis and others.[43] For the purposes of this inquiry, positing an anthropocentric human imagination in opposition to Scripture is an invalid approach at the foundational level.

David Bryant attempts to refine Kaufman's implicit definition of imagination and render it less anarchic by establishing a dialogic relationship with Christian tradition. However, his unwillingness to treat the Bible as the ultimate authority creates an unresolved dichotomy. On the one hand, there is a persuasive case for an imagination thoroughly informed by the biblical text, and, on the other, the postulation of Hans Georg Gadamer's 'fusion of horizons,' which in his hands results in a relativism unconditioned by any criteria for discriminating what is acceptable and what is not.[44] Here Bryant demonstrates affinities with Amos Wilder in his groundbreaking exploration, *Theopoetic*, which for the theological milieu of its time, emphasised quite radically the centrality of imagination to being, worship and apologetics. Wilder's plea for a deep engagement with contemporary secular culture is salutary, but again, his syncretistic approach, while paying more respect to the biblical witness than Bryant, undermines its unique claim to authority. Imagination unrestricted is given free reign: a small attempt is made to come to terms with the biblical emphasis on sin, and its real effects on human imagining and creativity, but this is neither comprehensive, nor sufficient.[45] Dealing with the possibility of evil uses of the imagination remains problematic for those

---

[42] Geoffrey Kaufman, *The Theological Imagination: Constructing the Concept of God* (Philadelphia: Westminster Press, 1981), 14-16.

[43] Paul Avis, *God and the Creative Imagination: Metaphor, Symbol and Myth in Religion and Theology* (London: Routledge, 1999); David J. Bryant, *Faith and the Play of Imagination: On the Role of Imagination in Religion* (Macon: Mercer University Press, 1989); Kathleen R. Fischer, *The Inner Rainbow: The Imagination in the Christian Life* (New York: Paulist Press, 1983).

[44] Bryant, *Faith and the Play of Imagination*.

[45] Amos Wilder, *Theopoetic: Theology and the Religious Imagination* (Philadelphia: Fortress Press, 1976).

who seek to combine an optimistic Romantic celebration of the power of imagination, with the moral imperatives of Scripture, whether on aesthetic or other grounds.[46] The necessity of holding together the essential unity of the biblical text in its propositional, ethical and aesthetic elements, if one is to develop a truly biblical understanding of the imagination as an aspect of human nature, is explored in the following chapter.

Garrett Green seeks to bridge the gap between imagination and authoritative revelation on a philosophical basis, through his development of 'the paradigmatic imagination.' The terminology of his title *Imagining God* is reminiscent of Kaufman, but the theological enterprise he outlines is very different. Green deploys discoveries in the philosophy of science, such as Thomas Kuhn's concept of paradigm shifts, and the *Gestalt* theory of Ludwig Wittgenstein, to argue that all beliefs, despite the positivist contentions of the Enlightenment, are taken on trust. Data is inevitably theory-laden, because what we see and how we see it are determined by the holistic perspective that informs our consciousness. The issue here is not the persuasiveness or otherwise of Green's thesis, but rather its implications for his understanding of imagination. Following Paul Ricoeur, he suggests that it is necessary for theologians to adopt a 'second naiveté' in their approach to Scripture. This involves recognising the claims of historical-critical scholarship concerning the authorship and transmission of the Bible, and reconstruing its authority in a new way. Instead of being valued as the inerrant, 'breathed out' Word of God, it becomes a canonical paradigm informing the imagination of believers so thoroughly that it acts as the determining framework by which they interpret the world and direct their lives.[47] This grants a degree of authority and integrity to the biblical text, but it still presents some problems. Green's appeal to the cohesive shaping power of a biblically informed imagination implicitly denies Scripture's own testimony to its authority, which is conceptual and historical as well. In addition, he fails thoroughly to resolve the dichotomy between reason and imagination that troubles both Bryant and Wilder, by neglecting the more rational dimensions of belief and practical application.

The potential implications of this indeterminacy find clearer expression in the work of Kathleen Fischer and Paul Avis, who share similar presuppositions to Green about the biblical text and also advocate a 'second naiveté' when

---

[46] A similar difficulty lies in David Jasper's use of Coleridge's distinction between 'fancy' and 'imagination' in order to overcome the same kind of problems in his discussion of literary imagination and the New Testament in *The New Testament and the Literary Imagination* (London: Macmillan, 1987), 84-6.

[47] Garrett Green, *Imagining God: Theology and the Religious Imagination* (Grand Rapids: William B. Eerdmans, 1989). It is an approach shared by Luke Timothy Johnson, "Imagining the World Scripture Imagines," *Theology and Scriptural Imagination*, eds. L. Gregory Jones and James J. Buckley (Oxford: Blackwell, 1998), 3-18.

engaging with it.⁴⁸ In *The Hidden Rainbow*, Fischer allows the meanings of 'imagination' and 'faith' and the relationship subsisting between them to remain obscure. Like Bryant, she asserts the need for an imagination faithfully informed by the biblical text, but couples this with borrowings from process theologians like Alfred Whitehead, who argue that God needs to be renamed for the current generation. Given the context provided by her persuasive analysis of the intricate role that images play in our consciousness this is a telling move. It is impossible to create new names and images for God, without completely reconfiguring our understanding of his Person, since the language in which human beings speak of God is inescapably analogical. The invitation to make new names or, as Whitehead suggests, choose from among the biblical images that seem most appropriate, is, according to Scripture, idolatry. Fischer herself earlier notes the need to hold all biblical images of God simultaneously in play, in order to prevent the occurrence of mental idolatry.⁴⁹ Otherwise, 'God' becomes simply a counter conceived according to the image and likeness of the creature (Romans 1:21-23). The kind of imaginative adherence to Scripture that Green postulates lacks the necessary clarity of definition to inoculate against such tendencies. As a consequence, the imperatives of contemporary theory or philosophy can easily assume a preeminent role in shaping the imagination, over and above the witness of Scripture.⁵⁰

Paul Avis has a more adventurous philosophical agenda than Fischer in his book, *God and the Creative Imagination*. He identifies imagination as central to all Christian experience and seeks to construct an understanding of truth that moves beyond the reductive positivism spawned by Enlightenment theology. To this end he draws upon the Romantics, particularly Coleridge, William Wordsworth and Henry Newman, redefining myth, symbol and metaphor in order to establish an 'imaginative truth.' While he is more sensitive than Green to the differences between imagination and faith, his fine distinctions render the adoption of even a 'second naiveté' when approaching Scripture a complex business. His literary analysis is superb, but the theological and practical conclusions he seeks to draw from it are intensely problematic from a biblical perspective. One is left wondering to what extent the historical veracity of the gospels, particularly the incarnation and resurrection of Jesus Christ, become a

---

⁴⁸ Fischer, *The Inner Rainbow*; Avis, *The Creative Imagination*.
⁴⁹ Fischer, *The Inner Rainbow*, 110-27.
⁵⁰ This observation does not negate the fact that all readers inevitably approach the text with presuppositions that shape the process of reading and interpretation. It is simply attempting to acknowledge that certain reading strategies are more prone to 'appropriate' the text for their own agenda than others. Imagination is always a central component of the reading process, different constructions of its role in relation to text and reader, have significant hermeneutic implications. For a persuasive argument of the case that alternative readings and roles cannot be reductively understood in terms of power see Vanhoozer, *Is There a Meaning in This Text?*, 148-95, 367-452; Anthony Thiselton, *Interpreting God and the Postmodern Self* (Edinburgh: T & T Clark, 1995).

matter of personal experience and discernment. Their real power is located in the influence of their narration as 'myth' upon lives now, rather than in the faithfulness of their witness to actual historical events. This does not sit easily alongside the tangible and evangelistic testimony of the apostle John:

> That which was from the beginning, which we have heard, which we have seen with our eyes, which we looked upon and have touched with our hands, concerning the word of life – the life was made manifest, and we have seen it and testify to it and proclaim to you....These are written so that you may believe that Jesus is the Christ, the Son of God, and that believing you may have life in his name (1 John 1:1-2; John 20:31)

This critique draws a distinction between myth and historical veracity, which much of Avis's argument is designed to deconstruct. He explicitly positions himself in the line of Romantic literary critics and theologians, producing an account of biblical authority and the role of the imagination where the final point of reference is located in the ability of the imaginative self to respond to the aesthetic qualities of the biblical text. This is essentially the position adopted by David Jasper in *The New Testament and the Literary Imagination*. Such denials of the importance of historical reference and verisimilitude are legitimately open to the wry challenge issued by T. S. Eliot: 'Those who talk of the Bible as a 'monument of English prose' are merely admiring it as a monument over the grave of Christianity....[T]he Bible has had literary influence not because it has been considered as literature, but because it has been considered as the report of the Word of God.'[51] The concept of truth in relation to a text as complex and literary as the Bible obviously cannot be simply equated with rational assent, and needs to incorporate the role of imagination in interpretation and appropriation. However, Avis's concluding explication of the way in which one may affirm faith in the Bible or Christian creeds with integrity is far more equivocal than Scripture warrants:

> The figurative language of the creed, based on the normative images of scripture, is...intended to be cognitive though not veridical. It is realist but not definitive. It denotes but does not describe. It speaks the truth but not literally. As metaphor, symbol and myth of the identity of Jesus with God, the incarnational doctrine of the creed is something which (in a realist but not literalist sense) we can and should gladly believe.[52]

Avis's argument, like that of John Coulson in *Religion and Imagination*,[53] is

---

[51] T. S. Eliot, "Religion and Literature," *Selected Essays* (New York: Harcourt, Brace & World, 1964), 344-45.
[52] Avis, *The Creative Imagination*, 174.
[53] John Coulson, *Religion and Imagination: 'in Aid of a Grammar of Assent'* (Oxford: Oxford University Press, 1981).

implicated in tensions inherent in adopting the Romantic hermeneutic of Victorian forbears, such as Matthew Arnold, where biblical inspiration remains located in the creative imagination of the individual self. Defining the language of religion and Scripture as 'poetic' provides helpful insights into the way in which it operates upon the reader and is a reminder of the necessity for a sensitive and astute reading practice. But, underneath this 'literary' approach to Scripture, evident in Fischer also, is an attempt to naturalise the concept of divine revelation, through the use of psychoanalysis to explain conversion and sanctification, or by deploying Romantic concepts of language and the imagination as these mediate the relationship between human beings and the world. Avis employs this Romantic tradition deliberately, in Fischer it remains implicit. The power of Scripture as an authoritative and transformational text is located in its distinctive literary qualities, and these are rendered effective in the life of an individual by the activating power of the human imagination. Avis radically inverts the theological assumptions of deconstruction and invests the actual words of Scripture and liturgy with a sacramental, almost magical quality. Fischer tends to focus upon the imagination as the faculty by which the temporal, physical world is rendered sacred.

Logos, Language and Literary Criticism

The biblical doctrines that lie behind such discussion are primarily those of creation, the incarnation and the eucharist. Theologians and literary critics often move by analogy from Christ as the Word made flesh, to the words of Scripture. Longstanding theological traditions lie behind such analyses, and this analogy between the divine-human relation and hermeneutics is integral to many configurations of the relationship between imagination and the Bible. David Brown and Ann Loades extend this analogical notion and explore it more thoroughly when introducing *Christ: The Sacramental Word*. There is a danger, however, in equating the lexicographical signifier too closely with that which is signified, as it can lead to a kind of idolatry of the word or text fetishism. Metaphor, image and narrative, by their very nature facilitate readings of great richness, but this does not render all the discoveries of a creative allusiveness either enlightening or appropriate. As in the parallel between 'intensive' and 'extensive' definitions of the 'poetic' which Prickett shows ultimately tend to collapse into one another,[54] so an intense devotion to the aesthetic depth and opacity of the written text results in a reading process remarkably similar to the 'hermetic' hermeneutics of deconstructionists.[55] Language, or the particular textual artefact under consideration, in its self-referential opacity, eventually assumes the functions of deity. Thus, Jasper can

---

[54] Prickett, *Words and the Word*, 201-2.
[55] I am indebted to Vanhoozer for the use of this theological term in characterising such reading practices. Vanhoozer, *Is There a Meaning in This Text?*, 122-3.

conclude that there is no real distinction between the Bible as the Word of God and a personal knowledge of Jesus Christ, despite denying the fact that the New Testament refers in any real sense to historical persons and places; for it is the text that matters. It bears an eerie familiarity to the Derridean aphorism: 'There is nothing beyond the text.'[56]

An obsession with the sign (literal or metaphoric) can render it opaque, particularly when words are graphically recorded and thus assume a more permanent status that enables them to be considered apart from their original context. George Steiner offers a more persuasive thesis in *Real Presences*, focusing on the performative dimension of creative works of art, he suggests that such acts of communication themselves attest to the existence of God. The very process of writing implies a Pascalian wager upon transcendence: before speech, there is being.[57] The importance of recognising a relational context in all acts of communication, whether spoken or written, with a carefully nuanced understanding of the connection between author and text, signifier and signified, has been developed by a number of theologians, including Kevin Vanhoozer, Trevor Hart and Nicholas Wolterstorff. Their arguments integrate the insights of deconstructionist and speech-act theory, within a clear biblical context, positioning imagination centrally as the means by which a text is read, interpreted and understood: the ethical high-ground is taken from deconstructionists, who continually assert the need for the other to speak, while simultaneously affirming that it is impossible for any self to transcend its own solipsistic understanding of the world.[58]

The Holy Spirit and Artistic Inspiration

Some of the difficulties that arise when considering the relationship between word and being can be resolved by moving the focus from Jesus Christ as the *logos* to the person of the Holy Spirit. This draws the discussion into an explicitly theological dimension. However, as Prickett observes, the inspiration and interpretation of the scriptural text in biblical studies has been paradigmatic, whether directly acknowledged or not, when considering the

---

[56] Jasper, *The New Testament and the Literary Imagination*, 20, 71. This is not surprising given that Jasper's subsequent work engages far more explicitly with deconstructionist literary theory.
[57] George Steiner, *Real Presences: Is There Anything in What We Say?* (London: Faber and Faber, 1989), 3.
[58] Vanhoozer, *Is There a Meaning in This Text?*; Trevor Hart, "Imagination and Responsible Reading," *Renewing Biblical Interpretation*, eds. Colin Greene, Craig Bartholomew and Karl Moller, vol. 1 (Carlisle: Paternoster Press, 2000); Nicholas Wolterstoff, "A Response to Trevor Hart," *Renewing Biblical Interpretation*, eds. Colin Greene, Craig Bartholomew and Karl Moller, vol. 1 (Carlisle: Paternoster Press, 2000).

creation and interpretation of literary texts generally in the Western tradition.[59] There is an inevitable transition, therefore, between biblical and artistic, or theological and literary accounts of inspiration. Romantic aesthetics effectively replaced the internal testimony of the Holy Spirit as the One who enlightened and assured the reader of the external authority inherent in the Word of God, with a subjective imaginative apprehension of its special status as a text of 'poetic' authority:

> the link between poetry and religion was that both relied on passion and supernatural persuasion to restore the inner harmony disrupted by the Fall. Above all, the insistence upon religious language as 'poetic' takes the debate away from the unarguable fanaticisms engendered by theories of inspiration, and places it firmly within the realm of aesthetics and psychology....Literary criticism is substituted for revelation as the guarantee of authenticity. Behind this redefinition of poetry in terms of passion lay an essentially psychological theory of how the head and heart, representing the most powerful human faculties, combined to produce through art a unique form of psychic integration....For [Coleridge]...the language of the scriptures was the *locus classicus* for the 'poetic.'[60]

In this account the role of the Holy Spirit is replaced by the imagination and the transcendence of a personal triune God, rendered immanent by the intimate working of Holy Spirit, is 'naturalised.'

This bears upon the subject in hand in several ways. Insofar as the biblical doctrine of the Incarnate Word is analogically transferred to all communication, a reexamination of scriptural teaching concerning the Holy Spirit can redress the tendency to treat the text as a fetish. Jesus himself taught his disciples that it was better for them that he be absent physically, as this enabled him to send the Helper, who would bring to their remembrance what he had said (John 16:6-15). This clarifies the relationship between Christ, the Bible, and the believing reader: there is an eschatological dimension to the hermeneutic process; 'For now we see in a mirror dimly, but then face to face. Now I know in part; then I shall know fully, even as I have been fully known' (1 Corinthians 13:12). The Holy Spirit enlightens the believing reader, leading them irresistibly to a true (though inevitably partial) knowledge of Christ. Direct personal knowledge – 'face to face' – will be realised at the *eschaton* (Cf. 2 Peter 1:19-21). The question remains though, to what extent can the paradigm of biblical interpretation, particularly as it incorporates the role of the Holy Spirit, be transferred to the reading of other literature? A similar problem is evident in the tendency to appropriate the biblical model of the inspired prophet as the most suitable parallel for the creative genius of the secular poet, which began in the

---

[59] Prickett, *Words and the Word*. See also Cunningham, *In the Reading Gaol: Postmodernity, Texts and History*, 3; David Lyle Jeffrey, *People of the Book: Christian Identity and Literary Culture* (Grand Rapids: Eerdmans, 1996).
[60] Prickett, *Words and the Word*, 43.

Renaissance and became far more widespread during the Romantic period. The question again arises, to what extent can biblical teaching on the inspiration of its authors, be transferred to, or equated with, the 'inspiration' of individual artists, and of what does the latter consist?

These issues are crucial to defining the 'imagination' as it is popularly conceived today, that is, the creative ability of individuals expressed in artistic enterprises. They are difficult to resolve as they cross the disciplinary *Gletscherwall* (between literary and theological studies) that Prickett explores,[61] requiring the integration of theological and literary inquiry on the very points where they initially parted company. George MacDonald, in a seminal essay upon the subject, goes so far as to equate the imagination of God with the person of the Spirit. This may initially appear to be little more than a modulated version of the 'natural supernaturalism' evident earlier in Avis and Fischer. However, MacDonald's emphasis on the transcendent and personal nature of God, as One who can and must be known, shapes his treatment of this issue. It prevents him from offering an uncritical affirmation of the more optimistic of Romantic notions of inspiration and the role of the artist.[62] Further clarification of the relationship between the Spirit and imagination has been initiated at least by John McIntyre in a highly suggestive work, *Faith, Theology and Imagination*. He explicates the different roles played by imagination in the epistemological and hermeneutical paradigms of the various theologians previously discussed, illuminating both its importance and the pervasive role it plays in theological discourse: it is neither seen in opposition to traditional theological endeavour, nor quarantined as a specialised category.

McIntyre begins his analysis of the imagination with the scriptural text. He carefully considers the parables of Jesus and the implications of their structure for theological endeavour. This is similar to the literary analysis undertaken by David Jasper; both offer a pregnant model for developing a biblical theory of the imagination.[63] Given the literary focus of this book, a full discussion will have to engage also with the narrative and other genres of the Old Testament, as well as the gospels and epistles in the New Testament.[64] McIntyre demonstrates how inserting imagination as an additional category within

---

[61] Prickett, *Words and the Word*, 1.
[62] George MacDonald, "The Imagination: Its Function and Culture," *A Dish of Orts* (1907). Kerry Dearborn offers a concise and thorough overview of MacDonald's theology of the imagination; her exploration overlaps in significant ways with the concerns of this present study. Kerry Dearborn, *Baptized Imagination: The Theology of George MacDonald* (Aldershot: Ashgate, 2006), see especially 67-120.
[63] John McIntyre, *Faith, Theology and Imagination* (Edinburgh: Handsel Press, 1987), 19-39; Jasper, *The New Testament and the Literary Imagination*.
[64] Vanhoozer has broken fruitful ground by analysing the *cognitive* dimension of biblical genres, drawing upon both Paul Ricoeur and Mikhail Bahktin. Further work needs to be done in order to deduce their specific implications for the imagination. Vanhoozer, *Is There a Meaning in This Text?*, 336-50.

traditional theological concepts can illumine their depths and resolve the seeming conundrums that emerge when theologians restrict themselves to empirical categories of thought (unsurprisingly, his prime example is interpretations of the eucharist).[65] Unlike most contemporary champions of imagination, however, he does not advocate the abandonment of propositional doctrinal statements as ossified relics, but shows how a judicious combination of conceptual and imaginative discourse can work within a biblical framework to illuminate the Word of God and its implications for daily life. This complementary rather than oppositional approach helps to melt the aforementioned *Gletscherwall*, facilitating a definition of imagination that does not simplistically equate it with faith.[66] It also lays the groundwork for further consideration of the role of the Holy Spirit in relation to ethical behaviour and artistic inspiration.[67]

The nature of the artistic imagination, whether discussed in terms primarily theological or biblical, remains a matter of controversy amongst artists and scholars. Once again, the historical turning point is the eighteenth-century and the popularisation of the Romantic notion of the poet. Lundin helpfully identifies the key metaphors that characterise the shift: 'Rather than being a mirror held up to nature, art became a lamp illuminating an otherwise darkened world; instead of attempting to represent reality, the artist now sought to express himself or herself—that is, to press out to the surface whatever was in the self.'[68] The most regal claim made for the artistic imagination on the theological premise of human creation in the image of God, which has clear affinities with Romantic aesthetics, and yet is firmly grounded in trinitarian doctrine, is that of Dorothy Sayers in *The Mind of the Maker*. She examines the mind of the artist in the process of operation, through analogy with the three persons of the Trinity in the act of creation: *ex nihilo, ex verbo, ex continuo*. She offers an original attempt to clarify aspects of creativity often consigned to a 'numinous darkness' and simultaneously renders an often abstruse doctrine more accessible. The analogy becomes forced at points though, when Sayers identifies various artistic weaknesses with different trinitarian heresies. The main strength of her thesis is the insightful intellectual and spiritual grounding that it provides for a practical theory of the artist at work.[69] Yet, her approach has several difficulties. Taking the talented artist as a paradigm for what it

---

[65] McIntyre, *Faith, Theology and Imagination*, 41-64.
[66] McIntyre, *Faith, Theology and Imagination*, 37.
[67] McIntyre, *Faith, Theology and Imagination*, 61-4, 75-83. The most pertinent and thorough discussion of this isssue is that of Patrick Sherry, *Spirit and Beauty: An Introduction to Theological Aesthetics* (Oxford: Clarendon Press, 1992).
[68] Lundin, *The Culture of Interpretation*, 51. Lundin is here, of course, drawing on the prior analysis of M. H. Abrams in *The Mirror and the Lamp: Romantic Theory and the Critical Tradition* (Oxford: Oxford University Press, 1971).
[69] Dorothy L. Sayers, *The Mind of the Maker* (London: Methuen, 1941).

means to be created in the image of God has the potential to develop into a dangerous elitism where, as with certain strands of Romanticism, the possession of a powerful artistic imagination is seen to be spiritually meritorious, liberating one from the normal moral boundaries of human behaviour, and providing a unique mode of access to the divine. The artistic imagination effectively becomes separated from the operations of imagination in daily life, establishing a deceptive dichotomy that cannot be maintained from a biblical perspective.

The creative artist of 'original genius' rapidly becomes synonymous with the independent, world-creating (post)modern self. The desires, aspirations and dreams of this individual establish competing didactic claims, which have made the relationship between religion and art a turbulent one, especially in the Western tradition. Lundin critiques the pervasiveness of this model in contemporary Christian aesthetics, stating that it is inconsistent with a biblical view of the human person. He draws on the hermeneutics of Hans Georg Gadamer and the theological anthropology of Richard Niebuhr in order to undercut the notion of the isolated, empirical Kantian subject. He takes C. S. Lewis as his paradigmatic example, arguing that while Lewis recognises the relational and inevitably 'prejudiced' perspective of human beings in his theological writings; his literary criticism simply assumes without question the Romantic preconceptions of his secular contemporaries.[70] Sayers is open to the same objections.

In terms of the imagination, however, the situation is a little more complex than the foregoing discussion implies. While in some of his work as an academic Lewis assumes the uninhibited Kantian subject, he also expresses serious reservations about the kind of Romantic terminology that informs literary criticism, on the grounds that it is inconsistent with the ethos of the New Testament. He suggests that models of reflection or imitation offer a more biblical approach, along the lines of J. R. R. Tolkien's concept of human beings as 'sub-creators' and in sharp contradiction to the position of Sayers explored above.[71] This nuanced notion of 'sub-creation' is certainly more in line with a

---

[70] Lundin, *The Culture of Interpretation*, 212-35.
[71] C. S. Lewis, "Christianity and Literature," *C. S. Lewis: Essay Collection and Other Short Pieces*, ed. Lesley Walmsley (London: Harper Collins, 2000); J. R. R. Tolkien, "On Fairy-Stories," *Tree and Leaf; Smith of Wootton Major; the Homecoming of Boerhnoth* (London: Allen & Unwin, 1975). Trevor Hart explores the longevity and theological resonance of Tolkien's concept of 'creativity' in "Tolkien, Creation and Creativity, " *Tree of Tales: Tolkien, Literature, and Theology*, eds. Trevor Hart and Ivan Khovacs (Waco: Baylor University Press, 2007), 39-53. See also the recent discussion of creativity in community by Diana Glyer in *The Company They Keep: C. S. Lewis and J. R. R. Tolkien as Writers in Community* (Kent, Ohio: Kent State University Press, 2007), especially 206-229 and Gregory Bassham's overview in "Lewis and Tolkien on the Power of the Imagination," *C. S. Lewis as Philosopher: Truth, Goodness and*

biblical understanding of the role of human beings, as made uniquely in the image of God and entrusted with the creation mandate to be faithful stewards and developers of the earth (Genesis 1:27-30).[72] Jeremy Begbie attempts to develop this position on a theological and philosophical basis. He critiques the masterful Enlightenment concept of an order imposed upon the external world through the superior cognitive processes of the individual human mind. Drawing upon Michael Polyani's notion of 'indwelling,' Begbie argues that human beings do not shape reality according to their desire; rather individuals discover aspects of the external world through inhabiting it. Artists recognise and respond to this, representing the encounter in ways that allow their audiences to appreciate the real world more deeply.[73] The imagination plays a synthesising role, bringing together diverse elements into a meaningful whole that allows the finished work to convey truths for the cognitive apprehension of its audience in a distinctive way. This offers an innovative and promising direction for the development of a biblical view of the imagination.[74]

Biblical Perspectives on the Imagination

Cheryl Forbes assumes the context of authoritative biblical revelation that theologians such as Green, Bryant, Wilder, Fischer and Avis are contesting, or seeking to establish. This biblical framework and her specific focus upon imagination enable her to foreground more definitively the nature of this function and its role. Like McIntyre, she differentiates between imagination and

---

Beauty, eds. David Baggett, Gary R. Habermas and Jerry L. Walls (Downers Grove: IVP Academic, 2008), 245-60.

[72] An extensive literature on the relationship of human beings to creation and its implications for artists and aesthetics has developed in recent years. See, for example, Robert Banks, *God the Worker: Journeys into the Mind, Heart and Imagination of God* (Sydney: Albatross, 1992); Michael Card, *Scribbling in the Sand: Christ and Creativity* (Downers Grove: InterVarsity Press, 2002); Adrienne Chaplin and Hilary Brand, *Art and Soul: Signposts for Christians in the Arts* (Downers Grove, Illinois: Piquant, IVP, 2001); Richard L. Pratt, *Designed for Dignity: What God Has Made It Possible for You to Be* (Phillipsburg: Presbyterian & Reformed Publishing, 1993); H. R. Rookmaaker, *The Creative Gift: Essays on Art and the Christian Life* (Westchester, Illinois: Cornerstone Books, 1981); Francis A. Schaeffer, *Art & the Bible : Two Essays* (Downers Grove, Ill: InterVarsity Press, 1973); Calvin Seerveld, *Bearing Fresh Olive Leaves: Alternative Steps in Understanding Art* (Toronto: Tuppence Press, 2000); Gene Edward Veith Jr., *State of the Arts: From Bezalel to Mapplethorpe* (Wheaton, Illinois: Crossway Books, 1991).

[73] This assumption – of an external, objective reality beyond the self as a gratuitous overflow of God's goodness – parallels George Steiner's assumption of presence prior to speech.

[74] Jeremy Begbie, *Voicing Creation's Praise: Towards a Theology of the Arts* (Edinburgh: T&T Clark, 1990), 241-9.

faith, whilst simultaneously demonstrating their interdependence:

> We cannot have faith (belief in that which is unseen) unless we have imagination; imagination is the vehicle through which faith is expressed. Nor can we understand our world without active imaginations – our world view that sees God as creator and controller, caretaker and lover....Our metaphors and paradoxes attempt to make concrete – at least a little – the faith presented in Scripture.[75]

This capacity of the imagination to render faith concrete, to integrate disparate parts into a coherent whole, and to embody the ethical in a persuasive form, with its implications for literature, will be considered in some detail in separate chapters on John Bunyan, Samuel Rutherford and Jane Austen.

Forbes examines Jesus himself as the prime exemplar of an imaginative life: in his relationship with others, he saw the hidden potential, drawing it out with an empathetic insight conceived through imaginative identification. His entire life was focused upon others, culminating finally in an act of self-sacrifice. Forbes argues that biblical language invites its readers to envisage themselves as metaphors, replacing and correcting the false images that so often govern human consciousness, the most devastating being: 'I am god.' This hearkens back directly to the distinction between a biblically informed imagination and the unencumbered, world-projecting (post)modern self. The biblical text acts as the standard against which alternative metaphors are measured; the true original remains the Incarnate Word. The purpose of developing the imagination, she concludes, is not ultimately self-satisfaction or fulfilment, but rather to enable one to conceive and worship God with one's entire being, following Jesus as 'a living sacrifice, holy and acceptable to God' (Romans 12:1).[76]

This empathetic, ethically engaged imagination that I am arguing is biblical, needs to be distinguished from an influential trend in literary criticism that stems from George Eliot's notion of 'moral sympathy.' This doctrine became a substitute for the Evangelical tradition that Eliot rejected as a young woman. She suggests that one can maintain a moral imagination in life and literature, without accepting the theological framework with which it has historically been associated in Christian thought.[77] Ironically, it is Friedrich Nietzsche who most

---

[75] Cheryl Forbes, *Imagination: Embracing a Theology of Wonder* (Portland: Multnomah Press, 1986), 46.
[76] Forbes, *Imagination*, 61-3, 174-5.
[77] For an analysis of the relationship between imagination and sympathy in George Eliot see Forest Pyle, "A Novel Sympathy: the Imagination of Community in George Eliot," *Novel*, 27.1 (1993), 5-23. Bernard J. Paris outlines her understanding of moral sympathy and its disassociation from traditional religious orthodoxy in "George Eliot's Religion of Humanity," *George Eliot: A Collection of Critical Essays*, ed. George R. Creeger, (Englewood Cliffs: Prentice Hall, 1970), 11-36. For an exploration of the link between religious symbolism and George Eliot's 'ethic of humanity' see Ruth Jenkins, *Reclaiming Myths of Power: Women Writers and the Victorian Spiritual Crisis*

clearly identifies the problem with Eliot's concept of the moral imagination and that which isolates it from the definition of imagining biblically established in this study. He notes in *Twilight of the Gods*:

> G. Eliot.— They have got rid of the Christian God, and now feel obliged to cling all the more firmly to Christian morality: that is English consistency, let us not blame it on little bluestockings à la Eliot. In England, in response to every little emancipation from theology one has to reassert one's position in a fear-inspiring manner as a moral fanatic. That is the penance one pays there. With us it is different. When one gives up Christian belief one thereby deprives oneself of the right to Christian morality.[78]

Whilst Nietzsche is undoubtedly reducing the complexity of Eliot's thought to a caricature, informed by nationalistic prejudice, his central insight that the moral imagination or sympathy cannot be divorced from the biblical theology that has traditionally undergirded it is crucial to my argument. It provides one of the central rationales for combining literary and theological analysis when developing the concept of what it means to imagine biblically. It is also one of the reasons why the novels of Jane Austen and Charlotte Brontë have been chosen to explore the function of imagination, as they remained committed intellectually and emotionally to an understanding of morality informed by the biblical narrative. Unlike Eliot, who wrote of the Bible: 'I regard these writings as histories consisting of mingled truth and fiction, and while I admire and cherish much of what I believe to have been the moral teaching of Jesus himself, I consider the system of doctrines built upon the facts of his life...to be most dishonorable to God and most pernicious in its influence on individual and social happiness.'[79] Eliot's doctrine of moral sympathy rejects the necessity for any external transcendent criterion to maintain moral values and sympathy; she believed that these qualities were immanent within human nature and society.[80] However, the understanding of imagination developed in this study is based on the opposite contention, voiced by Nietzsche, that the moral and theological are inextricably linked to one another. This issue is explored further in Chapter 2, which outlines the theological foundations of what it means to imagine biblically; whilst the moral dimension of the imagination is explored more particularly in Chapter 5.

A biblical understanding of the imagination integrates its ethical and practical dimensions alongside its artistic expressions in a holistic

---

(Lewisburg: Bucknell University Press, 1995); this text also examines similar issues in relation to other Victorian women writers including Charlotte Brontë.

[78] Cited by Alan Jacobs, "George Eliot: Good Without God," *First Things*, 102, April (2000), 50-3.

[79] George Eliot in a letter to her father explaining why she no longer considers herself a Christian, cited by Jacobs, "George Eliot," 50-53.

[80] Paris, "George Eliot's Religion of Humanity," 11-19.

understanding of the human person as created in the image of God. Thus the Romantic ideal of the solitary genius creating masterpieces from riches within also finds no support in the biblical text: the figure of the prophet ostracised by his people, due to their distaste for his preaching, is certainly a reality; but such prophets are inspired by God, carrying a message of judgement and hope, centred upon law communally revealed, and often weeping over the rebellion of their contemporaries. The prophets did not create their own moral standards; they remained subject to the same commandments as those which governed their neighbours, unlike the poetic genius who was seen to exist on a different level to ordinary human beings, and thus viewed as exempt from customary rules and responsibilities. Bezalel is the biblical paradigm of the artist *par excellence*:

> I have called by name Bezalel...I have filled him with the Spirit of God, with ability and intelligence, with knowledge and all craftsmanship, to devise artistic designs, to work in gold, silver, and bronze, in cutting stones for setting, and in carving wood, to work in every craft. And behold, I have appointed with him Oholiab, the son of Ahisamach, of the tribe of Dan. And I have given to all able men ability, that they may make all that I have commanded you (Exodus 31:2-7).

The word for 'calling' here is the same as that used for the divine vocation of the prophets. Bezalel is gifted, but he works to the design that God has given, within the context of the Israelite community, producing something that will glorify the Lord and benefit others. Far from being isolated, he works alongside people like Oholiab, and is given a responsibility to teach.

Central to a biblical understanding of imagination and the arts is the concept of beauty, and Edmund P. Clowney utilises this in order to further explicate the holistic perspective of Scripture, and the impossibility of separating aesthetic and spiritual concerns. The divine works of creation, redemption and ultimate glorification are seen to be manifestations of physical and spiritual beauty that God has showered upon the world. Similarly, God's providential government of history in his covenant dealings with Israel, reflect his love of order and design. Though the Israelites had to draw skilled craftsmen from neighbouring Tyre in order to build the Tabernacle, they 'did not lack artistic gifts....The art of Israel was the art of narrative, of poetry and song, of reflective wisdom, and of prophetic proclamation...their delight is in the Lord. It is this religious center of the life of the people of God...that shapes the understanding of beauty in the Old Testament.'[81] The Bible refuses to separate what is automatically regarded

---

[81] Edmund Clowney, "Living Art: Christian Experience and the Arts," *God and Culture: Essays in Honor of Carl F. H. Henry*, ed. J. D. Woodbridge (Grand Rapids: William B. Eerdmans, 1993), 239-40. For a more extended discussion of Christ as the form of beauty, or of 'the Incarnation as the archetypal manifestation of beauty' see Francesca Aran Murphy, *Christ the Form of Beauty: A Study in Literature and Theology* (Edinburgh: T&T Clark, 1995), 208 and passim.

as distinct in secular criticism: abstract terms such as beauty, glory, wonder and praise find their meaning only when related to God. Hence, the radiant transcendence of this deliberately suppressed divine 'Other' must be positioned at the centre when developing a biblical view of the imagination. The scriptural claim upon the imagination is first a claim upon the being and life of the individual, and only secondarily upon the creative work which they produce.

> Artistic expression is not an elitist pursuit, encoded for a restricted circle of initiates. It cannot be limited to what we speak of as "the arts," for its root is spiritual and the highest art is the exercise of what Jonathan Edwards called the "religious affections"....Our aesthetic response is also creative. Life-style artistry explores in freedom the richness of styles and of media that are offered in our cultural setting...it affirms, imagines, explores.[82]

This biblical perspective thus clearly critiques the tendency towards elitism that has characterised particular approaches to the artistic imagination, which see it as offering a form of salvation to the cultured devotee. Such attitudes have their roots in John Ruskin and Walter Pater's interpretation and extension of Wordsworth's Romanticism.[83] Pater, in particular, while teaching at the University of Oxford, articulated the notion that the experience of art is essential to a true or full life; it is known by those who have a sufficiently delicate sensitivity to its appeal. 'To burn always with this hard, gem-like flame, to maintain this ecstasy, is success in life.'[84] And later in the conclusion to *The Renaissance: Studies in Art and Poetry* he observes:

> Some spend this interval [i.e. life] in listlessness, some in high passions, the wisest, at least among 'the children of the world,' in art and song. For our one chance lies in expanding that interval, in getting as many pulsations as possible into the given time. Great passions may give us this quickened sense of life, ecstasy and sorrow of love, the various forms of enthusiastic activity, disinterested or otherwise, which come naturally to many of us. Only be sure it is passion – that it does yield you this fruit of a quickened, multiplied consciousness. Of such wisdom, the poetic passion, the desire of beauty, the love of art for its own sake,

---

[82] Clowney, "Living Art: Christian Experience and the Arts," 252-3. Edward Farley provides a strong theological and philosophical argument to support the basic claim that '[b]eauty is intrinsic to the life of faith because it is a feature of the divine image which is distorted by sin and restored by redemption.' Edward Farley, *Faith and Beauty: A Theological Aesthetic* (Aldershot: Ashgate, 2001), viii and passim.

[83] See Kenneth Daley, *The Rescue of Romanticism: Walter Pater and John Ruskin* (Athens: University of Ohio Press, 2001) for an exploration of the relationship between Ruskin, Pater and Romanticism.

[84] Walter Pater, *The Renaissance: Studies in Art and Poetry* ed. Adam Phillips, (Oxford: Oxford University Press, 1986), 152.

has most. For art comes to you proposing frankly to give nothing but the highest quality to your moments as they pass, and simply for those moments' sake.[85]

The passion aroused by such works of art – the Mona Lisa, the masterpieces of the Renaissance – is accessible only to those with the leisure and money to enjoy and appreciate them. There is thus an inherent elitism in the argument that 'our one chance' in experiencing life lies in multiplying the occasions for encounters that 'yield [the]...fruit of a quickened, multiplied consciousness.'[86]

This elitism in Pater's notion of 'the love of art for its own sake,' also influenced later versions of aestheticism, from the celebration of the decadent imagination by Oscar Wilde (a student of Pater's) in the *fin de siècle* to the more recent postulate by Jean-François Lyotard's of the postmodern sublime. Lyotard argues, 'the real sublime sentiment...is an intrinsic combination of pleasure and pain: the pleasure that reason should exceed all presentation, the pain that imagination or sensibility should not be equal to the concept.'[87] Emily Lutzker explicates this as an essentially ethical experience, which is later rationalised aesthetically: 'The sublime event is the confrontation with our humanity....We put ourselves in a situation to experience the sublime, to see the sublime because for that instant, through a contradictory experience, we gain an illusive insight about how to live a good life.'[88] The affinities with Pater's thought are evident. Although Lyotard takes care to note that: 'The sublime feeling is neither moral universality nor aesthetic universalisation, but is, rather, the destruction of one by the other in the violence of their differend [i.e. the incommensurability between reason and imagination].'[89] He continues: 'This differend cannot demand even subjectively to be communicated to all thought.'[90] Consequently, neither critical thought, nor the artistic imagination should be constrained by an overly restrictive concern for truth, on Lyotard's model, nor by the limitations imposed by various metanarratives.

The emphasis on the moment of encounter, privileging the capacity of an emotive or subjective response that exposes the gap between what is desired and what is perceived, within which an ethical appreciation of the 'good life' is realised and then dissolves, continues the trend of a 'secular' salvation achieved through art implicit in Pater's thought. But, in the absence of the accountability established by living in response to a particular metanarrative, what constitutes

---

[85] Pater, *The Renaissance: Studies in Art and Poetry*, 153.
[86] Pater, *The Renaissance: Studies in Art and Poetry*, 153.
[87] J-F. Lyotard, *The Postmodern Condition: A Report on Knowledge* trans. G. Bennington and B. Massumi (Manchester: Manchester University Press, 1984), 81.
[88] Emily Lutzker, "Ethics of the Sublime in Postmodern Culture", A Talk From the International Conference Aesthetics and Ethics (1997). <http://www.egs.edu/mediaphi/Vol2/Sublime.html>, 26 August 2008.
[89] J-F. Lyotard, *Lessons on the Analytic of the Sublime*, trans. E. Rottenberg, (Stanford: Stanford University Press, 1994), 239.
[90] Lyotard, *Lessons on the Analytic of the Sublime*, 239.

human 'ethics' or defines 'art' becomes exhilaratingly (or terrifyingly) malleable. An extreme example of the way in which this relativist notion of an ethical postmodern sublime can be applied is evident in the opinion reputedly voiced by the *avant-garde* composer Karlheinz Stockhausen following the terrorist attacks of September 11, 2001. He described this event as 'the biggest work of art anywhere, for the whole cosmos.' 'Picture what occurred. Five thousand people are concentrated on a performance and are pushed, in one moment, towards resurrection. I could never manage to obtain this result.'[91] Here the historic combination of the sublime and the terrible, initiated by Edmund Burke in the aftermath of the French Revolution, has been divorced from any ethical accountability; a mass tragedy, a supreme act of terror can potentially provide the 'intrinsic combination of pleasure and pain' which is central to Lyotard's definition the postmodern sublime.[92]

In contradistinction to such a conception of the artistic imagination, this study aims to develop an understanding of the imagination which remains accountable to the ethics implicit in the biblical metanarrative. As noted above, this incorporates both life and art, refusing the separation between spiritual and aesthetic, or the relativism of ethical norms; it thus contests the elitism that privileges either high art, extreme tragedy, or whatever feature may be seen as constituting the sublime moment, as a defining feature of imagination and artistic experience.

A Brief Synopsis

The following chapter will begin with a wide-angle lens in its consideration of the imagination. This is done in order to be faithful to the nature of the biblical text, which draws no artificial distinctions between literature and life, thus seeking to reflect the comprehensive biblical vision of the human person. It also provides a theological framework that contextualises the various dimensions of the imagination that are considered in the chapters on individual authors that follow; a common base that enables them to be integrated into the overarching argument. Francis Schaeffer, Leland Ryken, Hans Rookmaaker, Calvin Seerveld, Richard Mouw and Kevin Vanhoozer have established a comprehensive biblical approach to the arts in general over the past three decades, seeking to critique and overturn an ambivalent or indifferent attitude towards the imagination that has historically characterised various Christian traditions.[93] To this end, they draw frequently upon the Calvinist heritage

---

[91] Christine Battersby, "Terror, Terrorism and the Sublime: Rethinking the Sublime After 1789 and 2001," *Postcolonial Studies*, 6.1 (2003), 67.

[92] Battersby, "Terror, Terrorism and the Sublime."

[93] Schaeffer, *Art & the Bible*; Leland Ryken, *The Liberated Imagination: Thinking Christianly About the Arts* (Colorado Springs: Shaw Books, 1989); Leland Ryken, "Literature in Christian Perspective," *God and Culture: Essays in Honor of Carl F. H.*

developed by Dutch theologians such as Abraham Kuyper, Herman Bavinck and Herman Dooyeweerd earlier in the twentieth century. This study is indebted to the broad theological contours that inform their writings in defining a biblical concept of the imagination.

The definition of imagination that is employed in this study is developed in Chapter 2 from an examination of biblical words and concepts, sharpened and refined for the purpose of discussion through engagement with the work of John McIntyre, Richard Kearney, Mary Warnock and Garrett Green.[94] Given the complex nature of the imagination and the various ways it can be construed as operating (cognitively, philosophically, creatively, perceptually and so on) this definition will be complemented by a consideration of the biblical metanarrative and genres, as well as specific issues of contention, in order to position the examination clearly within the parameters of the biblical text. The concept of imagining biblically, by its very nature, is fluid and open to a range of interpretations and definitions. In an attempt to capture this within the methodological structure of the following argument, various aspects are treated thematically through a close reading and analysis of relevant literary texts.

Following the theoretical outline, I will look at John Bunyan's exploration of the nature of creativity as it is dealt with in *The Pilgrim's Progress*. On his own account, given in the 'Apology' which prefaces the work, this literary classic developed in the margins of another dialogue with Scripture. This engagement affords important insights into a biblical understanding of the imagination, as the literary artefact which Bunyan produced, necessitates a rethinking of Puritan definitions of aesthetics, poetics and imagination. The foundations for a more positive understanding lie in Bunyan's own account, but the limitations and implications of his approach will be modified through reference to Paul Ricoeur, J. R. R. Tolkien and others. I then turn in Chapter 4 to the *Letters of Samuel Rutherford*, a Scottish Covenanter and near contemporary of Bunyan. The posthumous collection of his letters facilitate a consideration of the scriptural distinction between faith and imagination, and the role of the imagination in understanding both human and divine relationships within the context of a biblical hermeneutic. This is crucial as faith and imagination are

---

Henry, eds. J. D. Woodbridge and D. A. Carson (Grand Rapids: William B. Eerdmans, 1993); Leland Ryken, ed, *The Christian Imagination* (Colorado Springs: Shaw Books, 2002); Rookmaaker, *The Creative Gift*; Richard J. Mouw, *He Shines in All That's Fair: Culture and Common Grace* (Grand Rapids: Eerdmans, 2000); Seerveld, *Bearing Fresh Olive Leaves*; Kevin J. Vanhoozer, "The World Well Staged? Theology, Culture and Hermeneutics," *God and Culture: Essays in Honor of Carl F. H. Henry*, ed. J. D. Woodbridge (Grand Rapids: William B. Eerdmans, 1993).

[94] McIntyre, *Faith, Theology and Imagination*; Richard Kearney, *The Wake of Imagination: Ideas of Creativity in Western Culture* (London: Hutchinson, 1988); M. Warnock, *Imagination* (London: Faber & Faber, 1976); Green, *Imagining God*; Garrett Green, *Theology, Hermeneutics, and Imagination: The Crisis of Interpretation at the End of Modernity* (Cambridge: Cambridge University Press, 2000).

often equated, a position not tenable scripturally; it also renders concrete issues concerning language, reference, accountability and relationships, which are implicated in a biblical treatment of imagination.

Incorporating a female perspective, the next two chapters will focus on Jane Austen and Charlotte Brontë respectively. Austen, in *Pride and Prejudice*, manages to create a narrative that has enchanted generations of readers, yet despite the celebrated relativism of the novel as a genre, she invokes a clearly defined framework of moral absolutes, against which the characters are measured. This has close affinities with the genre of historical narrative in the Bible: implications for the role of the imagination in understanding the self and its connections to moral criticism will be explored. Brontë writes in a very different style from Austen, nevertheless *Jane Eyre* also engages directly with the ethical role of the imagination. Brontë conducts an incisive theological critique of the dangers inherent in simply indulging the imagination, which can result in idolatry. Nevertheless, the novel also valorises its power in the familiar terminology of high Romanticism. This provides the opportunity to examine further the Bible's treatment of positive and negative uses of the imagination and how one may discern between them.

The following chapter on C. S. Lewis engages with the eschatological dimension of Scripture and the way this shapes a biblical understanding of the imagination by providing simultaneously a sense of closure or an ultimate boundary to finite human existence, and a sense of limitless possibility beyond the reach of time. Eschatology is a recurring theme in the critical, fictional and theological writings of Lewis, who developed a complex though nebulous theory of imagination. While he did not believe the imagination can provide direct access to divine truth, intimations of transcendence, a sense of the world beyond this world, can be grasped through this function, piercing the reductive empirical mind-set of contemporary secularism and awakening a sweet desire that only God can ultimately satisfy. These chapters each explore a different aspect of the imagination. They are designed to interact fluidly with the more clearly defined understanding of this crucial human function given in Chapter 2, inviting connections and further dialogue about the issues raised. The Conclusion will draw together the various threads which these chapters contribute to the concept of what it means to imagine from a biblical perspective.

Chapter 2

Towards a Biblical View of the Imagination

This chapter outlines a biblical context for understanding and defining the imagination. Linking Scripture and the act of imagining has been regarded as problematic, even antithetical, in the history of biblical interpretation. The purpose of examining and defining the concept denoted by the noun 'imagination' from a biblical perspective is to demonstrate that imagination is viewed as a powerful and necessary constituent of human nature in Scripture. Further, while imagination has assumed a complex and manifold array of definitions and associations, it remains the key term in literary studies for the aspect or function of human nature that I am considering in this study. This chapter sets out some of the ways in which the biblical text contributes to an understanding of imagination. It enables a fruitful link to be established between the biblical data and contemporary perspectives on the imagination within the field of literary studies. It also provides a framework within which the various trajectories of 'imagining biblically,' explored in the following chapters, can be situated.

I begin with a brief word study of imagination in the biblical text, detailing the limitations that such a methodology presents for defining this function. In order to overcome these, I then examine the more securely grounded concept of the 'heart,' which is integral to biblical anthropology. It is possible to integrate this inclusive term with imagination as it is commonly understood within contemporary cultural contexts; this will be explored and elaborated with particular reference to the philosophical work of Mary Warnock, the theological approach of John McIntyre, and the biblical hermeneutics of Paul Ricoeur. Together they provide a flexible definition of imagination. However, given the complex nature of the biblical text and the multifaceted ways in which it intersects with the creation and interpretation of works of literature, this definition needs to be positioned within a theological framework set by the ethical, relational and narrative dimensions of Scripture. In this chapter I will focus on the metanarrative of the biblical text; its pluriform structure; and the way in which its eschatological hope shapes the role of the imagination.

Finally, there are several aspects of imagining biblically which need to be further defined and clarified, as they have provoked significant debate. A biblical understanding of imagination cannot simply be conflated with faith; this separates a biblical definition of imagination from theories which see the two as synonymous and view art as a means of salvation. Patrick Sherry gestures towards a more helpful figuration of the relationship between art and the doctrine of salvation, by differentiating between the salvation achieved by the work of Christ on the cross and the effect that a work of art may play at a different level in one's life and relationship with the Divine:

> If the Cross is believed to atone for our sins, is it not blasphemous to speak of music in a similar way? And is not [there a] danger of confusing evanescent moods or emotions with something much greater?....In English the word 'atonement' means 'at-one-ment', i.e. reconciliation and the verb 'to atone' is originally derived from the noun. [The concern is] with how we may become 'at one' with God, or how this may be communicated....This...disposes of the suspicion of idolatry, I think. Nevertheless, we are left with other difficult questions....[1]

The biblical text undercuts elitist theories of imagination and creativity, recognising that imagining is an activity that occurs in all areas of life, and invokes issues of ethics and relational accountability whether one is creating an artistic masterpiece, or redecorating one's home. I conclude by exploring the nature of human creativity and the notion of artistic originality at some length, as this has also been viewed as problematic when defininig what it means to imagine and create from a biblical perspective.

Defining 'Imagination': Biblical Word Study

There is no direct correlate in either Hebrew or Greek for our English word imagination. Various English translations of the Bible have rendered different words from the original by this term or its cognates, but they are not consistent. A study of their occurrence frequently reveals more about the way the word was used in common parlance amongst English speakers at the time of translation rather than providing a firm etymological base for a biblical perspective on the subject. This does not mean that the Bible has nothing to say on the function that we now refer to as the imagination. A brief examination of the text, with the predominance of genres such as historical narrative, poetry, parable and song, and the rich use of metaphor and imagery that characterises biblical language refutes this assumption. But it is necessary to recognise scriptural definitions of what it means to be human or the way the mind, soul and body relate to one another, follow a pattern quite distinct from the more

---

[1] Patrick Sherry, *Images of Redemption: Art, Literature and Salvation* (London: T&T Clark, 2003), 16. This is similar to Jonathan Edwards's argument that there are structural affinities between affections inspired by art and those aroused by the contemplation of spiritual beauty, although Edwards draws a much starker contrast between the realms of 'common' and 'special' grace than is allowed for here. See Chapter 4 for a fuller elucidation of these issues.

familiar configurations in contemporary disciplines of science, psychology, medicine and religious studies.

Predominant among the Hebrew words used to connote imagination is *yatsar*. Richard Kearney takes this term to define generally, what he calls 'the Hebraic imagination.'[2] Its basic meaning is to form, frame or purpose. It is used of God, in the creation of human beings from the dust of the earth (Genesis 2:7,8,19; Psalm 103:14; Isaiah 64:8), and of people, as when the potter forms vessels from clay (Isaiah 29:16). It also refers to intellectual frameworks as manifested in purpose, imagination or devices (Genesis 6:5; 8:21).[3] The application of this word to God (Isaiah 37:26; 43:7; 45:18; 46:11) makes clear that it is not, in itself, a pejorative term, but rather an aspect of human nature (due to creation in the image of God) which can be used for good or ill. *Yatsar* appears in a wide range of situations demonstrating that the basic features of what we term 'imagination' find expression biblically in the common aspects of daily material existence, and the planning of future actions, as well as in great artistic works (Isaiah 22:11; 37:26; 43:1; 44:9,24; 46:11; 54:17).[4]

Other Hebrew words rendered as imagination or one of its cognates include *machashabah*, which connotes thought or device, including the concept of planning, purpose or invention (Exodus 31:4; 35:32,33,35; Proverbs 6:18; 12:5; 15:22).[5] *Maskiyth*: a show-piece, figure, imagination, image, idol or picture; it can denote both the carved figure (of idols), a show-piece, or the intellectual imagination or conceit (Leviticus 26:1; Psalm 73:7); revealing the biblical definition of idolatry as an evil use of the imagination.[6] *Shriyruwth*: stubbornness, hardness or firmness (Deuteronomy 29:19; Psalm 81:12), occasionally translated as 'imagination' by older English versions. Now largely obsolete, it is suggestive in that it shows how persistence in delusive or self-focused habits of imagining can become entrenched, leading to spiritual hardness and eventual apostasy (Jeremiah 11:8;13:10).[7] These various dimensions are all contained by and originate within the final word sometimes translated as 'imagination' in the Old Testament: *leb* (derived from *lebab*), the heart. It is one of the richest terms in the Hebrew Scriptures and, contrary to the predilection of modern scientific analysis, it insists on treating as a whole,

---

[2] Kearney, *The Wake of Imagination*, 39-61.
[3] Francis Brown, S. R. Driver, Charles A. Briggs and William Gesenius, eds, *A Hebrew and English Lexicon of the Old Testament* (Peabody, Mass.: Hendrickson Publishers, 1979), Hebrew Lexicon Entries for 'Yatsar' (3335) and 'Yetser' (3336).
[4] Brown et al, eds, *A Hebrew and English Lexicon of the Old Testament*, 'Yatsar', 'Yetser.'
[5] Brown et al, eds, *A Hebrew and English Lexicon of the Old Testament*, Hebrew Lexicon entry for 'Machashabah' (4284).
[6] Brown et al, eds, *A Hebrew and English Lexicon of the Old Testament*, Hebrew Lexicon Entry for 'Maskiyth' (4906).
[7] Brown et al, eds, *A Hebrew and English Lexicon of the Old Testament*, Hebrew Lexicon Entry for 'Shriyruwth' (8307).

aspects of human thinking and being that are often segregated. It denotes the inner person, mind, will, heart and understanding, inevitably encompassing what we now categorise as imagination.[8] Two key texts will illustrate this point:

> Keep your heart (*leb*) with all vigilance, for from it flow the springs of life (*leb*) (Proverbs 4:23).

> And the LORD your God will circumcise your heart (*lebab*) and the heart (*lebab*) of your offspring, so that you will love the LORD your God with all your heart (*lebab*) and with all your soul, that you may live (Deuteronomy 30:6).

The inextricable connections between the heart, imagination and ethical action are indicated in the highly suggestive, repeated phrase of the King James Version: 'the imagination of the thoughts of the heart (*leb*)' (Genesis 6:5; 1 Chronicles 29:18).

The standard literal translations of the Greek New Testament only render a few words as 'imagination' or its cognates. These include *meletao*, which means to meditate, devise, or contrive (Acts 4:25); the Greeks used it to describe the meditative pondering and practice of orators and rhetoricians.[9] *Dianoia*: the mind as a faculty of thinking, understanding or desiring, whether good or bad (Ephesians 2:3;4:18).[10] *Dialogismos*: the thinking of one deliberating within themselves; a thought, inward reasoning; purpose, design; a deliberating, questioning about what is true; hesitation, doubting; disputing, arguing. It is translated 'imagination' by the KJV in Romans 1:21: 'Because that, when they knew God, they glorified him not as God, neither were thankful; but became vain in their imaginations (*dialogismos*), and their foolish heart was darkened.'[11] This again connects the heart and the imagination. In fact, the Greek *kardia* is essentially a continuation in the New Testament

---

[8] Brown et al, eds, *A Hebrew and English Lexicon of the Old Testament*, Hebrew Lexicon Entries for 'Leb' (3820) and 'Lebab' (3824); G. Johannes Botterweck, Helmer Tinggren and Heinz-Josef Fabry, eds, *Theological Dictionary of the Old Testament*, vol. 7 (Grand Rapids: Eerdmans, 1995), Entry for 'Leb', 412-36.

[9] Blue Letter Bible. "Dictionary and Word Search for *meletaō (Strong's 3191)*". Blue Letter Bible. 1996-2008. 30 August 2008. <http:// cf.blueletterbible.org/lang/lexicon/lexicon.cfm? Strongs=G3191&t=KJV>

[10] Thayer and Smith. "Greek Lexicon entry for Dianoia". "The New Testament Greek Lexicon," 26 August 2008, <http://www.searchgodsword.org/lex/grk/view.cgi?number=1271>

[11] Blue Letter Bible. "Dictionary and Word Search for *dialogismos (Strong's 1261)*". Blue Letter Bible. 1996-2008. 30 August 2008. <http:// cf.blueletterbible.org/lang/lexicon/Lexicon.cfm? Strongs=1261&t=KJV&cscs=Phl>, Cf. Luke 1:51; *logismos*, 2 Corinthians 10:5 (KJV).

Scriptures of the Old Testament concept of *leb*.[12] When positioned in the full context of biblical revelation it incorporates the same richly suggestive semantic field,[13] illustrating the necessity of moving beyond the reductive analysis of words in the originals translated 'imagination,' to a more holistic engagement with biblical teaching concerning human nature. The New International Version uses 'imagine' in a more positive way, which nevertheless indicates the limits of even an imagination sanctified by grace: 'Now to him who is able to do immeasurably more than all we ask or imagine (*nooumen*), according to his power that is at work within us, to him be glory in the church and in Christ Jesus throughout all generations, forever and ever! Amen' (Ephesians 3:20-1).[14]

This survey is not exhaustive, but it is sufficient to show that the aspect of human nature, which we identify as imagination, is recognised and treated in the biblical text. A brief examination of the way in which 'imagination' is used over the history of English Bible translation and paraphrase is also instructive. It appears frequently to denote a wide range of cognitive activities in the KJV: purpose (Deuteronomy 31:21), self-will (Jeremiah 7:24), idolatry (Jeremiah 18:12), conceit (Luke 1:51). (See also Genesis 6:5; 8:21; 11:6; Deuteronomy 29:19; 1 Chronicles 28:9; 29:18; Job 6:26; 21:27; Psalm 2:1; 10:2; 21:11; 38:12; 62:3; 140:2; Proverbs 6:18; 12:20; Jeremiah 3:17; 9:14; 11:8; 13:10; 16:12; 23:17; Lamentations 3:60-1; Hosea 7:15; Nahum 1:9, 11; Zechariah 7:10; 8:17; Acts 4:25; Romans 1:21; 2 Corinthians 10:5). The use is almost always pejorative, with the significant and telling exceptions of David's instruction to his son Solomon, and the latter's subsequent prayer:

> And thou, Solomon my son, know thou the God of thy father, and serve Him with a perfect heart (*leb*) and with a willing mind (*leb*); for the LORD searcheth all hearts and understandeth all the imaginations of the thoughts. If thou seek Him, He will be found of thee; but if thou forsake Him, He will cast thee off forever....
> O LORD God of Abraham, Isaac, and of Israel, our fathers, keep this for ever in the imagination of the thoughts of the heart (*lebab*) of Thy people, and prepare their heart (*lebab*) unto Thee (1 Chronicles 28:9; 29:18 KJV).

The gradual reduction of this range of reference in the Revised Standard Version and the American Standard Version (1901) (Genesis 6:5; 8:21;

---

[12] Colin Brown, ed, *The New International Dictionary of New Testament Theology*, vol. 2 (Carlisle: Paternoster Press, 1975-78), Entry for 'Heart', 180-4. Gerhard Kittel and Geoffrey Bromiley, eds, *Theological Dictionary of the New Testament*, vol. 3 (Grand Rapids: Eerdmans, 1965), Entry for 'Kardia,' 611-13.

[13] Blue Letter Bible. "Dictionary and Word Search for *kardia (Strong's 2588)*". Blue Letter Bible. 1996-2008. 30 August 2008. <http:// cf.blueletterbible.org/lang/lexicon/lexicon.cfm? Strongs=G2588&t=KJV>

[14] Cf. 1 Corinthians 2:9, which the English Standard Version renders 'imagination', the NIV 'mind' and the NASB 'heart.'

Deuteronomy 31:21; 1 Chronicles 28:9; 29:18; Proverbs 18:11; Luke 1:51; Acts 4:25; 2 Corinthians 10:5), continued by translators of the New King James Version (1982) (Genesis 8:21; Luke 1:51), the New American Standard Bible (1960) (Esther 4:13; Psalm 73:7; Proverbs 18:11; Jeremiah 23:16), and the New International Version (Psalm 41:7; Proverbs 18:11; 23:33; Isaiah 65:2; 66:18; Ezekiel 13:2, 17; Ephesians 3:20) reflects the loss of this wider cognitive denotation, as also does its replacement by synonyms such as 'intention' or 'mind.' However, when it is used, particularly in the more recent of these translations, including also the Contemporary English Version (1995) (Job 36:26; Psalm 139:17; Proverbs 28:22; Song of Solomon 6:12; Isaiah 53:8; 66:8; Jeremiah 14:14; 23:16; Ezekiel 13:2, 17; Acts 3:10; Ephesians 3:20; Hebrews 13:3; 1 Peter 4:17), the New Living Translation (1996) (Nehemiah 6:9; Job 37:23; Psalm 41:7; Proverbs 18:11; Isaiah 55:8; Ezekiel 13:3, 17; 16:19; Matthew 10:34; 1 Corinthians 2:9; 1 John 3:2), the English Standard Version (2001) (Psalm 41:7; Acts 17:29; 1 Corinthians 2:9; 8:2; 1 Timothy 6:5), and The Message (2002) (Genesis 6:5; Deuteronomy 4:32; Ruth 1:13; 1 Kings 10:7; 2 Kings 18:24; 2 Chronicles 9:6; Job 3:21; 11:8; 22:25; 36:26; 38:30; 39:10; Proverbs 18:11; 30:12; Song of Solomon 8:3; Isaiah 40:12, 28; 64:4; Jeremiah 3:19; Ezekiel 18:5; Mark 10:24; Luke 11:5; 14:31; 15:8; 23:31; John 21:25; Acts 28:15; Romans 5:17; 11:12; 1 Corinthians 2:9; 4:1; 8:7; 12:21; 14:36; 15:40; 2 Corinthians 12:6; Ephesians 3:20; 1 Thessalonians 2:18), it takes a less overtly negative form than that which results from the cumulative usage of the influential KJV (1611).

Problems of Definition and the 'Heart'

Such cursory observations of the actual incidence of this word, as noted earlier, do not yet establish a clearly defined biblical perspective on the imagination. Since a constellation of different words are translated as 'imagination' or one of its cognates, by differing versions of the Bible in English, a word study works best as a touchstone and point of departure. Insightful discussion has resulted from these etymological analyses, but it is dependent upon specific English translations of the terms above,[15] or others like *bara* (another word for creativity reserved exclusively for God), or the various terms for 'image' such as *eikon* or *charakter*, which soon bring in by implication the whole weight of biblical teaching on creation in the image of God, the sin of idolatry, and the incarnation of Jesus Christ.[16] Those studies which isolate a single term in order to denote what we understand as 'imagination,' including Richard Kearney's

---

[15] Dale Durie, "In Biblical Bounds: Using the Imagination within Biblical Limits," *Preaching to Listeners: Communication with Contemporary Listeners* (Evangelical Homiletics Society: 2002).

[16] Brown, ed, *The New International Dictionary of New Testament Theology*, Entry for 'Image', 284-93.

exploration of *yatsar*, ultimately end by referring to the more holistic term, central to all biblical anthropology, *leb* or *kardia*, the heart.[17]

The affinity between the biblical use of 'heart' and modern conceptions of imagination has been astutely analysed by Garrett Green. After noting the seemingly uncooperative nature of the biblical material when seeking to develop a positive idea of imagination through word analysis, Green moves to equate his own particular construction of the 'paradigmatic imagination' with the biblical use of 'heart.' He adduces apologetics as his motive, believing that translating the Scriptures into such philosophical terminology will enable contemporary readers and hearers to understand its teaching better. If Green's careful formulation is held continually in view, this could be a profitable enterprise, but imagination in common parlance does not incorporate all the diverse elements and attenuations that he outlines. In addition, when seeking to develop a biblical view, it is essential to remain as close as possible to biblical methods of categorisation, therefore 'heart' (as used in the Bible) will not simply be identified in this study with 'imagination' (as Green defines it).[18]

The 'heart' biblically, is the essence of the person, and this denomination is consistent for both the Hebrew *leb* and the Greek *kardia*, as the New Testament writers are far more indebted to the Old Testament usage of the term and development of the concept, than they are to the writings of their pagan Greek contemporaries.[19] While it is possible to identify certain emphases at times on the intellectual, volitional, emotional, ethical and imaginative aspects of human nature in references to the 'heart,' the other elements remain implicitly present, both through the rich and suggestive phrasing, the cumulative effect of the Bible's use of the term, and its uncompromising practice of subsuming all these categories within the spiritual. Even a brief examination of certain key texts makes the point clear. The heart is that which defines the essence of our nature as human beings:

> Keep your heart (*leb*) with all vigilance, for from it flow the springs of life (Proverbs 4:23).

The locus of intellectual determinations:

> The fool says in his heart (*leb*), "There is no God." They are corrupt, they do abominable deeds, there is none who does good (Psalm 14:1).

---

[17] Kearney, *The Wake of Imagination*, 72-3.
[18] Green, *Imagining God*, 108-13.
[19] Kittel and Bromiley, eds, *Theological Dictionary of the New Testament*, Entry for 'Kardia,' 611-13. In addition, the holistic biblical hermeneutic outlined in the Introduction entails that aspects of the human person, as treated in the Old and New Testaments, will be interpreted as supplementary (or complementary) parts subsumed under the wider hermeneutic frame of the scriptural canon.

The ultimate source of imaginative desire and consequent action, whether evil:

> The LORD saw that the wickedness of man was great in the earth, and that every intention of the thoughts of his heart (*leb*) was only evil continually (Genesis 6:5).

> Their eye bulges from fatness; the imaginations of their heart (*lebab*) run riot (Psalm 73:7, NASB).

> But what comes out of the mouth proceeds from the heart (*kardias*), and this defiles a person. For out of the heart (*kardias*) come evil thoughts, murder, adultery, sexual immorality, theft, false witness, slander. These are what defile a person (Matthew 15:18-20).

Or good:

> And you, Solomon my son, know the God of your father and serve him with a whole heart (*leb*) and a willing mind, for the LORD searches all hearts (*leb*), and understands every plan and thought. If you seek him, he will be found by you, but if you forsake him, he will cast you off forever....[Be] strong and do it (1 Chronicles 28:9-10).

> Blessed are the pure in heart (*kardia*), for they shall see God (Matthew 5:8).

The seat of purpose formation:

> Now it was in the heart (*lebab*) of David my father to build a house for the name of the LORD, the God of Israel (1 Kings 8:17).

> And Moses called Bezalel and Oholiab and every craftsman in whose mind the LORD had put skill (*leb*), everyone whose heart (*leb*) stirred him up to come to do the work (Exodus 36:2).

The seat of the emotions:

> Because you did not serve the LORD your God with joyfulness and gladness of heart (*lebab*), because of the abundance of all things (Deuteronomy 28:47).

> I do not say this to condemn you, for I said before that you are in our hearts (*kardiais*), to die together and to live together (2 Corinthians 7:3).

Most importantly, the part of human nature that must be transformed and renewed by God for salvation to come to any individual:

> And I will give you a new heart (*leb*), and a new spirit I will put within you. And I will remove the heart (*leb*) of stone from your flesh and give you a heart (*leb*) of flesh (Ezekiel 36:26).

Because, if you confess with your mouth that Jesus is Lord and believe in your heart (*kardia*) that God raised him from the dead, you will be saved. For with the heart (*kardia*) one believes and is justified, and with the mouth one confesses and is saved....The same Lord is Lord of all, bestowing his riches on all who call on him (Romans 10:9-10, 12).

This brief overview does scant justice to the richness and breadth of the biblical terminology. But it does underline the crucial fact that the heart is a 'comprehensive term for the personality as a whole, its inner life, its character. It is the conscious and deliberate spiritual activity of the self-contained human [being].'[20]

To equate imagination and heart in Green's terms is to replace this crucial biblical concept with a new word already heavily freighted with a different set of associations. Scripture recognises the function more generally denoted 'imagination' (rather than Green's idiosyncratic formulation) as an aspect of the entire human person, expressed in short-hand by the use of 'heart,' as seen above. But it is very rarely isolated in biblical terminology from other functions of the human person, including the rational, volitional, emotional, intellectual and above all spiritual. Imagination is one significant, inextricable part of the complex that makes up our humanity in biblical perspective. 'The imagination is the bridge between the heart and the mind, integrating both, allowing us to think/understand with our hearts and feel/emote with our minds.'[21] In the words of Ephesians it is 'the eyes of [the] heart' (1:18). Imagination is shown biblically to be both corrupt like every aspect of human nature since the Fall and thus intimately connected to intellectual and volitional acts of disobedience against God; but also necessary to a right application of the Word of God, as in the command to 'love your neighbour as yourself' (Matthew 22:39), which implies a degree of empathetic identification. Or to '[r]emember those who are in prison, as though in prison with them, and those who are mistreated, since you also are in the body'(Hebrews 13:3).

It is thus most consistent from a biblical perspective to view imagination as a function integral to the whole human person, but not as comprehensive of all human 'faculties.' For purposes of clarity and refinement, however, it is important to develop a more focused definition of this term, which must always be held in the wider context of a biblical anthropology centred in the heart. Recent analyses of human thought and behaviour have been returning to a more holistic, rather than strictly compartmentalised understanding of human psychology and spirituality, which would support such an approach; although, in this study, they cannot form the authoritative basis for it, given that I am

---

[20] Walter Eichrodt, *Theology of the Old Testament*, vol. 2 (London: SCM Press, 1961-1967), 143.
[21] Card, *Scribbling in the Sand*, 55.

exploring what it means to imagine biblically.[22]

Imagination Defined

Since it was first introduced into English in the thirteenth century, a wide range of definitions have been ascribed to 'imagination.' It has had a chequered history as a concept in philosophical thought from at least the time of Plato and for even longer in the theological speculations of Jewish exegetes. It has been regarded with deep suspicion over the centuries, frequently categorised in opposition to reason, on the outdated model of faculty psychology, or simplistically equated with fantasy and deceit. However, a close reading of its history in Western thought reveals a surprising consistency in the central features attributed to the imagination and offers the potential for a rehabilitation that is neither simplistically dismissive, nor unreservedly celebrative (as Romantic inversions of the Enlightenment valorisation of reason tended to be).[23] Contemporary analysis from a variety of fields including the philosophical, psychological and theological is increasingly emphasising the complex interdependence between human emotion and cognition, in which the imagination plays a central role. There is a general reaction against the tendency to compartmentalise the mind, and a deconstruction of the myth that reason is an objective, unbiased human power able to assess situations, ideas and persons in universal terms, unaffected by the particular complex of emotions, social background, religious allegiance or gender of an individual.[24] This integrated and visceral understanding of the human person is far more

---

[22] Avis, *The Creative Imagination*; Paul Crowther, *Philosophy After Postmodernism: Civilized Values and the Scope of Knowledge* (London: Routledge, 2003); George Lakoff and Mark Johnson, *Metaphors We Live By* (Chicago: University of Chicago Press, 1980); Mark Johnson, *The Body in the Mind: The Bodily Basis of Meaning, Imagination, and Reason* (Chicago: University of Chicago Press, 1987); Kearney, *The Wake of Imagination*; Richard Kearney, *Poetics of Imagining: Modern to Post-Modern*, New ed. (Edinburgh: Edinburgh University Press, 1998); J. D. Lyons, "Descartes and Modern Imagination," *Philosophy and Literature* 23.2 (1999); McIntyre, *Faith, Theology and Imagination*; Colin McGinn, *Mindsight: Image, Dream, Meaning* (Cambridge, Mass.: Harvard University Press, 2005); S. Mithen, "The Evolution of Imagination: An Archaeological Perspective," *SubStance* 30.1 and 2 (2001); Edward Robinson, *The Language of Mystery* (London: SCM Press, 1987); Warnock, *Imagination*; Wilder, *Theopoetic*.

[23] Warnock, *Imagination*.

[24] Avis, *The Creative Imagination*; Bryant, *Faith and the Play of Imagination*; Coulson, *Religion and Imagination*; Fischer, *The Inner Rainbow*; Green, *Theology, Hermeneutics, and Imagination*; Johnson, *The Body in the Mind*; Kaufman, *The Theological Imagination*; David Brown and Ann Loades, eds *Christ: The Sacramental Word* (London: SPCK, 1996); Mithen, "The Evolution of Imagination: An Archaeological Perspective"; Wilder, *Theopoetic*.

compatible with biblical anthropology, which defines the emotional, physical, mental, volitional and spiritual aspects of human nature holistically, centred within and directed by the relational allegiance of the heart. While contemporary analysts rarely acknowledge this final, specifically biblical assumption, their shared recognition of the integrated nature of the human person correlates well with scriptural emphases, and enables a definition of the imagination to be developed that synthesises with the biblical data.[25]

Mary Warnock traces the concept of imagination as it is explored by Hume, Kant, Coleridge, Wordsworth, Wittgenstein and Sartre, concluding after a careful consideration of these influential thinkers that 'there is...a power in the mind, which operates in our everyday perception of the world around us, in our thinking about objects and persons when they are absent from us, so that we endow them with a kind of presence; which enables us to perceive significance in the world around us...to interpret it and to communicate that interpretation to others, 'for them to share or reject'; and which finds expression in, and enables appreciation of, the work of the creative artist.'[26] This definition is useful in that it recognises the central role played by the imagination in our ordinary perception and understanding of the world, clearly demonstrating its importance in synthesising sense-data and interpretation.[27] Warnock shows that there is nothing mystical about the way imagination operates when a gifted individual is creating a work of art, or writing a poem; the same functions which imagination performs in the ordinary processes of perception and communication are simply operating in a heightened manner. Biblical teaching on the creation of all human beings in the image of God, the unique worth of each individual person, and a refusal to accord special aesthetic status to 'the arts' on the grounds that those involved in their pursuit are somehow above the rest of humanity, by affirming the worth of all callings, and the importance of beauty in every part of life, is consistent with such an account.

John McIntyre offers a similar, though less synthesised, analysis of the imagination with a particular theological emphasis, which renders it peculiarly appropriate to the interests of this study. Drawing primarily upon Hume and Sartre he observes that there are three ways of seeing and knowing, 'namely of perceiving, conceiving and imagining.' An image mediates to consciousness the object that the imagination is envisioning, 'the role of imagination...is one way of thinking about an object, distinguishable from the other two, and as much a part of our everyday thinking as they are. It is the mediating

---

[25] Eichrodt, *Theology of the Old Testament*, 143; C. Ryder Smith, *The Biblical Doctrine of Man* (London: Epworth Press, 1951).
[26] This helpful summary is given by John McIntyre in *Faith, Theology and Imagination*, 122.
[27] See Warnock's book for a detailed philosophical analysis of the processes involved; it is beyond the scope of this definition to attempt such an account of imagination. Warnock, *Imagination*.

consciousness by which the absent is envisioned as present, or the non-perceived is thought about and talked about.' Sartre, following Kant, identifies the imagination as 'an essential and transcendental condition of consciousness,' it 'posit[s] the world as a synthetic whole.' Imagination is thus 'contiguous with the real world...it has a very special part to play in the construction and maintenance of that real world,' that is by 'making explicit what is implicit in the meaning of the real...imagination [plays] an interpretative role in our relation to reality.' In addition, it is this same consciousness which 'by taking the step of imagining can escape from that world' by going beyond it.[28]

Uniquely, however, McIntyre also examines imagination as a biblical category of thought, focusing specifically upon the parabolic thinking which characterises Jesus's presentation of his message in the New Testament. He argues that 'the way in which we entertain these parables is exactly by employing that imaginative consciousness which Sartre has so carefully outlined for us.'[29] This is significant because McIntyre here demonstrates the way in which the literary structure of a central feature of the New Testament models a form of thinking that has implications for defining the imagination as a biblical category. Though his argument focuses primarily upon the parables, he does demonstrate briefly the way this 'realistic imagination' is also at work in the narratives of the Old Testament, such as the account of Elijah at Mount Carmel (1 Kings 18:20-40) and in the institution of the eucharist. He questions any interpretation of these narratives as acted parables

> on the ground that it dichotomises what is in fact a unity. There are not two things, the action and the parable, the one separated from the other by the relation which connects symbol and symbolised, example and the point being illustrated by the example. The acted parable is a unity, and it is so in virtue of what I call the 'realistic imagination,' which sees as one what we divide into the two components in a situation with an external reference.

McIntyre refuses to accept the modification drawn from Wittgenstein, which replaces the dualisms of sign/signified or symbol/symbolised with the concept of 'looking-on' or 'seeing-as,' since this also assumes a prior separation and cannot achieve a unity that has already been destroyed. This distinguishes him from many other theologians of the imagination who were reviewed earlier, such as David Bryant and Garrett Green. Turning to the paradigm that is implicitly or explicitly central to almost all discussions of language and reference (sacred and secular), McIntyre argues that Jesus's association of bread and body, blood and wine, effected an 'immediacy of identity...through the realistic imagination.' As the disciples receive the bread and wine, they are 'guided by Jesus's own use of realistic imagination' and by participation accept the identification. In order to further explicate the term 'immediacy of identity,'

---

[28] McIntyre, *Faith, Theology and Imagination*, 118-21.
[29] McIntyre, *Faith, Theology and Imagination*, 120.

McIntyre draws upon an event that is central to any truly biblical understanding of imagination, the incarnation. "Immediacy' here carries the connotation of being unmediated, that is, by such relationships as 'symbolising', 'illustrating', or even 'revealing', though the last term comes closest...very much as the humanity of Christ is both an element in the Revealer and a component in the Revelatum.'[30] In order to underline both the uniqueness of this mode of thinking, and the necessity of ascribing it to the imagination, McIntyre returns to Hume and Sartre's tripartite division of human cognition: 'Hume...ruled out the senses....The senses perceive only bread and wine. He ruled out reason which can reach only as far as regular succession....It is realistic imagination which makes the immediate identification.'[31]

McIntyre also provides a helpful summary of the various roles which the imagination plays, deduced from his consideration of its epistemological, philosophical and theological history as a concept. This functional approach synchronises well with the concrete and practical emphasis of the biblical text, providing a theoretical foundation for the way in which its literary forms and subject-matter can be utilised to develop a uniquely scriptural understanding of this human capacity. The imagination is able to perceive features of the world that go unnoticed in ordinary observation; it selects salient features from the mass of materials that confront the mind and arranges the mass around and in terms of the features selected. Imagination is creative and constructive thought, drawing diverse elements into unitary form; it is interpretive, observing analogical connections essential to explanation. Perhaps most crucially, imagination is cognitive, there are things that we could not know if imagination had not been employed; this is of particular significance when considering its relationship to literature.[32] The imagination is empathetic, allowing us to project ourselves affectively and emotionally, as well as intellectually, into a situation; this can involve making the absent present, whether past, contemporaneous or future, without eliding a consciousness of the immediate spatio-temporal condition in which we are currently situated. It is also communicative, the means by which we present our understanding of the world to others; artists have this capacity in a heightened measure. Finally, drawing upon an observation by Iris Murdoch, McIntyre concludes that imagination creates 'our-world,' the synthesis of our values, principles, prejudices, religious commitments and subjects of faith. It is the framework within which our

---

[30] McIntyre, *Faith, Theology and Imagination*, 32-9. There are important theological issues which this discussion raises concerning the relationship of imagination to faith. These will be dealt with at a later point. It is necessary to note here that the discussion of the eucharist is being taken as paradigmatic of the imagination as it functions 'realistically'; it is obviously not a fully explicated theology of the ordinance.

[31] McIntyre, *Faith, Theology and Imagination*, 39.

[32] See also Jeremy Begbie on the philosophical and theological implications of this function of imagination. Begbie, *Voicing Creation's Praise*, 238-9, 248-9.

decisions are made, our ambitions defined, our emotional reactions stimulated, and in most general terms our lives are lived.[33]

In order to tie these general observations about the imagination to the biblical text that underlies the theoretical claims of this study, elaborating its significance for the literary imagination in particular, it is useful to turn to the work of Paul Ricoeur. His sensitivity to the generic forms of scriptural discourse and careful elaboration of their philosophical, ethical and hermeneutical implications is invaluable when seeking to develop a biblical understanding of what is involved in the act of imagining, enabling the particular trajectories that the Scriptures invite one to consider to be identified and examined. While recognising the insights of the historical-critical method, Ricoeur brackets this level of analysis, in order to explore the biblical text as a *Sitz im Wort* of diverse literary genres.[34] These are identified as 'narratives, prophecies, laws, proverbs, prayers, hymns, liturgical formulas, and wisdom writings,' amongst others.[35] Ricoeur sees each of these genres as offering a unique way of thinking, or perceiving reality, which operate dialectically, modifying one another in a 'biblical polyphony'[36] that collectively forms a 'hermeneutic of revelation' and 'names God,' though never comprehensively.[37]

Ricoeur takes the intertextual nature of Scripture and the implicit hermeneutic which this embodies as his point of departure, suggesting that it provides a heuristic model for the operation of the imagination itself in interpretation, appropriation and creation.[38] This sensitivity to the form as well as the content of the canon enables an exploration of what it means to imagine biblically which avoids 'theory-heavy methods of biblical reading in favor of a text-immanent approach that projects possibilities of meaning occasioned by the texts themselves.'[39] Paradigmatic of the various trajectories of imagining at work in the biblical text, is narrative, particularly as seen in the parables. Ricoeur demonstrates the way in which McIntyre's analysis of biblical parables, with their implications for understanding the imagination, can be extended to incorporate other biblical genres in a kind of dialectical, heuristic polyphony.[40] Richard Eslinger puts forward a similar argument. He suggests

---

[33] McIntyre, *Faith, Theology and Imagination*, 159-68.

[34] Mark I. Wallace, "Introduction," *Figuring the Sacred: Religion, Narrative, and Imagination* (Minneapolis: Fortress Press, 1995), 24.

[35] Paul Ricoeur, "Naming God," *Figuring the Sacred: Religion, Narrative, and Imagination* (Minneapolis: Fortress Press, 1995), 224.

[36] Ricoeur, "Naming God," 223.

[37] Ricoeur, "Naming God."

[38] Paul Ricoeur, "The Bible and the Imagination," *The Bible as a Document of the University*, ed. H. D. Betz, (Chicago: Scholars Press, 1981).

[39] Wallace, "Introduction," 24.

[40] Paul Ricoeur, "Biblical Time," *Figuring the Sacred: Religion, Narrative, and Imagination* (Minneapolis: Fortress Press, 1995); Ricoeur, "The Bible and the Imagination." Kevin Vanhoozer outlines the implications of these various literary forms

not only that narrative is the primary genre, but that Scripture itself 'is best construed within the category of narrative.' Wisdom literature, parable and apocalypse, the genres which would appear to most stringently challenge this, are ultimately explainable only by an eschatological orientation grounded within the historical context of the gospel accounts. 'To the extent that a hermeneutic is being proposed...that seeks to integrate...both narrative and imagery, apocalyptic becomes a significant expression of this intersection.'[41]

The dimensions explored here illustrate clearly that a biblical understanding of imagination necessarily extends far beyond literature to incorporate every aspect of human life. The depth of the biblical definition and the explicit connection it makes between literature and life is demonstrated in the description Paul gives to the believers in Ephesus: 'For we are his workmanship (*poema*), created in Christ Jesus for good works' (Ephesians 2:10); they are invited to see themselves as poems being written by the divine Creator. In the biblical vision of reality, truth is ultimately relational, whether one is considering God, other people, or texts.[42] Though the primary focus of this study is upon the literary imagination in biblical perspective, it is important to recognise that the Bible does not separate artistic production from ethical responsibility, or the life led by an author or reader.

The Literary Form of Scripture

The Biblical Metanarrative

The Bible as a whole possesses a remarkable unity which is again being recognised, particularly through the increased attention given to the text by literary scholars, and the rise of narrative theology. This comprehensive plotline forms an entire worldview and has profound moral, social, political and ethical consequences when embraced. The focus of this section will be on the relationship of this plotline to the imagination. The working definition of imagination outlined earlier, emphasises that it is a function which operates both in relation to our experience of reality in nature and history, as well as to more fantastic dimensions that project us beyond our spatio-temporal existence. Given the strong cultural bias against any association between imagination and truth, it is important to emphasise again that imagination plays an integral role in our relationship to all phenomena as human beings. The Bible maps history,

---

for understanding the imagination biblically in *Is There a Meaning in This Text?*, 336-50 and *First Theology: God, Scripture and Hermeneutics* (Downers Grove: InterVarsity Press, 2002), 127-58, 347-50.

[41] Richard L. Eslinger, *Narrative and Imagination: Preaching the Worlds That Shape Us* (Minneapolis: Fortress Press, 1995), 21-3.

[42] Alan Jacobs, *A Theology of Reading: The Hermeneutics of Love* (Oxford: Westview Press, 2001); Thiselton, *Interpreting God and the Postmodern Self*, 41.

experience, judgement, eternity and every dimension of human existence in the context of a comprehensive plotline that shapes the imagination, forms its culture, and provides the framework for its interpretation and vision. As Iris Murdoch has observed, 'through the imagination, we all of us construct ourworld; we choose to live within this world, partly private, partly fabricated.'[43] In the Western tradition this has been so pervasively woven into the thread of daily life and common narratives, that it is difficult to trace the actual effects of the widespread biblical influence on the cultural imagination: in concepts of time, linear progression, purpose, moral absolutes and so on. Only with the advent of postmodern experimentation with narrative and an increasingly relativist and pluralist society antagonistic to such assumptions, have these foundations been exposed more clearly by parodies that nevertheless remain indebted to a consciousness of the prototypes for their meaning to be clear.

The biblical plotline can be outlined simply according to its most prominent features: creation, fall, redemption, sanctification and glorification. Between them these terms encapsulate the Bible's central message about God in relation to the universe, human beings, the current state of the world, and what lies beyond the end of time. To imagine biblically one needs a biblically literate imagination; one shaped structurally, hermeneutically, emotionally and volitionally by the overall pattern and paradigm of the biblical plotline.

> All imagination is embodied. Images differ from concepts in the clay that clings to them. Scripture itself imagines a world....[It] is rooted in the physical realm where humans live. But...is by no means simply to be identified with the physical realm where humans live and act....The world constructed by Scripture also provides an opening to new perceptions of the here and now, and provides options for disposing of this and that in ways not otherwise imaginable. By imagining the world as always and essentially related to God, Scripture reveals the world and at the same time reveals God. People act on the basis of the imagined world in which they dwell, and by acting on what they imagine, they help establish their worlds as real....[T]he way I have laid this out reflects our loss of that world imagined by Scripture, for if we really inhabited it wholly, we could not speak of it as one world among others, as one more or less attractive option to be entertained; it would be, if we inhabited it wholly, simply our world.[44]

The biblical imagination is an exclusive envisioning of the world: in this pluralistic postmodern era it does not, when taken on its own terms, allow a dizzying play of innumerable alternatives. Its claims upon the imagination incorporate history also, as the plotline finds its illuminating focus at a particular moment in time: the incarnation of Jesus Christ (Galatians 4:4-5).

These two dimensions, of a biblical plotline that forms a comprehensive worldview and an historical reference, are fused existentially in the present of

---

[43] Cited by McIntyre, *Faith, Theology and Imagination*, 125.
[44] Johnson, "Imagining the World Scripture Imagines," 3-5.

an individual by the typological imagination that Scripture fosters:

> It sees every moment in this kingdom-saga as linked mysteriously to every other, and it envisions itself as an actor in this drama. It reads life as a meaningful history, the structure of which ("that plan hidden since the beginning of the world") was revealed in Christ....In every era, in every life, it recognises the creation-death-resurrection pattern epitomized in Christ's life. And it interprets every event as an essential moment in the movement of time toward eternity....[It] does not thrive in the disconnected instant...does not seek intense shock nor orchestrate instant gratification. Rather it seeks to recognize the stamp of eternity in every present, and to reinsert the lived moment in the whole sweep of human history.[45]

Thus the biblical plotline becomes exemplary for the narration of personal and social histories. When typology is understood as a key feature of the biblical perspective on imagination, the plotline provides not only the governing imagery, but also a methodology or hermeneutic for narrating thought and being.

Pluriform Structure and Language

The Bible is not a systematic philosophical or theological treatise, but rather a collection of books incorporating a wide diversity of literary genres: a rich tapestry of historical narrative, poetry, parable and epistle. In addition, its language is studded with key images and metaphors, such as the garden, the way, the lamb, the cross, bread, blood, water and many others, that are crucial to its message, and help to link the diversity of literary genres into a cohesive whole. This poetic use of language and proliferation of genre both implicitly affirm the imagination as a means of communicating truth: they also demand an active use of imagination on the part of readers when interpreting and applying the text; particularly prophetic language, paradox and parables.[46] The biblical text incorporates a respect for form and style as well as content, as the book of Ecclesiastes records: 'The Preacher sought to find words of delight, and uprightly he wrote words of truth. The words of the wise are like goads, and like nails firmly fixed are the collected sayings; they are given by one Shepherd' (12:10-11). Here beauty and utility are combined with the purpose of engendering personal, affective transformation, underwriting the imagination from a scriptural angle. Indeed, it is the admixture of the biblical text as both an authoritative religious document and rich artistic model that has caused it to exercise such a powerful influence on the development of English literature.

To take just one instance amongst many, the Song of Solomon is a collection

---

[45] Janine Langan, "The Christian Imagination," *The Christian Imagination*, ed. Leland Ryken (Colorado Springs: Shaw, 2002), 67-8.
[46] Avis, *The Creative Imagination;* Card, *Scribbling in the Sand*, 54-61.

of poetry within the scriptural canon that 'proclaims the power of imagination' through the metaphors by which it celebrates love and lovers.

> The verb *damah* ("to be like") occurs with particular frequency; in one of its conjugations, *dimmah*, it means "to liken, to compare," but also "to conjure up a mental image, to imagine, to fantasize." The lover imagines the Shulamite as a mare (the verb here is *dimmitih*, 1.9) and a palm tree (dametah, 7:8); she imagines him as a gazelle or a stag (*domeh*, 2:9), and tells him to "be like" a gazelle or a stag (*demeh leka*, 2:17, 8:14). In using these verbs, as Robert Alter has observed, the poet is "flaunting the effect of figurative comparison," deliberately calling attention to the workings of simile and metaphor, and by extension, the workings of the imagination. We have already noticed the role of fantasy in the Song. It is often hard to tell what is real and what imagined; for that reason, many readers have found the poem to be dreamlike, with a freedom of movement, a dizzying fluidity, that conveys the intoxication of the senses.[47]

The repetitive use of simile and metaphor in the biblical text affirms the imagination and is central also to the technique of parallelism which, at least since Robert Lowth's lectures in the eighteenth century, has been viewed as the most uniquely distinguishing feature of biblical poetry.[48] Metaphor is crucial to understanding how the imagination functions and this will be explored further in the chapter on C. S. Lewis.

Eschatology of Hope

It is important to recognise that the metanarrative of the biblical text establishes a teleological perspective that reconfigures an individual's understanding of temporal experience. Anthony Thiselton speaks of the 'divine promise and agency' which opens the apparent desperation, constriction and injustice of the present to 'a hermeneutic of hope and expectation.'[49] This theological horizon is central to the structure of the New Testament, picking up and extending the messianic and millennial expectations that inspired the Old Testament prophets, and focused upon the resurrection of Christ as a 'first-fruit' of the ultimate restoration.

> But if there is no resurrection of the dead, then not even Christ has been raised....If in this life only we have hoped in Christ, we are of all people most to be pitied. But in fact Christ has been raised from the dead, the firstfruits of those who have fallen asleep. For as by a man came death, by a man has come also the

---

[47] Ariel and Chana Bloch, *The Song of Songs: A New Translation with an Introduction and Commentary* (New York: Random House, 1995), 14-15.

[48] Robert Alter, *The Art of Biblical Poetry* (Edinburgh: T & T Clark, 1985).

[49] Thiselton, *Interpreting God and the Postmodern Self*, 78. The second phrase is a quotation from Charles V. Gerkin.

resurrection of the dead...in Christ shall all be made alive (1 Corinthians 15:13, 19-22).

This faith in a Christocentric biblical vision opens a transcendent dimension upon human existence, which is integral to the scriptural understanding of reality.[50] It demands a hope which liberates, exercises and stretches the imagination in freedom and anticipation, based upon faith in the supreme Other who has declared: 'Behold, I am making all things new' (Revelation 21:5).[51]

Imagination and Faith

The relationship between imagination and faith is complex. However, there is a fine but crucial distinction that needs to be made when understanding and analysing the former from a biblical perspective. Paul Avis and John McIntyre offer carefully attenuated descriptions of this distinction.

> Faith is the act of the whole person and has as its object a personal God. Faith cannot be less than personal and personalist categories are required to interpret it. Provided that we remember this, we may speak of the role of various faculties in conducing to faith: reason, conscience and imagination....Faith is indeed the gift of God...but it operates through human faculties, among which the imagination is pivotal.[52]

> Faith does much that imagination can not be expected to do: for example, obey, trust, acknowledge, respond, decide, to mention but a few. What is being said is that a genuine contribution can be made to our understanding of the nature of faith, as well as of the subject to which faith is related...if we allow that imagination, realistic imagination of the kind that we have been describing, has a proper place within it.[53]

It is the synthesising power of the imagination that enables the emotive, intellectual and volitional aspects of faith to be meaningfully incorporated from a human perspective. George MacDonald encapsulates the central role that imagination plays in the human perception of truth:

> The truth of a thing, then is the blossom of it, the thing it is made for, the topmost stone set on with rejoicing; truth in a man's imagination is the power to recognise

---

[50] Ryken, *The Liberated Imagination*, 16-17.
[51] See also Richard Bauckham, *The Theology of the Book of Revelation* (Cambridge: Cambridge University Press, 1993), especially 51-3.
[52] Avis, *The Creative Imagination*, 78.
[53] McIntyre, *Faith, Theology and Imagination*, 37.

this truth of a thing. But far higher will the doing of the least, the most insignificant, duty raise him.[54]

Imagination is a function of all human beings, held by virtue of their creation in the image of God; it can be used either for good or evil. Faith, however, is a supernatural gift (Ephesians 2:8), biblically focused upon Jesus Christ in his saving work upon the cross (Acts 20:20-1), that engages, reorientates and transforms the heart of an individual, with the consequence that their mind, affections, will, and imagination are all directed by the Spirit of God in obedience to the commands of God (Romans 8:1-17). Saving faith, therefore, operates existentially through the imagination and other aspects of rational personhood, but it is not native to it, nor able to be generated by it (Ephesians 2:8-10; Hebrews 11:6): the Spirit of God is necessary to a truly saving transformation (Romans 8:9), resulting in a relationship of living, personal communion (John 14:17-18, 20-21, 23-26). This distinction between faith and imagination also enables a differentiation to be drawn between the empathy invited by fictional characters and the ethical demands of the living other. In both, imagination is crucial to understanding the identity of the other as other: however, in the first instance imagination is all that is required; in the second, faith must step in and do 'much that imagination can not be expected to do...obey, trust, acknowledge, respond, decide....'[55] The literary imagination in biblical perspective, does not require this additional dimension, though the broader accountability of the existential imagination does.

Inspiration and Creativity

This study draws a distinction between the inspiration of the biblical writers and the inspiration of creative artists: what then does the Bible have to say concerning the latter? In fact, the text offers little by way of objective analysis on this controversial matter. It is far more interested in focusing on the various uses people make of their imagination than it is in providing an analytic of the function. Lewis makes this point with characteristic trenchancy when observing that engagement with culture is directed by the same biblical principles as sweeping a room. Both are to be done to the glory of God.[56] It is possible, though, to deduce some salient features from the Scriptures that enable a biblical understanding of human creativity to be developed.

Human beings are made in the 'image of God' according to the creation account in Genesis. While there is much dispute as to what precisely this image

---

[54] C. S. Lewis, ed, *George Macdonald: An Anthology* (London: Geoffrey Bles, 1946), 82.
[55] McIntyre, *Faith, Theology and Imagination*, 37.
[56] C. S. Lewis, "Christianity and Culture," *C. S. Lewis: Essay Collection and Other Short Pieces*, ed. L. Walmsley (London: HarperCollins, 2000), 78-9.

consists of, the immediate context, as Dorothy Sayers points out, is creation. All that is known of God at this point is that he creates, and that human beings are made in his image.[57] It is reasonable to assume that this forms a part of the likeness. It is obviously not a one to one equation, all aspects of human knowledge of God are analogical to some degree, and the difference in this situation is emphasised by the use of two distinct Hebrew words for 'creation.' As noted earlier, *yatsar*, is employed to denote forming on the part of both God and humans. However, the word *bara*, meaning the creation of something completely new, *ex nihilo*, occurs several times in Genesis 1 and throughout the Old Testament, but it only ever refers to the work of God.[58] It is his sole prerogative and power to call things into being out of nothing, to constitute spiritual and material reality through the authority and energy of his word. In this sense he is the absolute and only Creator (Genesis 1:1-3; Psalm 51:10; Hebrews 11:3), as the writer to the Hebrews observes of the Incarnate Word: 'He is the radiance of the glory of God and the exact imprint of his nature, and he upholds the universe by the word of his power' (1:3).

This distinction between Creator and creature has led some, such as George MacDonald, to state that it is ridiculous (even blasphemous) to attribute creativity to human beings. Provided that this central biblical separation between the divine and human is recognised, though, it seems unhelpful to enforce a semantic purity that is valid in Hebrew, but cannot be maintained in English without the continual use of qualifying statements. Creativity is thus being treated here as an aspect of the human person involving the active engagement of the imagination, inherent in all individuals by virtue of the creation of man and woman in the image of God. The biblical concept of creativity is not limited to a narrowly defined sphere of aesthetics, or even the arts. Nor did it begin to operate only after the Fall, as the means by which humans devised compensatory alternatives in a world alienated from God and distorted by sin. Creativity is a comprehensive function that was exercised in Eden prior to the Fall, as Adam and Eve sought to fulfil the divine mandate God gave in the form of both a blessing and a command: 'Be fruitful and multiply and fill the earth and subdue it and have dominion over the fish of the sea and over the birds of the heavens and over every living thing that moves on the earth' (Genesis 1:28).

Something of the way in which this was to be practically worked out can be seen as God 'formed every beast of the field and every bird of the heavens and brought them to the man to see what he would call them. And whatever the man called every living creature, that was its name' (Genesis 2:19). Naming in Hebrew thought involved far more than arbitrary signification; it entailed

---

[57] Dorothy L. Sayers, *The Mind of the Maker*, (1941; reprint ed. Cleveland: World, 1956), 34.
[58] Philip H. Eveson, *The Book of Origins: Genesis Simply Explained* (Darlington: Evangelical Press, 2001), 23-25.

carefully considering each animal, encapsulating its essential nature in the name given.[59] There is a close affinity between this process, and a well-known statement by Shakespeare concerning the more familiar and specifically fictional power of the imagination:

> ...imagination bodies forth
> The forms of things unknown, the poet's pen
> Turns them to shapes, and gives to airy nothing
> A local habitation and a name.[60]

The ability to communicate in language is a key aspect of human creation in the image of God, and one of the ways in which the world is made habitable, 'subdued,' by Adam and Eve. Creative engagement with the natural order entailed stewardship, accountability, and a sensitively caring cultivation of that which was other: 'The LORD God took the man and put him in the garden of Eden to work it and keep it' (Genesis 2:15). This image of the cultivated garden is suggestive and its combination of observant response and perceptive innovation has exercised a potent influence upon understandings of the role of human creativity in life and art. The example of Adam's naming, when coupled with the image of the garden, makes clear the distinction between human and divine creativity. The 'making' denoted by *yatsar*, that is using existing material, is characterisitc of both God and human beings. Human creativity in all dimensions of life is a response to that which has been given, never like the creativity denoted by *bara* which involves a bringing of what is completely new into existence and biblically belongs to God alone.

The Fall complicates this picture of original sympathy between God, human beings and the natural world. Alienation in relationships, toil in labour, and pain, all become integral aspects of a world under the judgement of the Creator. However, the biblical narrative does not end in a dualism of original good and irrevocable evil. There is, in the midst of the curse, the initiation of a promise through the line of the woman that engenders hope (Genesis 3:15). What Michael Edwards, following Blaise Pascal, calls a 'ternary process':

> ...the *grandeur* and *misère*...a precise pattern for understanding the pattern of everything. All that is great about a man derives from his 'first nature,' given to him in 'the state of creation.' His wretchedness – blindness, 'concupiscence,' mortality – is constituted by his 'second nature,' which has resulted from the original sin of Adam. A man is therefore no longer a 'simple subject'; his condition is double, and he will appear plausibly great or wretched according to the perspective in which he is viewed....Because his dualism is based on the Fall,

---

[59] Eveson, *The Book of Origins*, 76-7, 111-12, 131; John McIntyre, *On the Love of God* (London: Collins, 1962), 108-11.
[60] William Shakespeare, *A Midsummer Night's Dream* (New York: Airmont Publishing, 1965), 5.1.14-17.

and describes a dynamic rather than a static world, it also opens to the future. The thesis of *grandeur* and the antithesis of *misère* are in motion, both logically and historically, and they culminate and are exceeded in Jesus Christ. Jesus is the supreme paradox. In his two natures he unites the greatness of God and the wretchedness of fallen man....Divine, he undergoes death. Yet in reconciling the contraries he also draws beyond them. By the extreme greatness of his extremely wretched death, he overcomes wretchedness, and initiates a renewed greatness.[61]

This captures the essential plotline of the Bible and the history of salvation subsequent to the Fall. It is the basic context for a biblical examination of all aspects of human nature including creativity. No longer pure in heart by nature, the tendency of human creativity as the Bible presents it is towards pride, corruption and the perpetration of evil. Human beings are still the image-bearers of God, able to create powerful civilisations, but these can be falsely directed: as is exhibited potently by the Tower of Babel (Genesis 11:1-9). Yet, the promise given after the Fall is further explicated and engenders a redemptive hope of ultimate recreation. Under the renewing and transforming power of the Spirit of God, individuals can be reestablished in communion with God through Jesus Christ. Living in eschatological hope of a 'new heavens and a new earth', entails existential tensions for those in the world, but not of it (2 Peter 3:13; 1 Corinthians 7:31), most poignantly expressed by Paul:

> If the Spirit of him who raised Jesus from the dead dwells in you, he who raised Christ Jesus from the dead will also give life to your mortal bodies through his Spirit who dwells in you....For I consider that the sufferings of this present time are not worth comparing with the glory that is to be revealed to us. For the creation waits with eager longing for the revealing of the sons of God. For the creation was subjected to futility, not willingly, but because of Him who subjected it, in hope that the creation itself will be set free from its bondage to decay and obtain the freedom of the glory of the children of God. For we know that the whole creation has been groaning together in the pains of childbirth until now. And not only the creation, but we ourselves, who have the firstfruits of the Spirit, groan inwardly as we wait eagerly for adoption as sons, the redemption of our bodies. For in this hope we were saved (Romans 8:11, 18-24).

The creation mandate still applies. The earth is to be renewed and reclaimed creatively in every sphere, under the direction of the Spirit, in hope of the ultimate moment, when 'the earth will be filled with the knowledge of the glory of the LORD as the waters cover the sea' (Habakkuk 2:14).

The Bible presents creativity as an aspect inherent in human nature in this fallen world, whether one is graciously restored to communion with God or not. The biblical portrait of human beings has, as Pascal notes, elements of both *grandeur* and *misère*. Thus, in outlining the multiplication and spread of human civilisation, it is the descendants of ungodly Cain, rather than the chosen Seth,

---

[61] Michael Edwards, *Towards a Christian Poetics* (London: Macmillan, 1984), 2-4.

that are described as being most artistically and technologically innovative: 'Jubal...was the father of all those who play the lyre and pipe. Zillah also bore Tubal-Cain; he was the forger of all instruments of bronze and iron' (Genesis 4:21-22). Such natural human creativity could be directed towards positive ends, and the Bible encompasses this within the providential framework of common grace: 'The God who made the world and everything in it...gives to all mankind life and breath and everything. And he made from one man every nation of mankind to live on all the face of the earth' (Acts 17:24-26). It can also, as the Bible frequently depicts, be directed towards evil, particularly arrogant self-exaltation: 'They said: 'Come, let us build ourselves a city and a tower with its top in the heavens, and let us make a name for ourselves...'(Genesis 11:4). This tendency is graphically characterised in the type of the wicked man in Proverbs (6:12-18). Such evil ingenuity can move beyond a malicious plotting of evil. Amos describes the way in which rich people oppress the poor in order to attain wealth that funds the creation of beauty; then art and music are embraced in order to conceal the absence and neglect of true righteousness (Amos 3:15-4:1; 5:23-24). Clearly human beings can express creative ability in a way that is artistically beautiful and ethically repugnant; biblically, whilst evil can clothe itself with a resplendent attractiveness, true beauty is characterised by purity, love and justice.

One complex aspect of developing a biblical perspective on the creative imagination, concerns the relationship between the Spirit and artistic inspiration. The Scripture clearly claims that its human authors are divinely inspired, giving unique authority and status to the biblical text. However, artists and writers also often claim inspiration: there are certain instances in the Bible when men and women are specifically described as being inspired by God for the artistic work he calls them to do. The most notable instance is Bezalel in the construction of the Tabernacle:

> Then Moses said to the people of Israel, "See, the LORD has called by name Bezalel the son of Uri...and He has filled him with the Spirit of God, with skill, with intelligence, with knowledge, and with all craftsmanship, to devise artistic designs, to work in gold and silver and bronze, in cutting stones for setting, and in carving wood, for work in every skilled craft. And he has inspired him to teach, both him and Oholiab....He has filled them with skill to do every sort of work done by an engraver or by a designer or by an embroiderer in blue and purple and scarlet yarns and fine twined linen, or by a weaver – by any sort of workman or skilled designer. Bezalel and Oholiab and every craftsman in whom the LORD has put skill and intelligence to know how to do any work in the construction of the sanctuary shall work in accordance with all that the LORD has commanded (Exodus 35:30-36:1).

This passage speaks of the Spirit of the Lord giving wisdom to Bezalel in a very practical sense at a key moment in Israel's redemptive history. Having just been rescued from Egypt, under Moses, the people are building a Tabernacle for the worship of God. The artistic gifts of Bezalel, Oholiab, and their fellow workers are described as coming from God, their hearts are stirred in the same way as those who gave materially to the work, and it is done 'in accordance with all that the LORD...commanded.' The prophet Daniel, similarly, was given 'learning and skill in all literature and wisdom and...understanding in all visions and dreams' (Daniel 1:17).

Obviously, this is quite a different model of inspiration to the intense self-oblation or frenzy that is so often paradigmatic in the modern mind. There is a specific reference to giftedness by the Spirit, that parallels biblical references to the calling of other men and women as prophets, apostles, or leaders (Judges 3:9-10; 1 Samuel 3:1-10, 19-20; 16:1, 7, 12-13; 1 Corinthians 12:28); but despite the uniqueness of this remarkable man, Bezalel is not described as an original genius, and though known by name, his work follows a God-given pattern. The sanctuary played a crucial role in the national life of Israel under the Old Covenant, biblical teaching in the New Testament era focuses almost exclusively upon the work of the Spirit in spiritual regeneration and renewal, a transforming of human beings into the image of Christ (John 16:8-11; Romans 8:1-27; 2 Corinthians 3:15-18; Ephesians 3:16-19). It is impossible to draw a clear line in human terms between the providential workings of God in natural events, and the supernatural infusion of grace in salvation, as Jeremy Begbie helpfully points out, particularly when one focuses upon the theological implications of the incarnation.[62] But there is no biblical warrant for using the model of prophetic and apostolic calling, authorisation and inspiration by the Spirit as an exact parallel for the role of the contemporary poet or artist. Even with Bezalel, the biblical focus falls upon his technical skills, the desire in his heart to serve, and the wisdom he shows in the creative work he produced. The artistic gifts were God-given and to be used responsibly.[63]

In biblical perspective all human creativity is clearly presented as a gift from God: 'Every good gift and every perfect gift is from above, coming down from the Father of lights with whom there is no variation or shadow due to change' (James 1:17). The temporal world is proclaimed good and to be enjoyed (Genesis 1:31; Ecclesiastes 3:11-13; 1 Corinthians 10:31; 1 Timothy 6:17): this includes poetic praise and celebration (Psalms 8, 19, 24, 29 and so on); artistic excellence in painting, architecture, landscaping, and love (Exodus 35-39; Song of Solomon 1-8); faithfulness in pursuing the vocation of artist, writer, poet, or musician to the glory of God, if that is what one is gifted in (Psalm 45:1-2; Acts 18:1-3; 1 Corinthians 10:31; Colossians 3:23-24). However, gifts by nature good can be used for evil (Colossians 3:25). There are no grounds biblically for granting artists a privileged position, either of inspiration by the Spirit of God

---

[62] Begbie, *Voicing Creation's Praise*, 150-55, 257.

[63] Roger Lundin offers a more modest, biblical account of the imagination as a creative response to the otherness of creation in "Skipping the History: The Question of Art as Sacrament," *Image: A Journal of the Arts* 35 (2002).

that guarantees the truth of what they create, nor which insulates them from the ethical and moral standards that apply to all human beings (Romans 2:6-11). The Romantic poets, particularly William Blake and Percy Bysshe Shelley, redefined the biblical role of the prophet and understanding of inspiration in such a way that it became a model for their own understanding of the privileged position that they, as contemporary 'legislators of the world,' held within British society. The poet, artist and writer biblically, of course, must speak the truth. However, if a privileged position of authority in speaking the truth is given in Scripture to any role, it is that of the preacher or prophet, not the poet (though these roles do not need to be seen as mutually exclusive).

It may be helpful, at this point, to consider one final issue of intense controversy in relation to human creativity: how important, and how achievable, is originality? Can human beings create or do they simply appropriate and imitate what is already given in various ways? This opposition may not be the best way of formulating the matter, as it imposes an unhelpful and potentially false dichotomy. It is, at least in part, an attempt to come to terms with artistic freedom, human capability and worth. Commentators using the biblical text as a point of departure have come up with very different answers, from the positive affirmation of originality and power in Sir Philip Sidney's *Defence of Poesie*, to the distaste for self-display, mistrust of originality, and emphasis on imitation and reflection that characterises the observations of C. S. Lewis. The contention of various commentators, including most notably Leland Ryken, that the biblical text supports a balanced position between the two views, appears to me at least best to acknowledge the full dimensions of its multivalent perspective.[64]

The Bible teaches that every human being is unique, made in the image of a God who creates, and accountable for their decisions to the One who created them. This suggests a real degree of freedom and possibility. However, the Bible also states that the human heart is sinful, by nature prone to evil. The gospel emphasises the need to turn from oneself and toward God with an openness that flows into relationships with others. *Grandeur* and *misère*, freedom and humility, nature and grace: these themes form the familiar contours of all human experience. Imagination can never, of itself, grant a privileged access to saving truth; nor can the experience of an artistic work by virtue of its own inherent power save anyone. Yet, human beings are gifted in diverse ways, the creation mandate was 'to fill the earth and subdue it' (Genesis 1:28), necessarily implying a responsible interaction with all aspects of the created order. The imagination of a gifted individual, open to the glory of creation, can truly and uniquely embody and mediate aspects of truth and reality to various audiences, enabling a greater appreciation of and sensitivity to the fulness of the natural and spiritual world. But its worth does not consist in the fact that it bears the unique *imprimatur* of the artist, as Paul demonstrates in

---

[64] Ryken, *The Liberated Imagination*, 65-70.

a rhetorical question to the Corinthians: 'What do you have that you did not receive?' (1 Corinthians 4:7). Certainly art can legitimately explore the self as well as other matters, but this does not render the rebellious, bohemian model of the artist biblical. 'Truth' to the authenticity of personal experience is an insufficient and narrow base for measuring and valorising a particular work (it automatically disqualifies much of the creative output of human societies from even being considered).[65] The notions of ethical and communal accountability apply to the artist, as to every human being.

Conclusion

Before proceeding, it will be useful to summarise briefly the biblical understanding of imagination developed in this chapter. Imagination is a function characteristic of all human beings due to their creation in the image of God. Like all natural gifts it is neither inherently evil, nor inherently good; the moral dimension depends upon the use to which it is put. Imagination is a comprehensive aspect of our nature as human beings; this is indicated in biblical anthropology through the pervasive use of the term 'heart' (*leb, kardia*). The 'heart' is the root of human willing, acting, thinking and being; as such the role of the imagination in all dimensions of temporal existence is rendered apparent. The primary concern of this study is with the literary imagination and thus the various genres within the biblical text have important implications for how it is understood. The metanarrative outlined in Scripture, summarised by creation, fall, redemption, sanctification and glorification, provides a wider framework beyond the individual self in terms of which a person can define their own identity and make sense of their own experience in the tradition of Israel and the church. Similarly, the language of metaphor, paradox, and parable which is so characteristic of the biblical writings, demands imaginative engagement on the part of its readers, implicitly endorsing this dimension of human being, and modelling the diverse forms it can take in terms of self-understanding, literary appropriation and creative genesis.

Given that the biblical text contains propositional truth as well as historical narrative and poetry, the primary commandments of love for God and love for neighbour, regulate the use of the imagination in literature and in life. This function is crucial both to a true, though partial comprehension of the nature of God as revealed in Scripture, of the complex nature of others in different situations, and of the multifaceted depths of a reality that is open to transcendence through the eschatological orientation of the biblical text. The theological concepts informing what it means to imagine biblically 'do not limp after reality, and gaze on it with the night eyes of Minerva's owl, but they illuminate reality by displaying its future. Their knowledge is grounded not in

---

[65] Lundin, *The Culture of Interpretation*, 49-52, 136, 221-65.

the will to dominate, but in love to the future of things…engaged in the process of movement [they] call forth practical movement and change.'[66]

---

[66] Jürgen Moltmann cited by Thiselton, *Interpreting God and the Postmodern Self*, 145.

Chapter 3

A Creative Imagination? John Bunyan and the Pilgrim's Unexpected Progress

It is difficult to credit the possibility, in our post-Romantic cultural context, that the imagination could be viewed in primarily negative terms. However, in early modern Europe, it was a faculty associated above all with temptation, falsehood and deception. The shift in perspective, of course, reflects major changes in cultural understandings of the self, God, sin and the natural world.[1] The way one defines 'imagination' is also crucial since, if one works on the premise suggested in the previous chapter, that it is a shared aspect of our nature as created in the image of God, then in practice it should be possible to identify consistent patterns demonstrated by this function, despite dramatic shifts in the way it is defined and evaluated. John Bunyan is a key figure in both analysing the imagination from a biblical perspective, and also in considering the role played by the biblical text in generating, or establishing heuristic patternings followed by the creative imagination, particularly in relation to literature. I will therefore begin this chapter with a consideration of *The Pilgrim's Progress*. This text is historically significant, being the first fictional work produced by an English Puritan to command widespread admiration and exercise profound influence. The 'Apology' which precedes the work marks Bunyan's attempt to justify the production and dissemination of such literature from a biblical perspective.[2] It offers suggestive ways of thinking about what it means to imagine biblically.

The power and success of the text itself undercuts some of the stipulations that Bunyan posits, suggesting that the imagination can play a unique role in the discovery and articulation of truth, without the mediation of an

---

[1] Lundin, "Skipping the History: The Question of Art as Sacrament." William A. Dyrness provides an historical overview of the complex and contested nature of the relationship between imagination and the Puritan tradition in *Reformed Theology and Visual Culture: The Protestant Imagination from Calvin to Edwards* (Cambridge: Cambridge University Press, 2004).

[2] Richard Greaves, following Neil Keeble, emphasises the importance of Bunyan's work for the imagination in both literature and allegory. Richard Greaves, *Glimpses of Glory: John Bunyan and English Dissent* (Stanford: Stanford University Press, 2002), 220-1.

accompanying didactic framework.³ Additionally, Bunyan's narration of the way in which his text 'came to be' provides an interesting case-study of the creative imagination at work. Paul Ricoeur's discussion of the relationship between the Bible and imagination, read alongside the 'Apology' enables a biblical understanding of this function to be developed in terms of *praxis*.⁴ It reveals patterns that facilitate a more realistic and modulated definition of the imagination, which is of pertinence to critics generally, even if they do not subscribe to the biblical basis underlying this study.⁵ In order to specify more particularly the possibility of a realistic perspective on the imagination, which recognises its place, without either denigrating or exalting it unduly, I will turn finally to the work of J. R. R. Tolkien, to outline a perspective on art and the creative imagination as ultimately derivative and celebratory.⁶

Biblical Aesthetics and *The Pilgrim's Progress*

The term 'biblical aesthetics' is used here to denote the particular aesthetics characteristic of the work produced by Puritan authors as a result of the specific hermeneutic they applied to the King James Version of 1611, (the English translation of the biblical text most widely available in the seventeenth-century). Puritans are frequently vilified for their supposed iconoclasm. However, the relationship between aesthetics and spirituality, or imaginative literature and the Bible, has been conceived as problematic by many in the Christian tradition. John Bunyan offers a unique contribution to this ongoing debate in *The Pilgrim's Progress*. Instead of reiterating the conventional dichotomy between fiction and truth, he carefully adapts the embodied hermeneutic of scriptural interpretation developed by Puritan divines, linking the aesthetic features of literature and an engaged imagination to the spiritual and moral transformation of the reader's life.⁷ Bunyan argues, on the model of the biblical text, that metaphor, types and figurative language may be necessary to the revelation of truth.⁸ His adaptation of Puritan hermeneutics enables him to deploy a holistic biblical aesthetic in his understanding of how fictional texts may be read and received.⁹ Right reading thus becomes an experience of

---

³ A possibility ultimately explored by C. S. Lewis after several attempts at more didactic fiction in his final novel *Till We Have Faces*, which will be considered in Chapter 7.
⁴ Ricoeur, " The Bible and the Imagination."
⁵ Edwards, *Towards a Christian Poetics*, 1-13.
⁶ Tolkien, "On Fairy-Stories."
⁷ Michael Davies, *Graceful Reading: Theology and Narrative in the Works of John Bunyan* (Oxford: Oxford University Press, 2002).
⁸ B. A. Johnson, "Falling into Allegory: The "Apology" to the Pilgrim's Progress and Bunyan's Scriptural Methodology," *Bunyan in Our Time*, ed. R. G. Collmer (Kent: Kent State University Press, 1989).
⁹ John Bunyan, *The Pilgrim's Progress* (Harmondsworth: Penguin, 1965), 36-7. All subsequent citations refer to this edition.

aesthetic pleasure and spiritual transformation. This juxtaposition is important, for while Bunyan undoubtedly modifies the general Puritan distrust of literature, his biblical aesthetic can only be used to justify a highly specialised selection of fiction. However, his willingness to use Scripture as a heuristic model for the creative genesis of texts (both written and experiential) has implicit and revolutionary potential. While he does not explore these possibilities, Bunyan's work gestures towards a more comprehensive biblical understanding of aesthetics and imagination.

It scarcely needs to be observed that the Bible was a privileged text for the Puritans, providing sufficient instruction for all aspects of personal and corporate life. Its authority depended not on the validation of the church, but rather upon its testimony to itself as the 'quick' and 'powerful' Word 'given by inspiration of God' (Hebrews 4:12; 2 Timothy 3:16). Scripture was held to contain its own rules directing how it should be interpreted, and the Puritan hermeneutic drew on biblical statements like that of the apostle Paul: 'ye are manifestly declared to be the epistle of Christ ministered by us, written not with ink, but with the Spirit of the living God; not in tables of stone, but in fleshy tables of the heart' (2 Corinthians 3:3). Right reading involved far more than a mere increase in mental understanding, it was affective; transformation of life was a crucial element of proper interpretation.

This ideal of experimental piety, or knowing in the heart, was the tradition in which Bunyan stood: a holistic understanding of hermeneutics that by extension entailed an inclusive aesthetic, linking what is beautiful, appropriate or satisfying, to a true knowledge of God, doing what is good and a right ordering of life. However, as the Puritan theologian William Ames makes clear, didactic understanding did not preclude an appreciation of Scripture as literature:

> In form of expression, Scripture does not explain the will of God by universal and scientific rules, but rather by stories, examples, precepts, exhortations, admonitions, and promises, This style best fits the common usage of all sorts of men and also greatly affects the will, by stirring up pious motives, which is the chief end of theology.[10]

Sensitivity to the aesthetic dimensions of the biblical text was rarely extended to other literature: the distaste of some Puritans for plays and romances is well-known, though they were not the only ones who castigated fictional literature.[11] In fact, rejection of such time-wasting pursuits figures prominently in the conversion narratives of eminent believers, like the prolific author Richard

---

[10] Cited by Leland Ryken, *Worldly Saints: The Puritans as They Really Were* (Grand Rapids: Zondervan, 1986), 149.
[11] Leland Ryken, *Triumphs of the Imagination: Literature in Christian Perspective* (Downers Grove: InterVarsity Press, 1979), 13-17.

Baxter, and Bunyan himself.[12]

It is within this cultural context that Bunyan wrote and published *The Pilgrim's Progress*. The narrative is preceded by a poetic prologue entitled, 'The Author's Apology for His Book,' which he structures in the form of a dramatic dialogue, answering the objections of anticipated critics, whose arguments he hopes to forestall. Bunyan knows that it is the form of his text and choice of language that will be contentious, and thus formulates a defence in aesthetic terms. He begins with disarming modesty, deploying rhetorical questions in order to suggest that metaphor and figurative language are pleasant, capable of communicating truth in their own way:

> May I not write in such a style as this?....
> Some men by feigning words as dark as mine,
> Make truth to spangle, and its rays to shine (32-4).

The imagined interrogator responds that metaphors 'want solidness,' 'drowned the weak', 'make us blind,' and presses the author with a patronising heartiness, 'speak man thy mind' (34). Bunyan responds by turning to the Bible, drawing on the literary features of the text, in order to justify his fictional narrative: 'was not God's laws,/ His Gospel-laws in olden time held forth/ By types, shadows and metaphors?' (34). To Old Testament typology, a central feature of Puritan biblical interpretation, he adds that the 'prophets used much by metaphors/ To set forth truth,' as did 'Christ' and 'his Apostles too' (34). The narratorial tone grows increasingly confident and he challenges his critic: 'Be not too forward therefore to conclude/ That I want solidness, that I am rude' (34). He valorises the 'dark figures, allegories' 'style and phrase' of Scripture, as that which 'puts down all wit' in a manner entirely consistent with the Puritan tradition, simultaneously authorising the aesthetics of his own text: 'there springs/ From that same book that lustre and those rays/ Of light that turns our darkest nights to days' (34).

Bunyan is more conscious than many Puritans of the implications that an appreciation of artistry in Scripture has for other literature,[13] but he retains the

---

[12] For an extended commentary on this matter see Richard Baxter, "Letter to the Reader," *A Breviate of the Life of Margaret, the Daughter of Francis Charlton of Apply in Shropshire, Esq.; and Wife of Richard Baxter* (London: Printed for B. Simmons, at the Three Golden Cocks at the West-end of St. Pauls, 1681). Martin Butler in his ground-breaking work *Theatre and Crisis 1632-1642* (Cambridge: Cambridge University Press, 1984) demonstrates the complexity and range of contemporary responses to drama in the period. See also Jonas Barish, *The Antitheatrical Prejudice* (London: University of California Press, 1981), 80-190; Margaret Heinemann, *Puritanism and Threatre: Thomas Middleton and Opposition Drama Under the Early Stuarts* (Cambridge: Cambridge University Press, 1980), 18-47.

[13] Lori Branch suggests further that Bunyan not only goes against convenional Puritan opinion by arguing that 'the imaginative, allegorical form of his story can be as

biblical association of beauty with truth and practical action.[14] The purpose of his elaborated aesthetic is unashamedly evangelical: to bait those fish, who 'must be groped for and be tickled too,/ Or they will not be catched, what e'er you do' (33). The allegorical mode he adopts is designed to 'let truth be free/ To make her sallies...Which way it pleases God' (36), conveying aspects of truth which cannot be apprehended in the implicitly privileged forms of 'solid' discourse that his imagined interrogator is imprisoned within (36). His fictional presentation is to be measured alongside Scripture and, insofar as they are consistent, Bunyan pleads for an embodied hermeneutic that parallels practices of biblical interpretation: 'Would'st thou read thyself...know whether thou are blest or not...?/ O then come hither,/ And lay my book, thy head and heart together' (37). His literary aesthetic is designed to 'divert', 'be pleasant', full of 'fancies' that 'will stick like burrs', in order to affect 'the minds of listless men' and enable the reader to read themselves aright, to behold beauty and become beautiful (36-7). This circular scriptural logic is encapsulated by Michael Card:

> The God who is beautiful is love. His unqualified love reaching out to us through Christ is what makes us beautiful, and in response to that reaching out we hunger for more of his beauty. Out of that hunger we reach back to him through our worship, which calls us into new creativity. Beauty and love, two colors in the spectrum of the Light that is God.[15]

Bunyan's distinctive aesthetic is not only articulated in the 'Apology,' but also exemplified in the narrative, which is filtered through the perspective of one who sees biblically. Temporal and eternal existence, individual characters and spiritual experience are all conceived and presented as known by the Puritan pilgrim *en route* to the Celestial City.[16] Thus, the apparently reasonable advice of Christian's wife and neighbours when he decides to flee his home is diagnosed as dangerous rationalising that will damage his soul and theirs if they

---

legitimate an evangelical tool as preaching or Bible study because its language contains the same valuable substance of truth that Scripture does'; his language in these opening pages 'presents the gospel as deeply compatible with value as figured in an emerging commodity culture.' Lori Branch, "'As Blood is Forced out of Flesh': Spontaneity and the Wounds of Exchange in *Grace Abounding* and *The Pilgrim's Progress*", *English Literary History*, 74 (2007), 286.

[14] Clowney, "Living Art: Christian Experience and the Arts."; William A. Dyrness, "Aesthetics in the Old Testament: Beauty in Context," *Journal of the Evangelical Theological Society* 28.4 (1985), 421-32.

[15] Card, *Scribbling in the Sand*, 33.

[16] Johnson, "Falling into Allegory: The "Apology" to the Pilgrim's Progress and Bunyan's Scriptural Methodology," 122-4, 128-9, 131-2; T. H. Luxon, *Literal Figures: Puritan Allegory and the Reformation Crisis in Representation* (Chicago: University of Chicago Press, 1995), 160.

remain within the City of Destruction.[17] Or the affable gentility of Mr Worldly-Wiseman, seeking to turn Christian from the narrow path to a legalistic form of moralism, leads to the deadly landscape of Mount Sinai and the threat of righteous judgement. Later as Christian and Faithful go through Vanity Fair, practices of merchandise, unrestrained pleasure and even nationalistic pride are satirised and condemned as fripperies that will enslave the unthinking inhabitants to their own peril. The allegorical mode of the text is thus an aesthetic vehicle at the service of Bunyan's theological purpose, as temporal earthly categories are persistently inverted in favour of biblical principle, enacting at a narrative level the spiritual demand, 'to walk by faith, not by sight' (2 Corinthians 5:7).

This coercive singleness of vision is reinforced and enriched by Bunyan's creative and tenacious adherence to biblical language, concepts and imagery in the structure and lexicon of his artistic work. His concentrated intertextual relationship with Scripture constitutes and affirms the biblical aesthetic so critical to *The Pilgrim's Progress*. Almost every sentence, circumstance and character alludes to a cluster of scriptural concepts and images that add depth and force to the narrative of Christian and his fellow pilgrims.[18] The central metaphor is that of 'the way', crucial to the structure of biblical narrative, and the experience of the spiritual life as a pilgrimage. This forms a framework around which a constellation of other key images and concepts, with rich cultural associations gather: the burden of sin, apocalyptic flames, the dragon Apollyon and the figure of Evangelist, to mention just a few.

The aesthetics of the narrative cannot be divorced from the hermeneutic Bunyan articulates in his 'Apology,' without deconstructing the entire fabric of the text through an alternative interpretive strategy, or reading it against the grain. This chapter follows the interpretation of Bunyan's theology, offered by Michael Davies, as one in which grace eventually triumphs over the paradoxes, anxieties and persecutory elements in the experience of the individual seeking salvation.[19] While John Strachniewski's analysis of the functional role that

---

[17] For an astute account of women in Bunyan and the tradition of Bunyan criticism see Margaret Ezell, "Bunyan's Women, Women's Bunyan" in *Trauma and Transformation: The Political Progress of John Bunyan*, ed. Vera J. Camden (Stanford: Stanford University Press, 2008), 63-80.

[18] Michael Austin argues further that the two parts of *The Pilgrim's Progress* can be seen as paralleling the relationship between the Old and New Testaments, particularly through the use of typology in "The Figural Logic of the Sequel and the Unity of *The Pilgrim's Progress*," *Studies in Philology*, 102.4 (2005), 484-509.

[19] Davies, *Graceful Reading*, 1-16; Davies's argument regarding Bunyan's pastoral theology is further explicated in "Sex and Sexual Wordplay in the Writings of John Bunyan" in *Trauma and Transformation: The Political Progress of John Bunyan*, ed. Vera J. Camden (Stanford: Stanford University Press, 2008), 100-119. Anne Dunan-Page situates the literary embodiment of Bunyan's pastoral concern in *The Pilgrim's Progress* explicitly within the context of Restoration (in particular Baptist) Dissent in

allegory plays in the context of Bunyan's theological purpose supports the union of 'Parnassus' and 'Conventicle' in Coleridge's terms, the predominant hermeneutic employed is that of a Freudian suspicion of religion as merely self-gratifying wish-fulfilment. Stachniewski's basic attribution of an almost Manichean teleology to Bunyan fails to take into account Part Two of *The Pilgrim's Progress*, privileging the acute tension of Bunyan's early anxiety in *Grace Abounding*, over the confidence he later testifies to when looking to the objective presence of Christ in heaven at the right hand of God as the basis of his assurance, rather than the fluctuating state of his own feelings. This complements the pastoral and communal emphases of Part Two of *The Pilgrim's Progress*, which recognises a wide range of conversion experiences and degrees of spiritual maturity.[20] Similarly, Stuart Sim argues that 'the only certainty that the Calvinist can countenance as regards the individual consciousness of salvation is the certainty of its *un*certainty.' He elides the careful distinction Puritans made between a once-for-all act of justification and the ongoing process of sanctification (particularly when dealing with the 'open-ended' conclusion to *The Holy War*).[21]

Critics who read the text in this way often construe central pieces of the narrative, like Faithful's lengthy discussion with Talkative about the experiential dimension of saving faith, or Hopeful's account of his conversion, as didactic flaws.[22] But to say that Bunyan unfortunately departed from the artistic simplicity of his allegory, in order to make a sectarian theological point through overt sermonising, is an anachronistic projection of alien literary criteria upon his text. An interesting inversion of this argument construes Bunyan as a solitary and prophetic Puritan apologist for the imagination, suggesting that fictional literature can operate as an effective substitute for theology and doctrine. This retains the same basic dichotomy. It is a long way

---

Grace Overwhelming: John Bunyan, The Pilgrim's Progess and the Extremes of the Baptist Mind (Oxford: Peter Lang, 2008).

[20] John Stachniewski, *The Persecutory Imagination: English Puritanism and the Literature of Religious Despair* (Oxford: Clarendon Press, 1991), 169-216.

[21] Stuart Sim, *Negotiations with Paradox: Narrative Practice and Narrative Form in Bunyan and Defoe* (Savage: Barnes & Noble, 1990), 1-11, 44-70. Galen Johnson suggests that Bunyan's theology can be integrated with an historical understanding of his spiritual development as a Christian and pastor in "Glimpses of Glory: John Bunyan and English Dissent," *Christianity and Literature* 52.4 (2003), 557-61. See also Gaius Davies, "Grace Abounding: John Bunyan (1628-1688)," *Genius, Grief and Grace* (Fearns: Christian Focus, 2001), 52-90. Beth Lynch attempts such a reintegration of Bunyan's pastoral and narrative writings in her study of his *oeuvre* probing the difficulties he faced as an author constrained to 'make sense of his own spiritual identity' and to present 'himself as a spiritual authority to, and over, others' (165) in *John Bunyan and the Language of Conviction* (Cambridge: D. S. Brewer, 2004).

[22] C. S. Lewis, "The Vision of John Bunyan," *Selected Literary Essays*, ed. Walter Hooper (Cambridge: Cambridge University Press, 1969), 146, 152.

from Bunyan's fear that critics would fault his text's fictional nature as an impediment to the presentation of biblical truth, or as affording literary pleasure without fostering spiritual growth. He would have identified attempts to valorise his text in spite of its theological message,[23] or deliberately against its theological presuppositions, as the most serious of mis-readings.[24]

This is not to say that Bunyan must be read prescriptively according to his own directions given in the 'Apology,' but a careful attention to his argument does allow an appreciation of the didactic and expository elements of the text, as integral components in a complex strategy designed to instruct and encourage the reader. Doctrine and theology are not seen as unpalatable discourses that need to be replaced by an allegorical aesthetic, nor is fictional narrative viewed simply as an expendable embellishment of truth. Rather, Bunyan seeks to forge a method of presenting the truth in an aesthetically pleasing manner, designed effectively to motivate the reader.[25] The shift from adventure story to sermon-like exhortation can be seen as a deliberate authorial ploy, alerting the reader in a quite contemporary sense to the fictive status of the narrative, and seeking to forestall simple escapism, returning from the world projected by the text to that of the reader's own experience: 'Would'st thou be in a dream, and yet not sleep..../Wouldest thou lose thyself, and catch no harm/ And find thyself again without a charm?....This book will make a traveller of thee,/ If by its counsel thou wilt ruled be' (36, 37).[26] Such an awareness positions Bunyan's literary work firmly within the Puritan culture from which it emerged: it was the purpose of all pastors so to present the beauty of Christ, as to draw the affections and motivate the wills of their congregations;[27] Bunyan is determined that the pleasure of the text further and never subvert this ethical and experiential dimension.

Bunyan draws heavily upon Old Testament aesthetics in the body of his text.[28] Edmund Clowney has observed: 'Beauty is not comprehended as an

---

[23] See for example, Vincent Newey, ed, *The Pilgrim's Progress: Critical and Historical Views* (Liverpool: Liverpool University Press, 1980); Roger Sharrock, *John Bunyan: The Pilgrim's Progress* (London: Edward Arnold, 1966), 25-6.

[24] For example, Stanley Fish, "Progress in the Pilgrim's Progress," *Self-Consuming Artifacts: The Experience of Seventeenth-Century Literature* (Berkeley: University of California Press, 1972).

[25] Davies, *Graceful Reading*, 194-203.

[26] The rich theological and affective potential inherent in Bunyan's choice of allegory and its affinities with Renaissance emblems has been explored by Brenda Machosky in "Trope and Truth in *The Pilgrim's Progress*," *Studies in English Literature, 1500-1900*, 47.1 (2007), 179-99.

[27] This tradition reached its culmination in the writings and practice of Jonathan Edwards. Sherry, *Spirit and Beauty*, 15-16.

[28] Luke Ferretter offers a concise overview of the aesthetics of the Hebrew Bible in "The Power and the Glory: The Aesthetics of the Hebrew Bible," *Literature and Theology* 18.2 (2004), 123-38.

abstraction. Israel's inspired poets are not delighted with their own delight; their delight is in the Lord. It is this religious centre...that shapes the understanding of beauty in the Old Testament.'[29] Crucial to a biblical understanding of imagination is a preoccupation with the beauty of the ultimate Other, God, and human beings in all their manifold distinctness. This ethos informs Bunyan's depiction of the aesthetic dimensions of biblical spirituality in relation to conversion, sanctification and eschatological anticipation. The biblical presentation of the works of God in creation and redemption has a clearly aesthetic aspect. After the creation of the world, it is recorded: 'God saw every thing that he had made, and, behold, it was very good'; satisfaction and rest follow the consummation of his cosmic artistry (Genesis 1:31; 2:1,2,9). Human beings are exhorted to respond to this display of glory and beauty with adoration and delight. Similarly, human redemption has a definite aesthetic element as portrayed in Scripture, resonating in the overarching providential pattern of promise and fulfilment that permeates both Testaments.[30] Paul, for example, after providing a brief synopsis of biblical history, declares 'when the fulness of the time was come, God sent forth his Son' (Galatians 4:4). He is drawing out the eschatological implications of the single Greek word uttered by Jesus upon the cross, *tetelestai*, 'It is finished' (John 19:30).[31] The paradox of Calvary consists partly in the fact that the ultimate restoration of glory and beauty is achieved through suffering and crucifixion. This divine inversion of human aesthetics is mirrored in Bunyan's narrative strategy, both encapsulating the Pauline formulation, 'hath not God made foolish the wisdom of this world?' (1 Corinthians 1:20). The biblical terms for beauty thus refuse simply to be equated with Greek idealism or modern aesthetics, Yahweh is not conceived in the image of Apollo. However, to position Israel's praise of Yahweh's glory outside the sphere of aesthetics, because of this paradoxical difference, would be to impoverish both worship and art; the infinite transcendence of divine glory and suffering preserves the depth and integrity of the artistic enterprise.[32] From a biblical perspective the imagination is necessarily both realistic in its apprehension of suffering and death and redemptive. As Jürgen Moltmann has noted: 'unless it apprehends the pain of the negative [that is in the crucifixion of Christ], Christian hope cannot be realistic and liberating as hope.'[33] In this particular sense Bunyan can be seen to present a 'crucified aesthetic' in *The Pilgrim's Progress*.

---

[29] Clowney, "Living Art: Christian Experience and the Arts," 239-40.
[30] Clowney, "Living Art: Christian Experience and the Arts." Frank W. Boreham, "Hudson Taylor's Text," *Developing a Christian Imagination: An Interpretive Anthology*, ed. Warren W. Wiersbe (Wheaton: Victor Books, 1995), 199-206.
[31] Boreham, "Hudson Taylor's Text," 201.
[32] Clowney, "Living Art: Christian Experience and the Arts," 242. Paul Tillich calls this transcendence 'ultimate reality.' Begbie, *Voicing Creation's Praise*, 256-7.
[33] Thiselton, *Interpreting God and the Postmodern Self*, 148.

These dimensions of biblical aesthetics and beauty provide an important context when considering Bunyan's treatment of spiritual experience. Divine satisfaction with a complete and fitting work of redemption is a necessary precondition enabling the response of Christian when he finally comes to the cross. There is a pause in the narrative as 'he stood still a while, to look and wonder; for it was very surprising to him that the sight of the Cross should thus ease him of his burden. He looked therefore, and looked again, even till the springs that were in his head sent the waters down his cheeks' (70). In this scene, as Christian looks in faith upon the cross, he is cleansed and transformed. 'Three Shining Ones' meet him, strip off his rags and give him new clothes, a mark upon his forehead and a roll with a seal (70). Bunyan explores the biblical paradox of spiritual beauty in its supreme manifestation of self-sacrifice bringing about salvation. The One who in the words of the Song of Solomon is 'altogether lovely' (5:16), as the Suffering Servant, had 'no beauty that we should desire him' (Isaiah 53:2). It is through the disfigurement of the One 'full of grace and truth' (John 1:14) that beauty is granted to those whose 'righteousnesses are as filthy rags' (Isaiah 64:6). Christian muses: 'He hath given me rest, by his sorrow, and life, by his death' (70), a personal example of the cosmic restoration celebrated by Paul.[34] The simplicity of this faithful gaze is categorised aesthetically when the character Hopeful later narrates his conversion (183), with a child-like assurance that has roots in Bunyan's own experience. As his autobiography *Grace Abounding* demonstrates, he wrestled intensely with doubt, fear and corrosive introspection, before being able to look to Christ and declare him, all-sufficient and 'altogether lovely.'[35]

Conversion, in the biblical schema of salvation, is intimately linked to the process of sanctification, and Bunyan presents this also in distinctively aesthetic terms. In the most obvious set-piece exemplifying this theme, the allegorical Palace Beautiful, Bunyan draws upon traditional medieval moral discourse in the naming of its inhabitants, 'a grave and beautiful damsel...Discretion,' and her family, 'Prudence, Piety and Charity' (79-80), while Christian sleeps in a chamber called Peace (86). The theme recurs overtly later in the 'Bath of Sanctification' where Christian's wife, children and Mercy wash, before leaving the House of the Interpreter. They bathe at the will of their Master, and holiness is described in tactile and affective terms, which present it as an aesthetic ideal: 'they came out of that Bath not only sweet and clean; but also much enlivened...they looked fairer a deal' (256). This is followed by the Interpreter placing his seal upon them: 'this seal greatly added to their beauty,' they are clothed in 'fine linen, white and clean' (256). Drawing on the biblical themes of glory and beauty, often seen together, 'the women...thus

---

[34] Clowney, "Living Art: Christian Experience and the Arts." Boreham, "Hudson Taylor's Text," 199-206.
[35] Davies, "Grace Abounding: John Bunyan (1628-1688)," 52-90.

adorned...seemed to be a terror one to the other, for they could not see that glory each one on herself which they could see in each other' (256). This focus on the other induces humility, as each observed the fairness and comeliness of their companion.

For Bunyan, the supreme vision of this beauty in the One whose 'visage was so marred more than any man, and his form more than the sons of men' (Isaiah 52:14), was the central and necessary dynamic at the heart of all spiritual life, transformation and growth. His spiritual aesthetic is centred on the Person of Christ, and traces its eschatological trajectory to the final consummation. It is here, above all, that the transcendent depth or 'ultimate reality,' referred to earlier, consequent upon the inextricable biblical combination of divine glory and beauty finds narrative expression.[36] The consciousness of eternity that informs Bunyan's narrative is both terrifying and ecstatic. Thus complacent Ignorance, at the very gate of the Celestial City, is found to have no certificate, bound 'hand and foot' and taken away. The narrator comments at the end of Part One: 'Then I saw that there was a way to Hell, even from the Gates of Heaven, as well as from the City of Destruction' (204-5). Juxtaposed against this is the testimony of Mr Stand-fast, which forms the conclusion of Part Two:

> I see myself now at the end of my journey....I am going now to see that head that was crowned with thorns, and that face that was spit upon, for me. I have formerly lived by hear-say and faith, but now I go where I shall live by sight, and shall be with him, in whose company I delight myself....[W]herever I have seen the print of his shoe in the earth, there I have coveted to set my foot too. His name has been to me as a civet-box, yea, sweeter than all perfumes. His voice to me has been most sweet, and his countenance I have more desired than they that have most desired the light of the sun (372).

There are numerous biblical echoes in this passage, as Bunyan draws upon allegorical readings of the Song of Solomon; typological interpretations of the Messianic psalms; the apocalyptic declarations of Old Testament prophets; and the eager yearning of the New Testament epistles (2 Corinthians 3:18). The psalmist cries: 'One thing have I desired of the LORD, that will I seek after; that I may dwell in the house of the LORD all the days of my life, to behold the beauty of the LORD' (Psalm 27:4). Similarly, Isaiah prophesies, 'Thine eyes shall see the king in his beauty: they shall behold the land that is very far off' (33:17). While the ultimate fulfilment of this lies beyond the temporal linearity of his narrative, Bunyan does allow his pilgrims certain moments of aesthetic contemplation, in which the pressing weight of this world is suspended, and eternity floods in, reconfiguring present experience.[37] This occurs when Christian and Hopeful ascend the aptly named Delectable Mountains and gain a

---

[36] Begbie, *Voicing Creation's Praise*, 256-7.
[37] Henry E. Duitman, "Practical Aesthetics" <http://homepages.dordt.edu/~hduitman/musiced/practicalaesthetics.htm>, 26 August 2008.

ravishing, imperfect, intoxicating glimpse of the Celestial City.

> [The shepherds] had them to the top of an high Hill called Clear, and gave them their glass to look....[T]hey could not look steadily through the glass; yet they thought they saw something like the Gate, and also something of the glory of the place. Then they went away and sang (161).

Bunyan's emphasis on the crucified and risen Christ as the supreme embodiment of beauty, offers an alternative to the 'persecutory' or antithetical readings of his theology, where divine paradox is reduced to dualism. The unique artistic achievement of *The Pilgrim's Progress* is to suggest through its own structure and content that such paradoxes can only be understood and ratified experientially. The consolation and assurance that Christian gains from gazing at the cross; the sanctifying power of this concentrated focus, supplemented by the positive role of companionship and counsel; and the eschatological trajectory of the narrative, all provide an affirmative spiritual context that ameliorates the corrosive uncertainty that characterises Christian at the beginning of his journey. These elements also call into question an interpretation of Bunyan's theology which focuses exclusively on a negative reading of predestination. Bunyan does present two distinct eternal destinies in his text. However, his pilgrims do not live with a perpetual lack of assurance. Such uncertainty, far from being the necessary trademark of Calvinist theology, is in fact a demonstration of immaturity, as he shows through the character of Mr Fearing. The biblical aesthetic that Bunyan espouses is relational, didactic, experiential and transformative: the focused narrative structure of the adventure story, the humorous depiction and gracious tolerance of weakness and diversity in Part Two, and the ecstatic descriptions of Christ and heaven, are ultimately the aesthetic exemplification of an underlying theology that privileges grace and assurance over doubt and retribution.

However, while Bunyan moves beyond the traditional dichotomies between aesthetic and spiritual, fiction and truth, both at the level of the literary text and in his understanding of the spiritual life, he remains unwilling to venture too far on the insight that 'some...by feigning words as dark as mine,/ Make truth to spangle...'(33-34). Neither part of *The Pilgrim's Progress* is sent forth without a framing commentary from the author, designed to circumscribe modes of interpretation and preemptively disarm criticism. Nevertheless, the hermeneutic that Bunyan deploys in his reading of the biblical text, has generated a narrative of remarkable power, which suggests possibilities for a 'rule-governed' imagination exercised along the lines opened by the scriptural text.[38] Subsequent writers found the precedent set by Bunyan a liberating paradigm that prompted more venturesome works of literature within Puritan and later

---

[38] Ricoeur, "The Bible and the Imagination," 50.

Dissenting circles.[39]

A Biblical Understanding of the Creative Imagination

The implicit theoretical understanding of imagination, fusing hermeneutics, theology, experience and aesthetics, which characterises Bunyan's text can be articulated more explicitly and given a broader application through the lens offered by Paul Ricoeur. In a tightly argued essay he defines imagination as a 'rule-governed form of invention' with referential import due to its power of giving form to human experience, or redescribing reality. Ricoeur links these general features of the imagination to the process of reading the Bible. This is of great pertinence to Bunyan and the general theoretical concerns of this book.

> I would like to consider the act of reading as a dynamic activity that is not confined to repeating significations fixed forever, but which takes place as a prolonging of the itineraries of meaning opened up by the work of interpretation....[T]he act of reading accords with the idea of a norm-governed productivity to the extent that it may be said to be guided by a productive imagination at work in the text itself. Beyond this, I would like to see in the reading of a text such as the Bible a creative operation unceasingly employed in decontextualizing its meaning and recontextualizing it in today's *Sitz im Leben*. Through this...the act of reading realizes the union of fiction and redescription that characterizes the imagination in the most pregnant sense of this term.[40]

This is rather different to the imperious 'Poesie' lauded by Sir Philip Sidney in his *Defence of Poesie* (1595). In its mediation between the fact of the revealed text as given and a necessary degree of subjectivity when interpreting and appropriating, it provides an apt gloss on Bunyan's cryptic notes concerning the genesis of *The Pilgrim's Progress*: 'Before I was aware, I this begun,/ And thus it was: I writing of the way.../Fell suddenly into an allegory..../Still as I pulled it came...'(31). Ricoeur's emphasis on the experimental dimension of interpretation not only illuminates Bunyan's description of the creation of this particular literary text, more pregnantly he also indicates the latent potential in a biblical understanding of the productive imagination. By situating the germination of the creative process in the reading of the Bible itself, he suggests that he is placing himself 'at the starting point of the trajectory that unfolds itself into the individual and social forms of the imagination.'[41]

---

[39] This literary line can be traced ultimately to works like *Jane Eyre* by Charlotte Brontë, for example. Stachniewski, *The Persecutory Imagination*, 209-11. It is the affinity between the texts, not the conclusions that Stachniewski draws from this that is pertinent here.
[40] Ricoeur, "The Bible and the Imagination," 50.
[41] Ricoeur, "The Bible and the Imagination," 50.

Even if one does not necessarily agree with Bunyan and Ricoeur's emphasis on the central importance of the biblical text to an understanding of imagination, it is possible that the patterns, insight and balance which the text and its interpretation offer 'can also appeal, and appear true, to someone who rejects the specifically Christian doctrine that subtends it.'[42] The delicate interplay between indebtedness and inspiration, freedom and determinism, intertextuality and originality, 'drive deeply and variously enough into our reality to be recognised, whatever the source and the meaning we assign to them.'[43] Further, the biblical text is seminal in the Western tradition and remains a crucial factor in understanding the literary imagination in manifold and complex ways, whether one is considering narrative, eschatology, parable or hermeneutics and so on. The many dimensions of this relationship have been considered by literary critics and theologians including Northrop Frye, Stephen Prickett, David Jasper, N. T. Wright and others; some of these aspects, particularly the connection between morality and *telos*, narrative, metaphor and eschatology will be looked at in greater detail in subsequent chapters.

Bunyan's *Pilgrim's Progress* is a clear enactment of the 'reading of a text such as the Bible,' where 'a creative operation [is] unceasingly employed in decontextualizing its meaning and recontextualizing it in [the]... *Sitz im Leben*' of his own day.[44] Ricoeur specifies more clearly the 'form of imagination' at work in Scripture, giving primary place to narrative texts. This is because they enable a concrete meaning to be ascribed to his earlier definition of imagination as 'a rule-governed creation' and 'heuristic model.' The literary structure imposed by narrative form is well-documented theoretically, and narratives also demonstrate the power of fiction to redescribe reality, as it is through them that we give form to our experience both individual and communal. Ricoeur suggests further that it is at the point of intersection between the reader and the biblical text that imagination is engendered 'according to the Bible.'[45] These biblical narratives are viewed as privileged paradigms, acting as images which render other events intelligible: it is this that defines the heuristic nature of narrative fiction. '[T]he narrative-parable is itself an itinerary of meaning, a signifying dynamism, which transforms a narrative structure into a metaphorical process...while at the same time receiving in return a content of provisory meaning from the narrative structure.' For Ricoeur, this illustrates most concisely the biblical form of imagination: 'the process of parabolization working in the text and engendering in the reader a similar dynamic of interpretation through thought and action.'[46]

In order to prove that this 'process of parabolization,' whereby all other

---

[42] Edwards, *Towards a Christian Poetics*, 7.
[43] Edwards, *Towards a Christian Poetics*, 7.
[44] Ricoeur, "The Bible and the Imagination," 50.
[45] Ricoeur, "The Bible and the Imagination," 51.
[46] Ricoeur, "The Bible and the Imagination," 52.

experience is understood through the heuristic model of the biblical narrative-parables, is not reductionist, because limited to narrative-parables alone, Ricoeur introduces the notion of intertextuality: 'the work of meaning through which one text in referring to another text both displaces this other text and receives from it an extension of meaning.'[47] He argues that intertextuality is the operation that allows the narrative-parable to be metamorphosed into a 'heuristic model.' This principle, which can be seen evidently at work in the parables, is also characteristic of non-parabolic narratives, as for example in 'the intersection between narratives and laws in the Old Testament, and the overall intersection between the Old and New Testaments.' This demonstrates the process by which the biblical text becomes the framework that interprets our own history. Intertextuality reveals itself to be the key to 'the rule-governed imagination which, by the privileged way of narrative, invites the reader to continue...the Bible's itineraries of meaning.' The imagination which follows reading is rooted 'in the imagination that is the very act of reading.'[48] Ricoeur's earlier definition of the imagination is thus justified through the literary structure and theological principles of the biblical text itself, allowing a better understanding of the reading process, but also rendering it possible to articulate a biblical understanding of the imagination that is of relevance to the production and consumption of literary texts in general.

Though privileging narrative as the exemplary form of biblical imagination *par excellence*, Ricoeur supplements his analysis of the way in which the text as a whole intersects dynamically with the life of the reader through the principle of intertextuality, with a careful recognition of the other genres which compose a 'biblical polyphony.' The identification of these genres is far from being arbitrary and idiosyncratic: the basic distinctions between Law, History, and Wisdom were recognised by the Jewish rabbis prior to Christ. What is unique about Ricoeur's reading of the biblical text is the cognitive significance that he attributes to the generic form, as well as content: 'we miss what is unique about biblical faith if we take categories such as narrative, oracle, commandment, and so on, as rhetorical devices that are alien to the content they transmit.'[49] He describes the 'literary genres of the Bible, and behind these literary genres the acts of discourse characteristic of the Bible: narrations, legislations, prophecies, wisdom sayings and literature, hymns and psalms' as his 'guide,' attempting to trace both the structure of these acts of discourse and corresponding literary genres and the implications resulting from their interweaving, which constitutes the 'biblical intertext.'[50] He deploys this model, demonstrating the functioning of a biblical imagination at work, in his analysis of time, revelation and the character of God.

---

[47] Ricoeur, "The Bible and the Imagination," 53.
[48] Ricoeur, "The Bible and the Imagination," 53-4.
[49] Ricoeur, "Naming God," 224.
[50] Ricoeur, "Biblical Time," 169-71.

When considering time, for example, Ricoeur argues that the biblical genre of narrative establishes the notion of linearity.[51] However, this is instantly challenged by the phenomenon of intertextuality, as the giving of the law intersects directly with the great narratives of creation, election and deliverance in the Old Testament: 'the law qualifies not just the event of its giving but all the narratives in which this giving is encased, in such a way that the founding events become events that do not pass away but remain.'[52] The message of the prophets breaks the temporal structure of this narrative tradition, reversing the sense of closure that it provides. But the 'prophecy of misfortune' is complemented by the 'prophets of salvation,' where the interruption of the former becomes a necessary part of the dialectic that ushers in something new, 'not...radically different but as a sort of creative repetition of the old.' This intertextual hermeneutic, already at work in the Old Testament, is fully developed in the New: 'prophecy and its eschatology...open [the] initial surplus of meaning that...lies dreaming in the traditional narrative.'[53] The wisdom writings are nonnarrative, addressing 'the human condition in its universal aspect,' and affirm the importance of the everyday.[54] Finally, there is a time of the psalms, which is 'today and every day,' as worship reactivates salvation and its history in the present. Personal praise (expressed through the use of 'I' and 'we') can 'include the recitation of epic history and the time of recitation can envelop the time of the narrative.'[55]

Ricoeur follows this essential structure of paying close attention to the polyphony of literary genres that combine to form the text in order to explore many issues of philosophical and theological import. These will not be analysed here. Of more immediate pertinence is the way in which he understands the referential function of the biblical text, as this was a key component in his biblical definition of imagination. He identifies the biblical text as 'poetic,' but not in the sense of reducing its impact to an emotional function, based on the premise of an opposition between descriptive and nondescriptive discourse. Rather, he suggests that poetic literature generally 'suspends a first-order referential function, whether it is a question of direct reference to familiar objects of perception or of indirect reference to physical entities that science reconstructs as underlying' such objects, as the 'negative condition for the liberation of a more originary referential function.' Poetic discourse is a second-order function that 'refers to our many ways of belonging to the world before we oppose ourselves to things understood as "objects" that stand before a "subject."' It challenges 'the reduction of the referential function to descriptive discourse,' allowing nondescriptive reference to the world and

---

[51] Ricoeur, "Biblical Time," 171.
[52] Ricoeur, "Biblical Time," 172-3.
[53] Ricoeur, "Biblical Time," 173-6.
[54] Ricoeur, "Biblical Time," 176-8.
[55] Ricoeur, "Biblical Time," 178-9.

broadening the scientific understanding of truth as empirical verification. Poetic texts 'are precisely modalities of our relation to the world that are not exhausted in the description of objects,' they offer revelation, the concept of truth as manifestation, 'in the sense of letting be what shows itself. What shows itself is each time the proposing of a world, a world wherein I can project my ownmost possibilities.'[56]

Ricoeur shifts easily between a description of the power of poetic literature generally and the specific nature of biblical revelation. For the purposes of this section, which considers a biblical understanding of the creative ('productive' in Ricoeur's terminology) imagination, this does not really matter, as he carefully '[l]isten[s] to' the biblical text, in order to articulate an understanding of imagination deduced from its 'originary expressions...not a single tone, but polyphonic...diverse.'[57] It is not my purpose to develop an understanding of poetic revelation that applies specifically to Scripture, and attempt to distinguish this from the way in which other 'poetic' literature works. Rather, Ricoeur's discussion of what it means to imagine biblically, based on a literary reading of the text, provides a useful model for understanding the way in which the imagination functions, and a means of elaborating more explicitly the creative genesis of literary texts, such as *The Pilgrim's Progress*. At another level, though, it does create problems. Ricoeur's tendency to treat the biblical text, and particularly the gospels, as expressing 'human possibilities, waiting only for imaginative and ethical appropriation,' instead of recording 'the entry of the divine into the realm of the human...a prior action, a self-revelation of God, before humans can know him...[as he] is not generally available, either in nature or in human experience, but only as he breaks into these,' robs the incarnation of the unique status ascribed to it by the biblical text, and consequently impoverishes the understanding of creativity that results.[58]

It is not necessary to reject a literal historical reference for the gospel narratives, if one wishes to affirm their literary power evoked through 'poetic' language that 'incites the reader, or the listener, to understand himself or herself in the face of the text and to develop, in imagination and sympathy, the self capable of inhabiting this world by deploying his or her ownmost possibilities there.'[59] C. S. Lewis in a short essay, 'Myth Became Fact,' argues that the incarnation of Jesus Christ was the historical realisation at a particular moment in a particular place of that which fills the myths and legends of the pagan world: 'To be truly Christian we must both assent to the historical fact and also receive the myth (fact though it has become) with the same imaginative embrace which we accord to all myths. The one is hardly more necessary than

---

[56] Ricoeur, "Naming God," 221-3.
[57] Ricoeur, "Naming God," 224.
[58] Kevin J. Vanhoozer, *Biblical Narrative in the Philosophy of Paul Ricoeur: A Study in Hermeneutics and Theology* (Cambridge: Cambridge University Press, 1990), 149.
[59] Ricoeur, "Naming God," 232.

the other.'⁶⁰ In order to go further and explore the consequences of this for an understanding of human creativity, it is necessary to turn to J. R. R. Tolkien.⁶¹ While Lewis and Tolkien shared many ideas and religious convictions, producing their best work through collaborative interaction as part of a literary group known as the Inklings,⁶² Tolkien develops a biblical understanding of human creativity in the light of the biblical text more thoroughly and coherently than Lewis does.⁶³

Moving from Ricoeur's emphasis on the implications which the literary structure of the biblical text has for developing a definition of the human imagination, Tolkien focuses on the creation of man and woman in the image of God, and the biblical record of the incarnation, in order to sketch an understanding of the productive imagination as 'sub-creation,' which supplements the principle of intertextuality that Ricoeur outlines. Tolkien introduces an important distinction between the Primary World of created reality that is accorded Primary Belief, and the Secondary World produced when a 'story-maker proves a successful 'sub-creator,'' which is accorded Secondary Belief. This, he suggests, does not entail a 'wilful suspension of disbelief,' rather the Secondary World can be entered by the mind, and inside it all is 'true' according to the laws of that world.⁶⁴ The imagination is 'the mental power of image-making' and Tolkien posits further that it is inaccurate to restrict this to 'ideal creations,' and to distinguish between imagination and fantasy on the grounds of a difference in kind, as the 'perception of the image, the grasp of its implications, and the control, which are necessary to a successful expression, may vary in vividness and strength,' thus reflecting a difference in degree. Art is 'the operative link between Imagination and the final result, Sub-creation.'⁶⁵

Having taken issue with pejorative distinctions between fantasy and imagination, Tolkien proceeds to use the former as a general term which incorporates that which Ricoeur denotes as the productive imagination.⁶⁶ Even though Tolkien explicitly focuses on the genre of the fairy-story and privileges it over more 'realistic fiction,' his exploration of the way in which Secondary Worlds relate to the Primary World, and of the creative process, can easily be given a more general application. To make a Secondary World credible, commanding Secondary Belief, requires a close and consistent attention to

---

⁶⁰ C. S. Lewis, "Myth Became Fact," *C. S. Lewis: Essay Collection and Other Short Pieces*, ed. L. Walmsley (London: HarperCollins, 2000), 141.

⁶¹ Vanhoozer draws the link between these writers incisively in his discussion of Ricoeur in *Biblical Narrative in the Philosophy of Paul Ricoeur*, 282-4.

⁶² See Glyer, *The Company They Keep*, for a more detailed exploration of this phenomenon.

⁶³ As, for example, in his discussion of 'creativity' in "Christianity and Literature."

⁶⁴ Tolkien, "On Fairy-Stories," 40-1.

⁶⁵ Tolkien, "On Fairy-Stories," 49.

⁶⁶ Tolkien, "On Fairy-Stories," 50.

detail and facts, representing not a turning from the known world, but a different kind of engagement with it. It does not pretend to produce an alteration in the Primary World, that is the desire of the magician for power,[67] this occurs when the Secondary World is accorded Primary Belief, which is a delusion. Art is the human process by which Secondary Belief is induced and can be seen as a kind of Enchantment: it 'produces a Secondary World into which both designer and spectator can enter, to the satisfaction of their sense while they are inside; but in its purity it is artistic in desire and purpose....Uncorrupted it does not seek delusion...it seeks shared enrichment, partners in making and delight, not slaves.'[68]

The reciprocity and plenitude that characterise Tolkien's description are crucial, providing a way of mediating between the two extremes encapsulated in the metaphors of imitation and creation.[69] This is given poetic expression, ironically in response to the objections of C. S. Lewis, prior to his conversion:

'Dear Sir,' I said – 'Although now long estranged,
Man is not wholly lost nor wholly changed.
Dis-graced he may be, yet is not de-throned,
and keeps the rags of lordship once he owned:
Man, Sub-creator, the refracted Light
through whom is splintered from a single White
to many hues, and endlessly combined
in living shapes that move from mind to mind.
Though all the crannies of the world we filled
with Elves and Goblins, though we dared to build
Gods and their houses out of dark and light,
and sowed the seed of dragons – 'twas our right
(used or misused). That right has not decayed:
we make still by the law in which we're made.'[70]

In this account, fantasy is a universal aspect of human nature, by virtue of our creation in the image of God. Tolkien emphasises that it is not a flight from reality, because it 'is founded upon the hard recognition that things are so in the world as it appears under the sun; on a recognition of fact, but not a slavery to it.' However, the biblical account of the Fall also informs his analysis. Like all human faculties imagination can be put to evil use, indulged in to excess, or feed idolatry. But, with a scriptural affirmation of the hope of final redemption, it remains 'a human right: we make in our measure and in our derivative mode, because we are made...in the image and likeness of a Maker.'[71]

---

[67] Tolkien, "On Fairy-Stories," 51, 54-5.
[68] Tolkien, "On Fairy-Stories," 54-5.
[69] Lundin, *The Culture of Interpretation*, 5-6, 53-4, 75.
[70] Tolkien, "On Fairy-Stories," 56-7.
[71] Tolkien, "On Fairy-Stories," 56-7.

This sense of hope is extended further under Tolkien's notion of 'recovery,' which correlates almost directly with the referential function that Ricoeur accords to 'poetic' literature. It enables a seeing of things apart from ourselves, regaining a clear view, free from possessiveness. Fantasy draws upon the Primary World, but transforms the familiar, returning it enriched: 'For the story-maker who allows himself to be 'free with' Nature can be her lover not her slave....[Story can reveal] the potency of the words, and the wonder of the things, such as stone, and wood, and iron; tree and grass; house and fire; bread and wine.'[72] Again, Tolkien privileges the fairy-tale as the preeminent genre in which this occurs, but a similar transformation is effected by all well-wrought works of literature; what is needed is a more complex understanding of the multifaceted ways in which language refers to the created world and truth.[73]

Underlying this rich vision of creative plenitude and structured liberty is not only the biblical doctrine of creation and mandate to: 'Be fruitful and multiply and fill the earth and subdue it' (Genesis 1:28), but also the historical particularity of the incarnation, which reorientates the dialectic of human experience following the Fall with a trajectory of hope, centred upon the resurrection. Tolkien suggests, along the same lines as Lewis in 'Myth Became Fact,' that the gospels contain a 'story of a larger kind which embraces all the essence of fairy-stories....[T]his story has entered History and the primary world; the desire and aspiration of sub-creation has been raised to the fulfilment of Creation....[T]he Art of it has the supremely convincing tone of Primary Art, that is, of Creation.' In a final twist, Tolkien argues that the gospel not only forms the ultimate expression of what all art aspires to, it also verifies it: 'Legend and History have met and fused.' Far from negating all future sub-creation, the hope of ultimate joy contained in the resurrection liberates human imagination:

> So great is the bounty with which he has been treated that he may now, perhaps, fairly dare to guess that in Fantasy he may actually assist in the effoliation and multiple enrichment of creation. All tales may come true; and yet, at the last, redeemed, they may be as like and as unlike the forms that we give them as Man, finally redeemed, will be like and unlike the fallen that we know.[74]

It is unusual to juxtapose Ricoeur and Tolkien, but as Vanhoozer notes there are remarkable affinities in their understanding of poetic reference and the creative imagination.[75] Ricoeur provides a way of understanding the biblical text in terms of a polyphony of genres, which work together intertextually to intersect with the lives of those who read it, modelling in a dynamic manner the actual functioning of the productive imagination: this illuminates not only the

---

[72] Tolkien, "On Fairy-Stories," 60.
[73] Tolkien, "On Fairy-Stories," 60-7.
[74] Tolkien, "On Fairy-Stories," 70-2.
[75] Vanhoozer, *Biblical Narrative in the Philosophy of Paul Ricoeur*, 282-4.

way in which *The Pilgrim's Progress* emerged, but also allows one to articulate theoretically what it means to imagine biblically. The dialectical reciprocity that is so characteristic of Ricoeur's semiotics is extended and enriched by Tolkien's more doctrinally orthodox treatment of the creative imagination, or Fantasy. Creation *ex nihilo*, and consequently true originality, is the prerogative of God alone: the Primary Maker; but this does not mean that human beings are reduced to a robotic imitation that lacks any genuine creativity. The otherness of the created world extends an invitation to enrich and develop its abundance, 'making free' with Nature in the manner of the lover, rather than the slave. Similarly, the divine *eucatastrophe* recorded in the gospels is both a verification of all stories, and a mandate to continue imagining, in anticipation of a final redemption that will transcend all human imaginings: 'For the creation was subjected to futility, not willingly, but because of Him who subjected it, in hope that the creation itself will be set free from its bondage to decay and obtain the freedom of the glory of the children of God' (Romans 8:20-21). As Edwards's observes: 'literature is a privileged means...of contesting the Fall and of reaching towards possibility.'[76]

Thus Bunyan's acknowledgement of the capacity of the biblical text to generate fictions in the margins of its sacred page, juxtaposed alongside his recognition of the truth-bearing capacity of metaphor, provides a fruitful foundation for the development of a biblical understanding of the creative imagination. As we have seen, both Ricoeur's theoretical analysis of biblical discourse and genres, and Tolkien's theological explication of the creation of human beings in the image of God and the joyful anticipation of a new creation, allow Bunyan's tentative postulations to be extended, enabling a coherent expression of what it means to imagine creatively in the light of Scripture to be articulated. However, at the same time, the richly biblical imagination exemplified in *The Pilgrim's Progress* highlights the necessity of measuring all such secondary critical discourse alongside the biblical text. For it is in such imaginative responses to Scripture, as much as in attempts to paraphrase its theological teaching, that the trajectories its various genres open up can be traced, providing a heuristic model for the functioning of the creative imagination.

---

[76] Edwards, *Towards a Christian Poetics*, 8.

Chapter 4

The Eye of Faith: Imagination in Relation, the *Letters of Samuel Rutherford*

This chapter explores the role that the realistic imagination plays in negotiating the apparent divide between public and private, in defining and understanding interiority and in the relation of the self to others. These theoretical concerns emerge from the context of a close analysis of the *Letters of Samuel Rutherford*. Both the generic form and biblical content of this collection model an affective spirituality that draws upon the language, narrative and metaphors of the biblical text, in order to form a communal culture which bridges perceived dichotomies between public and private. The 'realistic imagination' denotes an act of perception 'which sees as one what we divide into the two components in a situation with an external reference,' it effects 'an immediacy of identity,' 'one of the functions of imagination is to picture the past-as-present, and when it does so realistically, it is in fact dealing with a present reality.'[1] I will therefore begin by considering the central biblical motifs, aesthetic claims and relational emphases of the *Letters*. I will then discuss these more generally, exploring the realistic imagination that they require of the reader, in order to develop further a biblical understanding of the role of imagination in communication and relationships, as expressed in the literary form of the letter. To this end it will be necessary to examine the ways in which Rutherford's encounters with the Divine Other, his passionate pastoral engagement with contemporaries, and his political career are undergirded and shaped by a faith commitment to the biblical text (as articulated in Reformed theology), in a way that both constrains and liberates his imagination.

Faith and imagination are sometimes understood to be synonymous terms in contemporary literary and theological discussion. The contention of this chapter is that while faith cannot operate without the imagination, faith is a central and clearly defined biblical concept, which is freighted with spiritual and relational denotations, particularly in the way individuals relate to the divine initiative in salvation, and thus cannot be equated with imagination. The incisive and helpful formulations of this relationship by Paul Avis and John McIntyre were cited in Chapter 2. Avis asserts the necessity for seeing faith as 'the act of the whole person,' it is 'indeed the gift of God...but it operates through human faculties, among which the imagination is pivotal.'[2] Similarly, McIntyre notes,

---

[1] McIntyre, *Faith, Theology and Imagination*, 33, 36, 38.
[2] Avis, *The Creative Imagination*, 78.

'faith does much that imagination cannot be expected to do: for example, obey, trust...respond,' but argues that it is possible to understand the nature of faith and the subject to which it is related better 'if we allow that...realistic imagination...has a proper place within it.'[3] This chapter explores that distinction by analysing the central role of the realistic imagination in the letters of Samuel Rutherford, and the implications which his literary expression of this concept has for defining what it means to imagine biblically.

Biblical Aesthetics and the *Letters of Samuel Rutherford*

Rutherford (c. 1600-1661) lived during one of the most tumultuous and formative periods in Scottish history, both political and religious. As a professor, pastor, preacher, prisoner, political thinker and statesman, he played a central role in determining the distinctive ecclesiastical shape of the Scottish Kirk, reforming the minds and hearts of its members, educating future leaders, resisting and reinstating Stuart monarchs, and defining the constitutional rights of the people, most notably in his treatise *Lex Rex*, which was burned by the public hangman and almost cost him his life.[4] However, none of these are the explicit focus of this chapter. Rutherford was also a prolific letter writer, and it is on the posthumous collection of these epistles, which he himself never intended for publication, that his reputation is primarily based.[5] The letters intersect in important ways with the public roles through which Rutherford became known to his contemporaries, but their focus is personal and

---

[3] McIntyre, *Faith, Theology and Imagination*, 37.
[4] Andrew Bonar, ed, *Letters of Samuel Rutherford* (Edinburgh: Banner of Truth Trust, 1984), 1-30. All subsequent citations come from this edition; J. K. Cameron, "The Piety of Samuel Rutherford (c. 1600-61): A Neglected Feature of Seventeenth-Century Scottish Calvinism," *Nederlands Archief voor Kerkgeschiedenis* 65 (1985); John Coffey, *Politics, Religion and the British Revolutions: The Mind of Samuel Rutherford*, Cambridge Studies in Early Modern British History (Cambridge: Cambridge University Press, 1997), 2-61; Robert Gilmour, *Samuel Rutherford: A Study Biographical and Somewhat Critical, in the History of the Scottish Covenant* (Edinburgh: Oliphant, Anderson & Ferrier, 1904); A. T. Innes, "Samuel Rutherfurd," *Studies in Scottish History, Chiefly Biographical* (London: 1892). This alternative spelling of the name is used consistently by Innes; Philip W. Lilley, "Samuel Rutherford, 1600-1661," *Transactions of the Hawick Archaeological Society* (1935); Marcus Loane, "Samuel Rutherford: The Saint of the Covenant," *Makers of Religious Freedom in the Seventeenth Century* (London: SCM, 1960); A. M. Machar, "A Scottish Mystic," *The Andover Review* 6 (1996); J. M. Ross, "Post-Reformation Spirituality 3: Samuel Rutherford," *The Month*. July (1975); A. Whyte, *Samuel Rutherford and Some of His Correspondents* (Edinburgh: 1894).
[5] Coffey, *Politics, Religion and the British Revolutions*, 5.

devotional. Like many other Covenanters and Puritans of his time,[6] Rutherford was a man of the Book. His *Letters* reflect and display in multiple, complex ways the shaping influence of the Bible in Scottish life, thought and ecclesiology; they are also intensely individual, mapping the unique devotional life and experience of a remarkable man.[7] I will explore his distinctive and influential exemplification of biblical aesthetics, language and imagination in the epistolary genre.

The first anonymous edition of the letters was published in Holland under the cryptic and allusive title, *Joshua Redivivus*, in 1664, by his former secretary Robert McWard.[8] This reference to Joshua probably draws upon one among the many examples of biblical metaphor that fill the *Letters*, where Rutherford states that God sent him into banishment in order to spy out the land of suffering and bring a report back to others;[9] a distinct echo of the account in Numbers 13 where Joshua and Caleb were sent to Canaan with ten others on a mission of espionage, on behalf of the Israelites. Numerous collections were subsequently published incorporating a greater number of letters as these were discovered, or made available. The first translation into Dutch was made as early as 1674, showing the close international links between those of a Reformed persuasion in Scotland and on the Continent.[10] The final and still authoritative critical edition was collated in 1891 by Andrew Bonar,[11] consisting of three hundred and sixty-five letters generally accepted to be authored by Rutherford.[12]

---

[6] The Scottish Covenanters and English Puritans can be identified as members of a common religious movement that manifested itself in the British Isles during the seventeenth century. Rutherford himself does not disown the label 'Puritan,' though he recognises it is intended in a derogatory sense, and the close working relationship between the two parties at the Westminster Assembly (1643-7) confirms their fundamental affinities in a day of intense spiritual division. Bonar, ed, *Letters of Samuel Rutherford*, 53, 134, 512.

[7] Loane, "Samuel Rutherford: The Saint of the Covenant," 73.

[8] Bonar, ed, *Letters of Samuel Rutherford*, 23-4.

[9] Gilmour, *Samuel Rutherford*, 14-15.

[10] Coffey, *Politics, Religion and the British Revolutions*, 5-6, 264-8. Rutherford twice refused calls to universities in Holland, Harderwyck and Utrecht, which were captivated by the learned works of Latin theology that flowed from his pen. Coffey, *Politics, Religion and the British Revolutions*, 55, 58.

[11] Though the critical quality of their transcription has been called into question. Hans H. Meier, "Love, Law and Lucre: Images in Rutherfurd's Letters," *Historical and Editorial Essays in Medieval and Early Modern English for Johan Gerritsen*, eds. H. Wirtjes and M.-J Arn (Groningen: 1985), 80-1. Meier also deliberately adopts the alternative spelling of 'Rutherfurd'; the common form used by scholars is an anglicised version of his name.

[12] Bonar, ed, *Letters of Samuel Rutherford*. Bonar is not as accurate as could be desired, making several mistakes in chronology and dating. Kingsley G. Rendell, *Samuel*

The publication history of these letters, which have remained in print since first issued, is remarkable,[13] and unique not only in Scottish literature, but British religious culture more generally,[14] where it is only in the past few decades that close attention has been paid to the social role of pastors and theologians in the seventeenth century. Their reading public has been specialised, interested primarily in the devotional quality of the collection;[15] but they have also attracted continuing interest from literary critics, who feel obliged to refer to them as a remarkable and influential phenomenon, even if they deplore Rutherford's idiosyncratic, impassioned and almost baroque prose.[16] This is most evident when he deals with the beauty, sufficiency, fairness, love and glory of Christ; the theme which consumed him and forms the central focus of the collection as a whole. The particular style and content of Rutherford's letters can also be considered within the context of Puritan and Catholic traditions of meditation. Louis Martz, for example, writes of the 'discipline' and 'creative imagination' required by the process of meditation, which can sometimes result in the creation of great poetry. Rutherford's commitment to the intellectual rigours and devotional emphases of Reformed theology worked in a similar way to produce the enraptured meditations of his letters.[17] Rutherford has even been described as a mystic; a quality rarely attributed to Scottish Covenanters.[18] However, they did share the Puritan commitment to experimental piety and Rutherford's language contains distinct echoes of a broad Catholic tradition, grounded in commentary and interpretation of the Song of Solomon, and demonstrated most notably by Bernard of Clairvaux.[19]

Rutherford's discourse upon the Person of Christ can be usefully categorised as a biblical aesthetic. This term is intended to denote a conception of what is beautiful and fitting as defined by the representation of Jesus Christ in the

---

Rutherford: A New Biography of the Man and His Ministry (Fearn: Christian Focus, 2003), 100-1.

[13] Coffey, *Politics, Religion and the British Revolutions*, 264-8.

[14] Gilmour, *Samuel Rutherford*, 10.

[15] Maurice Roberts, "Samuel Rutherford: The Comings and Goings of the Heavenly Bridegroom," *The Trials of Puritanism: papers read at the 1993 Westminster Conference* (1993), 119.

[16] Coffey, *Politics, Religion and the British Revolutions*, 107-10; Gilmour, *Samuel Rutherford*, 15-19; Meier, "Love, Law and Lucre: Images in Rutherfurd's Letters," 79-80.

[17] Louis Martz, *The Poetry of Meditation: A Study in English Religious Literature of the Seventeenth Century* (New Haven: Yale University Press, Revised Edition 1962), 321-30.

[18] Machar, "A Scottish Mystic."

[19] Coffey, *Politics, Religion and the British Revolutions*, 90-7. The helpfulness of the term 'mystic' in elucidating the nature of Rutherford's spirituality depends very much on how it is defined, though. Rendell, *Samuel Rutherford*, 130-4.

biblical text. Rutherford takes the hermeneutic principle articulated by Jesus in Luke 24:27: 'And beginning at Moses and all the prophets, he expounded unto them in all the scriptures the things concerning himself,' and draws upon the linguistic and metaphoric resources of the entire text, in order to express and represent his understanding and experience of Christ to his correspondents. Examples could be taken from almost any letter and the following is characteristic:

> Oh! oh! But we have short, and narrow, and creeping thoughts of Jesus, and do but shape Christ in our conceptions according to some created portraiture! O angels, lend in your help to make love-books and songs of our fair, and white, and ruddy Standard-bearer among ten thousand!....O glorified tenants, and triumphing house-holders with the Lamb, put in new psalms and love-sonnets of the excellency of our Bridegroom, and help us to set Him on high!....O fairness of creatures, blush before His uncreated beauty!....O sun in thy shining beauty, for shame put on a web of darkness, and cover thyself before thy brightest Master and Maker!....[E]njoy this Jewel of heaven's jewels!....Post, post, and hasten our desired and hungered-for meeting. Love is sick to hear tell of to-morrow (582-3).

The tone is one of rapture and reads strangely in a modern context that does not valorise a style of verbal extravagance. But, while singular in its accumulation of superlatives, stretching language taut to breaking-point in an attempt to convey a sense of the infinite, it is also richly biblical. Rutherford echoes the solicitations of the psalmists to angels to help them in praising God (for example, Psalm 148:2); there is a possible allusion to being 'compassed about with so great a cloud of witnesses,' mentioned in Hebrews 12:1, in the reference to 'glorified tenants'; whilst the call for 'new psalms' draws upon the Psalms, epistles and Revelation (Psalm 98:1; Colossians 3:16; Revelation 5:9-14). Also behind the passage is the image of the Bridegroom, taken from Revelation and Song of Solomon, supplemented by interpretations of David and the Messianic Psalms as typological precursors of Christ, seen in the attributions of 'ruddiness' and beauty (1 Samuel 16:12; 17:42; Psalm 45).

It is impossible fully to trace all the biblical sources in such an example, this text thoroughly nurtured and shaped the imagination and diction of Rutherford and many of his contemporaries, who defined their auxiliary discourse as 'the language of Canaan.' John Bunyan dramatically demonstrates the distinctive nature of this language in *The Pilgrim's Progress*, where the inhabitants of Vanity Fair are simply unable to comprehend the conversation of the pilgrims, Christian and Faithful:

> As they wondered at their apparel so they did likewise at their speech; for few could understand what they said; they naturally spoke the language of Canaan; but

> they that kept the Fair, were the men of this world: so that from one end of the Fair to the other, they seemed barbarians each to the other.[20]

There is more to this biblical aesthetic than a unique form of discourse. For Rutherford, Christ is the essence, object and definition of all that is truly beautiful; in his *Letters,* affective terminology is used to convey the surpassing loveliness of the Son of God. But the biblical source of his vocabulary and the invariably spiritual and relational contexts in which it occurs inevitably qualify the narrower understanding of aesthetics dominant in contemporary discussions.

Jonathan Edwards provides a helpful point of comparison in elucidating this issue, because while sharing the same broadly Calvinist theological heritage in which Rutherford stands, and possessing a similar temperament, both incisively logical and yet suffused with an intensely poetic sensibility, he is far more self-conscious about the aesthetic dimensions of spirituality and doctrine. Edwards carefully elaborates the Calvinist 'sense of the heart' that implicitly informs Rutherford's scriptural interpretation and its application to nature, physical or spiritual life and providence. This 'sense of the heart' is a gift of the Holy Spirit, enabling a kind of spiritual intuition, which allows the Christian to move from a recognition of the beauty of creation, to a transforming apprehension of spiritual beauty. Edwards observes:

> When we behold the fragrant rose and lily, we see [Jesus's] love and purity. So the green trees, and fields, and singing of birds are the emanations of His infinite joy and benignity. The easiness and naturalness of trees and vines are shadows of His beauty and loveliness. The crystal rivers and murmuring streams are the footsteps of His favor, grace, and beauty.[21]

Nature, created by God, is quasi-sacramental and reveals something of the beauty of his character and person. For Edwards, though, the spiritual sphere is higher. He takes the biblical phrase, 'the beauty of holiness' (Psalm 29:2; 96:9), and combines it with the perceptual, 'sense of the heart,' developing a theological aesthetic in which beauty becomes the term best able to unify and convey the intellectual, emotional and supernatural dimensions of the spiritual life.

> The beauty of holiness is that thing in spiritual and divine things, which is perceived by this spiritual sense, that is so diverse from all that natural men perceive in them: this kind of beauty is the quality that is the immediate object of

---

[20] Bunyan, *The Pilgrim's Progress*, 126-7.
[21] Jonathan Edwards, "The Covenant of Redemption," cited by Terrence Erdt, *Jonathan Edwards: Art and the Sense of the Heart* (Amherst: University of Massachusetts Press, 1980), 50.

this spiritual sense: this is the sweetness that is the proper object of this spiritual taste.[22]

In another place, ethics and volition are also embraced, 'it is this sight of the divine beauty of Christ that bows the wills, and draws the hearts of men.'[23] Beauty becomes a primary way of characterising and describing God himself:

> For as God is infinitely the greatest Being, so he is allowed to be infinitely the most beautiful and excellent: and all the beauty to be found throughout the whole creation, is but the reflection of the diffused beams of that Being who hath an infinite fulness of brightness and glory; God...is the foundation and fountain of all being and all beauty.[24]

Edwards provides a useful theological context that explains the peculiar deployment of biblical language to describe Christ which fills Rutherford's *Letters*; the sensual and tactile quality of Rutherford's nouns and adjectives are best categorised as aesthetic and affective. To cite just a few examples, he speaks of Jesus as 'the Beloved' (38), 'Sun of righteousness' (42), 'your Well-Beloved...ye feel the smell of His garments' (46-7), 'the King's wine-cellar' (55), 'the sweetest Master' (64), 'fair Chief Corner-stone' (67), 'that fair, lovely person, Jesus Christ' (70), 'lovely Christ' (71), 'that soul-delighting, lovely Bridegroom, our sweet, sweet Jesus, fairer than all the children of men, "the Rose of Sharon," and the fairest and sweetest smelled rose in all His Father's garden' (78), 'the fountain of living waters...the sweetest apple in all God's heavenly paradise, Jesus Christ, your life and your Lord' (79). This poetic sensibility, though, is inextricably linked to the strong ethical and doctrinal implications present in biblical images such as, 'Lord', 'Master,' 'Beloved' and 'Chief Corner-stone.' Rutherford himself makes this connection explicit when writing to the persecuted church in Ireland:

> If heaven and earth, and ten thousand heavens even...were all in one garden of paradise, decked with all the fairest roses, flowers, and trees that can come forth from the art of the Almighty Himself; yet set but our one Flower that groweth out of the root of Jesse beside that orchard of pleasure, one look of Him, one view, one taste, one smell of His sweet Godhead would infinitely exceed and go beyond the smell, colour, beauty, and loveliness of that paradise....If our Beloved were not mistaken by us, and unknown to us, He would have no scarcity of wooers and

---

[22] Jonathan Edwards, *Religious Affections*, cited by Erdt, *Jonathan Edwards*, 32.
[23] Jonathan Edwards, "True Grace Distinguished from the Experience of Devils," cited by Sherry, *Spirit and Beauty*, 15. Although Sherry is specifically attempting to define a theology of the Holy Spirit in relation to aesthetics, he acknowledges that Edwards gives an important role to both the Spirit and the Son in his Trinitarian understanding of beauty and the knowledge of God.
[24] Jonathan Edwards, *The Nature of True Virtue*, cited by Ryken, *The Liberated Imagination*, 70.

suitors....I earnestly desire to recommend this love to you, that this love may cause you to keep His commandments, and to keep clean fingers, and make clean feet, that ye may walk as the redeemed of the Lord....[L]et not His fairness be spotted and stained by godless living. Oh, who can find in their heart to sin against love? (573-74).

This passage has been quoted at length in order to give some idea of Rutherford's style, and also to demonstrate the way in which his Christocentric biblical aesthetic incorporates a spiritual and pastoral dimension; praise and a personal experience of Jesus are shown to lead necessarily, on the grounds of affection and loyalty, to a life of sanctified holiness. In Edwards's words, it is the sight of 'divine beauty' that 'bows the wills' and 'draws the hearts.'[25]

The exotic, sensual and impassioned extravagance of Rutherford's language and imagery has aroused equally strong responses of admiration and antagonism amongst his readers; though even sympathetic admirers often find it necessary to excuse certain metaphors as inappropriate or indecorous.[26] J. H. Millar decried 'the luscious and heady liquor purveyed by Rutherford and his astonishing jargon' as 'loaded and poisonous stuff.'[27] While to others, the letters are 'seraphic...exceedingly precious...full of comfort and inspiration,'[28] 'the nearest thing to inspiration that can be found in all the writings of mere men.'[29] It is preeminently the application of erotic relations between lover and beloved, to the relationship between the individual person and Christ, or the Kirk and Christ that amuses some and offends others. Here it is necessary to position Rutherford within a lengthy Christian tradition mentioned earlier, of drawing upon the language of human passion in the Song of Solomon to describe the spiritual relationship between the believer and Christ, or Christ and the church.[30] What makes him distinct amongst Puritan writers is the degree and consistency with which he draws upon this language, not his use of it.[31]

An apparent incongruity that has often troubled Rutherford's biographers is the fact that the individual who wrote these paeans of praise to his Saviour, was also the author of numerous weighty books in Latin of scholastic theology and

---

[25] Jonathan Edwards, "True Grace Distinguished from the Experience of Devils," cited by Sherry, *Spirit and Beauty*, 15.
[26] Bonar, ed, *Letters of Samuel Rutherford*, 24-5; Lilley, "Samuel Rutherford, 1600-1661," 12-13.
[27] Adam Philip, "The Golden Book of Love," *The Devotional Literature of Scotland* (London: James Clark & Co, 1920), 118.
[28] Lilley, "Samuel Rutherford, 1600-1661," 13.
[29] Faith Cook, *Samuel Rutherford and His Friends* (Edinburgh: Banner of Truth Trust, 1992), 145.
[30] E. Ann Matter, *The Voice of My Beloved: The Song of Songs in Western Medieval Christianity* (Philadelphia: University of Pennsylvania Press, 1990).
[31] Roberts, "Samuel Rutherford: The Comings and Goings of the Heavenly Bridegroom," 129.

doctrinal controversy.[32] Indeed, it was his theological rigour that made him eminent amongst his contemporaries, and perhaps led to his appointment as one of the five commissioners from Scotland present at the famous Westminster Assembly from 1643-7.[33] The aesthetic dimension explored earlier helps to resolve this seeming dichotomy, the Calvinistic 'sense of the heart' is intimately connected to the experiential piety that Covenanters and Puritans alike sought to enact, and which, as pastors, they repeatedly urged upon their congregations.[34] Rutherford identified himself primarily as a pastor. He states that apart from Christ, his supreme passion was to preach Christ (202), and the genre of the sermon fuses the doctrinal treatise with the divine love letter.[35] John Coffey insightfully observes: 'Rutherford was not aiming for literary grace, but for the maximum rhetorical effect on his audience. His language possessed a raw, colloquial energy precisely because it was intended to grab the attention of a congregation....In letters and sermons of great imagination, he fused the apocalyptic and the nuptial, the sublime and the homely, constantly surprising and assaulting the senses.'[36]

The *Letters* are characterised by a great diversity of imagery, and Rutherford rarely repeats himself.[37] However, a close analysis has revealed three spheres to be preeminent amongst the many drawn upon: 'love, law and lucre.'[38] To elaborate, the nuptial or erotic occurs most frequently, closely followed by the commercial and then forensic.[39] Of course, the boundaries between these spheres, particularly the last are fluid, and they reveal much about rural life in seventeenth-century Scotland, as well as becoming vehicles to convey pointed spiritual lessons. The semantic range and power of these allusions grows when one recognises how compatible these areas of life are with recurrent biblical imagery.[40] It was probably this affinity that directed Rutherford at either a conscious or subconscious level in his selection of various facets of contemporary life as illustrations. The juxtaposition of contemporary life with biblical metaphors could be mutually illuminating. When comforting a woman who had recently lost her husband, Rutherford observes: 'Know therefore, that the wounds of your Lord Jesus are the wounds of a lover, and that he will have compassion upon a sad-hearted servant...He

---

[32] Innes, "Samuel Rutherfurd."
[33] Coffey, *Politics, Religion and the British Revolutions*, 52. This Assembly was a gathering of Anglican, Puritan, Presbyterian and Independent divines, who sought to shape a uniform system of church government and creed for England, Scotland and Ireland.
[34] Coffey, *Politics, Religion and the British Revolutions*, 94-7.
[35] Loane, "Samuel Rutherford: The Saint of the Covenant," 91-96.
[36] Coffey, *Politics, Religion and the British Revolutions*, 110.
[37] Coffey, *Politics, Religion and the British Revolutions*, 103.
[38] Meier, "Love, Law and Lucre: Images in Rutherfurd's Letters."
[39] Meier, "Love, Law and Lucre: Images in Rutherfurd's Letters," 82.
[40] Meier, "Love, Law and Lucre: Images in Rutherfurd's Letters," 84-5.

loved you in your first husband's time, and He is but wooing you still. Give Him heart and chair, house and all...He will have all your love.'[41] Or fusing paternal and forensic discourses to convey a sense of his continual spiritual indebtedness to Christ: 'It is good to be ever taking from Him. I desire that He may get the fruit of praises, for dawting and thus dandling me on His knee: and I may give my bond of thankfulness, so being I have Christ's back-bond again for my relief...'(240).

As Meier notes, these three systems are highly fruitful due to the remarkable degree of correspondence between them, and the way in which it is possible to integrate and extend them metaphorically. In fact, the idea of Christ as 'husband', 'judge', or 'surety,' not only suggests significant parallels, but if one interprets the mutual relationships these imply in the legal framework of 'bonds' then their convergence forms 'a symbolic foundation of the 'covenanting spirit,' from which covenant or federal theology has sprung.'[42] This is important, as it illustrates the central role played by imagery in the logical development of thought in and between the *Letters*. It also links this literature, which is often confined to the 'devotional' or 'mystic' sphere firmly within the theological and political context of seventeenth-century Scotland. However, focusing on the 'commissive or mandatory'[43] clusters of imagery can result in a skewed portrait, creating the sense of an abject subject position under a tyrannous and arbitrary lord. There is a strong authoritarian strain in Rutherford, but as the earlier reference to being dandled on Christ's knee demonstrates, he deploys many gentler, more loving images, referring to 'bairns,' friendship (34), motherhood, lost sheep, and so on. Thus, in comforting a grieving wife he writes: 'he shall meet with the solacious company, the fair flock, and blessed bairn-teme of the first born....It is a mercy that the poor wandering sheep get a dyke-side in this stormy day...a sea-sick passenger a sound and soft bed ashore' (217). Or, in a more celestial strain to a mother who has lost her child: 'She is not sent away, but only sent before, like unto a star, which going out of our sight doth not die and evanish, but shineth in another hemisphere' (41).

Rutherford's language in these letters is vivid and peculiar, to a large extent this is due to his fusion of biblical language with the Scots dialect and it adds to the literary impact of his epistles, though it can also make them more difficult to follow.[44] This distinctive idiom is energised by his vivid imagination and gift for pithy and trenchant aphorisms, as well as lengthy rhapsodies on the person and work of Christ. Thus, the familiar image of the Beloved from the Song of

---

[41] Cook, *Samuel Rutherford and His Friends*, 6.
[42] Meier, "Love, Law and Lucre: Images in Rutherfurd's Letters," 84-5.
[43] Meier, "Love, Law and Lucre: Images in Rutherfurd's Letters," 85.
[44] The *Oxford English Dictionary* quotes him approximately 700 times to illustrate words now rare, colloquial or redundant. Coffey, *Politics, Religion and the British Revolutions*, 102.

Solomon is rendered uniquely, when Rutherford draws upon Scottish terms for a distant lover: 'He looked fremed and unco-like upon me when I came first here; but I believe Himself better than His looks' (148). Similarly, in seeking to apply the scriptural injunction to take up his cross when banished to Aberdeen he notes: 'Those who can take that crabbed tree handsomely upon their back, and fasten it on cannily, shall find it such a burden as wings unto a bird, or sails to a ship' (148). Finally, he describes himself in terms of a child, hungrily waiting upon Christ for food: 'I seek not an apple to play me with....I but beg earnest, and am content to suspend and frist glory whill supper-time....Will not a father take his little dawted Davie in his arms, and carry him over a ditch or a mire? My short legs could not step over this lair, or sinking mire; and, therefore, my Lord Jesus will bear me through' (225). The examples could be multiplied indefinitely, but sufficient have been cited to give a sense of the way in which seraphic strains of praise are welded to earthy imagery, and a distinctive Scottish idiom, which has made these *Letters* of literary interest, as well as devotional. It explains the observation of Richard Cecil, 'Rutherford's *Letters* is one of my classics....He is a real original.'[45]

The *Letters* are informed by the biblical text at many levels. Rutherford applies the dynamic hermeneutic of scriptural typology in order to understand the circumstances, often of intense suffering and deprivation, in which he and his correspondents found themselves. Of the three hundred and sixty-five extant letters written by Rutherford, more than two hundred were penned during his imprisonment at Aberdeen, where he had been banished by the bishops, for his 'newly printed book against Arminians' (then the ascendant party in the church), and for 'not lording the prelates' (135). The most galling part of this edict was his separation from his congregation at Anwoth, and being forbidden to preach (302). It was the latter that probably precipitated the extraordinary flow of epistles that emerged during this period of eighteen months in exile (1636-8).[46] Rutherford self-consciously interprets his situation on the basis of biblical models like the apostle Paul, imprisoned in Caesarea and Rome (Acts 24:24-27; 25:4; 29:30-31), or the beloved disciple John, exiled at Patmos (Revelation 1:4, 9). The affinities, of course, are accentuated, when one considers that many of the New Testament epistles were first sent by these men to various individuals or congregations during periods of imprisonment (Ephesians 4:1; Colossians 4:18; Philemon 1; 2 John 1; 3 John 1). Rutherford similarly writes to churches in Ireland and Anwoth (438-44, 521-24, 549-55), individual parishioners (323-34, 344-48, 378-80), friends (361-63), and those suffering acute persecution (418-20), during his period of exile. In his dedications and benedictions particularly, Rutherford models his language upon these biblical exemplars. He addresses John Fleming, Bailie of Leith, with the words, 'Grace, mercy, and peace be unto you' (292), a direct echo of Paul's

---

[45] Cook, *Samuel Rutherford and His Friends*, 144.
[46] Coffey, *Politics, Religion and the British Revolutions*, 45-8.

letter to Timothy (1 Timothy 1:2); he concludes his letter to Lady Busbie, 'I entreat you to think upon me, His prisoner, and pray that the Lord would be pleased to give me room to speak to His people in His name' (292), picking up Paul's plea to the Colossians, 'remember my bonds' (4:18) and 'praying also for us, that God would open unto us a door of utterance, to speak the mystery of Christ, for which I am also in bonds' (4:3). It can also be heard movingly in his oft-repeated phrase, the 'blessing of a prisoner of Christ be upon you' (285), 'remember my bonds' (244), again echoing Paul (Colossians 4:18).

In addition to his self-identification with the apostles in prison, and determination to fulfil his pastoral role through letters, when transferred 'eight score-miles' (141) to 'this northern world' (159) and consigned to 'dumb Sabbaths...like a stone tied to a bird's foot' (207),[47] the content of Rutherford's letters largely echo that of the New Testament epistles. This can be seen preeminently in his focus upon the person of Christ, and his exhortations to his readers to pursue him alone. But woven throughout are the recurrent themes of purification through suffering, the relationship between Christ and his Kirk, the need to pray for Zion, the prospect of imminent judgment, renunciation of the world, and an ecstatic hope of glory. These themes are by no means uniquely characteristic of Rutherford, they were often dealt with at the time, and frequently recur in the writings of Christians when under intense persecution or suffering; as the parallels with the New Testament make sufficiently obvious. Rutherford's *Letters*, however, in their entirety form a singular biblical response to a situation that has repeatedly occurred in the history of the church. His correspondents valued his pastoral insight and sympathy,[48] this, along with the vivid imagery, aesthetic and devotion previously explored, as well as the sheer number he wrote, cause his letters to stand out amongst other writings of a similar genre.

Many of Rutherford's letters were addressed to women, which also distinguishes him from other religious counselors who frequently resorted to this form of address, like John Calvin or Ignatius Loyola; their letters to women, in contrast to Rutherford, form only a small percentage of their total output.[49] This has provoked some infelicitous comments, like that of Meier: 'I was first struck by the extraordinary style of Samuel Rutherfurd's *Letters* among the other Scottish divines. By comparison, his qualities recalled one's first contact with women: they were softer, warmer, heavier, and sweeter than

---

[47] Bonar, ed, *Letters of Samuel Rutherford*, 207. It is necessary to note, though, that his frustration at being separated from his flock and his inability to preach is accompanied, and frequently overwhelmed, by joy in the presence of Christ, in 'my King's Palace at Aberdeen.' Bonar, ed, *Letters of Samuel Rutherford*, 131.
[48] John M. Brentnall, *Samuel Rutherford in Aberdeen* (Inverness: John G. Eccles, c. 1981), 15.
[49] Coffey, *Politics, Religion and the British Revolutions*, 97.

one had expected.'⁵⁰ Rutherford's style is certainly unique; its elaborate and luscious qualities can alienate even sympathetic readers. While gender is a useful tool of analysis, such stereotypical contrasts as those identified by Meier do not provide any real insights. Close relationships between pastors and women in their congregation, especially during times of persecution, when both pastors and people could be dismissed from their positions, imprisoned, beheaded, or burnt at the stake with little warning, were characteristic of Puritan and Covenanting circles, and a source of mutual encouragement.⁵¹ The temptation to read amorous sub-texts into such exchanges is present,⁵² but misses the intense spiritual dynamic at work in these tight-knit communities, as well as underestimating their serious and genuine hatred of adultery and fornication as sins that would bring about divine retribution. More significant in this present context is the obvious influence that these women could exert socially in Scotland for the cause they held to be biblically right for Kirk and country, and the way in which concerns peculiar to his female correspondents, as women, determined the subject-matter of Rutherford's *Letters*.

Most prominent amongst these is the reality of acute suffering and loss. Again and again Rutherford writes to women of high and low station, bereft of their husband or children. In his epistles to Lady Kenmure, to whom fifty-six of his letters were addressed,⁵³ he refers consistently to her young son, asking after the 'sweet child' and praying God's blessing upon him (132, 138, 149-50, 198, 200, 201, 202, 216, 402-4). This situation was particularly poignant as Lady Kenmure had lost several children and her husband (40, 100-1); while the young Viscount to whom Rutherford refers was also to die at four years of age (565-68). He himself had lost his first wife after a period of great sickness, and all but one of his children died before him (49, 50-54). It is in this context that many of his letters were written, and which made biblical teaching on suffering, sanctification, providence and glory of such pressing relevance and concern. Rutherford's biblical response to these agonising experiences was nuanced and complex, but always focused on the person of Christ.

I will consider here only two instances of the many clusters of scriptural images that informed his writing. In a letter to Barbara Hamilton upon the death of her son-in-law, he describes God as a Builder and Gardener:

> We see His working and we sorrow....[W]e see hewn stones, timber, and an hundred scattered parcels and pieces of an old house, all under-tools, hammers, and axes, and saws; yet the house, the beauty and use of so many lodgings and ease-rooms, we neither see nor understand for the present; these are but in the mind and head of the builder, as yet. We see red earth, unbroken clods, furrows, and stones; but we see not summer, lilies, roses, the beauty of a garden (623-4).

---

⁵⁰ Meier, "Love, Law and Lucre: Images in Rutherfurd's Letters," 77.
⁵¹ Coffey, *Politics, Religion and the British Revolutions*, 97-102.
⁵² Coffey, *Politics, Religion and the British Revolutions*, 99-100.
⁵³ Coffey, *Politics, Religion and the British Revolutions*, 97.

The argument of the passage is in the images, taking up the principle in Romans that 'all things work together for good to them that love God' (8:28). More introspectively, in an earlier letter to James Hamilton, he compares Christ to an Artist, shaping the 'unclean and impure channel' (Rutherford) so that it 'casteth such a lustre' to his glory:

> I see that Christ will be Christ, in the dreg and refuse of men. His art, His shining wisdom, His beauty speak loudest in blackness, weakness, deadness, yea, in nothing...no deserving, is the ground that Omnipotency delighteth to draw glory out of (471).

Here the process of sanctification is described in aesthetic terminology: the divine Artist shapes the 'black' human material into a vessel through which his 'shining wisdom and beauty' glow and 'casteth...a lustre.' It again clearly draws upon and echoes the biblical text, the 'base things of the world, and things which are despised, hath God chosen, yea, and things which are not....But of him are ye in Christ Jesus, who of God is made unto us wisdom, and righteousness, and sanctification, and redemption' (1 Corinthians 1:28, 30). Rutherford here takes up a biblical hint like that in Ephesians, that believers are God's *poema* (2:10), and traces the divine imagination at work weaving the events of daily life into 'the beauty of a garden,' through his artistic direction of providence, in order to shape the characters of his children through the crucified aesthetics of suffering into a beauty that reflects the image of the Creator: 'his art, his shining wisdom, his beauty' delights to write poems of grace transforming 'blackness, weakness, deadness' into 'glory.'[54]

It was thus out of an historical situation of deep suffering, uncertainty and ascetic deprivation that the exotic aesthetic and literary sensibility of Rutherford's *Letters* emerged. They represent an epistolary appropriation of the biblical text in the midst of a religious community where it held an authoritative role in all matters of faith, ecclesiastical discipline, structure, life and practice. They are unique, however, in their rapturous Christocentric focus, which draws heavily upon the Song of Solomon and Revelation, in the tradition of authors like Bernard of Clairvaux, inviting their immediate and subsequent readership to a sensuous and tactile spirituality, centred on the Person of Jesus. Rutherford forges a unique language and stock of imagery, which can be most accurately categorised as a deeply spiritual biblical aesthetic. Built upon a Calvinist theology that united clear scholastic logic, with passionate devotion to the glory of God, this 'sense of the heart' present in the believer by grace, enabled a vision of Christ, to which purity of heart and life was the only adequate response. These features generated a biblical language, imagination and

---

[54] Patrick Sherry refers briefly to the 'paradoxical beauty of the Cross' and the way in which moral beauty comes out of the suffering of Christ in his revised edition of *Spirit and Beauty: An Introduction to Theological Aesthetics* (London: SCM Press, 2002), 172.

aesthetic which have made the *Letters* foreign and uncongenial to contemporary tastes. However, the influence they exercised upon the preaching and spirituality of Scottish culture in subsequent centuries is an incontrovertible testimony to their literary power, vision, and biblical passion.[55]

The Role of the Realistic Imagination in Communication and Relationships

As already noted, Rutherford's language of communion with God and others, is firmly grounded in a relational commitment shaped by his understanding of the biblical text, appropriated and acted upon in faith. To cite McIntyre again: 'Faith does much that imagination can not be expected to do: for example, obey, trust, acknowledge, respond, decide....'[56] However, here I shall consider more precisely the role that a 'realistic imagination' plays within the framework established by this faith commitment, in order to articulate concretely how Samuel Rutherford at least imagined biblically. It is possible to approach this from many angles, and I will focus on three aspects in the remainder of this chapter. Firstly, Jonathan Edwards's aesthetic application of Calvin's 'sense of the heart' provides a theologically sensitive means of elucidating Rutherford's understanding of imagination in relation to the self, others and God, enabling these insights to be developed and applied beyond the particular historical situation in which Rutherford wrote. Secondly, Rutherford's use of biblical narrative and metaphor, as the mechanics by which he actualises the 'realistic imagination' will be examined, drawing upon Alan Jacobs's development of an Augustinian hermeneutic in order to elaborate further.[57] Finally, the implicit relationship between word and thing which informs Rutherford's 'symbolic discourse...of affective intentionality' will be explored and articulated,[58] through drawing upon the work of a contemporary theologian in the Reformed tradition, Kevin Vanhoozer.[59]

In many respects Rutherford is an enigma: Scottish Covenanter and mystic, scholastic theologian and suffering saint, legal theoretician and passionate pastor, national politician and rural cleric; he embodies a series of contradictions that are often simplified into the dichotomy of 'public' and 'private.' While much of this is obviously the consequence of Rutherford's distinctive character, (which remained a puzzle to him also),[60] the 'problem' of the two sides of his personality is equally a product of frequently unquestioned beliefs concerning the relationship between interior and exterior, body and

---

[55] Stuart Louden cited by Coffey, *Politics, Religion and the British Revolutions*, 96-7.
[56] McIntyre, *Faith, Theology and Imagination*, 37.
[57] Jacobs, *A Theology of Reading*.
[58] Bernard McGinn, "The Language of Inner Experience in Christian Mysticism," *Spiritus: A Journal of Christian Spirituality* 1.2 (2001), 156.
[59] Vanhoozer, *Is There a Meaning in This Text?*, 238-40.
[60] Rendell, *Samuel Rutherford*, 129.

spirit, religion and spirituality in Western culture. Such simplistic oppositions occlude a crucial dynamic expressed propositionally in Reformed theology and articulated experientially in the lives of Rutherford and his correspondents: namely, that it is a personal experience of communion with God which enables, energises and compels an active engagement with others in the material world.[61] Philip F. Sheldrake expresses this Puritan theological conviction in theoretical terms that rework the relationship more constructively: 'the concepts of interiority and exteriority need to be held in creative tension. The heart of Christian spirituality may indeed be expressed in terms of this tension – a dialectic of the mystical-contemplative and transformative practice (the prophetic).'[62]

Sheldrake reevaluates traditional readings of Augustinian thought in order to rehabilitate a crucial distinction between 'privacy' and 'interiority.' To turn within is not necessarily to selfishly neglect the needs of others and the outer world, as it is by looking within that we find the *imago Dei* in which we are created. While 'sin is a withdrawal into privacy,' in the biblical text 'human...solidarity with others [is] expressed in the image of the undivided heart.' Thus, 'the language of the heart...[w]hat is interior to me is, for Augustine, where I am also united with the whole human family.'[63] This circular hermeneutic is given classic expression in John Calvin's *Institutes*, and is crucial to Rutherford's understanding of the self, God and others: 'Our wisdom...consists almost entirely of two parts: the knowledge of God and of ourselves. But as these are connected together by many ties it is not easy to determine which of the two precedes and gives birth to the other.'[64] In biblical terms the heart is the centre of the person, where all good actions must originate in purity before God, by the grace of God, if one is to do anything effectively for others.[65] It is possible to extrapolate Sheldrake's observations on the medieval Augustinian tradition and apply them to Rutherford and his circle:

---

[61] Constance Furey offers another way of envisaging the theological, spiritual and emotional values and bonds shared by Rutherford and his correspondents in her concept of 'the religious republic of letters.' Rather like the Catholic intellectuals she considers, Rutherford and his correspondents were '[c]atalyzed by the specific tensions and pressures of a particular historical moment' and they 'sought out friendships with one another in order to demarcate a realm of spiritual meaning – a new kind of religious community bound together by affective relationships and shared interests in spiritualized scholarship.' Constance Furey, *Erasmus, Contarini, and the Religious Republic of Letters* (Cambridge: Cambridge University Press, 2006), 5.

[62] Philip F. Sheldrake, "Christian Spirituality as a Way of Living Publicly: A Dialectic of the Mystical and Prophetic," *Spiritus: A Journal of Christian Spirituality* 3.1 (2003), 20.

[63] Sheldrake, "Christian Spirituality as a Way of Living Publicly: A Dialectic of the Mystical and Prophetic," 21-3.

[64] John Calvin, *Institutes of the Christian Religion*, 1.1.1.

[65] Erdt, *Jonathan Edwards*, 4.

'the purpose of interiority [is]...external action rather than the cultivation of an inner universe of private experience' and 'the *homo interior* was a shared human nature, made in the image of God' rather than 'a unique, particular, autonomous self.'[66] As Denys Turner notes, two metaphors complement one another in Augustine's understanding of the spiritual life 'interiority' and 'ascent.'[67] This dialectical notion of 'inwardness paradoxically leads beyond distinctions of inner and outer towards the eternal boundlessness of God.'[68] He is not only within, but above.[69]

Imagination and the various aspects of human being that fall under its rubric cannot be looked at biblically, without reference to the heart. The significance of this term to biblical anthropology was elaborated in the second chapter of this study; the purpose of the present discussion is to focus it more specifically by drawing on Jonathan Edwards's definition of the 'sense of the heart.' Terence Erdt has traced the evolution and mutation of this concept through the Calvinist tradition. Classically, as defined by John Calvin and his seventeenth-century Puritan heirs, it is the feeling of sweetness that arises in the heart of the believer upon realising that they have received the mercy of God in Jesus Christ. It is experimental, a 'regenerative change in the inclination of the heart' awakening a relish for God. It is the assurance that one has been saved by grace, elusive, yet of the essence of faith: the means by which the believer acquires 'an experiential knowledge of the nature of God and of divine providence.'[70] This is critical to a right understanding of the theology that undergirds the experiential mysticism of Rutherford expressed in the *Letters*. Delight in God, fellowship with other believers and the ability to trace God's hand in providence, are all attributed to this divinely initiated infusion of grace in the heart (108, 218-20, 460-63). The unique contribution of Edwards, according to Erdt, was to define this *suavitas* as an aesthetic response, drawing upon John Locke.[71]

Erdt's reading of Edwards enables one to explicate the implications of this

---

[66] Sheldrake, "Christian Spirituality as a Way of Living Publicly: A Dialectic of the Mystical and Prophetic," 21-3.

[67] Denys Turner, *The Darkness of God: Negativity in Christian Mysticism* (Cambridge: Cambridge University Press, 1995), 74-101.

[68] Sheldrake, "Christian Spirituality as a Way of Living Publicly: A Dialectic of the Mystical and Prophetic," 24.

[69] Paul Cefalu attempts to link the encounters of early modern poets with the elusive otherness of God in *English Renaissance Literature and Contemporary Theory: Sublime Objects of Theology* (Houndmills: Palgrave Macmillan, 2007), 2 and passim.

[70] Erdt, *Jonathan Edwards*, 11-15. Norman Pettit offers an historical account of regeneration, assurance and the importance of the heart in Puritan theology in *The Heart Prepared: Grace and Conversion in Puritan Spiritual Life* (New Haven: Yale University Press, 1966) and *The Heart Renewed: Assurance of Salvation in New England Spiritual Life* (Lampeter: The Edward Mellen Press, 2004).

[71] Erdt, *Jonathan Edwards*, 23.

theological concept for a biblical understanding of imagination, rooted in the heart.[72] According to his interpretation, Edwards held that the imagination, through nature, fantasy, or works of art, can evoke an aesthetic and emotive response that is very close to the spiritual 'sense of the heart' infused by grace, and provides a means by which the believer can reawaken these religious affections. Edwards (unremarkably for a Puritan) recognises a providentially ordered correspondence between spiritual truths and the natural world, and this structural analogy forms the basis of his argument for the importance of the imagination, moving from nature, to fantasy, to art. Erdt even postulates that Edwards's use of the conventions of romance in order to describe the rapturous communion his wife Sarah enjoyed as a child with God may be a deliberate attempt to experiment with the potential moral resources of the newly developing genre of the novel in order to awaken spiritual affections. Erdt compares Edwards to Richard Baxter, stating that the latter held images to be important, but finally dispensable. The Bible applies figurative language in order to communicate the otherwise inexpressible character of spiritual realities: form and content on this model are separable, and form ultimately irrelevant. Edwards, though, feels his way towards a theory of the imagination as cognitive rather than merely ornamental, and Erdt suggests that this aesthetic becomes a structuring principle in his sermon organisation, leading to the development of consistent metaphors, rather than a barrage of competing similes that assault and surprise the senses of the congregation.[73] While recognising the importance Edwards ascribes to the imagination in the apprehension of truth, I do not think that he ever goes so far in pursuit of this secondary means of awakening the heart as Erdt posits when observing, 'one's spiritual fate may well hinge upon one's power of imagination.'[74] For Edwards this would have been an unbiblical negation of the power and role of the Holy Spirit.[75]

This explicit discussion of the religious role of the imagination, as conceived by Edwards, provides the vocabulary to discuss what is going on implicitly in Rutherford's use of affectional language, biblical metaphor and narrative. Additionally, it is possible to extrapolate from the secondary function which Edwards ascribes to the imagination in awakening the affections of the heart, in order to formulate an understanding of how the imagination works more generally (that is beyond the specific confines of devotional experience and

---

[72] Though it entails inverting the direction of Erdt's argument, as he is concerned to demonstrate that Jonathan Edwards theorised a place for art and the imagination in order to stir up a 'sense of the heart' as similar as possible to that effected by the gracious work of the Holy Spirit in the soul.
[73] Erdt, *Jonathan Edwards*, 46-57, 63-82.
[74] Erdt, *Jonathan Edwards*, 73.
[75] Erdt himself recognises this fact at an earlier point in his analysis. Erdt, *Jonathan Edwards*, 50-2.

worship), in biblical terms. To both of these objects I will now turn.

The *Letters of Samuel Rutherford* are saturated with observations of the natural world as an image, reflection or analogy of the spiritual, and this has firm biblical roots. One could cite Romans 1:20: 'For his invisible attributes, namely, his eternal power and divine nature, have been clearly perceived, ever since the creation of the world, in the things that have been made.' Or the psalmist: 'The heavens declare the glory of God, and the sky above proclaims his handiwork. Day to day pours out speech, and night to night reveals knowledge' (Psalm 19:1-2). For Edwards, the recognition of this fact became the basis of his understanding of imagination, 'natural beauty...typifies spiritual beauty....It furnishes the mind with something tangible by which spiritual or intangible beauty can be conceived.' This is not quite the same as Dante's ladder, however, for he adds the crucial qualifier that 'secondary beauty is the greatest that the mind is capable of apprehending without divine assistance.'[76] God's works are evidenced not only in creation, but also in the providential direction of individual human lives. Rutherford explicitly compares Christ to an Artist: 'His art, His shining wisdom, His beauty speak loudest in blackness, weakness, deadness, yea, in nothing...no deserving, is the ground that Omnipotency delighteth to draw glory out of' (471). Again, Edwards provides a direct link, the greatest work of art is creation: 'the Son of God created the world for this very end, to communicate Himself in an image of His own excellency....[T]he beauties of nature are really emanations or shadows of the excellencies of the Son of God.'[77] These secondary beauties of nature can engender affections that bear a structural affinity to those of the believer when beholding primary spiritual beauty, and in Edwards's words, 'have a tendency to assist those whose hearts are under the influence of a truly virtuous temper to dispose them to the exercises of divine love, and enliven in them a sense of spiritual beauty.'[78]

In fact, to move further, and consider the biblical text itself, the imagination is necessary in order to be able to conceive the spiritual at all. Rutherford often exemplifies what Erdt identifies as the traditional Puritan aesthetic, of juxtaposing many images in order to convey higher spiritual realities. However, at times he develops a particular biblical image consistently and indicates the necessity of such images in order to speak of spiritual realities at all. This can be seen in a letter to Lady Kenmure dealing with heaven:

> But I cannot tell you what is to come. Yet I may speak as our Lord doth of it. The foundation of the city is pure gold, clear as crystal; the twelve ports are set with precious stones; if orchards and rivers commend a soil upon earth, there is a paradise there, wherein groweth the tree of life that beareth twelve manner of

---

[76] Erdt, *Jonathan Edwards*, 48.
[77] Edwards cited by Erdt, *Jonathan Edwards*, 49.
[78] Erdt, *Jonathan Edwards*, 50.

The Eye of Faith 99

fruits every month, which is seven score and four harvests in the year; and there is there a pure river of water of life, proceeding out of the throne of God and of the Lamb; and the city hath no need of the light of the sun or moon, or of a candle, for the Lord God Almighty and the Lamb is the light thereof. Madam, believe and hope for this, till ye see and enjoy. Jesus is saying in the Gospel, Come and see...(87).

The rhetoric of the Puritans against the imagination, which Rutherford shared in, does not entail a rejection of its importance, or a necessary dependence upon it. Again, Edwards's articulates it for us:

Such is our nature that we can't think of things invisible, without a degree of imagination....As God has given us such a faculty as the imagination, and has so made us that we can't think of things spiritual and invisible, without some exercise of this faculty, so it appears to me that such is our state and nature, that this faculty is really subservient and helpful to the other faculties of the mind, when a proper use is made of it; though oftentimes when the imagination is too strong, and the other faculties weak, it overbears 'em, and much disturbs them in this exercise.[79]

The warning with which he concludes is not surprising and it isolates a crucial issue about the functioning of the imagination that in our post-Romantic age is not often made: imagination can be a powerful form of enslavement, as well as liberation.[80] Edwards addressed this in an article on physics, speaking of the 'prejudice of the imagination': the more a person's power of imagination is limited, the less capacity they have to conceive the wonders of God's creation. He identifies it as one of the most powerful prejudices 'against truth of any kind', conjecturing 'how far imagination is unavoidable in all thinking and why.'[81] A deluded imagination is deadly. In biblical terminology it is often seen as a form of idolatry, and it is this that constitutes the burden of Rutherford's critique of imagination within the *Letters*. Ultimately though, even biblical images are unable to convey the full reality of eternal truths. It is this recognition that prompts Rutherford to proliferate images in quick succession.

---

[79] Edwards cited by Erdt, *Jonathan Edwards*, 52-3.
[80] Kerry Dearborn explores this when analysing George MacDonald's theology of the imagination which sees it as open to distortion in three ways: in the Romantic tendency to 'evaluate art on the basis of the strength of the emotion evoked by it, which may result from 'fanciful thinking and writing and have no real connection with Truth'; to reduce imagination to mere ornamentation, rather than allowing that 'the imagination contributed substantially in providing cognitive content'; as a source of illusion or superstition. If imagination is divorced from the context of worship MacDonald believed it could 'create distortions.' 'Rather than submitting to the servant role of the imagination, fancy becomes with the occult a tool of control and manipulation.' Dearborn, *Baptized Imagination*, 89-91.
[81] Edwards cited by Erdt, *Jonathan Edwards*, 54-5.

They complement and correct one another in order to convey something of the beauty and wonder of the love of God in Jesus Christ. As fallible human beings, both Edwards and Rutherford acknowledge that now 'we see in a mirror dimly' only at the *eschaton* will we see 'face to face' (1 Corinthians 13:12). Even though Rutherford lived in a generation where the distinction between 'tenor' and 'vehicle' in metaphoric discourse was understood far less rigidly,[82] the type could never adequately comprehend the antitype, because of the nature of the analogy: there is an immeasurable gulf between finite and infinite being.

To summarise: the biblical principle that the created world reveals aspects of God's character and spiritual truths forms a foundation for recognising analogies between natural and spiritual beauty. Edwards extends this to the fantasies of the imagination and works of art, which provide a means of tangibly conceptualising spiritual things that are by their very nature incorporeal and intangible. These functions of the imagination are seen at work in Rutherford's *Letters*, where he interprets both nature and providence as sites in which the hand of God as Supreme Artist can be traced, and in the use of biblical and idiosyncratic metaphors in order to understand and convey the otherwise incomprehensible truths about God. For Edwards, these uses of the imagination are important due to their ability to arouse an affectional response in human beings, which is akin to that stirred by the Spirit of God in response to grace. Nevertheless, his understanding of the role of imagination in 'bodying forth' or perceiving secondary beauty, is an important resource for developing an understanding of imagination that is rooted in the biblical concept of the heart. The poet W. H. Auden enables the biblical (and Puritan) warnings against corrupt or flawed imagination to be applied specifically to artistic creativity.

> It is just when the would-be proximity of mimetic art to truth fails that the distance of analogy, with its 'feebly figurative signs,' manages somehow to succeed....The imagination is to be regarded as a natural faculty the subject matter of which is the phenomenal world, not its creator.[83]

The inadequacy of the created artefact, (in distinction from the limited, but authoritative and sufficient biblical metaphors), is its saving grace, for 'it is just here, among the ruins and the bones, that we may rejoice in the perfected Work which is not ours.' For Auden, as for Rutherford and Edwards, communion with the divine, and communication of the divine, was achieved uniquely and finally through the incarnation of Jesus Christ.[84] The closest the human

---

[82] Michael C. Schoenfeldt, *Bodies and Selves in Early Modern England: Physiology and Inwardness in Spenser, Shakespeare, Herbert, and Milton* (Cambridge: Cambridge University Press, 1999), 8.
[83] Alan Jacobs, *What Became of Wystan: Change and Continuity in Auden's Poetry* (Fayetteville: University of Arkansas Press, 1998), 24.
[84] Jacobs, *What Became of Wystan*, 24.

imagination can come from a biblical perspective is the hopeful orientation of a crucified aesthetic anticipating the *eschaton*, when 'we shall be like him, because we shall see him as he is' (1 John 3:2).

In a sense this has brought us back to the initial point of departure: the role of the imagination as it is enacted in the *Letters*, whilst structured by a faith commitment to propositional truth, is essentially relational. The self gains its identity in relation to God. Maintaining this focus is necessary, according to the theological dynamic embodied by the *Letters*, if one is ever actively and effectively to serve others. Rutherford's choice of metaphors foregrounds this emphasis on the self in relation: when speaking of the vertical relationship to God, he refers to the individual believer or church as the Bride of Christ the Bridegroom. Similarly, when speaking of horizontal relationships with fellow believers, he often resorts to familial or agricultural terminology (flock, wheat and so on). This reciprocity is characteristic of the epistolary genre and is particularly significant in the case of Rutherford, where the remarkable commonality of experience which he shared with many of his correspondents was grounded in the 'interiority' of each shaped by their communion with God.

In his study, *A Theology of Reading*, Alan Jacobs juxtaposes Mikhail Bakhtin's theory of double-discourse in the novel alongside an Augustinian hermeneutics of love. Jacobs's description of the dynamic relationship subsisting between self and other bears a remarkable affinity to the interpersonal 'interiority' of the *Letters*. His argument enables the dialectical movement between 'public' and 'private,' grounded in Reformed theology, and modelled by Rutherford, to be articulated and extended in a discriminating and biblically informed manner. Rutherford has been categorised as a 'mystic' by many readers of the *Letters*, but this category is of limited use in discerning the particular quality of interiority and spiritual experience that the *Letters* delineate. In the words of Benjamin Warfield, the biblical view 'issues not in the destruction of self, but only in the destruction of selfishness; it leads us not to a Buddha-like unselfing, but to a Christ-like self-development.'[85] If the term 'mystic' is understood to mean pantheistic union with the deity, then Rutherford's 'mysticism was not the experience we usually associate with the word,' for he never lost his identity, 'not self absorption in his own individual experience, but that union with Christ which is the right of every Christian.'[86]

The tendency of mysticism in the Western tradition has been towards *kenosis*, where the individual seeks to annihilate the self in order to receive the other (God or neighbour). Bakhtin, however, rejects this interpretation on the grounds that an evacuated self cannot act responsibly. The key passage is Philippians 2:5-11, which describes the *kenosis* of Christ. Bakhtin offers an alternative reading that enables the dialectic of interiority and exteriority, self

---

[85] Benjamin Warfield, "Imitating the Incarnation," *The Savior of the World* (Edinburgh: 1991), 267.
[86] Rendell, *Samuel Rutherford*, 134.

and other (neighbour or God), to be conceptualised and enacted dialogically. He argues that it is impossible to fulfil the command to 'love your neighbour as yourself' (Matthew 22:39), if one has embraced an understanding of *kenosis* which entails the annihilation of the self, as it is essential to truly ethical action that there is an identifiable individual agent. Nevertheless, visualising 'one's own outward image in imagination,' attempting 'to 'feel' oneself from outside' is also an insufficient base for loving our neighbour, as 'we lack any emotional and volitional approach to this outward image that could vivify it and include or incorporate it axiologically within the outward unity of the plastic-pictorial world.'[87] For Bakhtin, the fault with this approach of self-evacuation lies in its conception of the self as a monadic kingdom which engages with others as self-sufficient entities. The self, for Bakhtin, is intrinsically dialogic or relational and thus, 'neither the self nor the other is expendable, since self cannot be purely self nor other purely other.'[88]

Jacobs takes this insight into the intrinsically relational nature of the self further, by noting that God in Christ has become the other for us, in his atoning death upon the cross. This enables an individual, by first answering to the divine Other, through grace to genuinely give themselves on behalf of other people. Through responsible action, Bakhtin suggests that the individual can live, not simply for themselves, nor by attempting to eliminate themselves, but rather 'from within'; as they expend themselves on behalf of others in this way they achieve a genuinely answerable personhood.[89]

> If I actually lost myself in the other (instead of two participants there would be one – an impoverishment of Being), i.e, if I ceased to be unique, then this moment of my non-being cannot become a moment in the being of consciousness – it would simply not exist for me, i.e, being would not be accomplished through me at that moment. Passive empathizing, being-possessed, losing oneself – these have nothing in common with the answerable act/deed of self-abstracting or self-renunciation. In self-renunciation I actualize with utmost activeness and in full the uniqueness of my place in Being. The world in which I, from my own unique place, renounce myself does not become a world in which I do not exist, a world which is indifferent, in its meaning, to my existence: self-renunciation is a performance or accomplishment that encompasses Being-as-event.[90]

For Bakhtin, references to loving one's neighbour as oneself are 'explicitly linked to other-regard.' '[O]ne gives by making oneself the other's guarantor rather than by virtue of abandoning one's own interests.'[91] Bakhtin illuminates

---

[87] Bakhtin in *Towards a Philosophy of the Act* cited by Jacobs, *A Theology of Reading*, 58.
[88] Jacobs, *A Theology of Reading*, 106.
[89] Jacobs, *A Theology of Reading*, 60-1.
[90] Bakhtin, "Discourse in the Novel," cited by Jacobs, *A Theology of Reading*, 108.
[91] Gene Outka cited by Jacobs, *A Theology of Reading*, 110.

the ways in which the horizontal command to love one's neighbour complements rather than opposes the vertical command to love God supremely. It is the 'divine signature' inscribed in the sacrifice of Christ upon the cross, which, 'once recognized by me, provides the ground for, or source of, my own determination to...'incarnate' my love for the other.' Thus a genuine relationship between human beings, a true *kenosis* of the self on behalf of the other, has 'three – not two' as 'the 'dialogical minimum,' as it must be underwritten by the self-sacrifice of Christ (2 Corinthians 5:21).[92] Bakhtin articulates the dynamic way in which Rutherford's communion with Christ is the foundation and catalyst for his epistolary relationships with others, and his pastoral, political and academic engagement in British society. It is evident from reading Rutherford's *Letters* that for him also the dialogical minimum is three.

Bakhtin's distinction between passive existence (traditional understandings of *kenosis* or embodiment) and authentic action ('self-renunciation' where 'I actualize with utmost activeness and in full the uniqueness of my place in Being' or incarnation) can be used as a way of defining human creativity. In the previous chapter, the derivative nature of creativity that humans possess, because we are made in the image of the Creator, was explored. The differentiation which Bahktin draws between 'incarnation' and 'embodiment' in order to define an ethical action, also provides the vocabulary to distinguish an imitation which is truly creative, in the derivative sense Tolkien describes of 'making free' with nature, from an unthinking reproduction.

> When we incarnate rather than merely embody the act in our lives we put our signature on it....Embodiment refers only to the change that an individual undergoes when he or she becomes consciously aware of the fact that all human lives are different; the actual deed of ethically integrating with others follows after this awareness...both a partaking...and an incarnation.[93]

Leland Ryken links this 'partaking' and 'incarnation' directly to the process of artistic creation: the 'Incarnation of Christ provides a superb model for what a work of art is. Art, too, is a little incarnation – an embodiment of meaning in the concrete form of images, sounds, and stories.'[94] When someone creates a work of art (incarnation), they draw upon that which is given in terms of their own particular abilities, the resources of the natural world, the culture into which they were born, the traditions in which they work and so on. However, the creative process does not involve an annihilation of their own particular subjectivity. They do not merely replicate or passively embody that which is given. As they draw upon these resources, the otherness of creation is shaped from a unique perspective; they produce an artefact that has their own

---

[92] Jacobs, *A Theology of Reading*, 110.
[93] Alexandar Mihailovic cited by Jacobs, *A Theology of Reading*, 62.
[94] Ryken, *The Liberated Imagination*, 17.

distinctive signature upon it; a responsible act. Rutherford's record of his own spiritual experience and pastoral counsel is a testimony to the way in which he lived from himself, on behalf of others, and this incarnation is underwritten and enabled by the *kenosis* of Christ.

It is necessary to keep this relational dimension (both divine and human) in mind when considering the peculiar language that Rutherford employs. Genuine communication with God and others is attested to in the *Letters*. A dialectical link is formed between the interiority of the individual believer, and the lives of others in the exterior world: but this presupposes the relational context outlined above. Rutherford's language can best be viewed as communicative action, to cite Coffey again: '[it] possessed a raw, colloquial energy precisely because it was intended to grab the attention....In letters...of great imagination, he fused the apocalyptic and the nuptial, the sublime and the homely, constantly surprising and assaulting the senses.'[95] It is an example of the 'realistic imagination' that McIntyre refers to at work. Rutherford purposefully uses biblical language and metaphor, in a way similar to Edwards's use of nature and art, motivated by a pastoral concern to ensure that he and his correspondents actively pursue the supreme spiritual beauty incarnate in Christ. The *Letters* work in several ways: they enable him to present his 'teachings about God's action in the transformation of consciousness' through the experimental form of the epistolary genre; they record his attempt to convey the interiority of his experience of God in a 'concrete and communicable way,' and effectively model a biblical spirituality which is 'fixed within [a] mode of symbolic discourse...presented as [a] form of affective intentionality.' Rutherford seeks in his *Letters* to speak the language of the sense of the heart, communicating interiority 'by utilizing language that tries to fuse feeling and knowing – *amor ipse intellectus est....*'[96] In the words of the psalmist, he continually offers a tactile invitation: 'Oh, taste and see that the Lord is good!' (Psalm 34:8). The success of his endeavour, not intended for posterity, can be seen in the profound influence which his *Letters* have had upon experimental spirituality in Scotland and further afield.

Before leaving Rutherford, however, it is worthwhile to pursue further the notion of language as a form of communicative action, rooted intentionally in a social context. While Rutherford does not reflect directly on the purpose of words as signs and how these relate to the objects (often immaterial spiritual entities) which they are intended to denote, his understanding of both word and sacrament is deeply informed by Reformed theology. This implicit understanding is pertinent in the contemporary context of literary studies, because it addresses one of the problematic issues raised in the Introduction: the tendency of critics either to read words as opaque signs that refer to nothing but other signs in an arbitrary manner, or to invest words with a charged

---

[95] Coffey, *Politics, Religion and the British Revolutions*, 110.
[96] McGinn, "The Language of Inner Experience in Christian Mysticism," 156.

symbolic valence of almost magical depth. This will be of great significance in future chapters, as the capacity of words to denote a world that one can inhabit through imaginative engagement with texts, and which can alter the way the reader interprets and acts within the actual world of human experience, is crucial to the overall argument (see especially the chapters on Jane Austen and C. S. Lewis). In order to outline a preliminary biblical foundation from the same tradition of Reformed theology as Rutherford, which neither deifies the sign, nor drains it of all significance, but rather views words as a form of communicative action within the context of relationship, I turn to the work of Kevin Vanhoozer.

Vanhoozer begins at the same point as Stephen Prickett, noting that the contemporary impasse in literary theory requires a reintegration of its critical concerns with the resources of theology.[97] He views secular attempts to formulate the relationship between word and world through the prism of Reformation debates over the nature of the eucharist. Vanhoozer categorises the approach of critics like Roland Barthes and Michel Foucault, who posit the 'author' as a projection of the best interpretation that a reader can offer in terms of the theology ascribed to the Swiss Reformer, Zwingli, who believed that the bread and wine were merely symbols of Christ's body and blood. At the other extreme, there are those who embrace a theology of immediate presence, or 'transubstantiation', which is equivalent to the critical conviction that 'the real author projects oneself into the implied author in a kind of literary incarnation.'[98] Vanhoozer suggests a third alternative, mediated presence, which reflects the theological conviction of Calvin, where the author is inferred.

> Though verbal marks may be all we have, it does not follow that meaning is nothing other than verbal marks....Meaning is neither read off nor read into language, but is rather encountered in it....For the Reformers, Christ is not physically, but spiritually, present in the sacrament....For Calvin, the physical elements are instruments that communicate Christ's real presence to faith. Similarly, the linguistic elements mediate the author's presence to participants in the covenant of discourse – to those with the faith that seeks textual understanding.[99]

This understanding of language validates its capacity as a tool to effectively, if imperfectly, mediate the interiority of one's experiences to others. It is pertinent here insofar as this model of a mediated authorial presence provides a theologically appropriate, and theoretically significant, explanation of the way in which imagination as exemplified in Rutherford's use of biblical language and metaphor relates to his faith in the propositional doctrines of the

---

[97] Vanhoozer, *Is There a Meaning in This Text?*, 30.
[98] Vanhoozer, *Is There a Meaning in This Text?*, 238-9.
[99] Vanhoozer, *Is There a Meaning in This Text?*, 240.

Reformation. For him, as for his correspondents, biblical language and metaphor referred meaningfully, if incompletely, to realities beyond their own opacity as signs. Belief in Christ as the Incarnate Word has significance beyond the devotional sphere, as Eugene Peterson has noted: Christ is 'the Word from beyond' that 'set[s] all others in an eternal grammar of meaning.'[100] Faith in biblical revelation, underwrites not only the possibility of a personal relationship with divine and human others, but also the possibility of communicating through the medium of language. For Samuel Rutherford, faith operated through and informed a biblically saturated imagination, which forged the necessary link between communion with God, fellowship with other believers, and a life of selfless service in seventeenth-century Scotland. A biblical understanding of the integral connection between word and world, theologically founded on the fact that God spoke the world into existence – 'he upholds the universe by the word of his power' (Hebrews 1:3) – and the incarnation of the Son of God as the human Word, is essential to the understanding of imagination developed in this study. Words are the only material which the literary imagination has to work with and, as will be argued subsequently, they enable a genuine encounter with the other (text or person) beyond the self. Jonathan Edwards, Alan Jacobs, Mikhail Bakhtin and Kevin Vanhoozer, provide insights into the way this unique collection of letters can act as a theoretical resource for understanding what it means to imagine biblically, illustrating the crucial role the realistic imagination plays in the interiority of spiritual experience, and the dialectical energy that such an experience has in forging relationships with others, and precipitating an active engagement with the material world.

---

[100] Eugene Peterson cited by S. K. Dennis, "*Sehnsucht* and the Island Motif in C. S. Lewis's *Out of the Silent* Planet and *Perelandra*," MA Thesis, Florida Atlantic University, 1978, 60.

Chapter 5

The Moral Imagination: Narrative, Character and Hermeneutics in Jane Austen's *Pride and Prejudice*

The term 'moral imagination' has become a central topic of interest for literary critics and philosophers.[1] However, discussions about the 'moral imagination' are often premised on an unquestioning acceptance of cultural pluralism. This tends to lead those exploring moral issues to valorise sensitivity and complexity in themselves as characteristic of the process of ethical decision-making, and revert to the dictates of 'political correctness,' or in certain instances personal preference, when the situation calls for a definitive stand on some issue.[2] Literature, particularly novels, has been drawn upon frequently by moral

---

[1] The potential range of this term can be illustrated, through citing one (amongst many) broad definitions: 'What I mean by the term is the depth and adequacy of the novelist's conception of experience: the degree to which he recognizes the complexities of decision or action or inaction and the effort or release involved in solving or ignoring or evading problems. A moral imagination...does not mistake the evasion for the solution, but it may be able to accept one as much as the other. It may disclose a level of motive that the characters do not suspect, but it need not find in their innocence a failure.' Martin Price, *Forms of Life: Character and Moral Imagination in the Novel* (New Haven: Yale University Press, 1983), xii. Berys Gaut offers a persuasive case for considering the importance of ethics or moral beauty as a necessary element in the aesthetic appeal of works of art. He links cognition with imagination and concludes that 'ethical evaluation of art is inescapable, since it is inextricably intertwined with some of the grounds on which we value art': 'its beauty, its cognitive role, its affective dimension.' Berys Gaut, *Art, Emotion and Ethics* (Oxford: Oxford University Press, 2007), 252 and passim. Paul Crowther argues for the critical role played by imagination in cognition and of the consequent importance of art in developing our understanding of human beings and the world we inhabit in *Defining Art, Creating the Canon: Artistic Value in an Era of Doubt* (Oxford: Oxford University Press, 2007).

[2] For an example of the first kind of argument see Jesse Wolfe, "Jane Austen and the Sin of Pride," *Renascence* 51.2 (1999). For an example (amongst many) of the second kind of argument see David Parker, "Introduction: The Turn to Ethics in the 1990s," *Renegotiating Ethics in Literature, Philosophy, and Theory*, eds. Richard Freadman, Jane Adamson and David Parker (Cambridge: Cambridge University Press, 1998). Similarly S. L. Goldberg emphasises the radical indeterminacy he sees as characteristic of the nature of morality in *Agents and Lives: Moral Thinking in Literature* (Cambridge: Cambridge University Press, 1993), 2-4, 13.

philosophers and those of other disciplines in order to model this subtly attenuated approach to determining what is right in a particular situation. The nuanced narrative voice and complexity of character typical of novels is seen as an ideal opportunity for exploring a kind of practical Aristotelian wisdom as to how one should live. Here, the arguments sometimes become peculiarly akin to those of educational conservatives in the humanist tradition of liberal individualism, who have asserted (at least since Matthew Arnold) that by reading 'the classics' one is somehow inoculated with values that fine-tune a person's moral awareness and (hopefully) shape one into a better person.[3]

This chapter intersects at certain points with the contemporary concerns mentioned above, but it takes issue with several of the fundamental assumptions that underlie the recent 'turn towards the ethical' in literary criticism and philosophy.[4] While I agree that all theoretical engagement with literature has an inescapable moral dimension, the implicit correlative that the complex nature of certain moral situations that arise in our cultural context of religious pluralism necessitates the rejection of any absolute or universal standards which can be simply expressed seems illogical and unnecessary. Gestures towards 'complexity' can often mask unwillingness on the part of an individual theorist to state the premises upon which they are working, or a desire to justify without careful argument the decision to embrace a moral relativism which is the cultural norm of the postmodern West. Every approach to the highly contested issue of the 'moral imagination' is necessarily grounded on certain presuppositions, which 'prejudice' in positive or negative ways the subsequent argument.[5]

---

[3] The enormous weight which Arnold placed upon Poetry and Culture as agents of moral, social and spiritual transformation can be seen in "Culture and Anarchy" and "The Study of Poetry." Matthew Arnold, *Culture and Anarchy: An Essay in Political and Social Criticism* (London: Murray, 1961); Matthew Arnold, "The Study of Poetry," *Four Essays on Life and Letters*, ed. E. K. Brown (New York: Appleton-Century, 1947). For a similar argument on the way literature can 'fine-tune' moral awareness, see for example, Goldberg, *Agents and Lives*, xiii-xvii, 1-15; Martha Nussbaum, *Love's Knowledge: Essays on Philosophy and Literature* (Oxford: Oxford University Press, 1990), 40, 209, 230, 253. Goldberg particularly evidences the way in which one's fundamental presuppositions inevitably shape an account of the moral understanding in relation to literature.

[4] Cited by Parker, "Introduction: The Turn to Ethics in the 1990s," 14. A useful overview and critique of certain aspects of this literature is offered by Liesbeth Korthals Altes, "Some Dilemmas of an Ethics of Literature," *Theology and Literature: Rethinking Reader Responsibility*, eds. Gaye Williams Ortiz and Clara A. B. Joseph (Houndmills: Palgrave Macmillan, 2006), 15-31.

[5] This argument has been made most forcibly in terms of 'prejudice' and various 'traditions' by Gadamer, *Truth and Method*; a similar approach can also be found in the 'pre-suppositionalist' school of Reformed apologetics.

> It is not enough to explore the appropriateness of forming moral attitudes toward fictional characters without first investigating the nature of morality, that is, without making and expressing one's choices on a range of issues in moral theory....The difficulties are greatly compounded when religious faith and skepticism become factors in the inquiry.[6]

Beginning with the biblical text in seeking to understand the moral dimensions of imagination inevitably means that 'religious faith and skepticism become factors in the inquiry.' From a biblical perspective, the nature of morality is summarised in the Decalogue and rearticulated in positive terms by Jesus when a Jewish lawyer asked him to identify the greatest commandment:

> 'You shall love the Lord your God with all your heart and with all your soul and with all your mind. This is the great and first commandment. And a second is like it: You shall love your neighbour as yourself.' On these two commandments depend all the Law and the Prophets (Matthew 22:37-40).

The relationship between the moral law enshrined in divine revelation and the notion of 'natural law' written in the heart and universally available to all human beings by virtue of their creation in the image of God has a complex and disputed theological and philosophical history. Romans refers to 'the work of the law' 'written on [the] hearts' (2:15) of all people whether Jew or Gentile, and the nature of God, revealed in creation, 'for his invisible attributes, namely, his eternal power and divine nature, have been clearly perceived, ever since the creation of the world, in the things that have been made' (1:20). On this basis John Calvin argued that 'the law of God which we call moral, is nothing else than the testimony of natural law, and of that conscience which God has engraven on the minds of men.'[7] In this framework, the specific commandments given to Israel are understood as binding upon all people. However, a 'proper understanding of the Decalogue,' Richard Mouw insists following Calvin, 'must see these commandments as containing more than 'only dry and bare rudiments'; we must view them as a unified display of 'all the duties of piety and love.''[8] As so many ethical theorists have noted, the statement of propositions must be balanced by a narrative context, and the Decalogue is prefaced by God's own story of his role as Israel's deliverer: 'I am the LORD your God, who brought you out of the land of Egypt, out of the house of slavery' (Exodus 20:2). Both narrative context and surrender to the divine will summarised in revealed propositions are integral to biblical morality. Mouw continues: 'To understand the meaning of divine commands is

---

[6] Diana Fritz Cates, "Ethics, Literature, and the Emotional Dimension of Moral Understanding: A Review Essay," *Journal of Religious Ethics* 26.2 (1998), 427, 429.

[7] Calvin, *Institutes of the Christian Religion*, 4.20.16.

[8] Richard J. Mouw, *The God Who Commands: A Study in Divine Command Ethics* (Notre Dame: University of Notre Dame Press, 1990), 129.

to grasp something of God's character, of the divine intentions in providing moral guidance to human creatures. And this in turn requires that we know the story of God's dealings with the creation.'[9] Obedience to the commands is thus designed to develop a maturity and beauty of character, which can only be adequately expressed in terms of a life narrative, rather than occasional capitulations to an arbitrary Lord: 'for everyone who lives on milk is unskilled in the word of righteousness, since he is a child. But solid food is for the mature, for those who have their powers of discernment trained by constant practice to distinguish good from evil' (Hebrews 5:13-14). Mouw carefully differentiates between Calvinist and Hobbesian understandings of the divine commandments given by God, 'whose imperatives aim at the creation of new possibilities for cultivating those virtues that God intended in creating human beings.'[10]

By emphasising the sovereignty of God as law-giver, revealing his will through creation and scriptural revelation, I do not mean to suggest that all moral decisions are simple; but rather to acknowledge that there are certain fundamental principles integral to understanding the moral imagination from a biblical perspective.[11] The complexities arise as individuals seek to apply these general principles to the particular situations that confront them in diverse cultural and historical contexts. It is here that the essential and necessary role ascribed to the imagination in current moral philosophy becomes so important: in accurately perceiving the nature of a situation, envisaging the various responses that can be made, or options that can be followed, and making a decision as to which is the most appropriate. Literature can help to educate the moral imagination, modelling in a unique way through concrete fictional situations, characters and narrative, the intricacies of what it means to be human in a fallen world.[12] However, any attempt to deduce a consistent

---

[9] Mouw, *The God Who Commands*, 129.

[10] Mouw, *The God Who Commands*, 115.

[11] It is this gospel interpretation of the Decalogue, already implicit in the Old Testament vocabulary of obeying from the heart, expressed practically in the wisdom spoken of in Proverbs particularly, which renders dismissals of the 'Mosaic Decalogue' as 'a merely behavioural code' problematic. The kind of union between cognition and affect that A. E. Denham sees as crucial to moral understanding and truth is precisely what these standards are intended to summarise (though not exhaustively). A. E. Denham, *Metaphor and Moral Experience* (Oxford: Clarendon Press, 2000), 141, 183-5.

[12] See, for example, Simon Haines, "Deepening the Self: The Language of Ethics and the Language of Literature," *Renegotiating Ethics in Literature, Philosophy, and Theory*, eds. Richard Freadman, Jane Adamson and David Parker (Cambridge: Cambridge University Press, 1998); Cora Diamond, "Martha Nussbaum and the Need for Novels," *Renegotiating Ethics in Literature, Philosophy, and Theory*, eds. Richard Freadman, Jane Adamson and David Parker (Cambridge: Cambridge University Press, 1998); Anthony Cunningham, *The Heart of What Matters: The Role for Literature in Moral Philosophy* (Berkeley: University of California Press, 2001), 1-5.

morality from literature is doomed to failure. It is impossible to define the boundaries of 'literature' itself in a water-tight way; even those texts which possess an unchallenged status as 'classics' embody a great variety of competing moral codes, which cannot necessarily be harmonised with one another.[13] Finally, each reader inevitably comes to the texts with certain presuppositions against which they measure and evaluate the worlds that open to their imaginations.[14]

It is not the purpose of this chapter to attempt to outline a particular moral code, which can be deduced from the biblical text and provide a standard against which the imaginative worlds of other works are measured.[15] However, moral principles are integral to an exploration of what it means to imagine biblically and the form of the text itself presents a synthesis between narrative and proposition which shapes the way an inquiry into the moral dimension of the imagination must proceed. In contrast, though, to much contemporary ethical criticism, the biblical text also offers a specific account of the nature of morality, which while inculcated in a manner similar to that which such critics trace as being performed by the genre of the novel, resists assimilation into a celebratory narrative of complexity and nuance at the expense of clarity. In order to explicate this, it is necessary to bear in mind that God gives specific commands summarised in the Decalogue and Sermon on the Mount, but also that:

> At many points in our Christian narrations the propositions which are either directly stated or implied are often the least important items being presented for our consideration and response. And even when specific cognitive claims can be rightly singled out for special attention because of their significance to a community that is called to live truthfully, it is necessary nonetheless to remember that they are but distillations from a much richer and more textured drama – and that to distance them for too long from that narrative context is to deprive them of the source of their life-directing power.[16]

---

[13] C. S. Lewis, *An Experiment in Criticism* (Cambridge: Cambridge University Press, 1961), 74-87.

[14] This is simply reiterating the point that all human beings are inevitably shaped by their historical, cultural and social context, rendering it impossible to come to any text with a *tabula rasa*, morally or intellectually, no matter how much one may be willing to subject oneself to the authority of the given work.

[15] For a thorough theological exploration of biblical ethics see Robertson McQuilkin, *Introduction to Biblical Ethics* (Wheaton: Tyndale, 1995); Stephen Mott, *Biblical Ethics and Social Change* (Oxford: Oxford University Press, 1982); Mouw, *The God Who Commands*; John Murray, *Principles of Conduct: Aspects of Biblical Ethics* (Grand Rapids: Eerdmans, 1957); Scott B. Rae, *Moral Choices: An Introduction to Ethics* (Grand Rapids: Zondervan, 2000); Brian S. Rosner, *Paul, Scripture, and Ethics* (Grand Rapids: Baker Books, 1994).

[16] Mouw, *The God Who Commands*, 127.

Narrative is the primary genre in which the biblical text is written, comprising a large part of the historical and also prophetic sections of the Old Testament, as well as the gospels and the Acts of the Apostles in the New. The particular way in which biblical principles are embedded in these narratives, with their implications for an understanding of the moral imagination will form the focus of this chapter. I begin by analysing the nature of biblical narrative as delineated by Robert Alter, which implies an imagination that is essentially verbal in nature, responsible to both divine and human others, and orientated in hope of ultimate redemption. The moral and philosophical dimensions of the concept will be further developed through the work of Frank Palmer, enabling the relevance of the biblical understanding to be directly related to literature. Then, in order to clarify the sharp distinction between a biblical understanding of the relationship between the reader, morality, and literature, and that outlined by Matthew Arnold and those of his ilk such as F. R. Leavis, I shall explore an observation on the link between morality and teleology which Alasdair MacIntyre makes of Jane Austen bringing out its inextricable connections with theology in the light of work by Alan Jacobs and Anthony Thiselton. This will be followed by a close reading of *Pride and Prejudice*, which draws together the various threads of the theoretical analysis, and integrates them in the examination of a classic literary text, that itself foregrounds the hermeneutic implications of 'prejudice.' Austen does not overtly link the moral principles that inform her fiction to their metaphysical foundations. For the purpose of this analysis, however, the connections between the moral imagination and her narrative art will be elaborated and explored in order to define how the biblical text shapes the moral imagination in this literary context.[17]

---

[17] I am aware that Austen's decision not to make the connection between metaphysics and morals explicit in her fiction, as many of her contemporaries did, can cause her treatment of moral transformation in her characters and the development of events to be read as a secularised 'doctrine of sanctification' or morality, which does not acknowledge God's providential direction or the role of the Holy Spirit in character formation. However, due both to the *telos* implicit in her narrative structure, the largely Christian cultural context in which she wrote, and also the references in her letters which evidence her own personal allegiance to these religious doctrines and standards, I assume the connection between her moral postulates and their metaphysical and doctrinal foundations in this chapter. Deirdre Le Faye, ed, *Jane Austen's Letters: New Edition* (Oxford: Oxford University Press, 1995), 146-7, 170, 171, 173, 278-81, 287, 322, 334. These references in the letters indicate Austen's attendance at church, her reading of sermons, her ambivalence towards Evangelicalism (alternatively positive and negative), but consistently demonstrate the active way in which Christian principles informed her life and writing. Due to the broad parameters of the argument in this chapter a more precise analysis of Austen's complex relationship with Evangelicalism is not necessary. A helpful overview of Austen's 'moderate...Anglicanism' is provided by Michael Wheeler in "Religion," in *Jane Austen in Context*, ed. Janet Todd (Cambridge: Cambridge University Press, 2005), 406-14. Sarah Emsley asserts more strongly that

Biblical Narrative and the Moral Imagination

Given this book is attempting to explore what it means to imagine biblically, recognising that a large portion of the biblical text is presented in the form of narrative rather than propositions, has important implications for understanding the imagination. Robert Alter in his now classic text, *The Art of Biblical Narrative*, beautifully illuminates both the particular nature of scriptural narratives, and the intimate connection between their literary form and the theological and moral concerns of the ancient authors. He cites with approval the observation of Erich Auerbach 'that the sparsely sketched foreground of biblical narrative somehow implies a large background dense with possibilities of interpretation,' but moves beyond the lack of specificity implied by 'somehow,' seeking to elaborate the features of biblical narrative that actively invite the imaginative engagement of the reader.[18] Through a close analysis of various biblical narratives he summarises these as:

> the deployment of thematic key-words; the reiteration of motifs; the subtle definition of character, relations, and motives mainly through dialogue; the exploitation, especially in dialogue, of verbatim repetition with minute but significant changes introduced; the narrator's discriminating shifts from strategic and suggestive withholding of comment to the occasional flaunting of an omniscient overview; the use at points of a montage of sources to catch the multifaceted nature of the...subject.[19]

What is most interesting about Alter's overall argument is the explicit connection he makes between the literary strategies adopted by the various biblical authors, and the theological or moral point of the text. The sparseness of detail and yet the simultaneous sense of complexity and mystery that surrounds the characters, evoked through the use of dialogue and shifts between internal and external representation, forces the reader to entertain a variety of hypotheses when interpreting motivation and events. Similarly, the focus of the biblical text on word and deed, rather than long narratorial digressions about characters, allows 'an abiding mystery in character...which they embody in their typical methods of presentation.' This can be observed in the way biblical personages are subject to change. There is 'a sense of the unknowable and the unforeseeable in human nature' that reinforces the moral responsibility and accountability of human beings in history.[20] Alter goes beyond the

---

'Christianity, not just the forms of the religion but also the deep faith in Christ's atonement for the sins of the world, underlies the way Jane Austen understands the virtues and shows them in action and in tension in her fictional characters' (10) in *Jane Austen's Philosophy of the Virtues* (New York: Palgrave Macmillan, 2005).

[18] Robert Alter, *The Art of Biblical Narrative* (New York: Basic Books, Inc, 1981), 114-115.

[19] Alter, *The Art of Biblical Narrative*, 176.

[20] Alter, *The Art of Biblical Narrative*, 126-7.

representation of character to explore the way in which biblical narration may be seen as an 'experiment in the possibilities of moral, spiritual, and historical knowledge, undertaken through a process of studied contrasts between the variously limited knowledge of the human characters and the divine omniscience quietly but firmly represented by the narrator.'[21] He makes the intriguing suggestion that for the biblical authors to adopt a full knowledge of their characters such as that assumed by the omniscient narrators of Victorian fiction, would involve an attempt to 'be like God, knowing good and evil' (Genesis 3:5). Thus the reticence and obliqueness of the narrative style is a

> typically monotheistic decision...to lead us to know as flesh-and-blood knows: character is revealed primarily through speech, action, gesture, with all the ambiguities that entails; motive is frequently, though not invariably, left in a penumbra of doubt; often we are able to draw plausible inferences about the personages and their destinies, but much remains a matter of conjecture or even of teasing multiple possibilities.[22]

Importantly though, Alter recognises that the narrative form of Scripture does not thereby endorse a kind of epistemological scepticism. There 'is a horizon of perfect knowledge in biblical narrative,' but it belongs to God rather than the reader, who can glimpse it only fragmentarily. This delicate balance is maintained by the narrator emphasising indirectly a meaningful pattern worked out through the events that unfold: the characters are thus enabled to retain an enigmatic dimension, whilst the omniscient narration provides a sense of stable significance, which is conveyed through the measuring of characters 'by the[ir] varying distances...from divine knowledge,' and the way some deepen in their awareness of themselves and God.[23] Here it is evident that the narrative structure of the text and its presentation of character is influenced by specific theological assumptions, which shape and mould the reader as they engage imaginatively with individual characters. The text invites an interpretation of reality that connects the workings of providence, human decisions and time as meaningful, due to God's involvement in the world, even if the significance is ultimately ambivalent to human eyes:

> The organization of the narrative...its lexical and syntactic choices, its small shifts in point of view, its brief but strategic uses of dialogue, produce an imaginative reenactment of the historical event, conferring upon it a strong attitudinal definition and discovering in it a pattern of meaning.[24]

The impassive narratorial voice is a 'theologically appropriate' means for the

---

[21] Alter, *The Art of Biblical Narrative*, 157.
[22] Alter, *The Art of Biblical Narrative*, 158.
[23] Alter, *The Art of Biblical Narrative*, 158-9.
[24] Alter, *The Art of Biblical Narrative*, 41.

representation of human lives under the overarching dominion' of an omniscient and 'ethical God.'[25]

The implications of this astute reading of the preeminent literary form of the biblical text for a consideration of what it means to imagine biblically are profound. The narrative quality of Scripture thus conceived implicitly endorses the imagination as a positive and absolutely essential aspect of human being; crucial to understanding other people, appreciating what it means to be a moral person within the complex exigencies of daily life, and also in recognising the patterns of God's action in history. Alter goes further, however, by specifying the particularly verbal nature of the biblical imagination: 'Articulated language provides the indispensable model for defining this rhythm of political or historical alternatives, question and response, creaturely uncertainty over against the Creator's intermittently revealed design, because in the biblical view words underlie reality.'[26] This, of course, is integral to any exploration of the literary imagination from a biblical perspective: by defining human beings primarily as creatures who use language, due to their creation in the image of the God who spoke the world into being (Genesis 1:3,26-28), a very different relationship between word and thing, character and novel, reader and text, to that postulated by poststructuralist critics emerges, with consequent moral implications for authors and readers alike.[27] Alter continues

> in words each person reveals his distinctive nature, his willingness to enter into binding compacts with men and God, his ability to control others, to deceive them, to feel for them, and to respond to them. Spoken language is the substratum of everything human and divine that transpires in the Bible, and the Hebrew tendency to transpose what is preverbal or nonverbal into speech is finally a technique for getting at the essence of things, for obtruding their substratum.[28]

To cite Hebrews: 'he upholds the universe by the word of his power' (1:3), and Deuteronomy, 'man does not live by bread alone, but man lives by every word that comes from the mouth of the LORD' (8:3). The correlation with the imagination as embodied in literature is obvious here. While the biblical text by no means minimalises mental images or the power of imagination to reconstitute 'the data of perception and memory so as to feed the fires of concupiscence,' an 'onanistic preoccupation of the will, through imaginative self-aggrandizement' that illuminates the 'evil imaginations of the heart';[29] it also emphasises the power of words to create and mould our perception and

---

[25] Alter, *The Art of Biblical Narrative*, 87.
[26] Alter, *The Art of Biblical Narrative*, 69.
[27] George Steiner traces through some of the implications of this in understanding the relationship between artist and creation, reader and text in *Real Presences*.
[28] Alter, *The Art of Biblical Narrative*, 70.
[29] Ray L. Hart, *Unfinished Man and the Imagination: Toward an Ontology and a Rhetoric of Revelation* (New York: Herder and Herder, 1968), 206.

understanding of reality, with the correlative responsibility of weighing them carefully. In Proverbs, for example, the writer observes: 'Death and life are in the power of the tongue, and those who love it will eat its fruits' (18:21).

Although Alter deliberately limits his discussion to the Hebrew Bible, this emphasis on the word as the defining feature of human being, reality, and the imagination is reinforced even more emphatically in the New Testament, where Jesus is described as the Word of God, embodied in flesh (John 1:1-18; Hebrews 1:1-3). The notion that characters and persons express themselves concretely through words, and that these words, written or spoken, offer us the opportunity as persons and readers to become acquainted with the textual or human other is central to a biblical understanding of the moral imagination. Frank Palmer has argued that when we truly engage with a fictional text, as readers, we interpret the characters conveyed through the textual marks upon the page on the model of persons, rather than as semiotic systems of signification. To follow the latter mode of interpretation is, in Ricoeur's terms, to confuse the semiotic and semantic levels of meaning in a text,[30] Palmer is interested in the latter, and makes a persuasive philosophical case for its ontological assumptions.

He takes issue with what he calls the 'semiotic' school of criticism, through which he intends to denote structuralism and post-structuralism, for their dismissal 'not only of the idea of characters as persons but more generally of the idea that the meaning of a literary work is reached through a humane interest in the representation of a human world.'[31] He suggests that it is impossible to separate a structural analysis of functions and roles from ethical or moral evaluation, as the latter is implicit in the former. Similarly, these 'secondary abstractions' (like roles or functions) can 'only begin to acquire descriptive force in relation to the concrete actions and events that are experienced by the reader as the representational content....Far from 'functional' interpretations 'coming first', we must think of characters as persons from the very beginning to obtain any idea of their function within the literary work as a whole.'[32] He concludes that poststructuralism reduces 'characters' even further by turning structuralism's 'type of technical apparatus' into 'illustrations or tools of ideology.'[33]

Palmer then turns to an older, but still influential approach to literature, which he designates the 'symbolic poem' school. This also encourages a

---

[30] Ricoeur, *Interpretation Theory: Discourse and the Surplus of Meaning*, 7.

[31] Frank Palmer, *Literature and Moral Understanding: A Philosophical Essay on Ethics, Aesthetics, Education and Culture* (Oxford: Oxford University Press, 1992), 2.

[32] Palmer, *Literature and Moral Understanding*, 5-6.

[33] Palmer, *Literature and Moral Understanding*, 6. I find Palmer's analysis of structuralist and poststructuralist thought a little thin. However, it is not this aspect of his argument that is central to the logic of this chapter, but rather his concept of the moral imagination implicit in our response to literary characters.

'debilitated view of character,' by reacting against the superfluous and unnecessary interest in the lives of characters (seen to be typical of 'character criticism') at the expense of the text as a work of art, assuming that 'to understand or appreciate the metaphorical or symbolic significance of a literary work is flatly incompatible with a 'naturalistic' approach to character.'[34] He does not take issue with the necessity of not going beyond the text, though 'only if a literary text is not simply 'words on a page' but a work of art having a representational content (or depicting a fictional world) that cannot be understood or appreciated without the imagination (imagination itself being grounded in some 'common expectations' of our experience of the actual world).'[35] He wishes to demonstrate that the 'metaphorical or symbolic levels of meaning in a literary work can only be appreciated by thinking of the characters as persons.'[36]

In order to justify his understanding of fictional characters on the model of real persons Palmer makes a distinction between 'internal' and 'external' perspectives on the world of a fictional text. He suggests that from within (the internal perspective) it makes sense to think of characters, events and places as if they were real, despite the fact that they have no objective existence in the actual world. From the external perspective they are simply non-existent. Complications arise when one attempts to conflate these two spheres of discourse, by saying for example, 'Hamlet has imaginary thoughts,' and Palmer draws upon Wittgenstein's notion of 'language games,' and the discourse appropriate to a particular kind of human activity in order to underwrite the logic of his argument. The two forms of discourse 'neither clash nor are wholly distinct,' as the internal convention draws upon the language characteristic of utterances in the external convention (as fictional worlds draw upon known aspects of the actual world), and what is said about characters such as Hamlet in the internal convention 'can only be said given that the external convention recognizes the existence of novels and plays.'[37] The point of Palmer's argument is to suggest that insofar as fictional characters can be said to exist 'they exist as individuals, and...that our responses to literature are founded upon this presupposition.'[38]

Similarly, our understanding of the people and places described by novelists and playwrights is defined by expectations taken from the actual world.

---

[34] Palmer, *Literature and Moral Understanding*, 7-11.

[35] In this he is supported by Martin Price, who argues, following Mary Warnock, that imagination is crucial to understanding 'the forms in our mind's eye' and 'the very forms in the world,' so characters and fictional worlds, though 'they differ from real persons' 'must refer to them and draw their force from what we know their experience to be like.' Price, *Forms of Life*, xiv, 37-64.

[36] Palmer, *Literature and Moral Understanding*, 11.

[37] Palmer, *Literature and Moral Understanding*, 12-21.

[38] Palmer, *Literature and Moral Understanding*, 27.

'Impossible' fictions make sense only against this 'background of assumptions which are normally legitimate,' so 'one might as well consider the 'world' of *Mansfield Park*...not as a self-contained cosmos belonging to another dimension, but as a realm of possibility within the actual world.'[39] Palmer states that it is impossible to account for the 'ontology of fictional characters in terms of possible worlds,' since a particular character exists only insofar as the existence of the fictional world containing them, that is as it is understood from the internal perspective.[40] He is careful to emphasise that while his argument appears to give the impression that 'fictional existence is merely a linguistic matter,' it cannot be reduced to semiotics. Like Ricoeur, he insists on the necessity of moving to the semantic level,[41] or as he puts it here, 'the fictional world is 'transcendental.'' It is the imagination that enables us to move from semiotics to semantics.

> Though our experience of the fictional world of a novel or play is mediated through the author's 'verbal arrangements', and if it is not mere fantasy it will be disciplined by close attention to them, the experience leads beyond 'the words on the page' such that we do not merely have an intellectual grasp of linguistic constructions but are able to 'feel into' and 'live into' the scenes, places, people, and events as they are now brought into focus.[42]

The artistic medium chosen is a shared understanding or orbit of interest, first to reduce the characters and worlds depicted to the semiotic level and then attempt to reconstruct a persuasive case for why they engage us at the semantic level is, Palmer argues, a 'self-defeating absurdity.' He suggests that in order to contemplate a fictional world, we must assume that the persons in it are of the same kind as ourselves, whilst also recognising that the language-game of the novel or play has an inbuilt assumption that we (as those from the external perspective) cannot intervene within the internal perspective of the text; this imposes a certain detachment which shapes our response to fictional characters and events.[43]

Palmer explores the implications of his discussion for understanding the imagination. He posits that the 'aesthetic context which distinguishes our experience of works of art' entails that '[t]he invitation of a work of art is addressed to the imagination rather than to our capacity for make-believe.' The former involves thinking of something rather like the latter simply asserting that it is so. As it is possible to entertain a thought without necessarily asserting that it is literally true, 'the concept of make-believe or pretence' is not necessary to 'compensate for, the absence of belief involved in the imaginative

---

[39] Palmer, *Literature and Moral Understanding*, 31.
[40] Palmer, *Literature and Moral Understanding*, 34.
[41] Ricoeur, *Interpretation Theory*, 7.
[42] Palmer, *Literature and Moral Understanding*, 35.
[43] Palmer, *Literature and Moral Understanding*, 36-9.

grasp of fictional worlds.'[44] Following Kant, Palmer suggests that in 'being directed to the imagination, a genuine work of art calls upon capacities for understanding which are not concerned' with the literal truth 'of what is represented.' This does not mean that art has no direct involvement with our 'practical and moral engagement with the world,' rather the 'disinterested' quality of our engagement with a work of art enables a contemplation of objects and occurrences, which would be neither possible, appropriate, nor occasionally morally justifiable, 'were the objects or occurrences actual.'[45] This liberation from 'literalism' does not mean freedom from truth to life and experience, though. Palmer quotes Alan White in order to differentiate: 'Pretence shows an ability to perform, whereas imagination shows an ability to conceive.'[46]

There is a moral corollary to this distinction. Whilst pretence is evidenced in works of shallow 'realism' that 'cater to and gratify the crudest levels of feeling or sentiment compatible only with the barest minimum of thought,' imagination involves participation in 'a fictional world where actions and consequences and the circumstances in which they arise demand some sort of emotional credibility,' finding 'in the representation something that compels a certain kind of assent' so that 'disbelief' in the Coleridgean sense is not a relevant category.[47] Engagement with the fictional world called into being through a work of art is an emotional and moral matter, since writers lead us, through the way they handle their medium, to experience the characters and events within a particular world-view.[48] 'In order to accept the invitation to the imagination we...must be prepared to enter into a relationship with the work, such that our understanding of the characters needs to be as genuine and convincing as our understanding of actual people.' This does not mean that our understanding of fictional characters can be simply equated with our understanding of people, since the 'human institution[s] of art' entail a degree of distance from what is artistically represented, though they also provide the 'traditions and practices' that make any relationship between the reader and work possible. The 'make-believe' view cannot provide an adequate account of this relationship due to the fact that it postulates a large gap between fiction and reality. Thus, instead of

---

[44] Palmer, *Literature and Moral Understanding*, 52-3.
[45] Palmer, *Literature and Moral Understanding*, 53.
[46] Palmer, *Literature and Moral Understanding*, 54.
[47] Palmer, *Literature and Moral Understanding*, 54-55.
[48] Berys Gaut similarly affirms the postulate that we can learn from imagination in the sense of 'entertaining a thought-content...without commitment to the proposition's truth (or falsity), or to the existence (or non-existence) of an object that instantiates the concept' (151). He suggests further that imagination plays an important role in the ethical domain (157-64) through enabling us to feel 'the wrongness, rightness or sheer imponderability of certain moral choices (164). Gaut defends 'the common-sense view that one can feel real emotions towards fictional events and be rational when one does so' (203-226). Gaut, *Art, Emotion, Ethics*.

deploying a set of conventions regulating games of 'let's pretend,' Palmer opts for a more Wittgensteinian understanding, suggesting that when responding to a work of art, 'the reader is immersed in…a community of feeling, thought, and sensibility that sustains and is sustained by the creation of, and response to, works that are only intelligible to beings who are initiated into that community.' He concludes with the further claim that '[l]iterary criticism' is thus 'intersubjective and testable…in virtue of how it enables the common reader to experience and reexperience a fictional world with greater understanding.' The connections he has established between imagination, the human institutions of art, and the involvement of the reader, provide a more plausible account than the 'make-believe' view. It also incorporates moral understanding as a crucial component in the creation of, and response to, works of literary imagination.[49]

The usefulness of Palmer's discussion consists in the fact that he provides a philosophical argument which accounts for the integrity and truth of the fictional worlds embodied in works of art, without immolating them in an 'aesthetic zone' that has no point of connection with the lives, experiences and moral understanding of readers in the actual world of time and space. He goes on to explore in a manner similar to Martha Nussbaum and other moral philosophers,[50] the peculiar kind of knowledge that literature imparts to the reader and the way in which it informs the moral imagination. The writer producing a work of art is motivated by love, even if the *Gestalt* of the text is primarily negative in its assessment of the human condition: an appreciation of that humanness in all its complexity is a precondition of the kind of creation that stands in its own integrity as a showing of characters, situations and events rather than a mere telling.[51] Similarly, in experiencing a work of art as readers, we receive a particular kind of knowledge which is more clearly conveyed through a distinction in French between *savoir* (knowledge about) and *connaître* (knowledge by acquaintance). It is the latter that literature grants access to: '[t]o have an understanding of fictional characters that goes beyond merely 'knowing about', we must therefore be in some sense acquainted with them via the power of the work to 'show.'' This is an imagined rather than an actual acquaintance, but it does not restrict 'our capacity to learn from it,' for the distance thus established provides 'the opportunity for discovering things we might be inclined to miss if the objects were actual.'[52]

Alan Jacobs makes a similar case to that of Palmer for active and loving engagement with characters and people, even to the point of following Iris

---

[49] Palmer, *Literature and Moral Understanding*, 55-8.
[50] Nussbaum, *Love's Knowledge*; Diamond, "Martha Nussbaum and the Need for Novels"; Cates, "Ethics, Literature, and the Emotional Dimension of Moral Understanding: A Review Essay."
[51] Palmer, *Literature and Moral Understanding*, 164-8, 197-9.
[52] Palmer, *Literature and Moral Understanding*, 200-1.

Murdoch in her observation that a failure to distinguish clearly between books and persons can be a 'productive and enabling confusion.'[53] He moves beyond Palmer's argument, however, by introducing several specifically biblical principles that further elucidate the relationship between love and discernment when responding to texts, through a consideration of scriptural teaching on charity. Like Palmer and Nussbaum, he emphasises the kind of knowledge that love alone can give, also drawing upon the distinction in French between 'knowledge of' and 'knowledge about,' which he explores through the way in which Beatrice responds to the accusations made against Hero by Claudio and Don Pedro in *Much Ado About Nothing*. Because she does not doubt the purity of her cousin, Beatrice is unable even to make a case, responding to the cruelty of the men with a series of wounded cries.[54] What distinguishes the '"practical" (or Aristotelian and dialectical)' questions of Jacobs from those of Palmer, Nussbaum and Murdoch, however, is his attempt to be 'fully theological (or kerygmatic)' in his claims.[55]

This theological dimension strengthens Jacob's argument and prevents his discussion of responses to literature from sliding into an Arnoldian claim that reading the right books makes one a better person. Jacobs weaves an elegant and complex argument. The two elements of particular interest to the current discussion are his suggestion that ultimately the model of *philia* between reader and text, or person and person, postulated by Wayne Booth and Nussbaum (following Aristotle) falls short: it is neither sufficiently generous in its capacity to entertain the other, nor sufficiently discerning in its ability lovingly to reject that which is wrong. The second is his biblical observation that human beings in and of themselves are incapable of consistently responding to texts and persons with the kind of charity that is summarised in the law of love and embodied in the life of Christ. Jacobs brings out the risk and cost of such loving engagement through a consideration of Aristotle and Mikhail Bakhtin:

> Though all genuine friendships in their full flower possess this mutuality [foundational to Aristotle's understanding of love], they had to *begin* by someone extending the offer of affection and attention without knowing whether the other would reciprocate. Given the evil that besets human life…*kenosis* is not just a risk but a "tragic risk," and though it is obvious that many people…choose to take that risk…it seems almost cruel to demand that people do so. Yet Christianity makes

---

[53] Jacobs, *A Theology of Reading,* 78. See also Cates, "Ethics, Literature, and the Emotional Dimension of Moral Understanding: A Review Essay." Iris Murdoch argues further that the artist 'is indeed the analogon of the good man, and in a special sense he is the good man: the lover who, nothing himself, lets other things be through him.' Cited by Megan Laverty in *Iris Murdoch's Ethics: A Consideration of Her Romantic Vision* (London: Continuum, 2007), 97.
[54] Jacobs, *A Theology of Reading*, 6.
[55] Jacobs, *A Theology of Reading*, 2.

just this demand, knowing...that in merely human terms the demand is unjustifiable.[56]

The venture is ultimately underwritten by the *kenosis* of God himself, who inspires and enables each human venture through grace. This love is by no means a blind commitment though, it gives meaning to practical morality and is defined through its pursuit of justice, which finds expression in biblical discernment. Jacobs conveys this through analysing the thought of an early Church Father, Basil the Great:

> For Basil, it is this framework of faithful obedience to the Gospel witness that liberates the reader to read more generously, according to the spirit rather than the letter. Absent such faithful obedience, such reading would exemplify license rather than liberty, antinomianism rather than the freedom of Christian charity.[57]

By considering the kerygmatic claims that underlie his practical exploration of hermeneutics, reading and charity, Jacobs has provided an opportunity for articulating some of the prejudgments that inform a biblical consideration of the moral imagination. He also illustrates how the basic principles, which Mouw designates as a 'divine command ethic' summarised in the Sermon on the Mount, can be fleshed out in order further to define the moral imagination biblically. Such prejudgements are by no means unique to a biblical approach. As Hans Georg Gadamer has shown, the 'prejudice' of particular traditions inevitably inform all intellectual inquiry and argument.[58] However, while I am suggesting that this theological account is necessary to a truly biblical understanding of the moral imagination it is possible to draw a distinction between an account of the virtues and the theological interpretation of reality that undergirds it, as Alasdair MacIntyre observes in his comments on Jane Austen:

> When Jane Austen speaks of 'happiness', she does so as an Aristotelian. Gilbert Ryle believed that her Aristotelianism – which he saw as the clue to the moral temper of her novels – may have derived from a reading of Shaftesbury. C. S. Lewis with equal justice saw in her an essentially Christian writer. It is her uniting of Christian and Aristotelian themes in a determinate social context that makes Jane Austen the last great effective imaginative voice of the tradition of thought about, and practice of, the virtues which I have tried to identify.[59]

---

[56] Jacobs, *A Theology of Reading*, 112.

[57] Jacobs, *A Theology of Reading*, 144.

[58] Gadamer, *Truth and Method*.

[59] Alasdair MacIntyre, *After Virtue: A Study in Moral Theory* (Notre Dame: University of Notre Dame Press, 1981), 223. Sarah Emsley has attempted further to elaborate this link between Aristotelian and Christian virtues in her reading of Austen's work in *Jane Austen's Philosophy of the Virtues*.

When reading the novels of Jane Austen, one is acutely conscious of a moral vision informing and shaping every aspect of character and situation: Anne Crippen Ruderman has persuasively demonstrated MacIntyre's observation that she offers an imaginative exemplification of practical Aristotelianism.[60] Austen is one of the least transparently 'religious' or transcendental of writers, and this has led to her being read as the creator of an atheistic system of purely human ethics.[61] However, the moral imagination evidenced in her chosen form of comedy at all points implicitly assumes a Christian *telos*, which evidences itself in the way she understands the self, the world and others.[62] To cite MacIntyre again:

> Jane Austen's moral point of view and the narrative form of her novels coincide. The form of her novels is that of ironic comedy. She writes comedy rather than tragedy for the same reason that Dante did; she is a Christian and she sees the *telos* of human life implicit in its everyday form. Her irony resides in the way she makes her characters and her readers see and say more and other than they intended to, so that they and we correct ourselves. The virtues and the harms and evils which the virtues alone will overcome provide the structure both of a life in which the *telos* can be achieved and of a narrative in which the story of such a life can be unfolded. Once again it turns out that any specific account of the virtues presupposes an equally specific account of the narrative structure and unity of a human life and vice versa.[63]

While never overt, 'for all the Aristotelian acuteness with which Austen delineates the virtues and vices distinctive to the tiny polis about which she writes...the *telos* of which MacIntyre speaks, and which informs all her work, is Christian charity.'[64]

Moral values are understood and receive meaning within the context of the narrative shape ascribed to a particular human life or text and this is inextricably related to the theological convictions of an individual. Anthony Thiselton clearly articulates this connection between theology and narrative in his biblical analysis of postmodern assumptions: 'Narrative opens up the notion of an entity who acts and suffers within a framework of continuity and change through the changes and continuities of time...a continuity of accountability as the action of this self.'[65] He notes that 'truth-claims [are] implicit in narrative' and that theology 'handles the transcendental issues' about their 'possible

---

[60] Anne Crippen Ruderman, *The Pleasures of Virtue: Political Thought in the Novels of Jane Austen* (London: Rowmand and Littlefield, 1995).

[61] Wolfe, "Jane Austen and the Sin of Pride."

[62] C. S. Lewis, "A Note on Jane Austen," *Selected Literary Essays by C. S. Lewis*, ed. Walter Hooper (Cambridge: Cambridge University Press, 1969).

[63] MacIntyre, *After Virtue*, 225-6.

[64] Jacobs, *A Theology of Reading*, 3.

[65] Thiselton, *Interpreting God and the Postmodern Self*, 74.

basis.'⁶⁶ Truth in the biblical text 'proves itself in relationships and thus has a personal character,' for which narrative is a key mode of communication:

> Like the postmodern self, Christian theology understands the relativities and constraints of historical situatedness. For Jesus of Nazareth was enfleshed historically....Nevertheless, contrary to the expectations of the postmodern self, the cross of Christ in principle shatters the boundaries and conflicts between [people]....[T]he resurrection holds out the promise of hope from beyond the boundaries of the historical situatedness of the postmodern self in its predicament of constraint.⁶⁷

Narrative then opens a possible understanding of life (whether expressed textually or existentially) in 'the wider frame of temporal relation between the past, present and future.' It projects possibilities which become 'part of the temporal logic of the narrative plot. A plot has a beginning and an end; a pattern of tension and resolution.'⁶⁸

Thiselton conjectures that 'the identity of 'the real self' emerges fully only in relation to purposes which transcend the self.'⁶⁹ Thus the eschatological dimension of biblical narrative (expressed through comic resolution) is necessary to give meaning to the experiences of individuals and texts caught within time, establishing the basis for 'moral agency' within the 'narrative plot' of temporal human existence.⁷⁰ The 'self' of the biblical account is neither the autonomous subject of empiricism, nor the 'mere flotsam' of a postmodern account, 'driven by the surface currents of the power-interests and language-worlds of society.' The biblical promise of resurrection engenders 'a hermeneutic of hope and expectation,' for 'what else is resurrection but a reconstituted selfhood of the same identity, or a reconstituted identity for the 'same' self?'⁷¹ This account of the theology implicit in literary form returns us to the issue of biblical narrative with which the chapter began. Thiselton helps to clarify the wider context within which the biblical narrative's particular structure, delineation of character and emphases shape and educate the moral imagination and epistemology of its readers; its particular connection between moral agency and a teleological orientation towards eschatological fulfilment.

So far it can be seen that the moral principles woven into the narrative form in which much of the biblical text is written has important consequences for what it means to imagine biblically. The self is understood within the context of a linear framework where the final meaning and resolution is dependent upon

---

[66] Thiselton, *Interpreting God and the Postmodern Self*, 27.
[67] Thiselton, *Interpreting God and the Postmodern Self*, 42-43.
[68] Thiselton, *Interpreting God and the Postmodern Self*, 76.
[69] Thiselton, *Interpreting God and the Postmodern Self*, 76.
[70] Thiselton, *Interpreting God and the Postmodern Self*, 77.
[71] Thiselton, *Interpreting God and the Postmodern Self*, 78. The first phrase is a citation from Charles V. Gerkin.

accountability to a Divine Other, who will ultimately draw temporal and earthly reality into a transcendent dimension. Thus, each moment is not understood in isolation, but rather as intimately connected to all that one has been before, and all one may be. This answerability carries as its corollary a necessary responsibility, to shape one's life according to the pattern imaged in the biblical narratives. This does not by any means remove the need for perceptive insight and decision-making. Alter's analysis clearly demonstrates that the biblical narratives emphasise human individuality and freedom through their deliberate reticence as to matters of motive and the like, leading to a roundedness of character that preserves a sense of mystery. As Mouw observes, the moral dimension of the biblical text is conveyed primarily in narrative form, indicating that Scripture recognises both the complexity of life as it is experienced existentially, and the centrality of the imagination in coming to terms with both the need for structure and the flux of daily life; a balance that the novel as a genre is peculiarly designed to meet. The unique style of the biblical narratives thus provide a context and shape that has been crucial in structuring literary works, moral influence and understanding of character in the Western tradition. In the section that follows the particular ways in which the biblical text shapes the moral imagination, narrative structure, characters and epistemology of Jane Austen's novel, *Pride and Prejudice*, will be explored.

Literary Form, Moral Imagination and Hermeneutics in *Pride and Prejudice*

Jane Austen has been described as the writer above all others whom it is hardest to catch in the act of greatness.[72] In this section I shall consider the way in which the third-person omniscient narration of her text provides a moral perspective, despite the supple use of free indirect discourse that enables the introduction of other subjective points of view. The shaping power of omniscient narration, as Austen uses it, balanced by dialogue, has affinities with the method of biblical narration described by Robert Alter and invites a similar kind of imaginative engagement. I shall then consider the moral vision that informs Austen's text and its relationship to biblical theology and a particular understanding of the ideal human *telos*, whether Aristotelian, relativistic, Christian, or a synthesis of perspectives,[73] examining particularly the form of the novel as comedy and its resolution in a marriage of romance and complementarity. Finally, I will look at Austen's presentation of prejudice and the way it intersects with the hermeneutical acuity and challenges that face

---

[72] Virginia Woolf, "Jane Austen," *The Essays of Virginia Woolf*, ed. Andrew McNeillie, vol. 4 (London: Hogarth, 1986), 155.
[73] Lewis, "A Note on Jane Austen"; MacIntyre, *After Virtue*; Ruderman, *The Pleasures of Virtue*; Wolfe, "Jane Austen and the Sin of Pride."

Elizabeth Bennett and Mr Darcy especially, in relation to the tiny polis of which they are a part, and their encounters with one another. There are many other moral dimensions which could be explored, but the concepts of *telos*, self-understanding, perception and action will be developed in this section. These patterns of engagement with the other and growth in self-knowledge are often modelled on a Christian narrative of self-awareness, repentance, and reconciliation leading to transformation and happiness, situating Austen's romance within the biblical metanarrative of ultimate salvation imaged in the marriage supper of the Lamb in Revelation 21.[74]

In *Pride and Prejudice* Austen uses the 'imaginative form' of 'dramatic prose,' which entails that the 'moral "sense" or "philosophy"' informing the text is implicit in its form. Any attempt to 'translate' this moral philosophy of necessity alters or reduces it;[75] the aim of this section is to consider the implications of this imaginative form when seeking to elucidate both Austen's moral vision and, more generally, the working of the literary imagination. In refusing to separate 'imaginative form' and 'moral "sense"' in this way, I am following the line of reasoning put forward by Martha Nussbaum:

> Style itself makes its claims, expresses its own sense of what matters. Literary form is not separable from philosophical content, but is, itself, a part of content – an integral part, then, of the search for and the statement of truth....[C]ertain truths about human life can only be fittingly and accurately stated in the language and forms characteristic of the narrative artist....The telling itself – the selection of genre, formal structures, sentences, vocabulary....Life is never simply presented by a text; it is always represented as something.[76]

Given this premise, the third-person omniscient narration developed by Austen, as she represents a particular fictional world in her novel, has significance in itself.[77] This kind of narration is by no means unique to Austen and the

---

[74] This discussion of *Pride and Prejudice* has some affinities with Emsley's argument in *Jane Austen's Philosophy of the Virtues*, 83-106, particularly in exploring the importance of humility and repentance. However, while Emsley focuses on the link between theological and classical virtues, including the importance of justice and the politics of Austen's novel, I am primarily interested in its connections with the biblical metanarrative and ethics.

[75] Wolfe, "Jane Austen and the Sin of Pride," 111. The affinities between Austen's art, her experience of dramatic performance and 'the moral and emotional fields of self-knowledge' (97) are explored by Penny Gay in *Jane Austen and the Theatre* (Cambridge: Cambridge University Press, 2002), see especially pages 73-97 for *Pride and Prejudice*. See also Paula Byrne, *Jane Austen and the Theatre* (London: Hambledon and London, 2002), 131-147.

[76] Nussbaum, *Love's Knowledge*, 3, 5.

[77] I am thus arguing for a less ideologically absolutist interpretation of third-person narration than that typical of post-structuralist theory as exemplified by Catherine Belsey, *Critical Practice*, 2nd ed. (London: Routledge, 2002), 52-77. While I agree that

observations made here can be equally applied to any number of other novelists. However, she was instrumental in forging this method of narration at the beginning of the novel's efflorescence in England,[78] and her use of it enables the connection between biblical and literary narrative art to be made explicit, also demonstrating the similar function attributed to the imagination in both.

It has frequently been recognised that Austen's method of narration was shaped by her familiarity with the epistolary fiction of the eighteenth-century. Joe Bray suggests that Austen displays her mastery of the style by shifting 'the tensions within consciousness' which the epistolary novel privileges to 'the interaction between character and narrator.' Her deployment of free indirect thought enables subtle transitions in point of view from the omniscient perspective of the narrator, to the subjective experience of various characters.[79] While the shift in form is not disputed, the significance and implications ascribed to Austen's choice have been interpreted in a variety of ways. Bray argues that 'the widespread infiltration' of omniscient narration 'by the perspectives of characters...hinders moral unity and closure, preventing rather than enforcing judgement.' Rather than restricting subjectivity, third-person narration, as Austen handles it, reveals the tension that defines subjectivity through the 'fraught debate' between the consciousness of the narrator and that of the characters revealed in free indirect thought.[80] April Alliston also observes the transition from epistolary form to free indirect discourse in Austen's novels, however, she claims that the omniscient narration 'frames for the reader the interiors inhabited by her heroines,' 'fixing [the heroine] more squarely in its exemplary frame,' and thus placing her in the tradition of criticism that suggests Austen's third-person narrative provides an authoritative voice offering 'clear moral judgements' in place of the moral anarchy and untrammelled subjectivity of epistolary fiction.[81] It seems unnecessary to dichotomise these two schools of interpretation so rigidly though. The self-effacing narrative voice of Austen's texts gains an omniscient authority similar to that present in the biblical narratives, through selective disclosure and a general opaqueness of presence. But this also foregrounds the individuality of various characters who are effectively dramatised through direct speech and action. Nevertheless, the form of third-person omniscient narration does appear

---

classic realism is an artful literary device, I do not agree with the deterministic understanding of 'ideology,' which manifests itself in more extreme readings of this narrative style, as an attempt by the bourgeoisie of Regency or Victorian England to impose their understanding of reality upon others less fortunate than themselves.

[78] Joe Bray, *The Epistolary Novel: Representations of Consciousness* (London: Routledge, 2003), 108-114, 131.
[79] Bray, *The Epistolary Novel*, 108-9.
[80] Bray, *The Epistolary Novel*, 117.
[81] Cited by Bray, *The Epistolary Novel*, 116-17.

to me at least to frame the interiors of Austen's heroines, in the sense of possessing ultimate moral authority in the context of the narrative as a whole.[82]

Jesse Wolfe explores the implications of this tension between objective morality and individual subjectivity in a slightly different form, which is more specifically related to Austen's method of narration, suggesting that her novels have a structure which 'encouraged moralizing of a supple kind. The suppleness grows from an honest and thoroughgoing exploration of human psychology. Ambivalence, partial knowledge, confused sexual longing, egocentrism....'[83] She argues that Austen represents a transitional phase in the history of ideas between 'traditional Christian metaphysics and moralism' and 'an amoral behaviorist-existentialist view of human conduct,'[84] as her novels do not assume the presence of God, even in the hand of a directing providence, and explore morality within the constraints of human psychological interiority, and an objective external standard summarised in Murdochian terms as 'love and justice' and concern for concrete others.[85] Wolfe celebrates what she sees as Austen's ability to 'depict psychological awakenings, or conversions, which have all the profundity, all the weight...of religious awakenings – but are nevertheless thoroughly mundane,' resulting in the curious anomaly of a 'view of reality and morality' that 'can be strategically described as Christian in its ethical outlook, but secular (i.e., strictly non-metaphysical) in its ontology.'[86] Additionally, Wolfe speaks approvingly of the complex interiority of the moral life as depicted by Austen, suggesting that such complexity is essential to the capacity for moral growth and development, and concluding with a stoic ideal that valorises the process of self-improvement as ennobling in itself and the best that can be hoped for.[87]

However, there are several problems with this account of Austen's novels. It is far easier to separate the ontological from the moral dimension when 'translating' Austen's vision into 'expository' form, as this inevitably entails a degree of abstraction from 'the determinate social context,'[88] which both MacIntyre and Jacobs see as central to her ability to unite the Christian and Aristotelian themes that Wolfe argues she successfully separates to achieve a supple secularised morality. Against Wolfe's postulation that 'an act of significant faith' is required 'on the part of the reader' to connect the ontological or metaphysical dimensions of Christian belief with Austen's

---

[82] April Alliston, *Virtue's Faults: Correspondences in Eighteenth-Century British and French Women's Fiction* (Stanford: Stanford University Press, 1996), 234-9. Alliston explores the way in which Austen creates a realised imaginative world with a narratorial voice that maintains moral authority through its ironic and comprehensive poise.
[83] Wolfe, "Jane Austen and the Sin of Pride," 130.
[84] Wolfe, "Jane Austen and the Sin of Pride," 111.
[85] Wolfe, "Jane Austen and the Sin of Pride," 126.
[86] Wolfe, "Jane Austen and the Sin of Pride," 113.
[87] Wolfe, "Jane Austen and the Sin of Pride."
[88] MacIntyre, *After Virtue*, 223; Jacobs, *A Theology of Reading*, 3.

novels, is the notion of a desirable *telos* that is written into the very genre of romantic comedy that Austen adopts, sitting oddly with Wolfe's thesis that process is to be celebrated over and above the ultimate hope of moral perfection, though eschatological consummation lies beyond the boundaries which Austen considers appropriate to fiction. For the purpose of analysis in this chapter, I will make the biblical substructure underlying Austen's work more obvious. The teleological orientation, itself dependent upon an implicit acceptance of the biblical metanarrative, can be seen to inform every aspect of the ordinary circumstances, transformation of character, and moral strivings which Austen depicts within concrete social situations: 'she sees the *telos* of human life implicit in its everyday form.'[89] Additionally, it is her commitment to Christian metaphysics or ontology as well as an Aristotelian practical morality that provides the notions of 'love' and 'justice' against which her characters measure themselves with content, undergirding also the standards that define their relationships to others. Finally, it renders rich and meaningful the 'intelligent love' that finds expression in the complementary union of Darcy and Elizabeth at the end of *Pride and Prejudice*.[90]

Complexity is not an essential prerequisite to moral growth, as Wolfe assumes, though it is often desirable. Jane Bennett's generous and at times indiscriminate charity, for example, stands as a critique of Elizabeth's arrogant pretensions to immediate discernment of character in relation to both Darcy and Wickham. Though quite simple in her goodness, she does achieve a degree of moral growth throughout the novel, by refusing to again become the dupe of Miss Bingley's regard. Thus, I would conclude with Lewis that

> [t]he hard core of morality and even of religion seems to me to be just what makes good comedy possible. 'Principles' or 'seriousness' are essential to Jane Austen's art....Unless there is something about which the author is never ironical, there can be no true irony in the work. 'Total irony' – irony about everything – frustrates itself and becomes insipid.[91]

Lewis's connection here between 'morality' and 'religion' is not inadvertent, the kind of supple relativism in ontology and teleology which Wolfe ascribes to Austen would prevent this hard core and consistent, full-blooded standard against which all characters are implicitly measured, creating the fixed boundaries that allow both the human depth and the delightfully ironic humour of *Pride and Prejudice*.

While it is easy to make generalisations about morality and genre, if Nussbaum's observations on the intimate connection between form and content, style and truth stand, then it is important to consider how the genre of

---

[89] MacIntyre, *After Virtue*, 226.
[90] Richard Simpson identifies 'intelligent love' as the ideal that informs Austen's work in a perceptive article in the *North British Review* 52 (1870).
[91] Lewis, "A Note on Jane Austen," 185.

romantic comedy shapes our understanding of Austen's novel. Some critics have seen her decision to end her novels in marriage simply as a concession to novelistic convention or the social norms of early nineteenth-century England. However, her realistic depictions of marriage, her consideration of the alternatives (it is not a foregone conclusion that each of her heroines will necessarily marry any man who comes along), and the mutuality and commitment to others which shape the way her heroes and heroines come together, indicate a genuine appreciation of marriage as a covenant of companionship and complementarity that helps to promote the development of a civil society. The notion of marriage as a covenant between two people which furthers the health of society is, itself, a logical deduction from the biblical text (Malachi 2:13-16).[92] Crippen Ruderman's careful analysis of the way in which Austen valorises happiness over self-fulfilment, interpreting the former to be found in the pursuit of virtue objectively defined, makes attending to the symbolic echoes of the portrayal of marriage in the biblical text that informs her novels a plausible venture. It is important to note, though, that the happiness which marriage brings to an individual heroine is never the supreme motivating factor in Austen's work. In true biblical spirit, her characters are required to acknowledge principles higher than their own happiness, often involving a denial of self: 'For whosoever will save his life shall lose it; but whosoever shall lose his life for my sake and the gospel's, the same shall save it' (Mark 8:35).[93]

Michael Edwards has commented on the scriptural significance of the 'marriage of the lovers,' which is, he suggests, 'the clearest and most traditional sign of the comic intention.' He argues further that a biblical interpretation would connect it to both the 'Edenic' marriage described in Genesis, and to the church. Adam's well-known observation, 'this is now bone of my bones and flesh of my flesh,' as he beholds the woman created from his rib, is accompanied by the narratorial comment: 'Therefore shall a man...cleave to his wife: and they shall be one flesh.' To marry is thus a recovery, in some measure, of the 'primal unity that preceded the Fall.' It can also be connected to the other end of the story: the hero winning the bride corresponds to Jesus acquiring a bride in the form of the church.[94] The relevant biblical reference, of course, is Paul's exposition of marriage in Ephesians 5:

---

[92] Ruderman, *The Pleasures of Virtue*, 10-14.

[93] For example, when Elizabeth is talking to Darcy at the inn in Derbyshire, and reflecting on whether or not it would be conducive to the happiness of both if she should 'employ the power, which her fancy told her she still possessed, of bringing on the renewal of his addresses', she discovers that Lydia has eloped. The supposed implications of this upon her relationship with Darcy are immediately apparent, but 'self though it would intrude, could not engross her,' Jane Austen, *Pride and Prejudice* (London: Oxford University Press, 1970), 234, 245. All subsequent citations are taken from this edition.

[94] Edwards, *Towards a Christian Poetics*, 47.

> Husbands, love your wives, even as Christ also loved the church, and gave himself for it; that he might sanctify and cleanse it with the washing of water by the word, that he might present it to himself a glorious church, not having spot, or wrinkle, or any such thing; but that it should be holy and without blemish....For this cause shall a man leave his father and mother, and shall be joined unto his wife, and they two shall be one flesh. This is a great mystery: but I speak concerning Christ and the church (vv. 25-27, 31-2).

Thus 'the marriage of the lovers, which is the success of the comedy, looks towards the supreme success...in so far as that too is a marriage, both spiritual and eternal.'[95] Following this kind of analogical correspondence, a recent study of the role of religion in *Pride and Prejudice* has read the idealised family party at Pemberley as an allusion to Paradise.[96] This also needs to be understood within the context of the biblical metanarrative: 'the redemption of our intimate human relationships, indeed like the redemption of our relationships with God, is an already – not yet phenomenon.' The biblical presentation of marriage begins with perfection in the Garden of Eden (Genesis 1); it acknowledges sin, tension and death introduced by the Fall (Genesis 3). However, it also presents through Christ the hope that relationships will be redeemed; the interim state for love, caught between sin and the hope of perfection, can be seen in the Song of Solomon.[97]

The concepts of fidelity, a paradise to be obtained, of values that must be cherished above one's own personal happiness when making decisions, are all biblical principles that structure the imaginative shape of Austen's work and exemplify important aspects of what it means to imagine according to the trajectories opened by the biblical text (Proverbs 5:15-21, 12:22; Psalm 16:11; Matthew 10:22,39). The celebration of marriage at the conclusion of Austen's novels often has a symbolic valence that suggests more than the happiness of two people:

> [Elizabeth] began now to comprehend that [Darcy] was exactly the man, who, in disposition and talents, would most suit her. His understanding and temper, though unlike her own, would have answered all her wishes. It was an union that must have been to the advantage of both; by her ease and liveliness, his mind might have been softened, his manners improved, and from his judgment, information, and knowledge of the world, she must have received benefit of greater importance.

---

[95] Edwards, *Towards a Christian Poetics*, 47.

[96] Michael Giffin, *Jane Austen and Religion: Salvation and Society in Georgian England* (New York: Palgrave Macmillan, 2002), 124-5. I have certain reservations about literalising these symbolic echoes too firmly in what is after all a fallen world, the resonances seem to me more appropriately applied in an eschatological, or typological sense.

[97] Tremper Longman III, *Song of Songs* (Grand Rapids: Eerdmans, 2001), 63-70.

> But no such happy marriage could now teach the admiring multitude what connubial felicity really was (275-6).

> ...she looked forward with delight to the time when they should be removed from society so little pleasing to either, to all the comfort and elegance of their family party at Pemberley (342).

> With the Gardiners, they were always on the most intimate terms. Darcy, as well as Elizabeth, really loved them; and they were both ever sensible of the warmest gratitude towards the persons who, by bringing her into Derbyshire, had been the means of uniting them (345).[98]

The importance of purity and faithfulness is underwritten by a commitment to principles understood to possess ultimate and eternal significance, orientating life in the temporal world in the light of a future beyond this world.

In addition to the theological and moral implications suggested by the biblical structure and *telos* of the novel, Austen explores other themes that are central to the concerns of this chapter: the relationship between moral development and the ability to interpret and relate to others; the necessity of linking principle to *praxis*; a vision that is both stringent in its standards and generous in its charity; the way these are incarnated in narrative. The earlier analysis of Robert Alter and the affinities between biblical narrative and the form of the novel as Austen developed it have already been explored. Michael Giffin takes the argument further, suggesting quite persuasively that *Pride and Prejudice* can be 'read as a novel of neoclassical hermeneutics....The heroine and the hero recognise the sins of pride and prejudice that influenced [their] first impressions, reason and reflect their way into maturity, and learn to give and receive love.'[99] As readers we are invited through 'the normative gaze represented by the unified narrator' to enter a 'fully imagined world,' which is the 'aesthetic effect' of the 'omniscient narration' of characters' thoughts through 'free indirect discourse,' and experience the 'interiors inhabited by [Austen's] heroines' and to a lesser extent her heroes.[100]

This deft combination of omniscient narration, incorporating the subjective individualities of characters through free indirect discourse, enables Austen to create the imaginative experience of each character for her readers, whilst simultaneously maintaining a framing moral vision. Charmed by Elizabeth, delighted by her wit and sympathetic to her frustrations as a dependent young woman and member of the Bennett family, it is easy to sympathise with her initial dislike of Mr Darcy, as she allows the prejudice inspired by her wounded pride to colour all her subsequent contact with him and knowledge about him. Austen clearly demonstrates that Elizabeth has sufficient information to

---

[98] Austen, *Pride and Prejudice*.
[99] Giffin, *Jane Austen and Religion*, 92
[100] Alliston, *Virtue's Faults*, 234.

question her settled opinion about him, but so wholly does the heroine engage us as readers, that it is not until her moment of 'undeception' (in Lewis's terms) that we actually realise just how prejudiced and wilful Elizabeth's response to Darcy has been. Here the balance between the subjective experience of the character and the authoritative moral frame of the omniscient narration plays a crucial role. As readers we are taken upon the same epistemological journey as the heroine, being educated in the process as to the way that a prejudice engendered by hurt pride can lead to unjust interpretations of others. Imaginatively we engage with Elizabeth's initial self-deception, growing self-awareness, repentance, and gradual reconciliation to Darcy as she herself learns to lay aside her initial prejudice when interpreting his character, through a 'hermeneutics of love.'[101]

The vocabulary with which Elizabeth registers both her mistake and the need for repentance indicates Austen's moral concerns and the theological presuppositions that underpin her text:

> Every line proved more clearly that the affair, which she had believed it impossible that any contrivance could so represent, as to render Mr Darcy's conduct in it less than infamous, was capable of a turn which must make him entirely blameless throughout the whole....
>
> She grew absolutely ashamed of herself. – Of neither Darcy nor Wickham could she think, without feeling that she had been blind, partial, prejudiced, absurd.
>
> 'How despicably have I acted!' she cried. – 'I, who have prided myself on my discernment! – I, who have valued myself on my abilities! who have so often disdained the generous candour of my sister, and gratified my vanity, in useless or blameable distrust. – How humiliating is this discovery! – Yet, how just a humiliation! – Had I been in love, I could not have been more wretchedly blind. But vanity, not love, has been my folly. – Pleased with the preference of one, and offended by the neglect of the other, on the very beginning of our acquaintance, I have courted prepossession and ignorance, and driven reason away, where either were concerned. Till this moment, I never knew myself' (182, 185).

Elizabeth recognises the self-centered preoccupation that has rendered her incapable of interpreting either Wickham or Darcy accurately, 'pleased with the preference of one, and offended by the neglect of the other.' In addition to this, she has succumbed to the vanity that is a perennial temptation for one as quick-witted and humorous as herself: to be 'uncommonly clever in taking so decided a dislike to him, without any reason. It is such a spur to one's genius...'(199).

As Lewis observes, Elizabeth employs the 'abstract nouns' of the moralists in order to define her own fault,[102] critiquing herself for a failure in 'generous

---

[101] I have taken this phrase from Jacobs's explication of Augustine's exegesis of the greatest commandment in *A Theology of Reading*.
[102] Lewis, "A Note on Jane Austen," 178

candour,' and concluding with a knowledge of self that will provide the foundation for a right appraisal, a more mature and just relationship with Darcy and Wickham, and the capacity to grow. This pattern can be seen as both classical and Christian, it fulfils the Socratic injunction to: 'Know thyself,' but also evidences the desire of the psalmist: 'Search me, O God, and know my heart: try me, and know my thoughts: And see if there be any wicked way in me, and lead me in the way everlasting' (139:23-24). Austen emphasises the need for 'generous candour' and 'humility' in order rightly to judge and understand others, the latter virtue is Christian rather than classical, and finds expression in the apostle Paul's injunction: 'Let nothing be done through strife or vainglory; but in lowliness of mind let each esteem others better than themselves. Look not every man on his own things, but every man also on the things of others' (Philippians 2:3-4). Elizabeth acknowledges that she has been motivated by a 'vainglory' which has blinded her to the needs and worth of others.

None of this is to suggest, however, that Elizabeth had no grounds for offence in her original encounter with Darcy. But, as she notes later when conversing with her friend Charlotte Lucas, her pride was wounded by his and it was this that made his refusal to dance with her so offensive. Darcy was at fault, but his masculine arrogance and class prejudice are no excuse, though they provide extenuating reasons, for Elizabeth's readiness to credit Wickham's tale and her own 'immoveable...dislike' (172). Darcy himself acknowledges a measure of justice in her emotional response to his behaviour: 'What did you say of me, that I did not deserve? For, though your accusations were ill-founded, formed on mistaken premises, my behaviour to you at the time, had merited the severest reproof' (326).

It is one of the charms of *Pride and Prejudice* that the hero and heroine are equally fallible and equally open to transformation, rendering the mutuality of Austen's ideal of 'intelligent love' in this novel more satisfying than if Darcy played the role of mentor-lover. While the coming to self-awareness and moral transformation of the hero is not represented with the same narrative intimacy as that of Elizabeth, Darcy also learns to recognise the blindness induced by his pride, and the 'unpardonable' arrogance of his behaviour towards a woman 'worthy of being pleased,' though she had relatives whom he could not respect (326, 328). The writer of Proverbs notes: 'When pride cometh, then cometh shame: but with the lowly is wisdom' (11:2). Darcy, like Elizabeth in relation to Jane, implicitly comes to endorse the more 'generous candour' of his friend Bingley, who had earlier observed of the elder Bennett sisters: 'If they had uncles enough to fill all Cheapside...it would not make them one jot less agreeable' (31). Darcy describes his growth into self-knowledge and gradual recognition of the need for repentance and moral development in the same strong vocabulary as Elizabeth. He acknowledges the force of her reproofs, 'though it was some time' before he was 'reasonable enough to allow their justice' (326). He refuses to credit the philosophy that the past should be thought of only 'as its remembrance gives...pleasure,' stating that the past cannot be thus ignored. He traces over his childhood and youth recognising that though taught right principles, he was never nurtured in right practice, following the moral and social standards his parents inculcated with motives of selfishness and disdain. It is humility that is the requisite virtue; this ultimately enables him to value the worth and gain the favour of 'a woman worthy of being pleased' (327-28).

The magnanimity and rectitude of the aristocrat is insufficient. Principles must be linked to practice, and action needs to be informed by love. In the words of 1 Corinthians 13:1,4: 'Though I speak with the tongues of men and of angels, and have not charity, I am become as sounding brass, or a tinkling cymbal....Charity suffereth long, and is kind...charity vaunteth not itself, is not puffed up.' Darcy, when reflecting upon the familial education that had shaped his character, recognised his inability to follow the 'good principles' he had received with a right heart. Only when his desire to act was tempered by humility could he truly respect and lovingly reach out to those 'beyond [his] own family circle' (328). Biblical love requires an empathetic, self-giving of oneself for the other, not a detached altruism: one may do, but not necessarily be, and the one who has not loved is still in debt to the other, 'for he that loveth another hath fulfilled the law' (Romans 13:8).

Humility, self-knowledge and love are crucial to the progress of both Elizabeth and Darcy in coming to a true knowledge and appreciation of each other that facilitates a complementary mutuality in 'all the comfort and elegance of their family party at Pemberley' (342). But the novel also probes further than their relationship, examining the connection between intelligence, love and discernment in interpreting or responding to others, and the necessity of linking conviction to action, through the characters of Mr Bennett, Mr Bingley and Jane. As noted earlier, Elizabeth and Darcy in a moment of self-revelation compare themselves unfavourably to the 'generous candour' of both sister and friend, recognising that had they allowed their own thinking of and relating to others to be shaped by such love, it would have prevented them from being blinded by the prejudices of pride and self-esteem (Romans 12:9; 13:8). However, the novel does not endorse an unthinking candour either. Austen's ideal is undoubtedly 'intelligent love,' in biblical terms, Jesus states: 'be ye therefore wise as serpents, and harmless as doves' (Matthew 10:16). It does not necessarily follow that goodness or virtue demands complexity of character or 'quickness of perception.' Jane for instance is virtuous, though not always discerning, as Elizabeth notes – 'to be candid without ostentation or design – to take the good of everybody's character and make it still better, and say nothing of the bad – belongs to you alone' (12). Yet a failure accurately to perceive the faults of others is seen as a weakness that must be rectified, an intelligence that renders love aware, whilst not preventing its exercise (12). Mr Bennett points out with typically wry humour the lack of discernment that characterises the love and generosity of Bingley and Jane: 'I have not a doubt of your doing very well together. Your tempers are by no means unlike. You are each of you so complying, that nothing will ever be resolved on; so easy, that every servant will cheat you; and so generous, that you will always exceed your income' (309).

A far more serious fault than generous love incapable of truly or quickly perceiving the nature of others is the power of discernment coupled with an unwillingness to act. Mr Bennett is able to discern the faults and virtues of others. He knows what his duties are as a father and a husband, and what he ought to do in order to protect, train and provide for his wife and daughters. But he fails to couple his discernment with action. Elizabeth recognises this and it grieves her, though she is 'grateful for his affectionate treatment of herself' (209). Mr Bennett forms a telling contrast to Darcy, he knows the principles, but through an ironic, disappointed (or possibly embittered) indifference, fails to act. There is the suggestion that this apathetic withdrawal from his family ultimately begins to affect his ability intelligently to evaluate the characters and situations of those around him, even as Darcy's recognition of his false dignity and pride leads him to become actively involved in the lives of those he had previously despised. Elizabeth, moved by a real love for Lydia and her family, strongly urges upon her father the dangers of allowing her younger sister to go to Brighton. Mr Bennett, simply wanting to avoid trouble, fails to pay any real attention to her concern: only in the aftermath of Lydia's flight with Wickham is he able to acknowledge Elizabeth's more perceptive reading of the situation; 'Lizzy, I bear you no ill-will for being justified in your advice to me last May, which, considering the event, shews some greatness of mind' (264). However, Elizabeth does not so much evidence 'greatness of mind,' as the perceptive insight of an emotionally involved member of the family, concerned with what is right, and anxious to preserve the reputation of an ill-governed sister. The contrasting responses of Mr Bennett and Elizabeth when they receive the news of Lydia's elopement, shows the importance of loving involvement in promoting true discernment and effective action. Mr Bennett was 'shocked...could not speak a word' and subsequently angry and unforgiving (257, 277); Elizabeth, initially also shocked, felt most of all for others, 'self, though it would intrude, could not engross her. Lydia – the humiliation, the misery, she was bringing upon them all, soon swallowed up every private care,' and later 'for the sake of [her] sister's feelings and consequence ...urged...earnestly, yet so rationally and so mildly' that Lydia be received by her father upon her marriage (245, 277).

The inextricable connection between self-knowledge, right perception and a willingness to act on behalf of others and in order to achieve happiness, which Austen presents in her novel, ultimately reflects a moral imagination informed by the biblical text and the *telos* it envisages for a fulfilled human life. This chapter considers some of the ways in which Austen traces the implications of these values in *Pride and Prejudice*: her fusion of omniscient third-person narration with free indirect discourse, offering an authoritative moral centre which mediates various individual subjectivities that invite the engagement of the reader; the hermeneutic challenges that confront Darcy and Elizabeth and the way they overcome these through a hard-won knowledge of self and judicious mixture of love and discernment; the juxtaposition of various characters in order to highlight the necessity of love, wisdom and *praxis* being combined in order rightly to interpret, understand and relate to others. The connection between liberty, love, well-being and the wholesome community that such virtues foster is thoroughly biblical, as can be seen in Paul's epistle to the Galatians (5:13-16; 6:1-3). While I do not wish to suggest that reading *Pride and Prejudice* inculcates moral values in the reader, it does model the way in which literature engages and shapes the imagination, through its representation of reality as something.[103] Austen achieves this by forging a unique narrative form, creating a cast of memorable characters, and assuming a moral code which is implicit in all judgements and the overall shape of the novel.

Finally, Gene Koppel has offered the plausible suggestion that the narrator in Austen's fiction exemplifies the same kind of charity that is celebrated in her main characters. He quotes Jan Fergus who observes

> Morality...is not a code, or norm, or principle, which one can live and die by. Instead, it is a way of seeing which includes within its definition some sort of candor or affection. Judgment is seldom conclusive, never infallible. So we understand best and judge best when aided by sympathy and imagination. Austen lets us understand [her characters] by allowing us, for a little while, to live in [their] mind[s].

He suggests that this type of 'sympathy and imagination' can be connected to Christian love, and as has been argued throughout this section, 'perception' is 'an epistemological as well as a moral question.'[104] This is directly in line with Paul's interpretation of love in Romans, where liberty and freedom of conscience are never to be exercised at the expense of another: 'Be kindly affectioned one to another with brotherly love; in honour preferring one another....For none of us liveth to himself, and no man dieth to himself' (Romans 12:10; 14:7).

Thus Alan Jacobs's kenotic interpretation of the moral law is the controlling vision embodied in the narrator of Austen's novel, demonstrating both a generosity of spirit in evaluating her characters, but also a firm adherence to objective standards of right and wrong. To take the next step and suppose that Austen would have 'consciously...striven to incorporate these insights...into...her fiction' is not an implausible conjecture. Koppel offers in support of his thesis the fact that 'the narrative that generates the idea of the

---

[103] Nussbaum, *Love's Knowledge*, 5.
[104] Gene Koppel, *The Religious Dimension of Jane Austen's Novels* (London: UMI Research Press, 1988), 48.

person called Charlotte Lucas in our imaginations endows our conception of Charlotte with enough vitality and coherence to allow us to speculate legitimately' on what kind of person she would be like in situations beyond what the narrative relates. The 'unwritten possibilities for Charlotte's character must exist since the illusion of her reality is strong enough to compel us to contemplate her as we would an actual human being.'[105] This returns us to Palmer's notion that artistic creation is to some extent engendered by love and that our response to characters in fiction must first and foremost be as if responding to persons, fully realised in a fictional world that engages our imagination and inevitably has a moral component.[106] Nevertheless, the illusion of personhood which the text creates entails that even with Charlotte Lucas, 'though we do not hesitate to condemn the spiritual and moral blindness and the psychological callousness revealed by her actions,' the love which inspired the imagination of her creator grants a sense of possibility, which invites an imaginative empathy on the part of readers that prevents a 'completely negative opinion.'[107]

Implications for a Biblical Understanding of the Moral Imagination

So where does this excursus through biblical narrative, moral philosophy and *Pride and Prejudice* lead us in terms of understanding what it means to imagine along the trajectories opened by the biblical text? Robert Alter's analysis of biblical narrative presupposes Nussbaum's claim that philosophy is implicit in literary form. His reading of the theological intention embodied in the structure of the biblical text offers an important pointer for thinking through what may be deduced concerning the imagination from the predominance of narrative in Scripture, and how we respond to the characters embodied in imaginative literature. Alter notes that in biblical narration 'character is revealed primarily through speech, action, gesture, with all the ambiguities that entails; motive is frequently, though not invariably, left in a penumbra of doubt,' much is left to the imagination of the reader, as they conjecture as to plausible motives, possible inferences.[108] This failure to provide the kind of detail given by a Victorian novelist is not due to a lack of knowledge on the part of the narrator, but rather works to remind readers that they are flesh-and-blood, with limited access to the fullness of divine reality. It also helps to preserve a sense of the

---

[105] Koppel, *The Religious Dimension of Jane Austen's Novels*, 47-9.

[106] Palmer, *Literature and Moral Understanding*, 1-39, 164-8.

[107] Koppel, *The Religious Dimension of Jane Austen's Novels*, 48. The contrast between Elizabeth's response to Mr Collins, and the appreciation which the narrator has for the good motives which also inspired him to propose to his cousin is perhaps an even more telling example.

[108] So also A. D. Nuttall on Shakespeare's method of characterisation, cited by Price, *Forms of Life*, 57-8.

depth and mystery of human character, the possibility of change, and the responsibility of individuals to act. This sense of interplay between freedom and necessity that characterises human existence is engendered by 'studied contrasts' on the part of the biblical writers 'between the variously limited knowledge of the human characters and the divine omniscience quietly but firmly represented by the narrator.'[109] The biblical text thus requires that readers engage their imaginations thoroughly and freely if they want to understand what it means to live as a human being, created in the image of God, acting responsibly in time; imagination, in this account, is crucial to theological and moral understanding and growth. Austen's fusion of omniscient narration and free indirect discourse requires a similar response from the reader: we are invited to engage with the characters as individual people, full of possibility, but also provided with a framing moral perspective that guides our interpretation and shapes the range of imaginative response.

C. S. Lewis goes a step further in his analysis of Austen, suggesting that the kind of ironic imagination at work in her novels is only possible due to a 'hard core of morality and even of religion [it is]...just what makes good comedy possible. 'Principles' or 'seriousness' are essential to Jane Austen's art. Where there is no norm, nothing can be ridiculous....'[110] This assertion of the need for an objective moral standard, against which characters are implicitly measured and in order to achieve a comic resolution, can be equally applied to the biblical text and the way moral principles stated propositionally in other parts of Scripture are woven into the structure of the narrative sections.[111] The metanarrative articulated by the biblical text is ultimately comic in its resolution: 'unless there is something about which the author is never ironical, there can be no true irony in the work.' So, in a very real sense, if there were not clear moral principles defining righteousness and love in the biblical text, the comic resolution of true joy and everlasting life at the 'marriage supper of the Lamb,' achieved through the self-sacrifice of the Bridegroom, would not be possible (Revelation 19:6-10). It is this that sets even the failings of various characters in comparatively light relief; grace and mercy beget joy. To articulate it in terms of the literary imagination, if a work is not to become completely relativistic, there must be something which the author values and will not compromise. The biblical text liberates the imagination, by establishing the moral boundaries that give meaning to human being and relationships. This is expressed in creation through the image of the cultivated garden in the opening chapters of Genesis (1-2).

---

[109] Alter, *The Art of Biblical Narrative*, 157-8.

[110] Lewis, "A Note on Jane Austen," 185.

[111] In this use of the term 'objective' I am referring back to the earlier discussion by Richard Mouw citing John Calvin, where the moral law enshrined in the Decalogue and the Sermon on the Mount are seen as a divine revelation of the natural law written upon the heart of every human being by virtue of their creation in the image of God.

Palmer has argued, 'there is a fastidiousness of genuine art which is a creativity rooted in love.'[112] In this chapter, I have attempted to outline some of the ways in which the biblical text defines love, through narratives which reveal the character of God, and moral propositions 'whose imperatives aim at the creation of new possibilities for cultivating those virtues that God intended in creating human beings.'[113] The biblical imagination is simultaneously stringent and generous, rather like George MacDonald's characterisation of God as 'easy to please, but hard to satisfy.'[114] This Christian charity is the attitude which informs the vision of Austen's narrator. The art that results does not always eulogise human nature, nor display follies with a forgiving eye. But the biblical valorisation of creation as good, even though fallen, and of human beings as created in the image of God, whilst never unrealistic about evil and its horrific implications, 'does seem to be antithetical to the idea of artistic creation' that presents 'a vision of life that malevolently revels in the worthlessness of life itself.'[115] The moral standards are there to preserve dignity and purity, not to inhibit creativity or freedom: a biblical imagination is motivated by love, always reaching out sacrificially towards the other in empathy; clear-sighted and honest in self-examination. Simone Weil observed: 'artistic creation (that sort which is not demonic but simply human) is nothing but love.'[116] Returning to the intimate interconnection between narrative and proposition in the biblical text, this love is given concrete definition through the gospel narratives about the person of Jesus Christ. This radicalises the discussion of the moral role of literature, as the biblical text assumes that human beings are unable to achieve the standards that it sets out in and of themselves (John 15:5; Romans 7:7-25; Ephesians 2:1-10). The moral imagination of Scripture is contextualised and transformed by a crucified aesthetic (explored in Chapter 3) that is dependent upon the cross, which confounds human wisdom and moral endeavour, defining and enabling a *telos* which Austen's novels suggestively gesture towards, but never explore (Galatians 2:20).

---

[112] Palmer, *Literature and Moral Understanding*, 164.
[113] Mouw, *The God Who Commands*, 115.
[114] Cited by C. S. Lewis, *Mere Christianity* (Glasgow: Fontana Books, 1952), 170.
[115] Palmer, *Literature and Moral Understanding*, 168.
[116] Cited by Palmer, *Literature and Moral Understanding*, 164-8.

Chapter 6

An Idolatrous Imagination? Biblical Theology and Romanticism in Charlotte Brontë's *Jane Eyre*

In *Jane Eyre*, Charlotte Brontë explores from a biblical perspective the ways in which imagination is involved in idolatrous desire and eschatological anticipation. She draws upon the discourses of Romanticism and Evangelical theology, in order to critique the possible excesses of the Romantic imagination, through anatomising its potential to promote idolatrous attachments or desires. She also demonstrates the positive role of imagination in envisaging the future, defining a space for women in ways that were not socially acceptable in Victorian society, and orientating the restless energy and passion that drives Jane Eyre (and in some respects her cousin, St John Rivers) through the eschatological vision offered by the apocalyptic literature of the Bible (which was Jane's favourite reading material as a child).[1] Biblically the nature and direction of the imagination is always traced back to the relational allegiance of the heart (Proverbs 4:23; Matthew 15:9). This gives a distinctive shape to the role of imagination in love, desire and anticipation. It is exemplified in particular patterns (both literary and existential) that define and situate the imagination in the broader context of Scripture's metanarrative and moral emphases. In both these positive and negative aspects, Brontë draws upon a biblical understanding of the imagination. The centrality of Brontë's critique of idolatry to the structure of *Jane Eyre* has recently been explored by Essaka Joshua and Kathleen Vejvoda.[2] Brontë's attempt to balance this fear of idolatry with a positive appreciation of the imagination – particularly its eschatological dimension – equally rooted in biblical theology has not yet been examined in significant detail.[3]

---

[1] Charlotte Brontë, *Jane Eyre* (Leicester: Galley Press, 1987), 43. All subsequent quotations are from this edition.

[2] Essaka Joshua, "'Almost My Hope of Heaven'": Idolatry and Messianic Symbolism in Charlotte Brontë's *Jane Eyre*," *Philological Quarterly*, 81.1 (2002), 81-107; Kathleen Vejvoda, "Idolatry and *Jane Eyre*," *Victorian Literature and Culture*, 31.1 (2003), 241-61.

[3] Debra Gettelman offers a penetrating analysis of the dialectic 'between Brontë's allegedly riotious daydreams and supposedly obsessive interest in self-control' (578), showing how 'Jane's daydreams prove to be the healthy antithesis of those pathologized in nineteenth-century psychology treatises: rather than eclipsing her duties, they

Ray L. Hart outlines the way in which imagination is related to desire and the will, rooted in the heart, usefully explicating the definition of this function as modulated by the context of biblical anthropology.

> As regards its mental form....It is in the mode of dominant intention that the imagination is to be found in the nearest thing to a pure state. That is so because in the mode of dominant directionality the will projects forward its patterns of concern without specificity of content; or perhaps one could say, projects the will's patterns with respect to wholeness of value rather than in connection with the immediacy of particular acts. The historical future has no environment, and thus no contents upon which directionality may exercise itself....In the intention of dominant directionality the imagination projects something like the pure patterns of the will's teleological drive. Indeed in this form of intention is to be found the nearest thing to the coalescence of imagination as modality of mind and the will as potential ontological power....It follows from what has been said about lack of specific contents that intentions of dominant direction themselves are never fully concentrated into particular acts....This is the foundation of the commonplace that one is ignorant of nothing so much as his own deepest motives.[4]

This notion of imagination preceding action and comprising a surplus of mental or volitional energy can be seen in Jesus's interpretation of the Decalogue (Matthew 5:17-32). The corollary that aspects of the human imagination remain ultimately impenetrable to reason is also biblical: 'The heart is deceitful above all things, and desperately sick; who can understand it?' 'For the inward mind and heart of a man are deep!' (Jeremiah 17:9; Psalm 64:6).

In this chapter I will first of all consider the theme of idolatry as it is developed by Brontë in *Jane Eyre*, exploring its relationship to the Romantic imagination and the potential of this function to become implicated in false perceptions, imprisoning fantasies, or overweening pretensions. Effectively by this presentation, Brontë is performing a biblical critique of the Romantic imagination through her consideration of the scriptural theme of idolatry. The novel 'invokes imagination....[It] is informed by the energies of high romanticism, by its visions of quest, of conquest, of 'incident, life, fire, feeling' – of the aspiring ego, of creative vigour, and of restless desire.'[5] This is countered by a critique of the potential excesses of such a 'high' Romantic imagination, shaped by Evangelical theology, which contested the idolatrous attachments and desires cherished by such aspiring egos.[6] I will also consider

---

punctuate her working life with refreshing privacy' (572). Debra Gettelman, "'Making out' Jane Eyre," *English Literary History* 74.3 (2007), 557-81.
[4] Hart, *Unfinished Man and the Imagination*, 223-4.
[5] Heather Glen, *Charlotte Brontë: The Imagination in History* (Cambridge: Cambridge University Press, 2002), 235.
[6] Brontë's relationship with 'Romanticism' was variable and multi-faceted. This analysis draws upon the detailed study by Heather Glen, *Charlotte Brontë: The Imagination in*

the positive role of the imagination in desire: anticipating a future open to hope and envisaging alternatives that allow Jane to imagine and follow a path for herself not circumscribed by the poverty and pain of her childhood. Imagination in this sense plays a mediating role between the perceiving subject and the otherness of the created world, human beings and God, which is rooted in the biblical distinction between Creator and creature. Finally, I will explore the way in which the scriptural virtue of hope underwrites imagination, finding expression in a restless desire for transcendence.

Before turning to *Jane Eyre*, it will be useful to consider briefly Charlotte Brontë's own religious position in the complex and variegated structure of denominational allegiance characteristic of England in the mid-nineteenth century. Her father Patrick Brontë was an Evangelical clergyman in the Church of England, and this integration was of crucial importance in shaping the environment within which all of his children grew up. In contrast to portraits of Patrick as a repressive and sternly Calvinistic (in the most pejorative sense of that term) father, Marianne Thormählen has described the domestic environment he fostered as one of 'physical, emotional, intellectual and religious freedom.'

> It was a freedom allied to an ethos of labour and effort, informed by affection for fellow humans and by personal commitment to a religion which not only allowed for, but demanded, the engagement of the passions. It would be hard to think of a more favourable climate for creative imagination and intelligence to mature in at the time, and it was very much a product of that time.[7]

Despite this positive assessment of Evangelicalism, though, Thormählen suggests that Brontë herself cannot be characterised simply as an Evangelical,[8] as her commitment to intellectual freedom and the necessity of asking rigorous questions rendered her more adventurous in her search for truth than was generally acceptable to nineteenth-century Evangelicals. Thormählen states it 'was a movement...that...revived the spiritual and emotional dimensions of

---

History, in its particular understanding of what 'Romanticism' is and how it informs *Jane Eyre*; it does not consider Brontë's different explorations of her relationship with key Romantic figures, especially Byron, and their literary works in her other novels. The 'Romantic imagination' thus defined incorporates aesthetic, moral and emotional elements – its very complexity rendered it vulnerable to theological critique, especially from a biblical perspective that scrutinised 'every imagination of the thoughts of the heart' (1 Chronicles 29:18). Brontë's religious position is here interpreted as being broadly, though not unproblematically Evangelical, along the lines argued by Marianne Thormählen, *The Brontës and Religion* (Cambridge: Cambridge University Press, 1999), 20, 23, 42-3 and Vejvoda. On the issue of idolatry, with which this chapter is primarily concerned, Brontë is definitely rearticulating Evangelical Protestant polemic.

[7] Thormählen, *The Brontës and Religion*, 23.

[8] Thormählen, *The Brontës and Religion*, 20.

religious worship; but it did not offer much in the way of innovative thought....None of the Brontës fits in with this absence of mental drive and acumen.' But its encouragement of 'an undenominational temper' promoted the 'individualistic licence' of Brontë's movement in the sphere of religion, and renders the characterisation of her as an intellectually curious believer of broadly Evangelical convictions valid.[9]

Idolatry

Brontë's most famous novel, *Jane Eyre*, is enshrined in the canon as a sublime exemplification of the Romantic and feminist imagination. Various readings have been ascribed to the career of its 'heroine...plain and small':[10] Charlotte Brontë is seen as part of a tradition of English novelists, who substitute faith in human love for a traditional Christian dependence upon God. In this reading Jane and Rochester find their ultimate satisfaction in each other.[11] Feminist readings, of which there are many, typically foreground Jane's passionate assertion of independence and unwillingness to compromise the integrity of her selfhood through relationships with the powerful men whom she encounters:[12] this is undoubtedly a strong element in Brontë's characterisation of her heroine, but it fails to acknowledge the broader narrative context provided by the rich intertextual relationship with Scripture, and also the providential framework informing the story as a whole.[13] While it can definitely be argued that the power of the Cinderella love-story which lies at the centre of the novel overwhelms or effectively negates this larger narrative during the process of reading,[14] a thorough attentiveness to the text reveals that it works to deconstruct the mythic claim of romantic passion fully to satisfy any human being. This chapter will explore the fraught relationship that Brontë attempts to negotiate in her text between a strong valorisation of the imagination and a deep awareness of the ease with which it can lead individuals into spiritual idolatry.[15] Her critique of the Romantic imagination follows the lead of classic Christian theology, from Paul to Augustine, to the Evangelical clergymen of

---

[9] Thormählen, *The Brontës and Religion*, 42-3.

[10] Elizabeth Gaskell, *The Life of Charlotte Brontë* (London: Penguin, 1997), 235.

[11] Robert M. Polhemus, *Erotic Faith: Being in Love from Jane Austen to D. H. Lawrence* (Chicago: University of Chicago Press, 1990).

[12] Elaine Showalter, *A Literature of Their Own: British Women Novelists from Brontë to Lessing*, Expanded ed. (Princeton: Princeton University Press, 1999), 112-23.

[13] Jerome Beaty, *Misreading Jane Eyre: A Postformalist Paradigm* (Columbus: Ohio State University Press, 1996), 196-211; Catherine Brown Tkacz, "The Bible in *Jane Eyre*," *Christianity and Literature* 44.1 (1994); Joshua, ""Almost My Hope of Heaven": Idolatry and Messianic Symbolism in Charlotte Brontë's *Jane Eyre*."

[14] Micael M. Clarke, "Brontë's *Jane Eyre* and the Grimm's Cinderella," *Studies in English Literature 1500-1900* 40.4 (2000).

[15] Jennifer Gribble, "Jane Eyre's Imagination," *Nineteenth-Century Fiction* 23.3 (1968).

her own day, with whom Brontë had a certain degree of sympathy.[16] My fundamental thesis is that the feminism, faith, and imagination of *Jane Eyre* are primarily biblical in their principled independence, transformative aspiration and restrained passion.[17]

The seductive power of the romantic narrative that *Jane Eyre* relates, namely the relationship of the heroine to Rochester and her gradual empowerment as a writing subject, has enticed critics to read it as either a secular celebration of erotic attachment, or the achievement of one female's search for independence. Although more recent critics have tempered this celebrative appraisal with the recognition that it implicitly affirms discourses of class, race and power, which simultaneously disenfranchise other females, such as the 'madwoman in the attic,' the French-woman Celine Varens, her daughter Adele and others. Polhemus suggests that 'the intention of [Brontë's] text is to reconcile human love and Christian faith....This novel of religious yearning reads like a *Pilgrim's Progress* of Victorian love....[S]he uses the tone and forms of religious writing to explore erotic faith....Everything in it exists in a double context: Christian and erotic.'[18] In this nuanced expression, his general thesis appears both cogent and persuasive. Brontë undoubtedly draws upon the religious language of sermons, tracts and novels in order to convey the overwhelming strength of the attachment that bonds Rochester and Jane.[19] However, the two spheres 'Christian and erotic' are not simply superimposed upon one another in *Jane Eyre*, nor can the conflict that emerges between their distinctive claims be identified as an unproblematic choice between equal alternatives, intense and agonising though the experience may be.[20] The notion of the heroic female subject and her suppressed other is most famously articulated by Sandra Gilbert and Susan Gubar in their classic work of feminist criticism, *The Madwoman in the Attic*. This reading privileges the 'passionate sanity' of Jane in her rage against a dominant patriarchal order, aligning it with the madness of her suppressed double, Bertha Mason, imprisoned in the attic. Interestingly, they also recognise another doubleness of discourse, not simply that of female rage and passion, but also between the Christian and erotic

---

[16] Joshua, ""Almost My Hope of Heaven": Idolatry and Messianic Symbolism in Charlotte Brontë's *Jane Eyre*"; Thormählen, *The Brontës and Religion*, 13-23.

[17] By 'principled independence' I am referring to Jane Eyre's determination to follow her understanding of biblical principles and how they should be applied, despite the alternative and often oppressive interpretations given to these by Victorian society and other characters in the novel.

[18] Polhemus, *Erotic Faith*, 110. Heather Walton offers a more general theoretical critique of the relationship between reading literary texts and the construction of feminist theology in *Literature, Theology and Feminism* (Manchester: Manchester University Press, 2007).

[19] Elisabeth Jay, *The Religion of the Heart: Anglican Evangelicalism and the Nineteenth-Century Novel* (Oxford: Clarendon Press, 1979), 257-8.

[20] Polhemus, *Erotic Faith*, 110.

spheres in the title of their chapter on the novel: 'A Dialogue of Self and Soul: Plain Jane's Progress.' This invites their readers to see *Jane Eyre* as a continuation of and commentary upon Bunyan's seminal fictional work of Puritan autobiography.[21]

The problem with these interpretations and their various permutations is not that they cannot be justified by the text – their basis is fairly self-evident. Rather they fail to pay close attention to the discourse of biblical theology that pervades *Jane Eyre*, critiquing the excesses of romantic attachment, providing the rationale for Jane's resistance to Rochester and St John, and ultimately enabling the double-ending, which remains either inexplicable, or ideologically unpalatable in the erotic and/or feminist frameworks discussed above. Jerome Beaty provides an insightful analysis of this wider framework, identifying it as '[t]he providentialist ontology...insinuated into the narrative,'[22] that on an 'authorial' reading decentres both Jane and St John, 'to reveal the real center, which in the authorial world of Brontë's novel, is everywhere, God.'[23] Beaty also offers a theoretical rationale that enables the reader to choose between the 'misreadings' above, or the authorial reading, which he also suggests is a 'misreading' in his final chapter. I will argue, however, that by listening to the biblical critique of idolatry which structures the text, the 'authorial' reading enables a more coherent and complete understanding of the narrative than various other misreadings, and also leads to a different interpretation of the character of St John at the end of the novel to that provided by Beaty. He argues that Brontë concludes by offering two alternative pathways of service to God, the way of *eros*, followed by Jane and Rochester in an exemplary marriage, and that of *agape*, pursued by St John in his missionary service in India.[24] Again, this reading is accurate, but partial: Brontë does not ascribe to St John the same process of sanctification through chastening that enables Jane and Rochester to enjoy human love in the context of divine love at the end of the novel. His motive for converting the heathen in India is a mixture of holy zeal, personal ambition and confident imperialism.[25] St John thus remains

---

[21] Sandra M. Gilbert and Susan Gubar, "A Dialogue of Self and Soul: Plain Jane's Progress," *The Madwoman in the Attic: The Woman Writer and the Nineteenth-Century Literary Imagination* (New Haven: Yale University Press, 1979). Ronald Thomas, similarly, reads 'the novel...as a version of Pilgrim's Progress in which the heroine moves through a series of stages that strengthen her identity' (16). Elsie B. Michie, "Introduction," *Charlotte Brontë's Jane Eyre: A Casebook*, ed. Elsie B. Michie (Oxford: Oxford University Press, 2006), 3-21; Ronald Thomas, "*The Advertisement* of Jane Eyre," *Charlotte Brontë's Jane Eyre: A Casebook*, ed. Elsie B. Michie (Oxford: Oxford University Press, 2006), 47-77.
[22] Beaty, *Misreading Jane Eyre*, 213.
[23] Beaty, *Misreading Jane Eyre*, 211.
[24] Beaty, *Misreading Jane Eyre*, 196-222.
[25] Joshua, ""Almost My Hope of Heaven": Idolatry and Messianic Symbolism in Charlotte Brontë's *Jane Eyre*," 81-4, 100-2.

proud and to some extent fixed within an idolatrous commitment to the legalistic framework of his theology, which Jane earlier resists as unbiblical, even ungodly and this is not resolved completely by the encomium to St John with which Jane concludes, though she extends to him the charity of hope and a generous imagination.[26] Implicit in this comparison is a recognition of the importance of an imagination, open to the direction of the Spirit, in order to facilitate a true and free exercise of biblical religion. John McIntyre observes along these lines: 'I would venture to say that the Holy Spirit is God's imagination let loose and working with all the freedom of God in the world, and in the lives, the words and actions, of…men and women.'[27]

In order to explicate the foregoing argument, it is necessary to outline the biblical allusions and theological critique of idolatry that structure the narrative of *Jane Eyre*. In this I am pursuing a similar argument to that of Catherine Tkacz, Essaka Joshua and Kathleen Vejvoda, who have analysed in detail both the biblical allusions and the theological context of the novel.[28] In scriptural terms, idolatry is a transgression of the first commandment, where God states: 'I am the LORD thy God, which have brought thee out of the land of Egypt, out of the house of bondage. Thou shalt have no other gods before me' (Exodus 20:2-3). It thus involves putting a created person or object in the place that rightfully belongs to God as the Creator and Redeemer. According to Paul's Epistle to the Romans, this is the pervasive and deliberate choice of the human heart:

> Because that, when they knew God, they glorified him not as God, neither were thankful; but became vain in their imaginations,[29] and their foolish heart was darkened. Professing themselves to be wise, they became fools, and changed the glory of the uncorruptible God into an image made like to corruptible man, and to birds, and four-footed beasts, and creeping things. Wherefore God also gave them up to uncleaness through the lusts of their own hearts, to dishonour their own bodies between themselves: Who changed the truth of God into a lie, and worshipped and served the creature more than the Creator, who is blessed for ever. Amen (1:21-25).

---

[26] I am thus largely following Joshua's argument here, though with Thormählen I have to agree that his fault is both religious pride *and* a false ordering of loves. Beaty's suggestion that St John's path is a valid alternative to *eros* is, I think, more justified by the novel than Joshua allows. But I think Brontë's text itself remains somewhat equivocal on the spiritual status of St John. Thormählen, *The Brontës and Religion*, 204-20.

[27] McIntyre, *Faith, Theology and Imagination*, 64.

[28] Tkacz, "The Bible in *Jane Eyre*"; Joshua, ""Almost My Hope of Heaven": Idolatry and Messianic Symbolism in Charlotte Brontë's *Jane Eyre*."; Vejvoda, "Idolatry and *Jane Eyre*."

[29] As noted earlier, *dialogismos* is translated as 'imagination' in the KJV, though it is often given the interpretation of 'reasoning' or 'disputing' in later English versions of the biblical text. The KJV is quoted, as it is the version to which Brontë had access.

This was rearticulated by Jesus in positive terms as the greatest commandment: 'Thou shalt love the Lord thy God with all thy heart, and with all thy soul, and with all thy mind' (Matthew 22:37). Understood in the light of this New Testament context, idolatry involves, as well as Paul's worshipping and serving, loving someone or something more than God; it is not that love for others is wrong, in fact it is consistently required throughout the Bible; rather a supreme love and desire for God, must energise and direct all other loves.

The second commandment applies the principle of the first to idolatrous images of the Divine Being, whether physical or mental, in a way that has direct bearing on a biblical functioning of the imagination: 'Thou shalt not make unto thee any graven image,[30] or any likeness of any thing that is in heaven above, or that is in the earth beneath, or that is in the water under the earth' (Exodus 20:4). The New Testament also links idolatry to desire, through a connection with covetousness: 'Mortify therefore your members...inordinate affection...and covetousness which is idolatry;' 'but every man is tempted, when he is drawn away of his own lust, and enticed' (Colossians 3:5; James 1:14).[31] Imagination biblically is located within the heart and must be understood fluidly within the denotative field of this key scriptural term, consequently the notion of the idolatrous heart is the most useful concept for understanding evil uses of the imagination. John Calvin, for instance, speaks of 'the human heart' as 'a factory of idols...everyone of us is, from his mother's womb, expert in inventing idols.'[32] In Ezekiel 14:4, God refers to one who 'setteth up his idols in his heart, and putteth the stumblingblock of his iniquity before his face.' Undoubtedly, idolatry also involves false worship and patterns of behaviour. But the Bible locates the source of these other elements in the conceptions of the heart, and it is here, most intimately, that imagination comes into play. Charlotte Brontë shared this understanding of idolatry as a false prioritising of desire, love and imagination within the heart; it was common amongst Evangelicals in Victorian Britain. It is clearly seen in a letter she wrote to an old school-friend, Ellen Nussey, at the age of 21: 'Why are we to be divided? Surely, Ellen, it must be because we are in danger of loving each other too well; of losing sight of the Creator in idolatry of the creature.'[33] That this potential for falsely ordered loves and idolatry was connected with the imagination is evidenced in Calvin's subsequent observation: 'After such a figment is formed, adoration forthwith ensues: for when once men imagined

---

[30] Again, the KJV provides a reading of this word that is not accepted as the most accurate of translations now, though it is the version that Brontë had access to and which shaped her understanding of this scriptural theme. *Tesel* is more accurately rendered 'graven thing' than 'image.'

[31] See also 1 Corinthians 10:14; Galatians 5:20; 1 Peter 4:3.

[32] Calvin, *Institutes of the Christian Religion*, 1.11.8.

[33] Cited by Glen, *Charlotte Brontë: The Imagination in History*, 244, n. 182.

that they beheld God in images, they also worshipped him as being there.'[34]

Such references, at first sight, may seem to have no explicit connection with the characterisation and plot of Brontë's novel. In fact, the theme of idolatry structures the teleology of the entire narrative: identifying and overcoming the sin of idolatry is central to the spiritual development of Jane, Rochester and St John, though the final triumph of the latter remains ambivalent due to the mixture of ambitions that motivate his missionary endeavour. Right from the beginning of the novel, Brontë draws upon the discourse of biblical theology, in order to alert the reader to the fact that Jane's passionate craving for human love and initial indifference to divine love, is a weakness in her character. The first reference comes during her time at Gateshead:

> I always took my doll; human beings must love something, and in the dearth of worthier objects of affection, I contrived to find a pleasure in loving and cherishing a faded graven image, shabby as a miniature scarecrow. It puzzles me now to remember with what absurd sincerity I doated on this little toy, half fancying it alive and capable of sensation (38-9).

There is undoubtedly a strong and unhealthy psychological dimension to Jane's situation here; the passion given to a 'graven image' with its overtones of religious affection and worship, fostered by fancy, presage her later relationships with Helen Burns, Miss Temple, her cousins, the Rivers and preeminently Rochester.[35] Helen particularly warns Jane that she must restrain her passions, neither loathing the Reeds and Mr Brocklehurst, nor loving herself and Miss Temple so intensely and intemperately. Her life is characterised by a pattern of disordered emotions: 'Hush, Jane! You think too much of the love of human beings; you are too impulsive, too vehement: the sovereign hand that created your frame, and put life into it, had provided you with other resources than your feeble self, or than other creatures as feeble as you' (80). The novel, overall, does not endorse the stoic universalism of Helen at the expense of feeling, but the more mature Jane recognises the need to restrain and discipline her affections, by having God first in her heart, as all creatures inevitably fail.

The key discussion of this issue comes in connection with the passionate attachment which Jane and Rochester form for one another. It undercuts the claim made by Polhemus that an 'erotic faith' replaces Christianity as the central conviction regulating the lives of Brontë's characters, and consequently provides the framework for her text. *Jane Eyre* in actual fact deconstructs the absolute and totalitarian claims of romantic love as a dangerous idolatry. Rochester's love for Jane is idolatrous almost from the very beginning:

---

[34] Calvin, *Institutes of the Christian Religion*, 1.11.9.
[35] The patterns characterising Jane's relationships with male figures as both a child and an adult are explored by Cicely Palser Havely in "Troubles With Men," *The English Review* 17.2 (2006), 21-3.

knowing that it is an illegitimate passion for him to pursue as a married man, he arrogates to himself the right to revise divine laws on the basis of his own passion and sees his role as that of the atoning sacrifice, which biblically can be fulfilled by Christ alone (1 Timothy 2:5):[36]

> By what instinct do you pretend to distinguish between a fallen seraph of the abyss and a messenger from the eternal throne – between a guide and a seducer?....I know what my aim is, and what my motives are; and at this moment I pass a law, unalterable as that of the Medes and Persians, that both are right (149-50).

> God pardon me!...and man meddle not with me: I have her and will hold her....It will atone....Have I not found her friendless, and cold, and comfortless?....Is there not love in my heart, and constancy in my resolves? It will expiate at God's tribunal. I know my Maker sanctions what I do (272).

Jane resists both this lack of discrimination concerning the source of his messenger and his pride which assumes the power to rewrite divine law, reminding Rochester of the fallibility of human beings. Following the aborted marriage ceremony, she also refuses to play the role of saviour that Rochester construes for her, ultimately finding the freedom to relinquish the burden of responsibility for his damnation, which he implicitly places upon her:

> "Then you condemn me to live wretched, and to die accursed?....Then you snatch love and innocence from me? You fling me back on lust for a passion – vice for an occupation?"

> "Mr Rochester, I no more assign this fate to you than I grasp at it for myself" (334-5).

Jane's temptation is different to Rochester's, although it results in the same sin of idolatrous romantic love. She is unwilling to assume the role of saviour, so commonly attributed to female heroines in the Victorian novel, which Rochester urges upon her and she does not attempt to rationalise an alternative moral code on the basis of love; the kind of erotic faith that Polhemus anatomises. But, in the light of the first commandment, she fails rightly to prioritise her loves: passionate and craving the love of other human beings, she gradually, almost inexorably, allows her entire happiness to become rooted in her relationship with Rochester. Jane herself in a fateful, self-reflective moment prior to the disastrous wedding ceremony observes:

> My future husband was becoming to me my whole world; and more than the world: almost my hope of heaven. He stood between me and every thought of

---

[36] Joshua, "'Almost My Hope of Heaven': Idolatry and Messianic Symbolism in Charlotte Brontë's *Jane Eyre*," 85-6.

religion, as an eclipse intervenes between man and the broad sun. I could not, in those days, see God for his creature: of whom I had made an idol (291).

This could almost be a classic illustration taken from a theological textbook to exemplify the sin of idolatry;[37] it is the mature narrator Jane, commenting on her earlier self and signals an instance of '[t]he providentialist ontology...insinuated into the narrative,' referred to by Beaty.[38] I will cite one instance as a point of comparison from John Wesley's sermon on the text, 'Little children, keep yourselves from idols' (1 John 5:21):

Setting then pagan and Romish idols aside, what are those of which we are here warned by the Apostle?....[T]he idolizing a human creature. Undoubtedly it is the will of God that we should all love one another....Let this be carefully considered, even by those whom God has joined together; by husbands and wives, parents and children....How frequently is a husband, a wife, a child, put in the place of God....They seek their happiness in the creature, not in the Creator....Now, if this is not flat idolatry, I cannot tell what is.[39]

Ultimately both the lovers come to recognise their idolatrous affections and rightly order their loves under the guidance of providence. This section of the narrative, both Jane's period of wandering in the wilderness and Rochester's trial by fire in which he tellingly loses both right eye and hand (Matthew 5:27-30), are rich in biblical imagery and the common New Testament theme of sanctification through suffering (1 Peter 1:6-9; 4:12-19). It is not until Rochester humbly acknowledges his fault before God and turns to his Maker, rather than Jane, that he is able to enjoy a fulfilling and satisfactory relationship with her:

...my heart swells with gratitude to the beneficent God of this earth just now. He sees not as man sees, but far clearer: judges not as man judges, but far more wisely. I did wrong: I would have sullied my innocent flower – breathed guilt on its purity: the Omnipotent snatched it from me...disasters came thick on me: I was forced to pass through the valley of the shadow of death....I was proud of my strength: but what is it now....Of late, Jane – only of late – I began to see and acknowledge the hand of God in my doom. I began to experience remorse, repentance; the wish for reconcilement to my Maker. I began sometimes to pray (469-70).

---

[37] See for example John Wesley's sermon on "Spiritual Idolatry", based on 1 John 5:21: 'Little children, keep yourselves from idols.' From <http://wesley.nnu.edu/john_wesley/sermons/078.htm>, Copyright 1993-2007 by the Wesley Center for Applied Theology, 30 August 2008.
[38] Beaty, *Misreading Jane Eyre*, 213.
[39] From <http://wesley.nnu.edu/john_wesley/sermons/078.htm>, Copyright 1993-2007 by the Wesley Center for Applied Theology, 26 August 2008.

It is in this context that he gives the call that arrests Jane at such a distance and reunites them.[40] Jane, similarly, though never resisting and rebelling against God's law in the sense that Rochester does, learns through her time of exposure to the elements that she must entrust the man she loves to God: 'I had risen to my knees to pray for Mr Rochester....I felt the might and strength of God....Mr Rochester was safe: he was God's and by God would he be guarded' (343). It is through her relationship with other human beings, whom she can love and who love her, particularly her cousins, that Jane gains a more balanced and biblical notion of human interdependence and integrity. This helps to heal the unhealthy psychological obsession with objects, such as the doll she cherished in childhood, which could become a dangerous substitute for necessary human and divine relationships. It was her determination to stand up for her purity and integrity as a woman before God on the basis of scriptural principle that enabled her to break free of Rochester in the first instance. Similarly, a wholesome confidence in her ability to discern rightly the path of God's choosing and the memory of having been passionately loved, allowed her to recognise the foibles as well as the strengths of her newly discovered family and ultimately to resist an idolatrous preoccupation with their good opinion.

This form of idolatry needs to be considered further. Brontë introduces the psychological and spiritual dangers of excessive solitude, emotional dependence and insecurity, as a counterpoint to the absolutism of Jane and Rochester's idolatrous romantic attachment. 'The fear of man bringeth a snare: but whoso putteth his trust in the LORD shall be safe' (Proverbs 29:25). Interestingly, it is in the context of a close relationship with another male that Jane is confronted with this second challenge. During her time with her cousins, the Rivers, St John, who is determined to be a missionary, tells Jane that God is calling her to serve in India as his wife. If she rejects the role that he is offering, then she is effectively turning from heaven. Jane mistrusts this argument, not simply because she sees it as another more subtle attempt by a man to coerce her independence as a woman, but rather because St John is claiming to know the will of God for her life. Jane is convinced that it is possible God might call her to be a missionary, but if so, she would have an assurance of it in her own heart. The importance of such a call for Jane can be seen in the emphasis that she places on a vision that fires her imagination when making the important decisions in her life: in the words of Proverbs, 'where there is no vision, the people perish: but he that keepeth the law, happy is he' (29:18). Jane, as Rochester points out, is a 'passionate creature,' and her imagination needs to be engaged by her conception of the future in order for her to feel sure that it is right:

---

[40] The fact that Jane here is not aware of the death of Rochester's first wife does not invalidate a 'providentialist' reading of the passage, as her immediate resolve at this point is to find out how he is, not necessarily to resume a relationship with him that will end in marriage.

> the restlessness was in my nature; it agitated me to pain sometimes. Then my sole relief was to walk along the corridor of the third story...and allow my mind's eye to dwell on whatever bright visions rose before it – and, certainly, they were many and glowing...and best of all, to open my inward ear to a tale that was never ended – a tale my imagination created, and narrated continuously; quickened with all of incident, life, fire, feeling, that I desired and had not in my actual existence (121).

Without a calling that at least inspired her imagination, to follow St John would in fact be a sin against God: pursuing a misplaced course of direction for her life, a rejection of the priorities God had assigned to her, and even a failure in stewardship of the body and gifts he had entrusted to her; since she knew life in India would lead to her early death.

However, Jane for a time allows St John to have an idolatrous role in her life: she strives to please him through learning Hindustani, represses much of her character in an attempt to win his approval, and knows nothing of the peace or freedom that marks the life of one following God, because she is preoccupied with the creature, entangled in a bondage to the requirements of legalism: 'There is no fear in love; but perfect love casteth out fear: because fear hath torment. He that feareth is not made perfect in love' (1 John 4:18 cf. Galatians 5:22; Philippians 4:7; Colossians 2:18-23). Ironically, this is exactly the same fault that Rochester had mistakenly thought would mark the attitude of Jane and the other girls at Lowood towards Mr Brocklehurst. In that instance Jane's commonsense and clear-headedness instantly dismissed such idolatry:

> "And you girls probably worshipped him, as a convent full of religieuses would worship their director...."
>
> "I disliked Mr Brocklehurst: and I was not alone in the feeling. He is a harsh man; at once pompous and meddling; he cut off our hair" (135-6).

However, St John's classical Greek beauty, purity of life, and (most persuasively for Jane) his relationship as her cousin, cloud her ability accurately to appraise the situation. The words a mature Jane applied earlier to Rochester could equally at this point be applied to St John: 'He stood between me and every thought of religion....I could not, in those days, see God for his creature: of whom I had made an idol' (291).

Jane is able, in retrospect, to identify her feelings and even to recognise a parallel to the earlier situation with Rochester. As St John speaks with her, proposing marriage on the heath, she sees that he is not an exalted being but a man, and in terms reminiscent of the demystification of a false god observes: 'I saw his fallibilities...on the bank of heath, and with that handsome form before me, I sat at the feet of a man, erring as I. The veil fell from his hardness and despotism' (428). However, it is only with the call from Rochester that she is able to break free from the spiritual fascination that St John exerts over her, paralysing her ability to act and effectively blocking her personal communion with God. It is not that the path of action to which he was calling her was wrong in itself, but if she had followed she would have been at fault, because it was not God's purpose for her life.[41]

> I felt veneration for St John....I was tempted to cease struggling with him – to rush down the torrent of his will into the gulf of his existence, and there lose my own. I was almost as hard beset by him now as I had been once before, in a different way, by another. I was a fool both times. To have yielded then would have been an error of principle; to have yielded now would have been an error of judgment (440).

Again, the problem can be described as idolatry, insofar as the creature stands in the place of the Creator, violating in this case the integrity and individuality of a human being equally created in the image of God. It is only in renouncing this final temptation, that Jane is able to act, returning to Rochester, and find both satisfaction and freedom in serving another whom she loves, and by whom she is loved, with rightly ordered affection (1 Corinthians 7:3-4).

Surprising though it may seem, the other character who is caught in idolatry is St John himself.[42] Free from all danger of falling into the kind of 'erotic faith' that troubles Rochester, as St John clearly shows in his resistance to the gentle encouragement of Rosamond Oliver, he is nevertheless at fault. Still struggling with her own desperate longing to return to Rochester, Jane is more capable of truly assessing St John's spiritual condition than that of hers in relation to him: 'I was sure St John Rivers – pure-lived, conscientious, zealous as he was – had not yet found that peace of God...no more...than had I; with my concealed and racking regrets for my broken idol and lost elysium...'(371). This assessment is given as Jane listens to her cousin preach, he is detailing the logical points of Calvinistic theology, but they remain an intellectual abstraction. St John idolises the system, he is a legalist; not knowing the purity of heart, humility of spirit, peace and freedom to love that comes from a

---

[41] Hoyle provides a thorough theological and historical contextualisation for the notion of vocation and call, so crucial to Victorian Protestantism, and informing the presentation of Jane's decision-making process. This is not simply a rationalisation of her own deepest desires. Lydia Huffman Hoyle, "Nineteenth-Century Single Women and Motivation for Mission," *International Bulletin of Missionary Research* 20.2 (1996); Thormählen, *The Brontës and Religion*, 213, 268 n. 19; Cf. Carolyn Williams, "Closing the Book: The Intertextual End of *Jane Eyre*," *New Casebooks: Jane Eyre*, ed. Heather Glen (New York: St Martin's Press, 1997), 240-2.

[42] Readings which unproblematically ascribe the status of elect saint to St John, in effect simply adopt his own categorisation, however critically, failing to pay attention to the complex and nuanced theological framework through which he is presented. See, for example, Peter Allan Dale, "Charlotte Brontë's 'Tale Half-Told': The Disruption of Narrative Structure in *Jane Eyre*," *New Casebooks: Jane Eyre*, ed. Heather Glen (New York: St Martin's Press, 1997).

personal, experiential relationship with Jesus Christ, he is striving in Paul's words to establish his 'own righteousness, which is of the law' rather than 'that which is through the faith of Christ'; 'for if righteousness come by the law, then Christ died in vain' (Philippians 3:9; Galatians 2:21). In many respects he is reminiscent of the Pharisees: the same stern integrity, self-righteousness, commitment to law rather than love, and determination to go to great lengths in order to save one soul to his way of thinking (Matthew 23:15,23-24). He is unable to enjoy God's good gifts, even of family and friends on Christmas Eve, embracing an extreme asceticism that takes one thread of biblical teaching and emphasises it at the expense of others.

It is the lack of peace, tendency towards authoritarianism, and focus on his determination to obey the teachings of Christ, which through his manner of speaking sounds more like the creed of pagan philosophers (as Jane observes), that cause St John, in his pride and restless ambition, to fit the picture of a self-righteous formalist, sincere, but ultimately not trusting in Christ alone, that figures in so many Evangelical sermons of the period.[43] However, this portrait of an idolater, putting the system in place of a relationship with God, resting in himself rather than Christ is complicated at the end of the novel. In the final paragraphs, Jane compares St John to Great-heart, one of the mature and gracious pilgrims in Bunyan's classic text; his ambition has been disciplined and channelled to serve the divine purpose, his reward is sure. I do not think that this passage is intended ironically, nor does Joshua's argument that St John's way of *agape* is presented by Brontë as inferior to Jane's way of *eros* resolve the issue. Jane at no point critiques St John's denial of earthly ties in order to pursue missionary service, she objected to his attempt to coerce the conscience of one who was not called (Romans 14:12-23), and his refusal to enjoy natural human bonds when they were the environment in which God placed him (1 Timothy 4:1-6; 6:17; James 1:17). Beaty's postulation that we are shown at the end of the novel two alternative paths, both of which are appropriate avenues of service, seems to me valid. The problem that Thormählen wrestled with remains, however, at what point does St John undergo a change of heart which allows Jane to speak of a man so proud,

---

[43] Henry Martyn, the famous Evangelical missionary to India, can be cited as an example: '[The deceitful heart] tells us...that we have Zeal; which zeal is often no other than bitterness and ill temper. We are violent against the misconduct of others; not because they have sinned against God, but because they trouble and interfere with ourselves. We are zealous for Christ...but cannot rejoice if the work be not done by ourselves and friends: nay, are often so wicked as to wish the work may not be done at all, if it cannot be done in our own way. Now if our zeal is of this nature, it is evidently pure worldliness.' Thormählen, *The Brontës and Religion*, 216. See also "The Cross of Christ," a sermon by J. C. Ryle exegeting Galatians 6:14: 'God forbid that I should glory, save in the cross of our Lord Jesus Christ.' J. C. Ryle, *Old Paths: Being Plain Statements on Some of the Weightier Matters of Christianity* (Cambridge: James Clark & Co., 1972), 239-62.

legalistic, authoritarian and self-willed in the laudatory tones with which she ends? There is an ambiguity in the presentation of his character that none of these readings fully resolve. In her dual *dénouement*, Brontë powerfully presents the complexity of motive and experience that marked those who were pursuing the salvation of souls during this period of imperial expansion. However, there is no doubt that she also affirms the mutuality of human love, when regulated by a supreme love for God, in the bond of marriage as a fulfilling and right choice of action (Ephesians 5:22-33).[44] This narrative conclusion thus underwrites the imaginative acuity of Jane in perceiving the appropriate shape for her life and refusing the image of the future offered by St. John, though it also offers a tempered endorsement of his desire to reach Britain's colonies with the gospel.

Biblical Balance: The Mediating Imagination

In many respects Brontë's critique of the absolutist claims of romantic love, idolatrous imagination and legalism is typical of one from her period and religious milieu. What is so intriguing about this instance is the fact that it becomes the structural framework of a novel which has achieved the status of a myth in Western culture, precisely as a manifesto for romantic love and the imagination. Some of the reasons behind this tendency to partial readings, arguably misreadings, have been explored above, another is cultural amnesia. Contemporary readers simply do not have the familiarity with the biblical text that infuses almost every sentence and character of *Jane Eyre* with allusive depths.[45] The interpretation offered here is indebted to the plethora of critical works and articles on Brontë's novel over the past few decades that have revealed the rich range of cultural discourses upon which she drew in order to create her classic work of fiction. However, I would argue that despite this plurality of voices, biblical theology remains the predominant and controlling

---

[44] St John's disparagement of Jane's desire to marry Rochester as a denial of her calling as a Christian does not appear to be supported by the text as a whole. Brontë at no point indicates that Jane abandons her faith or commitment to God; to take St John's assessment of her spiritual condition as an authorial comment seems an extremely dubious process. Joshua helpfully contextualises the choice of *eros* as an avenue of service, through considering a letter of Henry Venn to his wife, indicating that the issue is not marriage or singleness, so much as the avoidance of an idolatrous love: 'Both for myself and you, I would always pray that God may be so much dearer to us, than we are to each other....By this means we shall be most likely to continue together, and not provoke the stroke of separation by an idolatrous love to one another. But by this means we shall love one another in God and for God.' Joshua, ""Almost My Hope of Heaven": Idolatry and Messianic Symbolism in Charlotte Brontë's *Jane Eyre*," 99; Cf. Dale, "Charlotte Brontë's 'Tale Half-Told': The Disruption of Narrative Structure in *Jane Eyre*."

[45] Tkacz, "The Bible in *Jane Eyre*," 3-4, 20-5.

religious discourse within the text, providing a crucial focalising counterpoint to the Romantic imagination which shapes *Jane Eyre* both implicitly and explicitly: the dialogue is a mutually enriching and liberating exchange.

The term 'Romantic imagination' instantly leads one into a strongly contested field of definition: a critical controversy in which *Jane Eyre* has been an important text at least since the 1970s.[46] Virginia Woolf first suggested in *A Room of One's Own* that the novel was an artistic failure at points, because Brontë's anger interfered with the free and detached functioning of her imagination.[47] Gilbert and Gubar invert the terms of this equation without really progressing beyond it, suggesting that Brontë's (and Jane's) feminist anger against a patriarchal order is the origin of her creativity, madness and passionate sanity (that is Bertha and Jane are two sides of the same complex female character): the means through which Brontë attains a degree of freedom from the repressive model of 'the angel in the house.'[48] Elaine Showalter gives a less emotional reading to the working of Charlotte Brontë's imagination: *Jane Eyre* occupies a central position in her attempt to trace a female literary tradition, and she suggests that Brontë offers a powerful analysis both of the social conditions that oppress women and the transformative possibilities that enfranchise them from these.[49] Such universalist and positive accounts of the 'female imagination' have been energetically and persuasively challenged by more recent feminist criticism, through the now familiar grid of class, gender and race.[50]

But these contemporary concerns, whilst they engage meaningfully with the text can occlude important motifs and contexts that would have directed, governed and unified various threads for the initial readers of *Jane Eyre*, in a real sense robbing the text of its historical 'otherness.' Even the nature of Brontë's feminism as expressed in *Jane Eyre* assumes a biblical form that does not neatly fit into modern narratives of its priorities, nature and development. As was seen in the previous section, Jane asserts her identity as an individual woman accountable to God and his commands, which provides her with the energy to resist the role of saviour scripted for her in romantic terms by both Rochester and Victorian culture. She also eventually refuses to have her imagination brought into captivity by the overweening authority of her cousin, St John, who attempts to usurp the role of the Holy Spirit in guiding and

---

[46] Heather Glen, "Introduction," *New Casebooks: Jane Eyre*, ed. Heather Glen (New York: St. Martin's Press, 1997).

[47] Virginia Woolf, *A Room of One's Own*, ed. Hermione Lee (London: 1991), 65, 68.

[48] Gilbert and Gubar, "A Dialogue of Self and Soul: Plain Jane's Progress."

[49] Showalter, *A Literature of Their Own*, 112-29, 139-42; Glen, "Introduction," 11.

[50] Jina Politi, "*Jane Eyre* Class-Ified," *New Casebooks: Jane Eyre*, ed. Heather Glen (New York: St. Martin's Press, 1997); Susan Meyer, "Colonialism and the Figurative Strategy of *Jane Eyre*," *New Casebooks: Jane Eyre*, ed. Heather Glen (New York: St. Martin's Press, 1997); Amit S. Rai, "The Black Spectre of Sympathy: The "Occult" Relation in *Jane Eyre*," *Literature Interpretation Theory* 14.3 (2003).

directing her (2 Corinthians 10:5). In a very real sense imagination is the aspect of human being upon which the Spirit is seen to work biblically, providing an understanding of and vision for the future that can inflame and direct the heart: 'ourselves also, which have the firstfruits of the Spirit, even we ourselves groan within ourselves, waiting for the adoption, to wit, the redemption of our body' (Romans 8:23). Or again, 'Eye hath not seen, nor ear heard, neither have entered into the heart of man, the things which God hath prepared for them that love him. But God hath revealed them unto us by his Spirit: for the Spirit searcheth all things, yea, the deep things of God....Now we have received...the spirit which is of God; that we might know the things freely given to us of God' (1 Corinthians 2:9-12). The freedom, passion and imagination so characteristic of Jane is not simply, or even primarily, an attempt to be free of the stranglehold of patriarchy, so much as a desire to fulfil her vocation as a woman in terms of her spiritual understanding of the biblical text. Jane's experience was mirrored in the life narratives of many Victorian women of Evangelical convictions, such as Mary Anne Cooke an English missionary and teacher in India (who had previously been a governess), and some decades later, Amy Carmichael.[51]

In this section, I wish to explore Brontë's negotiation of the Romantic imagination in terms of the biblical context that frames the novel. Just as the theological analysis of idolatry exposed the potential of the imagination to be deceived by self-deluding fantasies, or illusions, and consequently enslaved (Romans 6:6; Galatians 4:3; 2 Peter 2:19), so Jane's visionary and inspiring imagination indicates the positive dimensions of this human function. Brontë particularly considers the way imagination is informed by and fosters the biblical virtue of hope, its role in accurately perceiving the world beyond the self, and also its orientation of desire by enabling the absent other or the future to be conceived and thus shape the present. This dynamic is of crucial importance to the biblical imagination and structures the form of Brontë's text: 'For we are saved by hope: but hope that is seen is not hope: for what a man seeth, why doth he yet hope for? But if we hope for that we see not, then do we with patience wait for it.' 'And every man that hath this hope in him purifieth himself, even as he is pure' (Romans 8:24-25; 1 John 3:3).

Jennifer Gribble, in an article on 'Jane Eyre's Imagination,' provides a useful point of entry, because she neither conflates Brontë and Jane Eyre into the same entity, reductively defining the imagination as a 'mad' resistance to patriarchal power; nor does she unravel the text into its complex and manifold discourses, reading it against the grain. Rather, deploying the famous Coleridgean definition of imagination that undoubtedly informs *Jane Eyre* to

---

[51] Clare Midgley, "Female Emancipation in an Imperial Frame: English Women and the Campaign against Sati (Widow-Burning) in India, 1813-30," *Women's History Review* 9.1 (2000); Elisabeth Elliot, *A Chance to Die: The Life and Legacy of Amy Carmichael* (Grand Rapids: Fleming H. Revell Company, 1987).

some extent, she analyses the way in which at its best this novel

> Examine[s] the workings of the creative imagination....[I]n concentrating attention on the significance of Jane's active and sensitive imagination and its relationship with, and responses to, what it encounters, the novel inevitably unfolds the processes by which art is made....Far from envisaging the imagination as an escape from the realities of life...it is only through the imagination that "reality" can fully be explored and understood....Charlotte Bronte...show[s] that her heroine's imagination is necessarily limited as well as extraordinarily powerful.[52]

She achieves this, Gribble argues, by revealing not only the desires and visions Jane shapes to herself as she paces the corridor of Thornfield: 'allow[ing] my mind's eye to dwell on whatever bright visions rose before it....[T]o open my inward ear to a tale that was never ended – a tale my imagination created and narrated continuously; quickened with all of incident, life, fire, feeling, that I desired and had not in my actual existence' (121). But also making evident, as a novelist writing in the tradition of realistic fiction 'that which is intractable, which challenges Jane's sense of herself, her desires, her imaginative domination.'[53] Tracing through several incidents in the novel: notably Jane's experience in the red-room; the first meeting with Rochester and her period in the wilderness communing, in a sense, with nature; Gribble illustrates the way in which, though tempted at points 'to be overinvolved in Jane's success,' generally Brontë demonstrates the necessity of an engaged imagination in order fully to explore and comprehend reality, whilst also respecting the 'otherness' of the world and society. She concludes by suggesting that it is the conventions of the nineteenth-century realist novel which allow the 'insights of romanticism' to be explored, illustrating 'the powers and limitations of the imagination' through the mind's relationship to the natural world.[54]

This understanding of the imagination as delicately poised between creation and discovery, can be seen to depend in several ways on the biblical theology that undergirds *Jane Eyre*, inflecting its particular Romanticism. The role of nature within the text reflects the general tendency of Romanticism to view it as a book of revelation, gently instructing hearts sympathetically attuned. This can be implicitly defined against a more didactic moralism, as in Wordsworth's famous formulation: 'One impulse from a vernal wood/ May teach you more of man,/ Of moral evil and of good,/ Than all the sages can.'[55] Some recent critics have suggested that like Wordsworth's pantheistic tendencies, Brontë's

---

[52] Gribble, "Jane Eyre's Imagination," 280-2.
[53] Gribble, "Jane Eyre's Imagination," 282-3.
[54] Gribble, "Jane Eyre's Imagination."
[55] William Wordsworth, "The Tables Turned," (1798), *Wordsworth: Poetical Works*, ed. T. Hutchinson (Oxford: Oxford University Press, 1973), 377.

references to nature, particularly the moon, embody an alternative feminine folk or pagan spirituality that is designed to complement or deconstruct the primary discourse of historical Christianity in the text.[56] However, within the context of the novel as a whole, nature (including the feminised moon), fulfils the role ascribed to it in the biblical text of testifying to God's power, the glory of his works and his character. This can be seen in the fact that during Jane's flight through the wilderness, as she rests on the heath, her view of the broad sky filled with stars brings peace, reminding her of an omniscient, omnipresent God. Many verses could be cited and two will suffice, illustrating that this is no pagan alternative to biblical Christianity:

> The heavens declare the glory of God; and the firmament sheweth his handywork. Day unto day uttereth speech, and night unto night sheweth knowledge (Psalm 19:1-2).

> For the invisible things of him from the creation of the world are clearly seen, being understood by the things that are made, even his eternal power and Godhead (Romans 1:20).

Similarly, when Jane receives instruction from a female personification of the moon, she is not commanded to follow her own desires, but rather receives an affirmation of biblical revelation: "My daughter, flee temptation!" "Mother, I will" (338). In these examples, nature points to the transcendent God of Scripture, instructs concerning his character and even provides portentous warnings against unconscious disobedience (for example, the lightening which strikes the oak tree at Thornfield when Rochester proposes). As a human being made in the image of God, Jane is able to trace the hand of the Creator in works which 'declare the glory of God,' but she does not equate these with God, nor lose her own individuality in a desire for union with the natural world. The biblical doctrine of creation, reflecting the divine nature, but separate from it, is essential to the poised imagination that Brontë conveys through her narration of Jane's experience and the understanding of this function articulated in her novel.

---

[56] Robert B. Heilman, "Charlotte Brontë, Reason, and the Moon," *Nineteenth-Century Fiction* 14.4 (1960); J. Jeffrey Franklin, "The Merging of Spiritualities: Jane Eyre as Missionary of Love," *Nineteenth-Century Literature* 49.4 (1995); Cf. Margaret Homans, "Dreaming of Children: Literalisation in *Jane Eyre*," *New Casebooks: Jane Eyre*, ed. Heather Glen (New York: St. Martin's Press, 1997). Alternatively, it is sometimes read, through the explanatory paradigm of psychoanalysis as an alternative supplementary voice to God the Father. However, this is explicitly positing a different, mutually exclusive theoretical explanation to the theological discourse that informs the text, and which was Brontë's primary context. Williams, "Closing the Book: The Intertextual End of *Jane Eyre*." For a theological appraisal of psychoanalytic theory see Ferretter, *Towards a Christian Literary Theory*, 83-99.

While the Romantic imagination itself is inflected by Christian thought due to the influence of its primary proponents – Coleridge and the German Romantics – Brontë modifies it more specifically through the framework of the broadly Evangelical theology that shaped her convictions. Thus, while she celebrates the liberating potential and visionary character of the Romantic imagination, the desires it engenders are always directed by scriptural principle. When its capacity to envision a particular course of action or state of affairs comes into conflict with biblical precepts, its powerful fancies are defined as idolatrous. This has been and can be read as a capitulation on Brontë's part to the bourgeois ideological norms of Victorian society: an alternative rarely entertained is that Jane and Rochester are choosing, through their ultimate submission to the biblical principle of monogamous union, to recognise both their finitude and accountability as human beings made in the image of God on the one hand, and divine power and authority on the other. It is a familiar theme in biblical theology: the paradox of law and grace, obedience bringing life, submission leading to fulfilment and liberty; in this case a rightly ordered love for one another is rooted in a personal relationship with God. It is this that provides the key, in a theological reading of the text, to Jane's resistance to Rochester's adulterous proposal (which has direct affinities with an otherwise remarkably different heroine, Fanny Price). Rochester himself acknowledges this on several occasions: when disguised as a gypsy and reading Jane's forehead, he observes, 'The forehead declares: "The passions may rage furiously...the desire may imagine all sorts of vain things....[B]ut I shall follow the guiding of that still small voice which interprets the dictates of conscience" (215). Similarly, when attempting to talk Jane into being his mistress, he recognises 'the hitch in Jane's character,' no matter how much she loves him, she will not allow the desires of imagination to direct her outside the divine laws laid down in Scripture (319, 335).

As with the connection between imagination and idolatry, imagination plays an important part in the biblical concept of desire. The consideration of adultery as a possible state of affairs already involves an act of imagination within the heart that has objectified another person and broken the law (Matthew 5:27-32). Jane herself affirms the power of the imagination in directing and shaping desire for good or evil in the way she describes the liberty she found in refusing the slavery of a 'fool's paradise' for the quiet of her village school:

> Whether it is better, I ask, to be a slave in a fool's paradise at Marseilles – fevered with delusive bliss one hour – suffocating with the bitterest tears of remorse and shame the next – or to be a village-schoolmistress, free and honest, in a breezy mountain nook in the healthy heart of England? Yes; I feel that now I was right when I adhered to principle and law, and scorned and crushed the insane promptings of a frenzied moment. God directed me to a correct choice: I thank His providence for the guidance! (379).

This does not mean though that Brontë associated imagination in purely negative terms with sinful desires, which lead one away from a rational, moral manner of life. The imagination is presented in *Jane Eyre* in biblical terms as a gift of God that can be used or abused by those who possess it. Just as an idolatrous imagination threatens to direct Jane into a luxurious slavery, 'a fool's paradise,' in the passage quoted above, it also enables her to perceive the path of God's call and guidance for her life. Images of a world beyond her knowledge and broader spheres of service are what initially prompt her to leave Lowood; her visions during lonely school holidays are transmuted into extraordinary works of art; her dreams at Thornfield evidence a perceptive imaginative apprehension of dangers to others and troubles that lie ahead; her appreciation of nature, as mentioned earlier, enables her to draw near to the God to which it bears witness.

Finally, her imaginative conception of the shape of her life under the divine plan, rooted in a sensitive reading of her own past and a commitment to a useful future, enables her to resist St John's stern assertion that it is God's will that she become his wife and travel to India, she chooses instead to return to Thornfield. Yet, remarkably, her imagination also enables her to engage sympathetically with the man she has resisted and refused, despite the fact that his nature and temperament are almost incomprehensible to her. This provides an explanation for the eschatological trajectory with which the novel concludes, drawing upon both the conclusion of *The Pilgrim's Progress* and John's apocalyptic vision in Revelation:

> As to St John Rivers, he left England....[H]is is the sternness of the warrior Greatheart, who guards his pilgrim convoy from the onslaught of Apollyon....[H]is glorious sun hastens to its setting...."My Master," he says, "has forewarned me. Daily he announces more distinctly, – 'Surely I come quickly!' and hourly I more eagerly respond, – 'Amen; even so come, Lord Jesus!'" (475-6).

As a child, Jane expressed a preference for the apocalyptic and narrative literature of Scripture: 'I like Revelations, and the book of Daniel, and Genesis and Samuel, and a little bit of Exodus, and some parts of Kings and Chronicles, and Job and Jonah' (43). This continues to inform her own understanding of her life, opening the temporal framework of Brontë's narrative to a broader vision in the light of the biblical metanarrative that *Jane Eyre* consistently alludes to. The final words of the text, expressing a prayer for the second coming of Jesus, are a citation of the concluding verse of the Bible. The significance of the hope engendered by the omnipresence of this biblical metanarrative, in both validating the imagination as it engages with the temporal sphere, and also in opening the natural to the ameliorating potential of a transcendent dimension will be considered in the final section of this chapter.

Heather Glen has recently analysed the particular ways in which Brontë engaged imaginatively with the more specific historical discourses that constituted her cultural context in early nineteenth-century England. She examines the shape of the narrative identifying two 'opposing and incommensurate' stories within the text, those 'of triumphant omnipotence and imminent annihilation,' which 'remain to the end unresolved...imaged in the potent yet death-bound figure both of romantic self-assertion and of evangelical self-immolation who has the novel's final word.'[57] This apparent contradiction reflects a similar tension to that explored earlier, where Jane's principled resistance led to spiritual liberty: 'For whosoever will save his life shall lose it: and whosoever will lose his life for my sake shall find it;' '...work out your own salvation with fear and trembling. For it is God which worketh in you both to will and to do of his good pleasure' (Matthew 16:25; Philippians 2:12-13). Glen is not prepared to interpret these biblical paradoxes as uniting mutually compatible, but logically incommensurate truths, preferring to situate them as contradictory discourses within their contemporary theological and cultural milieu as articulated by Evangelical tracts, female conduct books, annuals and romantic poetry.[58] However, she references in considerable detail the aspiring, Romantic imagination that Brontë attributes to Jane, which is nevertheless forced to respect the concrete social situations in which she finds herself. Indeed, sometimes it becomes a coercive instrument, and Jane exerts authority over others, subjecting them to the power of her own gaze, as for instance in the portraits she paints of Rochester, Blanche Ingram and Rosalind Oliver.[59]

But generally, as Glen observes, Jane's imagination fed by Romantic literature, is other-focused, continually pressing her to probe beyond the limits of her present knowledge, to test the extent of her capabilities. This restlessness grants her a 'preternatural' perceptiveness, fuels action, and through the very insatiability of its perpetual craving, suggests a need that no human circumstances, however blissful, can fully satisfy. Glen takes issue with an ahistorical figuration of desire, though, such as that postulated by twentieth-century psychoanalytic criticism, arguing that 'the desires that animate Jane's story...appear...in forms that would have been quite familiar' to its initial readers. While I agree that historical circumstances shape the form that these desires take and that St John Rivers 'seems still at the close of the novel to embody much of that 'restless' aspiration which has informed and is gone from Jane's story,' I do not think that in this instance we are presented with a division on the basis of gender, so that he has 'an aspiration that is emphatically other, and male.'[60] This does not seem fully to acknowledge the very real possibility that Jane could have gone to India, had she felt it to be God's call for her life; nor to recognise the historical fact that many women did travel

---

[57] Glen, *Charlotte Brontë*, 64.
[58] Glen, *Charlotte Brontë*, 65-143.
[59] Glen, *Charlotte Brontë*, 125-9.
[60] Glen, *Charlotte Brontë*, 130, 132.

throughout the British Empire and beyond as missionaries.[61] Jane's decision is related to the shape she imagines to be appropriate for her life, sensitive to a divinely overarching providential plan revealed through the guidance of the Spirit: 'And we know that all things work together for good to them that love God, to them who are the called according to his purpose' (Romans 8:28). Jane's restless probing desire finds expression in the way she first imagines and then enacts her return to Rochester, as she had earlier determined to leave Lowood and then Thornfield. In a very real sense it is her confidence in an ultimately beneficent providential plan, detailed in the scriptural narratives, which liberates her to imagine possibilities for herself as a woman that facilitated her decisions to act in ways that defied the specific social constraints limiting those of her class and gender.

The differing paths of *eros* and *agape* followed by St John and Jane, as Glen notes, are both ultimately incapable of satisfying these two 'restless,' 'aspiring' protagonists: the one with its apparent quiescence, the other in its inevitable solitariness. Brontë in the ambivalence of her ending reflects the paradox that characterises the existence of all human pilgrims in this life, whether married or single, expressed in the command to be amongst those 'that use this world, as not abusing it: for the fashion of this world passeth away' (1 Corinthians 7:31). This 'tale...is so equivocally ended as to evade an explicit recognition of the imagination's limits,'[62] suggesting that all human stories are necessarily inconclusive, anticipating the *eschaton*: 'For the earnest expectation of the creature waiteth for the manifestation of the sons of God....Because the creature itself also shall be delivered from the bondage of corruption into the glorious liberty of the children of God' (Romans 8:19, 21; Ephesians 3:20). This correlates with the way Glen locates the subversiveness of the novel in 'its central emphasis on absolute, primary need,' which 'more directly, more urgently questions the notion that self is or could be an autonomous entity.' The fact that the imagination evokes visions and arouses a restless desire, which inevitably transcends the possible social configurations designed to satisfy it, suggests the existence of an infinite, personal being that corresponds to this longing. Joshua argues that Brontë deliberately structured her novel in order to

---

[61] J. Haggis, "Ironies of Emancipation: Changing Configurations of 'Women's Work' in the 'Mission of Sisterhood' to Indian Women," *Feminist Review* 65.1 (2000); Hoyle, "Nineteenth-Century Single Women and Motivation for Mission"; Valerie Sherer Mathes, "Nineteenth Century Women and Reform: The Women's National Indian Association," *The American Indian Quarterly* 14.1 (1990); Dana Robert, "Evangelist or Homemaker? Mission Strategies of Early Nineteenth-Century Missionary Wives in Burma and Hawaii," *International Bulletin of Missionary Research* 17.1 (1993).

[62] Dale, "Charlotte Brontë's 'Tale Half-Told': The Disruption of Narrative Structure in *Jane Eyre*," 207. I agree with Dale's astute analysis of the open-ended quality of the narrative, though I am not so sure of the simple equation he implicitly draws between the imagination of Jane and her creator, and give a very different interpretation to this refusal on Brontë's part to recognise the limits of the imagination.

lead the reader to this conclusion: no human love or mission, however laudable in itself can still the restless yearning.[63] In the words of Augustine, 'you have made us for yourself, and our heart is restless until it rests in you.'[64] The ultimate inability of imagination to postulate a condition that satisfies desire uncovers a hunger for transcendence that the biblical text positions within the realm of hope (Romans 8:24-25).

Biblical theology is not the only framework within which Brontë's novel can be considered. However, it is rarely explored in contemporary criticism and offers illuminating insights into the structure of the plot, which on one reading is resolved through a rejection of the idolatrous imagination,[65] and a perceptive apprehension of the directives of divine providence. Similarly, the reasoning behind Jane's decision to leave Rochester, the functioning of nature, and the particular form assumed by the Romantic imagination within the novel can be coherently explained through a consideration of the biblical concept of creation, the relationship between law and freedom, and the providential direction of the Spirit. Thus, remarkably, though this text has been appropriated by many feminist, spiritualist, pagan and other readings (both positively and negatively), as can be seen it also portrays a passionate imagination, rightly ordered, functioning according to biblical principle, bearing fruit in mutual romantic fulfilment and eschatological anticipation.

Eschatology and Transcendence

A key issue which the apocalyptic allusions that structure *Jane Eyre* raise, is the distinction between an imagination fostered by faith in transcendence, open to hope, and that which deliberately restricts its aspirations to processes and possibilities immanent in the historical, natural and self-centred contingencies of contemporary human existence. This latter division can be refigured as the contrast between an imagination shaped by biblical eschatology, and a particular inflection of the secular postmodern imagination. The biblical description of 'vain...imaginations' bears a remarkable and instructive affinity to a diagnosis of the postmodern imagination by Trevor Hart and Richard Bauckham. They argue that the relativism embraced by many in the West following the failure of the Enlightenment project, with its faith in a history of progress leading to a secular utopia, has trapped contemporary society in an absolute present, engendering hopelessness. 'The death of truth threatens to lead inexorably to the death of human culture in the sense of 'a creative project in which human beings have an ethical, artistic and political role to play.''

---

[63] Joshua, ""Almost My Hope of Heaven": Idolatry and Messianic Symbolism in Charlotte Brontë's *Jane Eyre*," 96.
[64] Saint Augustine, *Confessions* (Oxford: Oxford University Press, 1998), 3.
[65] Joshua, ""Almost My Hope of Heaven": Idolatry and Messianic Symbolism in Charlotte Brontë's *Jane Eyre*," 96.

There is a retreat from the public sphere, with its concomitant ethical responsibility to the other, based on an apathetic conviction that any attempt to alter or improve the real world is useless.

The current tendency, they suggest, is to respond with a 'narcotic hedonism,' retreating to private worlds (available through phenomenal developments in technology) where the individual is in total control. However, this imagining is self-focused, it 'has no aspiration to transcendence, no forward moving and potentially liberating direction.' It produces fictional alternatives to reality that work like a narcotic to distract, rather than an inspiration to transform. They conclude that this renders the postmodern imagination thus defined unethical, for if nothing is true, images of the other can be ignored; no call to action that would draw us out of ourselves into complicating and costly relationships is heeded. Hopelessness (a failure of imagination) justifies the failure to act: the alternative, a comfortable deceptive world of illusion, 'which we are not even free to choose or create for ourselves...but which must be selected from a range...carefully imposed by the totalitarianism of the 'free' market.'[66] This process of dehumanisation resulting from a sense that everything is vanity, is thoroughly explored in Ecclesiastes: the moral conclusion drawn by those choosing to participate is the same, 'Let us eat and drink, for tomorrow we die' (1 Corinthians 15:32). Thus evil, like hopelessness, is seen to be a failure of imagination, turning in on itself as Satan does in *Paradise Lost*: the kind of condition Jane envisions herself in had she allowed the images of freedom, sexual pleasure and romantic bliss that Rochester presented on the night of their aborted wedding ceremony to beguile her imagination and lead her away from a commitment to biblical principle.

Hart and Bauckham position alongside the hopelessness of a postmodern imagination trapped in the closed universe of an absolutised present, the possibility of transcendence available to an imagination inspired by faith in the eschatological openness and hopefulness articulated by the biblical text. Instead of deducing the end of the human story from a reading that assumes the only possibilities available are those immanent in history and nature, the Bible offers the opportunity for a 'wager' of faith based on a transcendent God, who will 'make all things new,' transforming the present world in a way that can only be imagined. It is this hope (one of the three primary biblical virtues, 1 Corinthians 13:13) that encourages people to conceive of things as being other than they are at present: faith in 'the human capacity for invention and creativity as the source of all meaning' is insufficient. Rather, every communicative act of self-transcendence, including works of art:

> assumes the real presence of that which cannot...ever be demonstrated...which transcends the level of the symbolic and inheres in the nature of the real itself.

---

[66] Trevor Hart and Richard Bauckham, *Hope against Hope: Christian Eschatology at the Turn of the Millennium* (Cambridge: William B. Eerdmans, 1999), 52-61.

> Human creativity, artistic or otherwise, is never *ex nihilo*, but is a *response* to constant epiphanies through which reality impinges upon our existence.[67]

This imagination stretches after fulfilment, testing the limits of the possible, grounded in and fed by faith in a transcendent God who has revealed himself as the 'Father of our Lord Jesus Christ' (Ephesians 3:14, KJV), returning to the real with a dissatisfaction engendered by hope. This biblical imagination, Jürgen Moltmann, Hart and Bauckham argue, turns Marx's claim that 'religion is the opiate of the masses' on its head: 'Faith, wherever it develops into hope, causes not rest, but unrest....Those who hope in Christ can no longer put up with reality as it is, but begin to suffer under it, to contradict it....[F]or the goad of the promised future stabs inexorably into the flesh of every unfulfilled present.'[68]

The restlessness that Moltmann believes such hope inspires has affinities with the dissatisfied and transformative energies that a contemporary reviewer of *Jane Eyre* fearfully speculated that it would inspire. The reviewer expressed a preference for quietistic interpretations of the biblical text and was apprehensive of the passionate Romantic imagination that she (and many other readers since) found embodied in *Jane Eyre*.[69] The dynamic influence of biblical eschatology offers a theological context within which to interpret the 'restlessness' that critics have noted characterises both Jane and St John. The energy that these characters exemplify is not intrinsically valorised, for if it is channelled unwisely it can do great harm: as for instance, if directed inwards in corrosive, self-pitying dissatisfaction, or if projected outward in a self-glorifying, ambitious imperialism. If focused rightly, however, this biblically inflected version of the Romantic imagination, often self-centred and Promethean when unchecked, can be seen as positive, transforming and enriching. The hope and active anticipation that characterise it also further elucidate the puzzling double-ending of the novel. For, on the one hand, since this world is created by God it must be affirmed as good: a theological understanding demonstrated in the mutual exchange of spiritually regulated natural affection enjoyed by Jane and Rochester. On the other hand, however, the biblical emphasis on the shortness of this life and the importance of eternity is also acknowledged. Even marital bliss at Ferndean does not mark the ultimate end of the pilgrim. St John's citation of Revelation contextualises *Jane Eyre* within the biblical metanarrative, ensuring that the passionate imagination which motivated its heroine (and her cousin) is not ultimately contained or

---

[67] Trevor Hart and Richard Bauckham, *Hope against Hope*, 47-9.

[68] Trevor Hart and Richard Bauckham, *Hope against Hope*, 55. Hart has extended the theological analysis given here through fruitful deployment of the theatrical metaphor in a later essay: "The Sense of an Ending: Finitude and the Authentic Performance of Life," *Faithful Performances: Enacting Christian Tradition*, eds. Trevor A. Hart and Steven R. Guthrie (Aldershot: Ashgate, 2007), 167-86.

[69] Elizabeth Rigby cited by Glen, *Charlotte Brontë*, 121. Cf. also 135.

denied by the text: 'For this perishable body must put on the imperishable, and this mortal body must put on immortality....For in this hope we were saved' (1 Corinthians 15:53; Romans 8:24).

Chapter 7

Intimations of Transcendence: C. S. Lewis and the Eschatological Imagination

A biblical account of the imagination cannot ignore the eschatological orientation of the scriptural plotline, which reaches its consummation in the apocalypse of the apostle John. Paul writes in Romans of the creation which waits with 'eager longing' 'in hope that [it]...will be set free from its bondage to decay and obtain the freedom of the glory of the children of God' (8:19-20). Similarly, in Ephesians he refers to the fact that God 'is able to do far more abundantly than all we ask or think' (3:20). This expectation reconfigures conceptions of the present, transforming our understanding of created reality and experience in the light of the promised future. Scripture emphasises the virtues of faith and hope in relation to the *eschaton*. The imagination is central to the ways in which these virtues are fostered and realised, through the biblical text and in the hearts of its readers. The biblical account defines human beings as created in the image of God, but fallen. Through the incarnation of Jesus Christ, there is the possibility of redemption now, but the process will not end until 'the perishable puts on the imperishable, and the mortal puts on immortality' (1 Corinthians 15:54). Even if one rejects the theological explanation, as I have observed before, this pattern of despair and hope is so characteristic of our existence as human beings that it is possible to affirm the experiential structure under consideration.[1]

The purpose of this chapter is to explore the implications of this biblical definition of our human condition for an understanding of the functioning, role and possibilities of the imagination. In order to explicate this theoretically, I will draw on both Paul Ricoeur's definition of metaphor, which is shaped through his own engagement with the biblical text, and C. S. Lewis's theorisation of myth. Together they provide a way of comprehending biblically the structural operations of the imagination defined in Christological and linguistic terms. They also allow one to trace through the implications of this biblical concept of imagination for the creation, role and purpose of imaginative fiction in a fallen world. Following the theoretical exploration of metaphor and myth, I turn to a reading of what is arguably Lewis's most successful attempt artistically to realise these theoretical concepts, *Till We Have*

---

[1] Edwards, *Towards a Christian Poetics*, 1-11.

Faces, in order to deepen, enrich and aesthetically inform the contours of the discussion.

Paul Ricoeur on Metaphor and 'Poetic' Language

The scholarly fortunes of metaphor have undergone a dramatic shift over the past few decades. Rather than being characterised simply as an ornamental aspect of discourse, conveying what could be phrased more accurately and succinctly in literal terms, as it had been conceived from the beginnings of rhetorical criticism in ancient Greece, metaphor is now understood to be central to the processes of cognition and discovery in every field of intellectual endeavour. The literature on this topic is vast and formidable. For the purposes of this chapter I shall draw upon the theory of metaphor developed by Paul Ricoeur, as he explicates its role in terms informed by the revelatory potential of the biblical text, emphasising the referential function achieved by poetic language. Ricoeur equates the biblical text with other classic literature and thus 'does not...adequately account for the truth-claim which distinguishes the Biblical from literary texts...inasmuch as he presupposes the assimilation of the referential function of the Bible to that of poetic, or non-descriptive texts.'[2] However, his analysis of the way in which the biblical text works as literature and its similarity to the methods by which other classic texts signify, provides a useful model for understanding the centrality of metaphor to the functioning of the imagination, and the biblical justification for such an explication.

In *The Rule of Metaphor* Ricoeur argues that defining metaphor at the level of the individual word, is a reductive and inaccurate way of explaining how it works to create meaning. He suggests that there are two levels at which one can consider language: the semiotic, where language is seen as a system of potential meanings to be realised through a finite number of signs; and the semantic, whereby language is understood to refer to something beyond itself. The irreducible unit of analysis when considering the semantic level is the sentence, and thus Ricoeur suggests that the meaning of a metaphor can only be fully understood as a tensive interaction between the focus (the word upon which the metaphorical meaning is concentrated) and the remainder of the sentence. The way in which metaphor refers differs, however, from literal discourse, even when considered at the level of the sentence. It does not present a univocal proposition which is designed to correlate with the empirical world of our experience, and can be verified as true or false. The truth of metaphor is perceived only through the destruction of such first-order reference, in order to allow a second-order reference. Such language is equally engaged with the world of human experience, but it is liberated from the constraints of first-order reference in order to engage with reality at a deeper level.

What is of particular interest in Ricoeur's account of metaphor is the way he

---

[2] Ferretter, *Towards a Christian Literary Theory*, 129.

moves from the level of the sentence to the level of discourse, suggesting that the same structural mechanism is at work in the way a literary text refers to the world.

> Our concept of likeness as the tension between sameness and difference implies that a discourse which makes use of metaphor has the extraordinary power of redescribing reality. This is, I believe, the referential function of a metaphorical statement....[Similarly] the main operation of poetry...is the building of a mythos, of a fable....Therefore if we say that the function of poetry is to imitate nature, we must not forget that this mimesis is not a copying of reality, but a redescription in light of a heuristic fiction....If it is true that lyrical poetry suspends all didactic references and even abolishes the world, can we not say that this...is the negative condition for the disclosure of new aspects of reality which could not have been said in a more direct way?[3]

Poetry, and indeed all literature, thus abolishes the 'didactic description' or first-order reference offered by 'ordinary language,' yet maintains the mimetic function of all discourse 'in as much as it is a heuristic fiction preparing a redescription of reality.' While it does not add to our empirical knowledge of the world, 'it may change our way of looking at things...our way of dwelling in the world...we receive a new way of being in the world.'[4] Such language opens a world in front of the text, which we can dwell in whilst reading; offering new possibilities of being, new ways of dwelling in the world of our everyday experience. Ricoeur states that this metaphorical process, where the literal meaning is destroyed as a negative precondition enabling the intuitive grasp of resemblances or analogies, is the essence of the creative imagination. The moment of perception is, simultaneously, the moment of invention: 'the iconic element has therefore to be included in the predicative process itself.'[5] The tension between creation and discovery which we have come across before is again evident here. Ricoeur articulates the structural process through which such perceptions occur, both in the creation and appropriation of literary texts.

Ricoeur's assimilation of the biblical text into the more generic category of 'poetic texts,' needs to be qualified somewhat. This is so, not only because the biblical text contains certain genres, such as epistle, legal discourse, and theoretical argument,[6] which fall more appropriately under Ricoeur's definition of 'first-order reference' in the way in which they refer to the world, but also because the Bible makes truth claims concerning the world at both first and second order of reference, which are not shared by other fictional literature.

---

[3] Paul Ricoeur, "Creativity in Language: Word, Polysemy, Metaphor," *Philosophy Today* 17 (1973), 110-11.
[4] Ricoeur, "Creativity in Language: Word, Polysemy, Metaphor," 111.
[5] Ricoeur, "Creativity in Language: Word, Polysemy, Metaphor," 107.
[6] Frame, "Images of God," *Doctrine of God* (Philadelphia: Presbyterian and Reformed Publishing, 2002), 362-86.

'The world proposed by the Biblical texts...is distinct from those proposed by literary texts inasmuch as it claims to constitute the ground of the world of the reader's experience in general.'[7] The significance of this in terms of a biblical understanding of the imagination is that while the imagination works in the same manner, through the indwelling of proposed worlds, when reading either the biblical text, or other literary texts, the existential claims made by those worlds on the life of the reader are different. The biblical text becomes the paradigm world in terms of which all other worlds, possible or real, are measured. Otherwise: 'how can we discern which imaginative worlds to appropriate? The Bible is clear in its insistence that the imaginings of the heart may be evil....That is, the imagination itself has the potential for perversity.'[8]

Despite this qualification concerning the nature of the truth claims made by the Bible and other literary texts, and consequently the authority given to the possible modes of being in the world which they propose, the scriptural roots of much of Ricoeur's philosophical reflection make his theory of metaphor highly relevant to this study. This is especially so when considering the teleological framework, with its emphatically eschatological orientation, within which Ricoeur explores the role of imagination and poetic language. Whilst his limitation of the reference of the biblical text, and particularly of the gospel narratives relating the incarnation, compromise the uniqueness which Scripture attributes to the coming of Jesus Christ, and undercut (or at least render tenuous) the foundation of an eschatological hope grounded in the historical reality of the resurrection, the structure of his argument continues to be shaped by biblical revelation.[9] In this context, therefore, the imagination, defined by its unique ability to perceive resemblances or analogies on the negative condition of a destroyed literal meaning, can still be understood to be orientated in hope towards that which is not seen (Romans 8:24-25).

Lewis on Myth, Metaphor and Joy

The correlation between Ricoeur's theory of metaphor and the work of C. S. Lewis is not immediately obvious. There are, however, remarkable affinities between the thought of these two very different men on metaphor, myth, and the role of the imagination in referring to a transcendent reality that undergirds all that we are, though it may not initially be apparent to empirical observation. Ricoeur offers a careful philosophical defence of the centrality of metaphor to cognition, and as a way of defining the imagination, which elucidates Lewis's more occasional attention to these themes. In his essay, 'Bluspels and Flanlansferes,' for instance, Lewis argues that all language is metaphorical and, like Ricoeur, asserts that human beings must use metaphor if they wish to gain

---

[7] Ferretter, *Towards a Christian Literary Theory*, 130.
[8] Vanhoozer, *Biblical Narrative in the Philosophy of Paul Ricoeur*, 247.
[9] Vanhoozer, *Biblical Narrative in the Philosophy of Paul Ricoeur*, 224-266.

fresh cognitive insights into that which is new, or otherwise inexpressible.[10] However, Lewis complements this with a careful consideration of the theological implications of metaphor in a sermon, 'Transposition,' which, as Owen Barfield dryly observes, 'can be seen as a theory of the imagination...in which imagination is not mentioned.'[11] Closely allied to this theory of the imagination, are Lewis's lifelong preoccupations with 'joy' and 'myth.' References to these concepts are scattered throughout Lewis's entire *oeuvre* and are central to understanding how he conceives the role of the imagination, both in perceiving the transcendent dimensions of human existence, and also in defining the longing or homesickness he describes as a desire that ultimately leads the sincere seeker to God himself.[12]

In his sermon, 'Transposition,' Lewis begins with the account of the apostles speaking in tongues at Pentecost (Acts 2), noting that in many respects it resembles what we would call hysteria, and raises the question as to why this particular instance should be seen as consisting of something more. The problem centres around the fact that we can only describe experiences or states claimed to be beyond the merely natural (heaven, communion with God and so on) in terms derived from nature, suggesting that it is irrational to assert that any of these things we define as spiritual are in fact supernatural. Lewis responds to this conundrum by presenting an example which we can look at from both below and above. When experiences of intense pleasure or pain are 'transposed' from the richer realm of our emotions, to our sensations, the distinction is lost: in fact, the senses compensate for a lack of possible variations by using the same sensation to express opposite emotions. For example, the sensation of 'intense aesthetic delight' can be indistinguishable from that of being say 'in a rough channel crossing' when measured by the accompanying 'flutter in the diaphragm' at the level of the senses, even though in one situation the neural response is desired and in another it is dreaded. While not identifying Transposition as 'the only possible mode in which a poorer medium can respond to a richer,' Lewis suggests that it is 'not improbable that [it] occurs whenever the higher reproduces itself in the lower.' If in a description of spiritual things, elements of our natural life recur (eating in the eucharist, conjugal love to describe mystical communion and so on) this is only to be expected. However, in these instances we are unable to consider it

---

[10] C. S. Lewis, "Bluspels and Flalansferes," *Rehabilitations and Other Essays* (London: Oxford University Press, 1939).

[11] Cited by Walter Hooper, *C. S. Lewis: A Companion and Guide* (San Francisco: Harper, 1996), 574.

[12] Erik J. Wielenberg has critiqued the apologetic argument for Christianity that Lewis based upon his concept of Joy in *God and the Reach of Reason: C. S. Lewis, David Hume, and Bertrand Russell* (Cambridge: Cambridge University Press, 2008), 108-20. The focus of this chapter, however, is on the contribution that Lewis's concept of Joy made to his definition of the imagination.

from both 'below' and 'above.' '[T]he sceptic's conclusion that the so-called spiritual is really derived from the natural, that it is a mirage or projection or imaginary extension of the natural, is also exactly what we should expect.'[13]

Lewis thus identifies a relationship of analogy as the fundamental structure of the mind by which we perceive that which is beyond the immediate contours of our empirical existence. Like Ricoeur, he holds that such language, whilst rooted in the natural, may in fact refer truly to that which is beyond nature. Rather than leaving his argument in the hands of the sceptic, Lewis continues by observing that one can only verify the capacity of such language (that is metaphor and analogy) to refer truly to the spiritual through experience. This is critical to understanding imagination from a biblical perspective: the metaphors can demonstrate their cognitive truth and reference to reality through *praxis* alone. This notion of ordeal through embodiment is perhaps the only way of determining the 'goodness' or 'badness' of a metaphor, if one does not judge it by some external criteria, such as the authority of the biblical text as divine revelation. Of particular relevance to the concerns of this present chapter, Lewis identifies the importance of his doctrine of Transposition in developing 'the theological virtue of Hope. We can hope only for what we can desire.' He notes that it is difficult to conceive of heaven except by way of negation of the biblical images and situates imagination as absolutely crucial to the enactment of faith: '[w]e must believe – and therefore in some degree imagine – that every negation will be only the reverse side of a fulfilling.'[14] Citing the scriptural text: 'We know not what we shall be' (1 John 3:2), Lewis comments,

> we may be sure we shall be more, not less, than we were on earth....You can put it whichever way you please. You can say that by Transposition our humanity, senses and all, can be made the vehicle of beatitude. Or you can say that the heavenly bounties by Transposition are embodied during this life in our temporal experience. But the second way is the better. It is the present life which is the diminution....If flesh and blood cannot inherit the Kingdom, that is not because they are too solid....They are too flimsy....[15]

Thus, like Ricoeur, Lewis defines the imagination through its ability to understand the depths of reality, to enable a mode of being in the world, orientated towards that which lies beyond this world. Metaphor, or its close affiliate 'myth', is not fact, but the very condition of truth; that which enables us to think at all. What is more, Lewis bases his observations concerning the correlation between the metaphors by which we think, and the objective reality of the created world, 'a kind of psycho-physical parallelism (or more) in the

---

[13] C. S. Lewis, "Transposition," *C. S. Lewis: Essay Collection and Other Short Pieces*, ed. L. Walmsley (London: HarperCollins, 2000), 267-73.
[14] Lewis, "Transposition," 273-5.
[15] Lewis, "Transposition," 276.

universe,'[16] on the teaching of the biblical text: 'Nature is only the image, the symbol; but it is the symbol scripture invites me to use. We are summoned to pass in through Nature, beyond her, into that splendour which she fitfully reflects.'[17]

This essay and sermon, however, are exceptions for Lewis: two of the rare occasions where he gives full attention to a subject that is treated incidentally in his literary criticism, or more indirectly through the process of literary creation. In order to understand Lewis's concept of the eschatological imagination more fully, it is therefore necessary to explore his concepts of myth and joy. In 'Transposition' Lewis suggests that the miracle of the incarnation can be comprehended better through the doctrinal lens he has outlined:

> Transposition is not always symbolism. In varying degrees the lower reality can actually be drawn into the higher and become part of it....For we are told in one of the creeds that the Incarnation worked 'not by conversion of the Godhead into flesh, but by taking of the Manhood into God.' And it seems to me that there is a real analogy between this and what I have called Transposition: that humanity, still remaining itself, is not merely counted as, but veritably drawn into, Deity, seems to me like what happens when a sensation (not in itself a pleasure) is drawn into the joy it accompanies.[18]

Biblical teaching on creation and the incarnation are central to understanding the role of the imagination according to Lewis. He deliberately links the historical account of the gospels to pagan mythology, in order to explain both the literary power of the narrative of Jesus, its parallels in other stories, and the ontological basis that grounds and legitimises the yearning, desire, joy that he repeatedly describes as drawing every heart towards a fullness, home, Person, beyond the boundaries of the temporal world.[19]

In *The Pilgrim's Regress*, at a crucial point in his journey home, the protagonist John hears a divine Voice, which provides the clearest explanation of the importance of myth to Lewis, and its relationship to the gospel:

> Child, if you will, it is mythology. It is but truth, not fact: an image, not the very real. But then it is My mythology. The words of Wisdom are also myth and metaphor: but since they do not know themselves for what they are, in them the hidden myth is master, where it should be servant: and it is but of man's inventing. But this is My inventing, this is the veil under which I have chosen to

---

[16] Lewis, "Bluspels and Flalansferes," 158.
[17] C. S. Lewis, "The Weight of Glory," *C. S. Lewis: Essay Collection and Other Short Pieces*, ed. L. Walmsley (London: HarperCollins, 2000), 104-5.
[18] Lewis, "Transposition," 277.
[19] William Luther White, *The Image of Man in C. S. Lewis* (Nashville: Abingdon Press, 1969), 113.

appear from the first until now. For this end I made your senses and for this end your imagination, that you might see my face and live.[20]

For Lewis, as for Ricoeur, myth is not falsehood, but rather 'the best means of embodying those ultimates that transcend fact.' Lewis parts company with Ricoeur, though, in emphasising the historical veracity as well as the poetic reference of the gospels: 'Only once did myth ever become fact and that was when the Word became flesh, when God became a man...the summing up and actuality of them all.'[21] By understanding the gospel simultaneously as myth and history, Lewis renders the reference of the biblical text somewhat more complex than the distinction between 'first' and 'second' order reference that Ricoeur postulates: the hope to which joy entices, and the appetite which myth whets, is underwritten by a divine mythology, penetrating history, and assuring that while 'now we see in a mirror dimly,' we will then see, 'face to face' (1 Corinthians 13:12). In the light of the Prologue to the Fourth Gospel (John 1:1-18), all of created reality is 'ontologically worded,' the incarnation is the decisive event which reveals what the whole story has been about. 'To be 'unstoried' is to live in a world without windows. With the fading of the biblical drama, we are shut out to the transcendent and shut up in triviality. We have no Word from beyond to set all others in an eternal grammar of meaning.'[22]

Myth is the term that Lewis uses to describe the quality of literature that provides such intimations of transcendence, which break into the relative smallness of an empirical, naturalistic mindset, with the sense of something greater, more beautiful, eternal. As the earlier reference to *The Pilgrim's Regress* shows, it is the imagination that is able best to apprehend or 'taste' such glimpses of the numinous; a method of perceiving reality (through the use of metaphor) that is prior to rational thought, the essential precondition to reaching any understanding of truth:

> it must not be supposed that I am in any sense putting forward the imagination as the organ of truth. We are not talking of truth, but of meaning: meaning which is the antecedent condition both of truth and falsehood, whose antithesis is not error but nonsense....Imagination, producing new metaphors or revivifying old, is not the cause of truth, but its condition. It is, I confess, undeniable that such a view indirectly implies a kind of truth or rightness in the imagination itself. I said at the outset that the truth we won by metaphor could not be greater than the truth of the metaphor itself; and we have seen since that all our truth, or all but a few

---

[20] C. S. Lewis, "The Pilgrim's Regress," *C. S. Lewis: Selected Books* (London: HarperCollins, 2002), 190.

[21] Cited in Clyde S. Kilby, *The Christian World of C. S. Lewis* (Grand Rapids: Eerdmans, 1964), 156.

[22] Eugene Peterson cited by Dennis, "*Sehnsucht* and the Island Motif in C. S. Lewis' *Out of the Silent* Planet and *Perelandra*," 60.

fragments, is won by metaphor...it does follow that if our thinking is ever true, then the metaphors by which we think must have been good metaphors.[23]

While it is evident that Lewis sees metaphor (and to some extent myth also) as the essential precondition of all thought and perception, he defines myth in a more particular sense as a type of story with an extra-literary component, which is detected by its effect upon certain readers: '[i]t is not so much that they receive a message, but rather that they seem to have a fleeting contact with some remote unbroken world, one in which..."the silence is broken only to shout the Truth."'[24] The uniqueness and value of myth is that it offers a partial solution to the antithesis that 'we murder to dissect': 'we come nearest to experiencing as a concrete what can otherwise be understood only as an abstraction.'[25] In a sense, myth is a form of reference or experiential truth, which remains ambivalently poised between Ricoeur's two kinds of 'truth,' surpassed only in its ultimate exemplification, the incarnation: 'What flows into you from the myth is not truth but reality (truth is always about something, but reality is that about which truth is), and, therefore, every myth becomes the father of innumerable truths on the abstract level.'[26] The structural parallel between the part that Lewis attributes to metaphor in all thought, and myth in all truth, is obvious: in both, the imagination plays a crucial epistemological role.

Finally, though, the most important dimension, for Lewis, of both myth and imagination, is their eschatological orientation, which he explores in great detail under the rubric of Joy. The centrality of this theme to his life and thought can be amply demonstrated by the fact that he uses it as the unifying motif in his autobiography, *Surprised By Joy*. However, the most cogent and lyrical definition of Joy is found in another sermon, 'The Weight of Glory,' which potently expresses also the apologetic dimension of his dialectic of desire:

> In speaking of this desire for our own far-off country, which we find in ourselves even now, I feel a certain shyness....I am trying to rip open the inconsolable secret in each one of you...which pierces with such sweetness....We cannot tell it because it is a desire for something that has never actually appeared in our experience....The books or the music in which we thought the beauty was located will betray us if we trust to them; it was not in them, it only came through them, and what came through them was longing...they are not the thing itself; they are

---

[23] Lewis, "Bluspels and Flalansferes," 157-8.
[24] Rolland Hein, *Christian Mythmakers: C. S. Lewis, Madeleine L'Engle, J. R. R. Tolkien, George Macdonald, G. K. Chesterton, Charles Williams, John Bunyan, Walter Wangerin, Robert Siegel, and Hannah Hurnard* (Chicago: Cornerstone Press, 1998), 9. The quotation is taken from Flannery O'Connor.
[25] Lewis, "Myth Became Fact," 140.
[26] Lewis, "Myth Became Fact," 141.

only the scent of a flower we have not found, the echo of a tune we have not heard, news from a country we have never yet visited. Do you think I am trying to weave a spell? Perhaps I am; but remember your fairy tales. Spells are used for breaking enchantments as well as for inducing them.[27]

The reference to fairy tales is deliberate, highlighting the crucial role that story and myth play in gesturing towards the transcendent. But this longing does not have to be interpreted according to the teleological fulfilment that Lewis ascribes to it: Frank Kermode, following Franz Kafka, suggests that we can only live in perpetual uncertainty at the door of eternity, the best we can attain to are fictions that console our hunger for an eschatological certainty that gives meaning to human mortality; Derrida would maintain the structure of messianic expectation as the essence of religion, whilst denying all images that attempt to convey something of its imminent presence.[28] Lewis parts company, on the basis of biblical revelation. While he acknowledges the limited nature, and ultimate insufficiency of all images, both of God and heaven, as seen earlier in the summary of 'Transposition,' for him creation and history are given ultimate meaning through the historical event of the incarnation, attested to in Scripture. Such a foundation is necessary as these 'romantic longings cannot long be cherished and maintained in isolation from an ontology which provides a satisfactory frame for them.'[29] This unique concept of myth, realised in history, witnessed to by the presence of *Sehnsucht* in the human heart, supplements the general creation-based passion for the possible which Ricoeur's philosophy outlines, and illuminates the relationship between biblical teleology and imagination as it works structurally through metaphor and myth.

Narrative, Metaphor and Imagination in *Till We Have Faces*

Lewis's final novel, *Till We Have Faces*, may appear at first glance an odd choice for the discussion of biblical themes, given that it is less overtly didactic and apologetic than any of his other fictional works. However, despite its pagan setting, this signals a greater confidence in the power of the imagination to convey truth to the reader and a more consummate mastery of the relationship between message and story realised in myth, rather than any change in his overall purpose in writing.[30] In this novel Lewis takes the classical Greek tale of Cupid and Psyche, as narrated by Apuleius in *The Golden Ass*, and creatively transforms it, by narrating events from the first-person perspective of one of

---

[27] Lewis, "The Weight of Glory," 98-9.
[28] Ferretter, *Towards a Christian Literary Theory*, 30-35; Frank Kermode, *The Sense of an Ending: Studies in the Theory of Fiction* (New York: Oxford University Press, 1967), 3-31, 40, 144, 173.
[29] White, *The Image of Man in C. S. Lewis*, 113.
[30] Peter J. Schakel, *Reason and Imagination in C. S. Lewis: A Study of 'Till We Have Faces'* (Grand Rapids: Eerdmans, 1984), 88-182.

Psyche's sisters. In the process, he weaves into the story many of the themes and preoccupations that can be traced throughout his career including Joy, hope, sanctification through suffering, the nature of divine love as both jealous and irresistible, the necessity of a link between sacrifice and reason (or the concrete and abstract) at the centre of reality, and the teleological framework that reflects a providential directing in the lives of individuals and the history of the world.[31] These thematic concerns are saturated in the biblical perspective that governed Lewis's thought and work, coming through implicitly in his personal narration of the ancient Greek myth. The juxtaposition of narrative and metaphor provides a literary framework through which he structurally articulates many such ideas. Orual (the narrator) comes to self-knowledge through writing the story of her life as a case against the gods; her sense of justice compels a rewriting that transmutes the entire book into a testimony which has affinities with the genre of conversion narratives.[32] This section will explore the biblical themes in the text, particularly its eschatological orientation, and the understanding of imagination implicit in its fictional form.[33]

Perhaps the most overtly biblical aspect of *Till We Have Faces* is its teleological framework, starkly at odds with classical pagan concepts of time and history.[34] The trajectory of the narrative is precipitated and driven by the raw frustration of Orual, the central character, at the alleged injustice of the gods, and her commitment to an honest self-examination as she tells the story of her life:

> I am old now and have not much to fear from the anger of gods....I will accuse the gods, especially the god who lives on the Grey Mountain. That is, I will tell all he has done to me from the very beginning, as if I were making my complaint of him before a judge....Perhaps [the Greeks'] wise men will know whether my complaint is right or whether the god could have defended himself if he had made an answer (3-4).[35]

---

[31] For an interpretation of this as rooted in the 'tradition' of the Israelites see Tomoo Ishida, *History and Historical Writing in Ancient Israel*, Studies in Biblical Historiography (Leiden: Brill, 1999), 1-5; Noel Weeks outlines the central dynamic of biblical history, dependent upon its openness to God acting in the future, as expressed in the scriptural pattern of divine promise and fulfilment in *Gateway to the Old Testament* (Edinburgh: Banner of Truth Trust, 1995), 3-70.

[32] Mara Donaldson, *Holy Places Are Dark Places: C. S. Lewis and Paul Ricoeur on Narrative Transformation* (Lanham: University Press of America, 1988), xv-xxii.

[33] For a theological exploration of the relationship between eschatology and its transformation of the present see Trevor Hart and Richard Bauckham, *Hope against Hope*.

[34] R. G. Collingwood, *The Idea of History* (London: Oxford University Press, 1970), 14-52.

[35] C. S. Lewis, *Till We Have Faces* (San Diego: Harcourt, 1956). All subsequent citations are from this edition.

The first-person narrative voice, the retrospective nature of the account, the sense of need for a personal relationship between human individuals and the divine are signalled right from the beginning. Orual is searching for justice, the nature of her account presupposes the possibility of a rational explanation for the events in her life; this sense of divine patterning is biblical, it does not follow the cyclical concept of history that informed pagan culture.[36] Orual's account is divided into two parts: the first section is basically a linear narration of her coming of age in the small barbarian kingdom of Glome; the command given by the Priest of Ungit that her beloved sister Psyche be sacrificed to the gods for the well-being of the land; her reiterated grievance that she never received any reasonable evidence to prove that the god her sister longed for, loved and knew, was real; and finally, her just and competent rule of Glome following the death of her father.

However, Orual begins to encounter the unexplored depths of the self that she has struggled to put to death in her public role as queen through the very process of writing. She becomes open to other stories, aware of other readings of her life, memory is awakened and events she suppressed in her case against the gods come flooding back, undercutting her self-righteous stance and undoing her sense of self. Just before her death she begins part two of the text:

> Since I cannot mend the book, I must add to it. To leave it as it was would be to die perjured; I know so much more than I did about the woman who wrote it....The change which the writing wrought in me (and of which I did not write) was only a beginning – only to prepare me for the gods' surgery. They used my own pen to probe my wound (253-4).

This sense of accountability before the gods, of divine intervention leading to self-understanding, of circumstances sanctifying the individual and leading inexorably to a personal encounter with the Divine Being, as the ultimate purpose of existence and definition of reality is biblical rather than pagan (Psalm 139:23-24; John 17:3; Colossians 1:15-20). Its structure, as noted before, has a greater affinity with the conversion narratives of Augustine, John Bunyan and countless others, than the religious life and experience even of initiates of the Greek mystery religions in the pagan world a century or so prior to Christ.[37] For it is not only self-examination that leads Orual to question her reading of events, but also the prods to her conscience provided by a meeting with the eunuch Tarin, lover of her other sister, Redival; an encounter with the

---

[36] Collingwood, *The Idea of History*, 14-52; Kevin Mills, *Justifying Language: Paul and Contemporary Literary Theory* (New York: St. Martin's Press, 1995), 82.

[37] Peter Brown, *The World of Late Antiquity: From Marcus Aurelius to Muhammad* (London: Thames & Hudson, 1971), 63, 65-8; Everett Ferguson, *Backgrounds of Early Christianity* (Grand Rapids: Eerdmans, 1987), 237-40; Corbin Scott Carnell, *Bright Shadow of Reality: C. S. Lewis and the Feeling Intellect* (Grand Rapids: Eerdmans, 1974), 88, 116, 158-9.

Intimations of Transcendence 181

wife of her trusted servant, Bardia, who makes Orual aware of the self-centered voraciousness of her love. Finally, and most devastatingly, she realises that her love for Psyche was of the same nature, she is ugly within and without, incapable of transforming herself and this too is 'a stroke from without.'[38]

A tension runs throughout the entire narrative, centering upon the way events are read, what is perceived, akin to the biblical distinction between 'faith' and 'sight.'[39] Psyche represents the former, what Lewis called 'an instance of the *anima naturaliter Christiana*,'[40] longing for union with the gods from birth, willingly acquiescing in the necessity of sacrifice, delighting in the presence and palace of her divine lover, and filled with the strength of selfless love that comes from obedience to the divine will. Orual, however, lives by sight. Like her Greek tutor, the Fox, she is notionally committed to a concept of truth that will only accept what can be verified empirically and rationally. But, as the narrative unfolds, progressing inexorably to an encounter with the god she has denied, Orual reveals that her attachment to Greek rationalism masks an unwillingness to acknowledge various experiences and encounters, as these would entail relinquishing control of her own life and a remaking of the self in relation to the divine.[41] Psyche's response to her demand that she disobey her husband exposes the self-love and voracious affection that motivates Orual's intellectual commitment to rationalism:

> You are indeed teaching me about kinds of love I did not know. It is like looking into a deep pit. I am not sure whether I like your kind better than hatred. Oh, Orual – to take my love for you, because you know it goes down to my very roots and cannot be diminished by any other newer love, and then to make of it a tool...an instrument of torture – I begin to think I never knew you (165).

This kind of self-knowledge, where patterns of thought are traced back to the desires of the heart, is biblical and Augustinian (Psalm 14:1; Colossians 1:21-22), echoing the cries of the Hebrew psalmists as, confronted by God, they desired and came to a true knowledge of themselves: 'Search me, O God, and

---

[38] Lewis deals with the theological dimension of natural and divine loves in *The Four Loves* (London: Fontana Books, 1963).
[39] Jeff McInnis explores the counterpoint between faith and doubt in *Till We Have Faces* in *Shadows and Chivalry: C. S. Lewis and George MacDonald on Suffering, Evil, and Goodness* (Milton Keynes: Paternoster, 2007), 68-76.
[40] Letter to Clyde S. Kilby, 10 February 1957, from W. H. Lewis, ed., *Letters of C. S. Lewis* (New York: Harcourt Brace Jovanovich, 1966), 273-4.
[41] Hein, *Christian Mythmakers*, 248-9. Mervin Lee Ziegler defines this distinction in terms of a contrast between the 'horror of holiness' and the 'beauty of holiness.' Lewis thus requires his readers to contemplate two possible approaches to the Desirable Other. Mervin Lee Ziegler, "Imagination as a Rhetorical Factor in the Works of C. S. Lewis," (PhD Thesis, University of Florida, 1973), 113. See also Revelation 6:15-17; Psalm 27:4 for examples of these two responses to encounters with God.

know my heart! Try me and know my thoughts! And see if there be any grievous way in me, and lead me in the way everlasting' (139:23-24).

It is also inextricably connected to the eschatological orientation of the narrative. As Orual comes to a true knowledge of herself through the writing of part one, this generates the second part of *Till We Have Faces*, which is a rewriting of the first section. However, part two does not proceed chronologically; rather the gaps and absences of her original account are filled in, through dreams, visions and the voices of others.[42] Layer after layer of Orual's carefully constructed public persona, symbolised by the veil she wears, is stripped away. Finally she comes to an end of herself and her life, positioned liminally between time and eternity: 'Die before you die. There is no chance after' (279). This is a direct echo of the teaching of Jesus: 'Whoever finds his life will lose it, and whoever loses his life for my sake will find it' (Matthew 10:39). Orual can only understand her life and self truly in relation to the divine nature whose existence she has explicitly denied, and implicitly recognised all her life. Once all the rationalisations have been abandoned, she hears herself speaking in her true voice:

> We want to be our own. I was my own and Psyche was mine and no one else had any right to her. Oh, you'll say you took her away into bliss and joy such as I could never have given her, and I ought to have been glad of it for her sake. Why? What should I care for some horrible, new happiness which I hadn't given her and which separated her from me? (291-2).

It is here, as Orual recognises her true nature, that she encounters the divine, and the providential threads of her life come together in a pattern of repentance and joyous anticipation, that echoes the apocalypse of Revelation, and situates the narrative of her life in terms of the biblical intertext that establishes the framework for reality as a whole within Lewis's fiction: 'I saw well why the gods do not speak to us openly, nor let us answer....How can they meet us face to face till we have faces?....Joy silenced me. And I thought I had now come to the highest...which the human soul can contain. But now, what was this?...."He is coming," they said' (294, 306-7). It is the biblical text which provides the prototype and explication: 'Beloved, we are God's children now, and what we will be has not yet appeared; but we know that when he appears we shall be like him, because we shall see him as he is. And everyone who thus hopes in him purifies himself as he is pure' (1 John 3:2-3).

Till We Have Faces presents the narrative of a pilgrim, who comes to a true understanding of herself through writing a first-person testimony, where the temporal is reconfigured in the light of eternity and the Divine Nature at the heart of reality: the biblical themes of sanctification, hope and ultimate purpose come sharply into focus, despite the pagan context which is the ostensible

---

[42] Donaldson, *Holy Places are Dark Places*, 7-10, 67-82.

setting for this realistic novel. There is a danger that the historical setting will be dismissed as extraneous to the 'essence' of the text in such a reading of the novel, but that would be a grave injustice to Lewis's artistic achievement. 'Myth' is a concept of great significance to Lewis and its inclusion in the subtitle, 'A Myth Retold,' indicates integral links between the pagan context and the implicit biblical themes, orientation and narrative structure of the text. The term 'myth' encapsulates for Lewis the most desirable quality of a literary work. It is not intrinsic to a particular genre, but rather a sense of the numinous suggested by certain novels, plays and poems, that depends also to some extent upon the receptivity and experience of the individual reader.[43]

Myth was of such significance to Lewis and crucial to the integration between pagan stories and the gospel accounts of the incarnation, firstly, because a recognition of these affinities was instrumental in bringing him to faith in Christ. He saw the biblical writings as the supreme fulfilment of the various pagan mythologies of the dying god, Balder, Osiris and so on, with this crucial distinction that Jesus Christ was God's mythology, the moment when myth occurred in history; a divine intervention reconfiguring and fulfilling all that had gone before.[44] In this sense, reading the myth of Cupid and Psyche in the light of the gospel account, fits into the general pattern by which Lewis understood pagan mythologies in relation to Scripture. This myth had been 'thickening and hardening' in his mind for decades, it was only in his fifties that the right form for expression came to him, 'the central alteration in my own version consists in making Psyche's palace invisible to normal, mortal eyes – if 'making' is not the wrong word for something which forced itself on me, almost at the first reading of the story, as the way the thing must have been...and finally modifies the quality of the whole tale' (313).

Secondly, myth played a crucial aesthetic function for Lewis, with a correlative spiritual dimension: it is the means by which human beings are best able to experience the abstract and other in concrete terms, to 'taste' reality. Just as the incarnation fuses the necessity of sacrifice with the clarity of reason, represented in this novel by the barbarian priest of Ungit and the Greek Fox respectively; so myth fuses the universal and the particular.

> In the enjoyment of a great myth we come nearest to experiencing as a concrete what can otherwise be understood only as an abstraction....What flows into you from the myth is not truth but reality (truth is always about something, but reality is that about which truth is).[45]

When Lewis gives this novel the subtitle 'a myth retold,' he thus indicates that the tale originally narrated by Apuleius is carrying significant meaning. In

---

[43] Lewis, ed, *George Macdonald*; Lewis, *An Experiment in Criticism*, 40-9.
[44] Lewis, "Myth Became Fact," 141.
[45] Lewis, "Myth Became Fact," 140-1.

terms of Lewis's recontextualisation of pagan mythology, (a kind of secular analogue to the model of historical reinterpretation found in the New Testament), it can only be fully understood in the light of the incarnation, which 'transcends myth.' But also, in 'making his own version' of this particular myth, Lewis seeks to provide his readers with a 'taste' of that 'reality about which truth is.' As it is not an allegory like his earlier work, *The Pilgrim's Regress*, there is no simple one-to-one correspondence between characters and ideas,[46] but the themes that inform all his work are most effectively and aesthetically 'incarnated' in this historical novel. Myth, for Lewis, was not rooted in any particular literary form, but was rather a quality of the narrative as a whole, a work which enables the reader to experience 'the numinous' in Rudolph Otto's famous phrase, providing a glimpse of eternity in the shadows of time:[47] 'For now we see in a mirror dimly, but then face to face. Now I know in part; then I shall know fully, even as I have been fully known' (1 Corinthians 13:12).

The character who embodies this desire or Joy which suggests eschatological anticipation in *Till We Have Faces* is Psyche, Orual's youngest sister. For Lewis, the presence of 'desire for our own far-off country' in the human heart is a strong argument 'that such a thing exists and some' will enjoy it. His apologetics generally centre around this dialectic of desire, which is Augustinian, Platonic and biblical, assuming that since none of the beautiful things which this world offers can satisfy the desire in our hearts, which Lewis terms Joy, that there must be a reality beyond this natural world.

> We want so much more...the poets and the mythologies know all about it....We want something else which can hardly be put into words – to be united with the beauty we see...to become part of it...all the leaves of the New Testament are rustling with the rumour that....Some day, God willing, we shall get in.[48]

Till We Have Faces is the only one of Lewis's works in which an individual character embodies this poignant longing.[49] Ever since she was a little girl, Psyche has spoken of a golden palace where she will reign as consort to a god: it was at moments of happiness, rather than misery that she longed for this most. In fact, it is this hope that sustains her through the pain and fear of being sacrificed on the mountain to the Brute, or Shadow-Beast, since 'devouring and loving' are the same thing for the gods. She paced in the chamber on the eve of her death, saying to Orual:

---

[46] C. S. Lewis, *Allegory of Love: A Study in Medieval Tradition* (Oxford: Oxford University Press, 1936), 45-8.
[47] Lewis, ed, *George Macdonald,* "Introduction"; Lewis, *An Experiment in Criticism*, 40-9; Hein, *Christian Mythmakers*, 9; White, *The Image of Man in C. S. Lewis*, 37.
[48] "The Weight of Glory", 104.
[49] Carnell, *Bright Shadow of Reality*, 116.

> Do you remember? The colour and the smell, and looking across at the Grey Mountain in the distance? And because it was so beautiful, it set me longing, always longing. Somewhere else there must be more of it. Everything seemed to be saying, Psyche come! But I couldn't (not yet) come and I didn't know where I was to come to. It almost hurt me. I felt like a bird in a cage when the other birds of its kind are flying home (74).

This picks up on the longing for eternity that fills the pages and shapes the teleology of the New Testament, most notably, of course, in Revelation: 'But, as it is written, "What no eye has seen, nor ear heard, nor the heart of man imagined, what God has prepared for those who love him"' (1 Corinthians 2:9). Interestingly, it is this eschatological expectation, this captivity by faith to divine desire, which most radically separates Psyche from Orual and causes all the jealousy of the latter, turning her love for Psyche 'almost to hatred' and preventing her from delighting in the divine invitation to 'taste and see' (Psalm 34:8), until the end of her long life. Here Lewis is returning to an Augustinian theme that runs through many of his writings and which he treats in depth in *The Four Loves*: any natural human affection turns rank and despotic when it is not regulated and leavened by a supreme love and desire for God; the biblical allusion to the Golden Rule is self-evident.[50]

In attempting to convey both the quality of this expectation, the distinctive character of the Divine Nature (which is far more biblical than pagan) and the sense of an entire order of reality beyond that which can be perceived or explained in the light of Greek rationalism, Lewis balances the linear chronology of Orual's narrative, as we have seen, with the surreal dream-visions of part two. This is further modified, as Mara Donaldson observes, by a dependence on key metaphors, which reconfigure the narrative structure of the text. She identifies two. One is found in the significant words of the priest of Ungit as he responds to the Fox's charge that his account of the 'devouring' and 'loving' of the god is incoherent and therefore false:

> We are hearing much Greek wisdom this morning, King....[It does not] give them understanding of holy things. They demand to see such things clearly, as if the gods were no more than letters written in a book....I know that they dazzle our eyes and flow in and out of one another like eddies on a river, and nothing that is said clearly can be said truly about them. Holy places are dark places. It is life and strength, not knowledge and words, that we get in them. Holy wisdom is not clear and thin like water, but thick and dark like blood (50).

The metaphor is encapsulated in the phrase: 'Holy places are dark places.' Whilst narrative encourages a teleologically orientated understanding of the past, present and future, the logic of metaphor is a reminder that the past and future impinge upon the present in important ways, as in Donaldson's second

---

[50] Lewis, *The Four Loves*, see especially 107-28.

key metaphor, where the god tells Orual, 'You also shall be Psyche.' Temporality itself is challenged, as metaphor provides a means of conveying or 'transposing' something of the eternal present of that other world into Orual's understanding of her current situation.[51]

The closest Lewis came to actually developing a theory of the imagination was in exploring this metaphorical logic and its unique capacity to mediate between our present order of reality and the sense of something greater and higher, which we experience, 'taste,' but cannot truly describe, suggested primarily by the ever-present desire (or Joy) referred to earlier. Again, this interpenetration of the temporal by the eternal, realised linguistically through metaphor, and apprehended by an imagination captive to faith, is modelled upon the example of the biblical text.[52] Numerous examples can be cited, but the classic text is found in Hebrews 11, listing the heroes of faith who walked as 'strangers and exiles on the earth':

> These all died in faith, not having received the things promised, but having seen them and greeted them from afar...For people who speak thus make it clear that they are seeking a homeland. If they had been thinking of that land from which they had gone out, they would have had opportunity to return. But as it is, they desire a better country, that is, a heavenly one. Therefore God is not ashamed to be called their God; for he has prepared for them a city (vv. 13-16).

The logic of metaphor works both ways. As Donaldson argues, Orual understands her present and future in the light of a metaphorical prophecy uttered by the god in her past, 'You also shall be Psyche.' But, eschatological anticipation of the future, expressed through the metaphor of 'the city that has foundations, whose designer and builder is God' (v. 10), and presaged by the aching desire for something more, cause Psyche and the biblical pilgrims to understand themselves in the present as 'exiles and strangers' seeking their true country, when they would see 'face to face' and 'know fully' just as they 'have been fully known' (1 Corinthians 13:12).

In *Till We Have Faces* Lewis is willing for the first time in his career as a writer of fiction to trust the imagination as a means of conveying and receiving truth. For Lewis, myth is the means by which literature conveys 'reality, that about which truth is,' and this is apprehended by imagination, rather than reason. Many of his other works, preeminently *Perelandra* and 'The Chronicles of Narnia,' have something of the quality he defines as myth, but there remains a latent distrust of imagination, evidenced by the fact that he feels it necessary to appeal to reason through a didactic framework, or narratorial interpolations.[53] This final novel represents a fusion of the historical and aesthetic dimensions which he attributed to myth in his theoretical writings, realised artistically. He

---

[51] Donaldson, *Holy Places are Dark Places*, 91-6.
[52] Lewis, "Transposition," 267-78.
[53] Schakel, *Reason and Imagination in C. S. Lewis*, ix-xii.

remains faithful to the plotline of the classical myth which is the 'source' of his own tale, but he draws out its full potential in the light of the incarnation, as recorded in biblical revelation, which he believed transcended pagan mythologies. This is primarily evidenced in the eschatological orientation of the text, conveyed through the character of Psyche who desperately longs 'to reach the Mountain, to find the place where all the beauty came from...' (75). Orual's path is more complex, through faithful self-examination and divine providence, enacted structurally at the level of a first-person narrative and dream-visions, she gradually comes to a true understanding of herself, and the inexorable, jealous, ecstatic nature of divine love, drawing her into union with the Person at the centre of reality. The teleological trajectory of the linear narrative is rendered more complex through the transpositional logic of metaphor, as Lewis follows the biblical model, in order to provide 'glimpses of eternity.' *Till We Have Faces* is an invitation to taste imaginatively those realities which lie beyond the borders of the temporal world; 'Nature is only the image, the symbol; but it is the symbol Scripture invites me to use. We are summoned to pass in through Nature, beyond her, into that splendour which she fitfully reflects.'[54]

Lewis on the Imagination that 'Tastes and Sees'

Lewis used the term 'imagination' in several ways, which, as Peter Schakel observes in detail, altered over the course of his lifetime. 'Imagination' can mean therefore, depending on context, wish-fulfilling fantasies, the lower level artistic imagination (drawing on Coleridgean terms) denoting conscious invention, and imagination in the highest sense (that is the Primary Imagination). This latter type includes both the 'poetic imagination', the 'organic or intuitive power needed to write...both mythic fiction and great lyric poetry,' and Joy. This final term had a poignant significance for Lewis; his writings on the subject generally imbue it with a primarily eschatological orientation.

> Joy is imaginative in that it makes nonlogical (or superlogical) connections between outer and inner events, or between events in the present and the past. It is imaginative in that it is often set in motion by literature or music, which are the products of the imagination; it involves being transported beyond the physical and emotional to a rapturous state that could take place only in the imagination at an inspired level, and it usually depends on memory...as a remembered experience triggers a longing not for the past but for something of which a past experience is a symbol.[55]

---

[54] Lewis, "The Weight of Glory," 104-5.
[55] Peter J. Schakel, *Imagination and the Arts in C. S. Lewis: Journeying to Narnia and Other Worlds* (Columbia: University of Missouri Press, 2003), 5-8.

As noted earlier, Lewis used this theme as the organising motif of his autobiography, *Surprised by Joy*. He writes, 'I mean here only my life as concerned with Joy,' defined as 'the imaginative longing for Joy, or rather the longing which was Joy.'[56] Schakel conjectures that it was through the process of writing a personal account of his life that Lewis became aware of the problems that characterised his previous opposition between the perceiving self and objective reality. This allowed him, for the first time, to attribute a positive role to the inevitably subjective involvement of the individual in all acts of interpretation and communication. Previously he had seen this as an impediment it was necessary to try and overcome by positing an impossible kind of *kenosis*. *Till We Have Faces*, however, enacts in a Gadamerian kind of fashion the positive valence of 'prejudice.' The narrative is written as a personal autobiography, the same form as *Surprised By Joy*, and the self-reflexive nature of this style has a salutary effect upon the epistemological attitude of Orual, becoming the means by which she attains a true knowledge of herself and God.[57]

However, Lewis's myth does what his autobiography cannot, it not only provides a concrete 'taste' of Joy, which occurs often throughout his writings, it also embodies the paradoxical dialectic that characterises Joy in its artistic structure. This dialectic is engendered by a biblical understanding of time and eternity: the juxtaposition of creation and apocalypse; the command to be 'in the world, but not of the world.' It is a particular instance of the more general contrast informing *Till We Have Faces*, which was explored in an earlier section, namely the difference in interpreting reality by 'faith' or by 'sight.' This difference is initially represented through the distinction between Psyche and Orual, though the gap closes as Orual's reading of her experience is reconfigured in the light of an encounter with the divine. Psyche from the very first is wrung by longings, an agonising lack coupled with insatiable yearnings that project her beyond the temporal circumstances that constitute her reality at the moments when she is most happy.

This is identical to the experiences of Joy that Lewis describes minutely in his own autobiography, intimations of transcendence, or in the words of Jürgen Moltmann, 'the unquiet heart...the goad of the promised future' that 'stabs inexorably into the flesh of every unfulfilled present.'[58] It is in the context of anatomising as far as possible this experience of Joy that Lewis describes it as what 'the word imagination in...the highest sense of all' denotes. For him personally, it was first evoked 'by the memory of a memory,' the smell of a

---

[56] Lewis cited by Schakel, *Imagination and the Arts in C. S. Lewis*, 8.
[57] Schakel, *Reason and Imagination in C. S. Lewis*, 157-62.
[58] Jürgen Moltmann cited by Trevor Hart, "Imagination for the Kingdom of God? Hope, Promise, and the Transformative Power of an Imagined Future," *God Will Be All in All: The Eschatology of Jurgen Moltmann*, ed. Richard Bauckham (Edinburgh: T & T Clark, 1999), 62.

currant bush on a summer day, which reminded him of a toy garden in the nursery that had set him longing. 'It was a sensation, of course, of desire; but desire for what?...and before I knew what I desired, the desire itself was gone, the whole glimpse withdrawn, the world turned commonplace again, or only stirred by a longing for the longing that had just ceased. It had taken only a moment of time; and in a certain sense everything else that had ever happened to me was insignificant in comparison....something..."in another dimension."'[59] The Beatrix Potter books, Longfellow's *Saga of King Olaf*, Wagner's operas, these and many other things acted as the catalyst in Lewis's own life, forming the autobiographical basis for his characterisation of Psyche, with her sensitivity to incidents that gestured towards a realm of transcendence.

Orual, however, is initially walking by 'sight,' deliberately suppressing a reading of her temporal existence as exile, which comes naturally to Psyche.[60] In making this choice she is governed by self-centred fear: she wants to have her sister entirely to herself, caught in perpetual dependence. She is also afraid, sensing that the wager on transcendence may turn her into the senseless dupe of malicious divinities who offer false hopes only to dash them to the ground. Orual designates the grim stoicism with which she faces her world, seeking to destroy her individuality through adopting a public persona and put to death all memories of her sister, as a rational 'realistic' response to temporal reality: this is all there is. Lewis's indictment of the self-centred pride that lies at the root of such a choice against hope is a stringent theological critique of a human pose that has been glossed heroically again and again by the modern (and postmodern) imagination. Ursula Le Guin writes somewhat caustically about the way in which evil and pain are seen to be more 'interesting' and true to life than beauty and hope:

> The trouble is that we have a bad habit...of considering happiness as something rather stupid. Only pain is intellectual, only evil is interesting. This is the treason of the artist: a refusal to admit the banality of evil and the terrible boredom of pain....But to praise despair is to condemn delight, to embrace violence is to lose hold of everything else. We have almost lost hold; we can no longer describe a happy man, nor make any celebration of joy.[61]

However, as noted earlier, the process of writing causes Orual to begin to read her experience differently. Instead of affirming stridently that the gods sent riddling clues that could never enlighten, she begins to take an attitude of trust. The implicit 'faith' that characterised Psyche, seemingly from her birth, prompts Orual to reconfigure her life-experience. The intimations of

---

[59] C. S. Lewis, *Surprised by Joy: The Shape of My Early Life* (Glasgow: HarperCollins, 1955), 18-19.
[60] Hein, *Christian Mythmakers*, 238-9.
[61] Ursula Le Guin, "The Ones Who Walk Away from Omelas," *The Wind's Twelve Quarters* (New York: Harper & Row, 1975).

transcendence that she had previously rationalised or dismissed as maliciously cryptic riddles, she understands as glimpses of eternity in a moment of time, which she chose to suppress. In old age, as she opens herself to the past, she becomes vulnerable and in this lies her potential salvation. Lewis observes in a theological work written just prior to his novel: 'To love at all is to be vulnerable. Love anything, and your heart will certainly be wrung and possibly be broken. If you want to make sure of keeping it intact....Wrap it carefully...avoid all entanglements; lock it up safe in the casket or coffin of your selfishness...it will become unbreakable, impenetrable, irredeemable. The alternative to tragedy, or at least to the risk of tragedy, is damnation.'[62]

The second part of the novel delineates Orual's vision of her life, reconfigured by an apprehension of Joy. This complicates rather than simplifies the reality she has been and is experiencing, because it is truer to the eternal dimensions of temporal existence than her prior commitment to a reductive stoicism. She becomes caught in the paradox that had governed Psyche's life, radically separating her from Orual's temporally bound 'sight' on the Grey Mountain, and providing her with a curious energy and courage when the command was given that she be sacrificed for the well-being of Glome. Moltmann again helps here by showing the specifically biblical paradox and eschatology that underlies Psyche's delight in the created world, suffering, self-sacrifice and irrepressible hope:

> ...[D]o the apocalyptic contradiction and the messianic correspondence of the kingdom of God to the conditions of this world constitute mutually exclusive ideas?...apocalyptic sects which cut themselves off from 'the wicked world,' and modern Christians who want to keep up with every movement of 'the spirit of the age'....Again and again there have been times when the people of God have been persecuted, and martyrdom has been enjoined. Then nothing more is possible in history...all that remains is the sole decision: to confess or to deny....Yet again and again there have also been, and are, times of open doors....Then we stand face to face with almost unlimited possibilities...the kingdom of God is at hand....Then hope turns into action, and we already anticipate today something of the new creation of all things which Christ will complete on his day.[63]

The taste of this Joy is paradoxical in essence; it defines temporal existence as a place of exile, separating a person from their true home. However, the promised paradise of which Joy is a foretaste simultaneously incorporates and therefore ascribes value to this present world which will also be transformed, for 'the creation itself will be set free from its bondage to decay and obtain the freedom of the glory of the children of God' (Romans 8:21).

---

[62] Lewis, *The Four Loves*, 111-12.
[63] Jurgen Moltmann, "Hope and Reality: Contradiction and Correspondence," *God Will Be All in All: The Eschatology of Jurgen Moltmann*, ed. Richard Bauckham (Edinburgh: T & T Clark, 1999), 84-5.

Orual begins to understand her present in the light of an openness to the future that is dependent upon hope in a transcendent God, in other words to walk 'by faith'. This transforms her previous experience of temporal reality as a cryptic emptiness into a condition of exile shot through with the promise of change, as the Old Testament prophet testified, 'the desert shall...blossom as the rose' (Isaiah 35:1, KJV). Bradley Baurain has argued that the 'exiled imagination' is as biblical as 'the paradisal imagination' and while the latter 'yearns onward and upward' the former 'interacts primarily with the state of exile itself.'[64] The two though are not necessarily antithetical, and it is the strength of the biblical vision of reality (reflected in Lewis's novel) that it neither denies the pain, dislocation and ambiguities of the present, nor does it shut out experiences of joy and the sense of anticipation for utopia that has characterised human societies over the millennia. Biblical reality is neither naively optimistic, nor reductively pessimistic: it is true to the manifold complexities of temporality and transcendence. 'The paradisal imagination remembers the loss or envisions the destination, while for the Christian believer the exiled imagination is absorbed with the journey.'[65]

It is this biblical definition of the disjunction between a fallen world, renewal begun in time on the basis of the resurrection of Christ, and the promise of ultimate consummation that evokes Joy in the particular sense defined by Lewis, of a longing more precious than any fruition this side of death. It is the consciousness of lack, of exile, complemented by a hope against hope (Romans 4:18) that underwrites, circumscribes and compels Lewis and others to imagine biblically, that is with the freedom inspired by hope. Following the model of the New Testament, which affirms creation as good, yet acknowledges the necessity and hope of a 'new creation,' Lewis and Ricoeur underline the centrality of metaphor and narrative in intimating the transcendent dimensions that reconfigure temporal reality. The imagination fosters the creation and perception of metaphor, narrative and myth. Trevor Hart notes:

> [T]he discontinuity and incommensurability...renders imagination absolutely necessary as the mode or capacity relevant to eschatological expectation and statement....It is precisely imagination, the capacity which is able to take the known and to modify it in striking and unexpected ways, which offers us the opportunity to think beyond the limits of the given....[66]

Lewis follows the biblical model, providing an explication and taste of this imagination at work: 'for now we see in a mirror dimly, but then face to face.

---

[64] Bradley Baurain, "By the Rivers of Babylon We Weep: The Exiled Imagination," *Christianity and the Arts* May-July (1997), 12.
[65] Baurain, "By the Rivers of Babylon We Weep: The Exiled Imagination," 14.
[66] Hart, "Imagination for the Kingdom of God? Hope, Promise, and the Transformative Power of an Imagined Future," 75-6.

Now I know in part; then I shall know fully, even as I have been fully known' (1 Corinthians 13:12).

Chapter 8

Conclusion

Often general principles arise in the biblical text from the discussion of a specific issue, sometimes of local importance, which then becomes a point of departure for more broad-ranging inquiry. For example, Paul moves from the treatment of spiritual gifts to their role in the unity of the church (1 Corinthians 12); or from the matter of food presented to idols to a discussion of conscience and liberty (1 Corinthians 8). Such a methodological structure has shaped most of the chapters in this study of the imagination so far. Although the first chapters sketched a broad biblical framework for considering the imagination, subsequent chapters have reversed the direction of the inquiry into what it means to imagine biblically, by beginning with an aspect of this process and exploring it in relation to a specific text. Thus the nature of creativity; the realistic imagination and its role in relation to faith, God, self, language and others; morality, aesthetics and narrative; the danger of idolatry and the potential of the Romantic imagination; metaphor, myth and the hopeful orientation of an imagination open to the eschatological vision of Scripture, have all been touched upon in order to explore the complex and multifaceted nature of imagination understood from a biblical perspective.

In this final section I wish to focus closely upon the imagination itself once more, particularly considering the issue of the nature of this function biblically. Earlier it was seen that imagination, from a biblical perspective, is best understood in terms of the heart, which avoids the debate over whether imagination should be defined in terms of the image or word. Since the biblical text is a written document that simultaneously presents many powerful images – the prophets often 'see' the visions that we read (Nahum 1:1; Habakkuk 1:1) – it is worth exploring the relationship between word and image as it relates to the imagination in more detail. These issues will be treated by closely analysing a verse that has been cited repeatedly throughout this study, with which Paul concludes his famous paean to love in 1 Corinthians 13: 'For now we see in a mirror dimly, but then face to face. Now I know in part; then I shall know fully, even as I have been fully known' (v. 12). The Greek in this passage is unusual, rendered literally Paul's phrase yokes together both visual and verbal elements: 'now we see through a mirror in a riddle.' The implications of this juxtaposition will be treated theoretically, through reference to the work of Richard Eslinger, as they offer an avenue into the rich synthesis which the biblical text forges between narrative and image, providing a unique and fruitful understanding of the imagination.

I will then turn to a second passage, often considered to be exemplary and central to theological discussions of the imagination, that has not yet been dealt with in this study. It comes from 2 Samuel 12, where the prophet Nathan confronts David, king of Israel, over his adulterous liaison with Bathsheba and subsequent murder of her husband Uriah the Hittite. It is one of the rare occurrences when an explicit allegory appears in Scripture (see also Galatians 4:24). More pertinently though it demonstrates the central role that the biblical text ascribes to the imagination; underlining its powerful capacity to promote a true understanding of self, others and ultimately God. This example enables certain conclusions regarding a biblical understanding of the literary imagination to be drawn, as it models the use of fictional narrative in a scriptural context. It links together many of the diverse aspects of imagination that have been treated separately in various chapters so far, integrating them in a single, poignant account that summarises much that has been asserted concerning what it means to imagine according to the trajectories opened by the biblical text and how this relates to literature.

'Through a mirror in a riddle': The Visual/Verbal Imagination

The relationship between text and image is a complex one in theoretical discussions of the imagination. Paul's celebrated chapter on love in 1 Corinthians 13 ends with an analysis of the form of knowledge open to believers prior to the fullness of revelation and personal encounter at the *eschaton*: 'then face to face.' He characterises the mode of perception available in the present by juxtaposing a visual image with a verbal, 'now we see through a mirror in a riddle.' Not only is this ambivalent, it suggests that a biblical understanding of the imagination, 'the eyes of [the] heart' (Ephesians 1:18), requires a move beyond the traditional definition of this function in terms of the 'image' to a more multivalent perceptual model. The inadequacy of a simplistic opposition between text and image, privileging one at the expense of the other, or attempting to set up a dichotomy is revealed in Paul's paradoxical yoking of 'mirror' and 'riddle.'

The kind of biblical imagining that Paul notes characterises the situation of his readers prior to the second coming of Christ is similar to the biblical imagination evidenced by the authors of Ezekiel and Revelation, and this correlation enables a more general theoretical deduction to be made concerning what it means to imagine biblically in a literary context.[1]

---

[1] The long passages of narrative in Daniel make it something of an exception in biblical apocalyptic literature.

> John's work is highly unusual in the sheer prolific extent of its visual imagery....The proportion of visual symbolism in Revelation is greater than in almost any comparable apocalypse....[I]nterpretations are rare in Revelation (7:13-14; 17:6-18), whose visual symbols are so described as to convey their own meaning. The symbols can thus retain a surplus of meaning which any translation into literal terms runs the risk of reducing....

The power, the profusion and the consistency of the symbols have a literary-theological purpose. They create a symbolic world which readers can enter so fully that it affects them and changes their perception of the world. Most readers were originally, of course, hearers. Revelation was designed for oral enactment in Christian worship services (cf. 1:3). Its effect would therefore be somewhat comparable to a dramatic performance, in which the audience enter the world of the drama for its duration and can have their perception of the world outside the drama powerfully shifted by their experience of the world of the drama.[2]

The images of this text 'are symbols with evocative power inviting imaginative participation,' but they do not work simply by 'painting verbal pictures.' Their precise literary formulation is essential to their meaning and 'saturated with verbal allusions to the Old Testament,' drawing the entire biblical canon into the repertoire by which Revelation appeals to the imagination.[3] The thin narrative and richly multivalent imagery characteristic of apocalyptic literature in the Bible stretches the resources of human language to the limit, in order to provide glimpses of transcendence.[4] The juxtaposition of visual and verbal elements is thus crucial to imagining biblically, whether envisioning one's own life, or creating a work of literature, as it is an essential structural mechanism, rather like Ricoeur's definition of metaphor, that enables the temporal, contingent quality of the natural and given, to be open to amelioration by that which is supernatural and transcendent.

Nevertheless, apocalyptic literature is not the predominant genre in Scripture. To provide an account of the way in which the biblical text connects the visual and verbal together as integral to a doctrine of imagination, rooted in the heart, that can be inferred from the literary and theological structure of the biblical text as a whole, it is necessary to consider narrative and image. Richard Eslinger has attempted to define this relationship from the perspective of a

---

[2] Bauckham, *The Theology of the Book of Revelation*, 9-10.
[3] Bauckham, *The Theology of the Book of Revelation*, 18.
[4] This multi-perceptual understanding of imagination is not limited to the genre of apocalypse in the Bible. A similar use of imagery which demonstrates the breadth of the biblical imagination can be seen in the descriptions of love that fill the Song of Solomon. '[T]he Song's imagery will exploit comparisons, not only of sight but of all the senses, including taste, touch, smell, and sound. Love excites all the senses, and the poet reflects this through figurative language.' Longman, *Song of Songs*, 13.

postliberal hermeneutic,[5] providing an understanding of the imagination that does justice to the unique contribution of Scripture in the light of contemporary imagination theory. He begins by critiquing the various attempts of narrative theologians to establish a 'foundationalist' position for biblical narrative external to the text itself: either through a 'cognitive' model based upon the assumptions of empiricism; or an 'experiential-expressive' model that assumes a common human interiority, where the biblical text becomes illustrative of a more general 'archetypal' experience, or is dispensable as humans progress to a more complete form of knowledge. In antithesis to this, he argues that the biblical text presents a narrative, which posits a world: this must form the determinative imaginative paradigm against which all personal experience and other world views are measured. Eslinger critiques the claim of liberalism that a genuine pluralism is possible, where there is a supposedly neutral point from which the various stories and symbols of different religious traditions can be evaluated, assuming that once symbols are abstracted from the specific narrative context in which they are situated that they retain the same meaning. Instead, he argues, genuine dialogue can be achieved only if a community of faith embraces the world posited by the biblical text, with all its 'scandal of particularity.'[6] This provides a theoretical basis for understanding the imagination in terms of the world projected by the biblical text (to use Ricoeur's terminology) and also to do justice to Paul's paradoxical formulation.

Having underlined the necessity of beginning from a community shaped and nurtured in the narratives of Scripture, Eslinger then goes on to argue that narrative is the primary mode of interpreting Scripture. He establishes this not only by referring to the 'remarkable plenitude of stories within biblical literature,' but also noting that nonnarrative literature such as 'the Pauline corpus and the covenant law portions of Deuteronomy' are concerned with questions as to how the narratives should be interpreted, or elaborations on the narrative in praise. Similarly, the wisdom literature and proverbs, which might appear to jeopardize an overarching narrative hermeneutic, are caught up in the web of expectation of the kingdom of God. The apocalyptic, despite its 'thin' use of narrative, integrates 'within a single field both narrative and imagery.' 'Only the narrative context of the Gospels is capable of locating this reworking of apocalyptic [in Revelation] with reference to Jesus and the nearness of the mystery of God's reign.'[7]

However, as this reference to the apocalyptic signals, Eslinger is attempting to develop a hermeneutic that does justice to both the narrative context and

---

[5] 'Postliberal' refers to a theological approach grounded in a neo-orthodox understanding of Scripture, that is, one that rejects the Enlightenment presuppositions of much nineteenth and twentieth-century biblical criticism in order to 'hear again' the primary text as a transformative narrative.

[6] Eslinger, *Narrative and Imagination*, 3-38.

[7] Eslinger, *Narrative and Imagination*, 21-3.

complex use of imagery characteristic of the biblical text, which makes his project so germane to a biblical understanding of the imagination. He shows that Paul's link between the visual and the verbal is an accurate characterisation of the contribution made by all the various genres of Scripture working together to a definition of imagination, due to the cohesive contextualisation provided by narrative, culminating in the event of Jesus Christ (Galatians 4:3-5). Eslinger continues via an exploration of imagination theory, beginning with more traditional definitions of the function that focus on the image, tracing through Mary Warnock's explication of the perceptual imagination construed as 'seeing as,' which both 'imagines how' and 'imagines that,' moving beyond the simple visual bias of older theories, in order to encompass all the sensual dimensions of human being involved in the act of imagining. He concludes by noting the linguistic turn that has enriched more contemporary accounts, such as Paul Ricoeur's definition of imagination in terms of metaphor (analysed in the previous chapter on Lewis) and Hans Georg Gadamer's concept of play. This latter Eslinger suggests 'takes up within itself the metaphor, since the game itself is only possible as it is performed as meaningful activity in contradiction to all definitions of meaningful activity by a world that does not know how to play.'[8] In order to imagine according to the trajectories opened by the biblical text, the Scriptures must operate as the definitive paradigm. The world 'wrought by the imagination' of the reader as they respond to the text is embraced as that in terms of which they understand the world of their existential experience and by which they measure the realms opened to their imagination through literature.[9] This, in fact, is precisely what Paul models in 1 Corinthians 13:12, as the present is understood in the light of the apocalyptic future that God has revealed.

Eslinger then moves to the crux of his argument, situating this understanding of imagination – 'now we see through a mirror in a riddle' – in the framework of biblical narrative. He begins by taking issue with Margaret Miles's polarity between 'text' and 'image,' arguing that because the narrative stories of Scripture share all the qualities that she attributes to the 'image' the biblical text deconstructs such an opposition as the basis on which imagination can be defined. These similarities are: that texts project a spatial dimension which correlates with the static offering of images; that it is reductionist to attribute a cognitive role to texts and an affective role to images, given that there is a 'spectrum ranging from concept to image,' which is applicable to both. Eslinger argues that 'the metaphoric act of imagination – with its linguistic turn – in no way finds the affective dimension of its performance diminished as compared to the more visual imagery.' Both text and image are open to an 'interpretive....span.' He continues, 'from the perspective of narrative hermeneutics...an often fluid affinity obtains between texts-as-stories and

---

[8] Eslinger, *Narrative and Imagination*, 46-71.
[9] Eslinger, *Narrative and Imagination*, 46-71.

images. The former evoke the latter; on the other hand, images imply the stories within which they were begotten.' The affective dimension is not dependent on the presence or absence of a visual component, no imaginative activity whether visual or linguistic is without a degree of affective significance. This combination of visions that are written (Habakkuk 1:1; Nahum 1:1), of potent images reconfiguring narrative, of narratives in terms of which as readers we come to understand ourselves and imagine according to the 'rule-governed productivity' and metaphors modelled in Scripture, helps to fill out the contours of Paul's cryptic summary – 'through a mirror in a riddle.'

The final polarity that Eslinger deconstructs is that of an 'aural-oral/visual impasse,' where texts are defined linguistically and images visually. This is of particular relevance when considering the biblical text which was and is often encountered aurally rather than visually by its readers/hearers. Thinking of texts as spoken rather than seen reorientates this simplistic dichotomy: the primacy of the text as a material product to be read, ironically emphasised the visual element of the linguistic artefact at the expense of a prior emphasis on hearing. This reverses Miles's privileging of the visual as affording intimacy; in this case it effects a distanciation. It is necessary to move beyond an either/or:

> Viewed from the perspective of biblical narrative – and the particular element of metaphor – image and language disclose an interplay of meaning-producing functions. This interplay offers immediacy and affective significance across the perspectual spectrum. Moreover, on some occasions the dichotomy between the senses is finally overcome in a unitive experience of self, God, and world. A phenomenon exists in which perception extends beyond its mundane compartmentalization – we may 'hear colors' or 'see sounds.'[10]

This evidences the same understanding of imagination described by Warnock as multivalent perception,[11] drawing on the whole person, as imagination plays an integral part in emotion and volition, as well as allowing us to project a vision of that which lies beyond the immediate present of our experience.

The paradoxical notion of hearing colours or seeing sounds in Eslinger's description above also has close affinities with the imagination of the biblical authors embodied in the apocalyptic segments of Scripture. Sinclair Ferguson has spoken, for example, of the 'alien world' described in Daniel through 'colorful, dramatic, and sometimes grotesque pictures,' suggesting in a resonant phrase that 'the visionary sections...contain God's picture book.'[12] Both Revelation and Daniel refuse to conform to a Western 'straight-line view of things,' the patterns of imagery present an outline of history from different viewpoints in a 'progressive parallelism' that 'one might liken to the structure'

---

[10] Eslinger, *Narrative and Imagination*, 76-85.
[11] Eslinger, *Narrative and Imagination*, 57-9.
[12] Sinclair Ferguson, *Mastering the Old Testament: Daniel*, ed. Lloyd J. Ogilvie (Dallas: Word Publishing, 1988), 20.

of 'a spiral staircase, turning around the same central point...yet rising higher....'[13] It is obvious that traditional definitions of 'image' as visual need to be reworked, as they are filtered through the verbal imagination of Scripture (defined in an earlier chapter through the work of Robert Alter).

> Names, images, and attributes, then, are perspectively related: they tell us the same truths...in different ways. The whole Bible may be seen as a literary image of God's nature and action. God's actions in history present images of him....When God creates he is an artisan; when he heals, he is a physician. So the whole Bible consists of divine images. But we have seen that the whole Bible is also an exposition of God's name....And it is also, in its entirety, a conceptual description of God's nature....[14]

Paul's own hermeneutic outlined for 'the present evil age' (Galatians 1:4) underwrites the same fusion of word and image when defining a biblical doctrine of the imagination, 'now we see through a mirror in a riddle.'

For the purposes of this chapter, Eslinger concludes his exploration by assessing the relationship between story and imagery. He confirms Alter's insistence on the verbal nature of the biblical imagination (both that evidenced by the authors and the conclusions concerning this function that can be deduced from the narrative), arguing that from the perspective of biblical narrative, '[t]he story is logically prior,' as the image derives from it. He specifies the logical priority of narrative to a theory of imagery in two ways: 'Narratives serve to name and thereby "locate" images such as their meanings remain diverse, yet not random.' If images are divorced from stories they 'grow ambiguous and opaque,' until they are named in a particular fashion 'they will not divulge their precise significance;' it is crucial to distinguish between 'imagery's multivalence and plain ambiguity.' However, he also emphasises the importance of images. They are capable of taking on a life of their own, as they move from one narrative context to another, creating echoes throughout the canon of Scripture. In specific instances the image may provide the clue to interpreting the narrative. Eslinger cites the eucharist as the paradigmatic instance, 'bread and wine....The image interprets the narrative and the assembly, which now is revealed as the body. The narrative interprets the image so that what we taste and see is not just bread but the body of Christ.'

Finally, he notes that certain images are of supreme importance as they 'provide a hermeneutic function' which shapes the way in which stories are heard:

> These components of vision, then, encompass all of the senses and their image-forming competencies. Included in the achievement of vision, moreover, is the vast and complex symbol system connecting these images and elevating some to

---

[13] Ferguson, *Mastering the Old Testament*, 22.
[14] Frame, "Images of God," 364.

the status of hermeneutic lenses. Still, the notion of vision is not fully explored without attending to language and the linguistic turn of imagination. Our vision is shaped as well by the ways in which we imagine-that and imagine-how, and by the metaphors and ironies of our stories. There is a distinctive sense of praxis within narrative hermeneutics that is implicit in these considerations.[15]

Praxis becomes the biblical determinative for establishing the truth of one's imagination. It is here that Eslinger, like Vanhoozer, takes issue with Ricoeur's theory of metaphor. The danger of this theory is that its ontological assumptions will assume a general 'archetypal' kind of authority of religious experience at the expense of the irreducible and scandalous historical particularity of the event of Jesus Christ recorded in the gospels.[16] For both Eslinger and Vanhoozer, following Moltmann, the historical resurrection of Jesus Christ is the necessary precondition to Kantian postulations of hope.[17]

Eslinger's analysis of narrative and imagery has opened up issues central to the formation of a biblical definition of imagination. These include the fact that the very concept of the Bible's doctrine of what we call imagination inevitably intertwines word and image, ultimately collapsing the distinction for all practical purposes and engaging individuals on the basis of a multi-perceptual model that addresses all the dimensions of personhood encapsulated in the biblical concept of the heart. Secondly, surrender is required to the narrative vision of the text in order meaningfully to participate and imagine the last things as the Bible speaks of them, as Eslinger notes by drawing on Gadamer's concept of play. Only by ascribing primacy to the world projected by the biblical text can the uniqueness and historical particularity of the event of Jesus Christ be given due weight. The Word enfleshed must be at the centre of a biblical understanding of imagination that attempts to incorporate both the Old and New Testaments. Finally, coherence is not a necessary aesthetic quality of the literature resulting from a biblical doctrine of imagination; in fact a certain incoherence is sometimes essential. This can be seen in the apocalyptic literature that distorts the presuppositions of our 'natural' vision through surreal juxtapositions in order to convey something of the transcendent that lies beyond the apprehension of human sense, through our senses. It is a familiar biblical tension, encapsulated by Paul in his discussion of the resurrection: 'flesh and blood cannot inherit the kingdom of God....For this perishable body must put on the imperishable, and this mortal body must put on immortality. When the...mortal puts on immortality...."Death is swallowed up in victory"' (1 Corinthians 15:50-54).

In exegeting the implications of Paul's account of our present vision – 'now we see through a mirror in a riddle' – for a biblical doctrine of imagination, it is

---

[15] Eslinger, *Narrative and Imagination*, 85-9.

[16] Eslinger, *Narrative and Imagination*, 116-7.

[17] Vanhoozer, *Biblical Narrative in the Philosophy of Paul Ricoeur*, 224-266.

important to recognise also that the metanarrative of Scripture positions the imagination in interim terms both logically and historically. Humankind, and thus the imagination, has been tainted by the Fall. However, through the death and resurrection of Jesus Christ, the imagination has been reorientated, looking in hope towards the coming of the new creation that will be revealed at the *eschaton*. This leads to a characterisation of human beings as 'no longer 'simple subject[s]''; [their] condition is double.'[18] Kevin Mills elucidates this in a meditation on the hermeneutical implications of faith, hope and love that follows the key Pauline verse under discussion here:

> Freedom in the light of hope, then, is freedom 'in spite of' death. The kerygma of the Gospels is read as: 'the living Lord of the Church is the same as Jesus on the cross.' The question of the identity of the crucified and the living arises in the 'hiatus between the Cross and the apparitions of the Resurrected. The empty tomb is the expression of this hiatus.' Hope must carry this discontinuity – the hiding of the kingdom under its contrary, the Cross. Hope, then, becomes paradoxical. It takes on the form of that not-yet-knowledge of 1 Corinthians 13:12.[19]

Mills emphasises the centrality of the historical advent of Christ in interpreting the biblical pattern of history and also in understanding what it means to see 'through a mirror in a riddle' when defining the imagination biblically. The precise historical positioning indicated by the 'now' and 'then' of Paul's discussion entails a crucified aesthetic: a dimness of perception is the inevitable corollary of finitude and sin, transcendence and truth penetrate the 'mirror' only in distorted fragments. However, the hope of ultimate revelation and encounter engenders an imagination which waits with 'eager longing:' God himself has 'subjected' it 'in hope that the creation itself will be set free from its bondage to decay and obtain the freedom of the glory of the children of God' (Romans 8:19-20). Paul writes in the previous chapter (Romans 7) of the poignant yearning that this paradoxical situation engendered, rendering him a riddle even to himself: 'I do not understand my own actions. For I do not do what I want, but I do the very thing I hate' (v. 15).

A crucified aesthetic denotes the implications of the death and resurrection of Christ, so central to the biblical metanarrative, for the concepts of imagination, art, beauty and so on. This was explored briefly in Chapter 3 when considering the doctrines of salvation and sanctification as Christian gazed upon the cross.[20] The notion of a crucified aesthetic indicates the ignominy and apparent ridiculousness or humility that can characterise all attempts to create beautiful lives, or works of art prior to the *eschaton*, particularly when confronted with the reality of sin and death (1 Corinthians 2:1-16). The brutal facts of evil cannot be avoided, as the death of Christ, the paradigm behind the

---

[18] Edwards, *Towards a Christian Poetics*, 3.
[19] Mills, *Justifying Language*, 90.
[20] See Chapter 3, 66-9.

concept of a crucified aesthetic, is intended to deal with nothing less (Romans 3:21-26). However, the resurrection holds out the promise of a final healing and restoration, achieved through the transcendent power of the One who will make all things new (Revelation 21:5). The imagination defined in these terms is also hopeful, but given the oppression and evil of the present, and the hiddenness of ultimate glory, it finds expression in the indirect denotations of metaphor, paradox and irony.

The pattern encapsulated in this crucified aesthetic, central to a biblical doctrine of imagination, can be traced in the experience of disciples seeking to pattern their lives after the paradigm of the biblical text, as Paul's tortured reading of himself makes evident (Romans 7). Mills goes on to explore how the eschatological fruition described in 1 Corinthians 13:13 – 'So now faith, hope, and love abide, these three; but the greatest of these is love' – which correlates with the fruit of the resurrection in the paradigmatic example of Christ, reconfigures the situation of those seeking to imagine and live, in the light of this biblical hope. This tension is encapsulated in the 'now...then' polarity of verse 12.

> [Paul] sees reflection as transformation because consciousness, in the act of interpreting, turns from itself towards the other, and in reflecting the other, the self is re-focused, re-created, transfigured: 'But we all, with open face beholding as in a glass the glory of the Lord, are changed into the same image from glory to glory, even as by the Spirit of the Lord' [1 Corinthians 3:18]. Understanding may still be 'through a glass, darkly', but the opacity grounds a reflection. The field of the unreflected is the otherness of God that cannot be subsumed under self-consciousness. Self-reflection becomes speculation on the 'same image', as the glory 'which was to be done away' is transformed into 'the glory that excelleth' – the other light which arrests, blinds, envisions and opens hope for meaning and maturity.[21]

The Bible thus locates imagination in relation to the ultimate Other, seeking through a complex linguistic interplay of word and image to capture something that will only be 'fully known' in the maturity of love which flowers in the *eschaton*, when faith will be sight (2 Corinthians 5:7). As has been evident throughout this study, transformation of life and the creation of literary texts operate on parallel principles, in this case the doctrines of the crucifixion and the resurrection shape both person and work. Ultimately, the Bible insists on a definition of imagination that is relational, accountable to God and others, shaped by a desire for transcendence, and committed to that which is other in empathetic love.

Gerald Manley Hopkins encapsulates something of this paradox at the heart of the crucified imagination and its essential humility (cf. John 13:1-17). The knowledge possessed now is fragmentary, transformation into the 'same image

---

[21] Mills, *Justifying Language*, 139.

from one degree of glory to another,' often unconscious (2 Corinthians 3:18). There are depths within and visions without that are beyond the grasp of conscious articulation. It is the imagination that catches glimpses in the opaqueness of the mirror, reflecting the fragments which reason cannot always grasp. Language itself is implicated in the Fall, but also, as Mills argues, gestures towards that plenitude and fulfilment, paradise restored, which the biblical text hints at, but cannot comprehensively reveal, 'betweenwhiles.'[22]

> Hope holds to Christ the mind's own mirror out
> To take His lovely likeness more and more.
> It will not well, so she would bring about
> An ever brighter burnish than before
> And turns to wash it from her welling eyes
> And breathes the blots off all with sighs on sighs.
> Her glass is blest but she as good as blind
> Holds till hand aches and wonders what is there;
> Her glass drinks light, she darkles down behind,
> All of her glorious gainings unaware.
>
> I told you that she turned her mirror dim
> Betweenwhiles, but she sees herself not Him.[23]

Paul's definition – 'now we see through a mirror in a riddle' – offers a biblical rationale through which one can come to terms with the juxtaposition of narrative and image throughout the biblical text, and the paradoxical nature of the interim stage by which Scripture defines history prior to the second coming of Christ, for developing a biblical doctrine of imagination: crucified, provisional, yet ever hopeful.

'The play's the thing wherein I'll catch the conscience of the king'

It is important to recall Eslinger's observation on the centrality of biblical narrative in 'naming' and 'locating' images, remembering also his stress upon the necessity of maintaining the 'scandal of particularity' which its exclusive claims establish as essential to participation in the world posited by the text. This is a necessary qualification, as it is easy to fall into the methodological trap of simply illustrating general principles with biblical narratives, or finding

---

[22] Mills, *Justifying Language*, 170-7. For a suggestive and powerful exploration of this passage and other of Paul's writings in relation to Rembrandt's self-portraits see Andrew W. Hass, "Seeing Through a Glass Face to Face," in *Believing in the Text: Essays from the Centre for the Study of Literature, Theology and the Arts, University of Glasgow*, eds. David Jasper, George Newlands and Darlene Bird (Oxford: Peter Lang, 2004), 57-73.

[23] Gerard Manley Hopkins, *The Poems of Gerard Manley Hopkins*, 4th ed. (London: Oxford University Press, 1967), 186-7.

contemporary secular parallels to biblical narratives, thus assuming a more general, authoritative and anterior theoretical framework, which undercuts a biblical hermeneutic.[24] With these provisos in mind, I will consider an exemplary instance of narrative in the Old Testament, where the role of the imagination is explicitly thematised, as it helps to think through the implications of a biblical understanding of this function.[25] Here is the story as recorded by the writer of 2 Samuel 12:1-10.

> And the LORD sent Nathan to David. He came to him and said to him, "There were two men in a certain city, the one rich and the other poor. The rich man had very many flocks and herds, but the poor man had nothing but one little ewe lamb, which he had bought. And he brought it up, and it grew up with him and with his children. It used to eat of his morsel and drink from his cup and lie in his arms, and it was like a daughter to him. Now there came a traveler to the rich man, and he was unwilling to take one of his own flock or herd to prepare for the guest who had come to him, but he took the poor man's lamb and prepared it for the man who had come to him." Then David's anger was greatly kindled against the man, and he said to Nathan, "As the LORD lives, the man who has done this deserves to die, and he shall restore the lamb fourfold, because he did this thing, and because he had no pity."
>
> Nathan said to David, "You are the man! Thus says the LORD, the God of Israel, 'I anointed you king over Israel, and I delivered you out of the hand of Saul. And I gave you your master's house and your master's wives into your arms and gave you the house of Israel and of Judah. And if this were too little, I would add to you as much more. Why have you despised the word of the LORD, to do what is evil in his sight? You have struck down Uriah the Hittite with the sword and have taken his wife to be your wife and have killed him with the sword of the Ammonites. Now therefore the sword shall never depart from your house, because you have despised me and have taken the wife of Uriah the Hittite to be your wife.'"

This passage acts as a paradigmatic case for understanding the role and power of secular literature biblically, as it affects and engages the imagination. The prophet Nathan uses a fictional allegory, specifically tailored as a moral analogue to David's experience. Although imaginative works of literature are not directly shaped to the situation of individual readers, literature works in a form similar to the story related here, by engaging and moulding the ways in which readers experience the world. What then does the biblical account add to this familiar (though not always generally accepted) understanding of the role of literature and its relationship to the imagination? The very fact that a prophet uses a secular story in order to 'catch the conscience of the king' legitimises

---

[24] This methodological flaw is evident, for example, in John Bausch, *Storytelling: Imagination and Faith* (Mystic, Connecticut: Twenty-Third Publications, 1984), 9-10.
[25] Bausch, *Storytelling*, 10-11, 52.

and underwrites the use and power of fictional literature to appeal to the imagination from a biblical perspective; something that has frequently been contested throughout the history of the church. It also evidences a faith in the capacity of the imagination to convey and receive truth leading to self-awareness. However, the imagination does not of itself work moral transformation, only the Spirit of God can do that, as David evidences in his prayer of repentance recorded in Psalm 51: 'Create (*bara*) in me a clean heart, O God, and renew a right spirit within me. Cast me not away from your presence, and take not your Holy Spirit from me. Restore to me the joy of your salvation' (vv. 10-11). It is noteworthy that the word translated 'create' here is the Hebrew *bara*, which is reserved throughout the Old Testament for God alone, and is used in Genesis 1 to describe creation *ex nihilo*.[26] Only God can create a universe out of nothing, and only God, the psalmist asserts can create a 'clean heart' and renew a 'right spirit' in human beings.

As has been observed numerous times, the imagination is located biblically in the heart, and has a particular language and mode of operation that simultaneously engages the mind, will and emotions of an individual. In this case, the story that Nathan presents to David invites empathy and appeals to his sense of justice: the rich man took the poor man's lamb, 'which was like a daughter to him.' The king responded with self-righteous vengeance and called upon the offender the full weight of Israelite law, 'he shall restore the lamb fourfold' (cf. Exodus 22:1). This brief incident draws together the various dimensions of imagination explored throughout this study. The biblical text endorses the imagination as an integral aspect of human beings made in the image of the Divine Creator. It is a powerful function, capable of great good or evil, Nathan here turns it to an astute moral purpose. Rooted in the biblical notion of the heart, imagination is integrally connected to desire and will, but of itself, it is incapable of transforming human beings spiritually. As Psalm 51 makes clear, this is the prerogative of the Holy Spirit.

Imagining Biblically

This study has explored many aspects of what it means to imagine biblically, that is how the Bible as both a literary and theological text defines and shapes an understanding of the imagination in the contemporary context of literary criticism. Central to this examination has been the concept of the heart, which, in biblical anthropology, is the essence of the person, where all thought, feeling, emotion and imagination originate. The relational allegiance of the heart is crucial to determining the overall shape and direction of an individual's life. This method of defining the location of what we classify in more specialised terms as 'imagination' is a crucial component of the unique perspective that the biblical text offers, as it categorically refuses to distinguish

---

[26] Eveson, *The Book of Origins*, 23-25.

the conceptual and aesthetic from the practical and moral, literature and life are considered within the same comprehensive framework. It also prevents 'the arts' or 'literature' from being isolated in a rarefied atmosphere. Imagination, rooted in the heart, is a function that all human beings possess by virtue of their creation in the image of God and shapes the making of pottery, the design of the temple, the writing of the Psalms, the selection of wise sayings, and the decision to break a bottle of expensive perfume over the feet of Christ (Genesis 1:27; Isaiah 64:8; Exodus 25-31; Psalm 45:1; Ecclesiastes 12:9-11; Mark 14:6).

The concept of the heart reworks traditional configurations of imagination by rendering the issue as to whether it should be defined in terms of image or word superfluous, as it incorporates both in a unique manner. Eslinger has helped to clarify this point, by emphasising the primarily narrative quality of the biblical imagination, whilst also recognising that images can reconstitute narratives and become the interpretive paradigm in terms of which texts (written or lived) are understood. The rich and repeated phrase of the King James Version encapsulates this holistic fusion of visual and verbal elements when referring to 'the imagination of the thoughts of the heart' (1 Chronicles 29:18). The heart is such a useful short-hand term for how Scripture defines imagination, as, even though it incorporates far more than this function, it allows the complex elements of volition, emotion and desire that are involved in acts of imagination to be considered as an integral whole. The biblical text defines the imagination in this way by describing individuals who demonstrate it, as for example, Bezalel, in the construction of the temple (Exodus 31:1-11); through the literary form of the text itself, which embodies in a variety of genres this imaginative fusion of the creative, aesthetic, admonitory and ethical (Ecclesiastes 12:9-14); by encouraging its readers to imaginatively perceive and appropriate these instructions and examples in their own particular cultural context (John 13:1-17; 1 Corinthians 4:16; Ephesians 5:1).

These three dimensions: the biblical imagination of the scriptural authors, the Bible's literary form, and the imagination of readers of the text, all inform what it means to 'imagine biblically' as the term is used in this study. The notion is fluid, but intended to denote what can be deduced from a consideration of the biblical text concerning the imagination in a literary context. Thus, it has been a deliberate methodological choice so far not to draw a hard and fast distinction between these possible interpretations of what I have called 'imagining biblically,' in order to do justice to the breadth and complexity of the ways in which the Bible informs our understanding of the imagination. For the sake of clarity and in order to sum up the argument of the book as a whole, I will now draw together the aspects of what it means to imagine biblically that have been analysed in the course of this study.

Creativity has been central to definitions of imagination in Western culture since the Renaissance. However, this is somewhat problematic from a scriptural perspective, as only God is able to create *ex nihilo* (Genesis 1-2). Some have responded by arguing that the biblical text presents humans as incapable of creating anything original; imitation is the highest that can be achieved, I suggest that a more balanced position does greater justice to the biblical data overall. Creation *ex nihilo* is indeed the prerogative of God alone (as the reservation of the Hebrew word *bara* for divine action indicates). But the creation mandate to exercise stewardship that Adam and Eve received – 'Be fruitful and multiply and fill the earth and subdue it' (Genesis 1:28) – incorporated a responsible care for the earth and its development, requiring discernment, initiative and creative action, as the task of naming the animals demonstrates (Genesis 2:19-20). The popular notion of the individual who creates original works of genius through drawing upon the illimitable riches within is certainly not consistent with biblical teaching, but the alternative suggestion that human beings simply imitate what is given also fails to do full justice to the scriptural view. The doctrine of creation in the image of God, juxtaposed alongside the creation mandate, suggests that a model of worshipful response and development (or 'effoliation and enrichment') is more appropriate.

In Chapter 3 the parallel that Paul Ricoeur draws with the 'other book' of revelation, namely Scripture was explored. Bunyan's *Pilgrim's Progress* enables Ricoeur's concept of the productive imagination, deduced from the biblical text, to be applied to the creation of other works of literature. He suggests that the various biblical genres model a 'productive imagination' that defines the 'norm-governed productivity' which characterises imagination more generally. This act of imagining, understood biblically, 'realizes the union of fiction and redescription' central to this function; the reading process is 'the starting point of the trajectory that unfolds itself into the individual and social forms of the imagination.' Thus the ways in which the biblical text shapes its readers act as a 'heuristic model' to define the dynamic operation of the creative (or productive) imagination in other contexts. Ricoeur demonstrates how the production of literary works and the transformation of human lives can be traced back to the paradigmatic operations of the imagination embodied and generated by the biblical text (especially in the genres of narrative and parable). '[T]he process of parabolization working in the text...engender[s] in the reader a similar dynamic of interpretation through thought and action.'[27] Ricoeur's definition attends carefully to the biblical text, allowing it to shape a concept of the imagination as 'rule-governed productivity.' This retains the crucial balance between response and initiative characteristic of the Bible's presentation of human creativity, and also recognises the inextricable connections it maintains between the creation of literature and the pattern of life modelled by artists and writers.

Imagining biblically necessarily entails negotiating complex theoretical issues that cut to the heart of literary criticism as a discipline. Roland Barthes's celebrated announcement of the death of the author almost a century after

---

[27] Ricoeur, "The Bible and the Imagination," 50-2.

Nietzsche proclaimed the death of God shows that secular critical theory and theology are not as far apart as they first appear. Kevin Vanhoozer draws upon the richly biblical resource of Reformed theology in order to negotiate the chasm between author and word, reader and text that has followed in the wake of deconstruction. He postulates a firmly Christocentric understanding of the relationship between author and text, word and meaning, on the model of Calvin's interpretation of the eucharist. Words, without which literature cannot exist, mediate presence: an act of faith enables meaning to be enacted. Behind such concepts is the biblical doctrine of the incarnation, the Word made flesh (John 1:14), that underwrites the venture of communication between person and other (text, human or God). It situates all utterance within a framework of meaning – death, coming to terms with the reality of deception and evil, and resurrection, inducing hope that one day we 'shall know fully, even as [we] have been fully known' (1 Corinthians 13:12). It is the hope engendered by this metanarrative, of which Christ is the historical culmination, that liberates imagination and engenders faith. The way this theology enables one to imagine according to the trajectories opened by the biblical text was explored through the literary form and covenantal Christocentric aesthetic manifested in the *Letters of Samuel Rutherford*. We saw that incarnation 'the actual deed of ethically integrating with others,' rooted in the supreme example of Christ, offers a model for the work of art:[28] an 'incarnation' embodying 'meaning in the concrete form of images, sounds, and stories.'[29]

Liberty, from a biblical perspective, however, is only attained through a respect for the structure of divine law, which is what makes Ricoeur's definition of imagination as 'a rule-governed productivity' so germane. Imagining biblically is an inescapably moral activity. The narrative form of much of Scripture is suggestive in its implications for an understanding of the process of self-formation, the necessity of ethical standards, and the shape of literary narratives in Western culture. Robert Alter has outlined the way in which the style of biblical narratives has an implicit theology that sees God as the One ultimately in control of all events and human beings as responsible and mysterious creatures. There is an implicit invitation in the biblical metanarrative to situate oneself in a story that stretches beyond time into eternity, providing a framework for the imagination in which past, present and future are all construed in terms of a transcendent horizon that lies in the hands of One who makes all things new (Revelation 21:5). This form of self-understanding is coupled in biblical narratives by a respect for moral principles that flesh out the propositional revelation given in other parts of Scripture. These 'imperatives aim at the creation of new possibilities for cultivating those virtues that God intended in creating human beings.'[30] Such 'new possibilities'

---

[28] Alexandar Mihailovic cited by Jacobs, *A Theology of Reading*, 62.
[29] Ryken, *The Liberated Imagination*, 17.
[30] Mouw, *The God Who Commands*, 115.

include the shape that an individual may imagine for their own life (past, present and future) according to the trajectories opened by the biblical text, or the use of their imagination to enrich and expand the world and possibilities of being through the creation of literary works. A moral dimension is characteristic of all our activities, including imagination, as human beings. Biblical morality is motivated by love and thus underwrites the conclusion of Frank Palmer that 'there is a fastidiousness of genuine art which is a creativity rooted in love.'[31] Love respects the otherness of the created world and aims to disclose and enrich. To this end Scripture emphasises the necessity of the moral imagination and a right degree of respect for it, in both literature and life. In literary terms this is achieved by the preeminence of narrative as a biblical genre, enabling the complex texture of human existence to be consistently presented from an ethical perspective that is objective without being reductionist.

The central position which the Bible ascribes to morality and the relational orientation of the heart renders it necessary to consider possible misdirections of the imagination leading to illusion and abuse. Charlotte Brontë analyses this powerfully in her novel, *Jane Eyre*. If someone or something other than God is given the primary place in a character's thoughts, affections and desires, this results in their fundamental inability rightly to envision life, the world and their relationships with others. Brontë's text thus reflects faith in the first of the Ten Commandments, to have no other gods before Yahweh (Exodus 20:2-3). Jesus defined this positively in terms of the settled affections of the heart, where the imagination is situated in Scripture (Matthew 22:37-40). Biblically, the notion of an idolatrous imagination is equated with covetousness, or evil desire. Allowing one's life to be characterised by the pursuit of such desires, originating in the heart, can lead to a gradual enslavement by futility and illusion, rather as Jane envisions her life at Marseilles had she acceded to Rochester's demands (Matthew 5:27-28; Romans 1:21-32; Ephesians 4:17-24; Colossians 3:5). However, the corruptions of the imagination that the biblical text identifies, namely idolatry and evil desire, also demonstrate the potential for good implicit in this human function if directed towards the transcendent depth and breadth of God, engaging empathetically with others, interacting perceptively with the world, and creatively envisioning the shape of the future both individually and in community (1 Corinthians 2:9; 2 Corinthians 3:17-18; Ephesians 3:14-20; Hebrews 13:3).

The biblical metanarrative and the virtue of hope, fostered by faith in a transcendent God who has promised to make all things new, are essential to establishing space for a creative imagination orientated towards the future, informed by the past, and capable of transforming the present (1 Corinthians 13:12-13; Revelation 21:5). C. S. Lewis analysed the presence of desire (which he termed Joy) in theological terms as intimations of transcendence, moments

---

[31] Palmer, *Literature and Moral Understanding*, 164.

when the temporal and mundane suddenly open up to depths and vistas that reveal a reality other and beyond the here and now. The biblical text ascribes an ontological basis to these yearnings. The imagination is the aspect of human nature, working primarily through the literary structure of metaphor, which allows this dimension of reality to be apprehended. Both Lewis and Ricoeur have developed a theory of metaphor on the model of biblical parable, poetic parallelism and narrative that offers a way of structurally defining what it means to imagine biblically for contemporary readers and writers. This fleshes out Ricoeur's definition of imagination as a 'rule-governed productivity.' Metaphor is an important complement to, and qualification of, the preeminence of narrative as a biblical genre, when defining the concept of imagining biblically. However, even the apprehensions of imagination are ultimately provisional, awaiting the fulness of revelation at the *eschaton*: 'What no eye has seen, nor ear heard, nor the heart of man imagined, what God has prepared for those who love him' – these things God has revealed to us through the Spirit' (1 Corinthians 2:9-10).

It is this horizon, sketched in the apocalypse of Revelation, that most sharply distinguishes imagining biblically from a characteristic form of the postmodern imagination, where all avenues out of the cultural, social and linguistic networks in which we find ourselves implicated are regarded as self-serving illusions. Consequently desire is focused on self and disconnected fragments of time, there is no basis upon which one can imaginatively conceive the world from the perspective of another, and there is nothing to inspire a creative communal effort towards transformation. To imagine biblically, in contrast, is both to recognise the evil and suffering that characterises the present, but also to anticipate the *eschaton* with a creativity simultaneously provisional and fostered by hope. Human beings, through the use of their imagination, 'may actually assist in the effoliation and multiple enrichment of creation. All tales may come true; and yet, at the last, redeemed, they may be as like and as unlike the forms that we give them as Man, finally redeemed, will be like and unlike the fallen that we know.'[32] To conclude with Paul:

> Love never ends....For we know in part and we prophesy in part, but when the perfect comes, the partial will pass away. When I was a child, I spoke like a child, I thought like a child, I reasoned like a child. When I became a man, I gave up childish ways. For now we see in a mirror dimly, but then face to face. Now I know in part; then I shall know fully, even as I have been fully known. So now faith, hope, and love abide, these three; but the greatest of these is love (1 Corinthians 13:8-13).

---

[32] Tolkien, "On Fairy-Stories." 72.

Bibliography

Abrams, M. H. *The Mirror and the Lamp: Romantic Theory and the Critical Tradition.* Oxford: Oxford University Press, 1971.
—. *Natural Supernaturalism: Tradition and Revolution in Romantic Literature.* New York: W. W. Norton, 1971.
Alliston, April. *Virtue's Faults: Correspondences in Eighteenth-Century British and French Women's Fiction.* Stanford: Stanford University Press, 1996.
Alter, Robert. *The Art of Biblical Narrative.* New York: Basic Books, Inc, 1981.
—. *The Art of Biblical Poetry.* Edinburgh: T & T Clark, 1985.
Altes, Liesbeth Korthals. "Some Dilemmas of an Ethics of Literature." *Theology and Literature: Rethinking Reader Responsibility.* Eds. Gaye Williams Ortiz and Clara A. B. Joseph. Houndmills: Palgrave Macmillan, 2006. 15-31.
Arnold, Matthew. *Culture and Anarchy: An Essay in Political and Social Criticism.* London: Murray, 1961.
—. "The Study of Poetry." *Four Essays on Life and Letters.* Ed. E. K. Brown. New York: Appleton-Century, 1947.
Augustine, Saint. *Confessions.* Oxford: Oxford University Press, 1998.
Austen, Jane. *Pride and Prejudice.* London: Oxford University Press, 1970.
Austin, Michael. "The Figural Logic of the Sequel and the Unity of The Pilgrim's Progress." *Studies in Philology.* 102.4 (2005): 484-509.
Avis, Paul. *God and the Creative Imagination: Metaphor, Symbol and Myth in Religion and Theology.* London: Routledge, 1999.
Banks, Robert. *God the Worker: Journeys into the Mind, Heart and Imagination of God.* Sydney: Albatross, 1992.
Barish, Jonas. *The Antitheatrical Prejudice.* London: University of California Press, 1981.
Bassham, Gregory. "Lewis and Tolkien on the Power of the Imagination." *C. S. Lewis as Philosopher: Truth, Goodness and Beauty.* Eds. David Baggett, Gary R. Habermas and Jerry L. Walls. Downers Grove: IVP Academic, 2008. 245-60.
Battersby, Christine. "Terror, Terrorism and the Sublime: Rethinking the Sublime After 1789 and 2001." *Postcolonial Studies* 6.1 (2003): 67-89.
Bauckham, Richard and Trevor Hart. *Hope Against Hope: Christian Eschatology at the Turn of the Millennium.* Grand Rapids: Eerdmans, 1999.
Bauckham, Richard. *The Theology of the Book of Revelation.* Cambridge: Cambridge University Press, 1993.

Baurain, Bradley. "By the Rivers of Babylon We Weep: The Exiled Imagination." *Christianity and the Arts* May-July (1997): 12-15.
Bausch, John. *Storytelling: Imagination and Faith*. Mystic, Connecticut: Twenty-Third Publications, 1984.
Baxter, Richard. "Letter to the Reader." *A Breviate of the Life of Margaret, the Daughter of Francis Charlton of Apply in Shropshire, Esq.; and Wife of Richard Baxter*. London: Printed for B. Simmons, at the Three Golden Cocks at the West-end of St. Pauls, 1681.
Beaty, Jerome. *Misreading Jane Eyre: A Postformalist Paradigm*. Columbus: Ohio State University Press, 1996.
Begbie, Jeremy S. *Voicing Creation's Praise: Towards a Theology of the Arts*. Edinburgh: T&T Clark, 1990.
Belsey, Catherine. *Critical Practice*. 2nd ed. London: Routledge, 2002.
Bloch, Ariel and Chana. *The Song of Songs: A New Translation with an Introduction and Commentary*. New York: Random House, 1995.
Bonar, Andrew, Ed. *Letters of Samuel Rutherford*. 1891. Edinburgh: Banner of Truth Trust, 1984.
Boreham, Frank W. "Hudson Taylor's Text." *Developing a Christian Imagination: An Interpretive Anthology*. Ed. Warren W. Wiersbe. Wheaton: Victor Books, 1995. 199-206.
Botterweck, G. Johannes, Helmer Ringgren and Heinz-Josef Fabry, Eds. *Theological Dictionary of the Old Testament*. 1982-4. Vol. 7. Grand Rapids: Eerdmans, 1995.
Branch, Lori. "'As Blood is Forced out of Flesh': Spontaneity and the Wounds of Exchange in *Grace Abounding* and *The Pilgrim's Progress*." *English Literary History* 74 (2007): 271-99.
Bray, Joe. *The Epistolary Novel: Representations of Consciousness*. London: Routledge, 2003.
Brentnall, John M. *Samuel Rutherford in Aberdeen*. Inverness: John G. Eccles, c. 1981.
Brontë, Charlotte. *Jane Eyre*. Leicester: Galley Press, 1987.
Brown, Colin, Ed. *The New International Dictionary of New Testament Theology*. Vol. 2. Carlisle: Paternoster Press, 1975-78.
Brown, Francis, S. R. Driver, Charles A. Briggs and William Gesenius, Eds. *A Hebrew and English Lexicon of the Old Testament*. Peabody, Mass.: Hendrickson Publishers, 1979.
Brown, Peter. *The World of Late Antiquity: From Marcus Aurelius to Muhammad*. London: Thames & Hudson, 1971.
Bruce, F. F. *The Canon of Scripture*. Downers Grove: InterVarsity Press, 1988.
Bryant, David J. *Faith and the Play of Imagination: On the Role of Imagination in Religion*. Macon: Mercer University Press, 1989.
Bunyan, John. *The Pilgrim's Progress*. Harmondsworth: Penguin, 1965.
Butler, Martin. *Theatre and Crisis 1632-1642*. Cambridge: Cambridge University Press, 1984.
Byrne, Paula. *Jane Austen and the Theatre*. London: Hambledon and London, 2002.

Calvin, John. *Institutes of the Christian Religion*. Vol. 1. Trans. Henry Beveridge. Edinburgh: Calvin Translation Society, 1845.
Cameron, J. K. "The Piety of Samuel Rutherford (c. 1600-61): A Neglected Feature of Seventeenth-Century Scottish Calvinism." *Nederlands Archief voor Kerkgeschiedenis* 65 (1985): 153-9.
Card, Michael. *Scribbling in the Sand: Christ and Creativity*. Downers Grove: InterVarsity Press, 2002.
Carnell, Corbin Scott. *Bright Shadow of Reality: C. S. Lewis and the Feeling Intellect*. Grand Rapids: Eerdmans, 1974.
Carson, D. A. *The Gagging of God: Christianity Confronts Pluralism*. Grand Rapids: Zondervan, 1996.
Cates, Diana Fritz. "Ethics, Literature, and the Emotional Dimension of Moral Understanding: A Review Essay." *Journal of Religious Ethics* 26.2 (1998): 409-31.
Cefalu, Paul. *English Renaissance Literature and Contemporary Theory: Sublime Objects of Theology*. Houndmills: Palgrave Macmillan, 2007.
Chambers, Oswald. "'Is Your Imagination of God Starved?' February 10." *My Utmost for His Highest*. Grand Rapids: Discovery House, 1963.
Chaplin, Adrienne and Hilary Brand. *Art and Soul: Signposts for Christians in the Arts*. Downers Grove, Illinois: Piquant, IVP, 2001.
Christensen, Michael J. *C. S. Lewis on Scripture: His Thoughts on the Nature of Biblical Inspiration, the Role of Revelation and the Question of Inerrancy*. London: Hodder and Stoughton, 1980.
Clarke, Micael M. "Brontë's *Jane Eyre* and the Grimms' Cinderella." *Studies in English Literature 1500-1900* 40.4 (2000): 695-710.
Clowney, Edmund P. "Living Art: Christian Experience and the Arts." *God and Culture: Essays in Honor of Carl F. H. Henry*. Ed. J. D. Woodbridge. Grand Rapids: William B. Eerdmans, 1993. 235-53.
Coffey, John. *Politics, Religion and the British Revolutions: The Mind of Samuel Rutherford*. Cambridge Studies in Early Modern British History. Cambridge: Cambridge University Press, 1997.
Collingwood, R. G. *The Idea of History*. London: Oxford University Press, 1970.
Cook, Faith. *Samuel Rutherford and His Friends*. Edinburgh: Banner of Truth Trust, 1992.
Coulson, John. *Religion and Imagination: 'in Aid of a Grammar of Assent'*. Oxford: Oxford University Press, 1981.
Crowther, Paul. *Defining Art, Creating the Canon: Artistic Value in an Era of Doubt*. Oxford: Oxford University Press, 2007.
Crowther, Paul. *Philosophy After Postmodernism: Civilized Values and the Scope of Knowledge*. London: Routledge, 2003.
Cunningham, Anthony. *The Heart of What Matters: The Role for Literature in Moral Philosophy*. Berkeley: University of California Press, 2001.
Cunningham, Valentine. *In the Reading Gaol: Postmodernity, Texts and History*. Oxford: Blackwell, 1994.
—. *Reading After Theory*. Oxford; Blackwell, 2002.

—. "The Best Stories in the Best Order? Canons, Apocryphas and (Post)Modern Reading." *Literature and Theology*. 14.1 (2000): 69-80.

Dale, Peter Allan. "Charlotte Brontë's 'Tale Half-Told': The Disruption of Narrative Structure in *Jane Eyre.*" *New Casebooks: Jane Eyre*. Ed. Heather Glen. New York: St Martin's Press, 1997. 205-26.

Daley, Kenneth. *The Rescue of Romanticism: Walter Pater and John Ruskin*. Athens: University of Ohio Press, 2001.

Davies, Gaius. "Grace Abounding: John Bunyan (1628-1688)." *Genius, Grief and Grace*. Fearns: Christian Focus, 2001. 53-90.

Davies, Michael. *Graceful Reading: Theology and Narrative in the Works of John Bunyan*. Oxford: Oxford University Press, 2002.

Davies, Michael. "Sex and Sexual Wordplay in the Writings of John Bunyan." *Trauma and Transformation: The Political Progress of John Bunyan*. Ed. Vera J. Camden. Stanford: Stanford University Press, 2008. 100-119.

Dearborn, Kerry. *Baptized Imagination: The Theology of George MacDonald*. Aldershot: Ashgate, 2006.

Denham, A. E. *Metaphor and Moral Experience*. Oxford: Clarendon Press, 2000.

Dennis, S. K. "*Sehnsucht* and the Island Motif in C. S. Lewis' *Out of the Silent Planet* and *Perelandra*." MA Thesis. Florida Atlantic University, 1978.

Diamond, Cora. "Martha Nussbaum and the Need for Novels." *Renegotiating Ethics in Literature, Philosophy, and Theory*. Eds. Richard Freadman, Jane Adamson and David Parker. Cambridge: Cambridge University Press, 1998. 39-64.

Donaldson, Mara. *Holy Places Are Dark Places: C. S. Lewis and Paul Ricoeur on Narrative Transformation*. Lanham: University Press of America, 1988.

Duitman, Henry E. 'Practical Aesthetics.' <http://hompages.dordt.edu/~hduitman/musiced/practicalaesthetics.htm> 26 August 2008.

Dunan-Page, Anne. *Grace Overwhelming: John Bunyan, The Pilgrim's Progess and the Extremes of the Baptist Mind*. Oxford: Peter Lang, 2008.

Durie, Dale. "In Biblical Bounds: Using the Imagination within Biblical Limits." *Preaching to Listeners: Communication with Contemporary Listeners*. Evangelical Homiletics Society: 2002.

Dyrness, William A. "Aesthetics in the Old Testament: Beauty in Context." *Journal of the Evangelical Theological Society* 28.4 (1985): 421-32.

Dyrness, William A. *Reformed Theology and Visual Culture: The Protestant Imagination from Calvin to Edwards*. Cambridge: Cambridge University Press, 2004.

Edwards, Michael. *Towards a Christian Poetics*. London: Macmillan, 1984.

Eichrodt, Walter. *Theology of the Old Testament*. Vol. 2. London: SCM Press, 1961-1967.

Eliot, T. S. "Religion and Literature." *Selected Essays*. New York: Harcourt,

Brace & World, 1935. 343-54.
Elliot, Elisabeth. *A Chance to Die: The Life and Legacy of Amy Carmichael.* Grand Rapids: Fleming H. Revell Company, 1987.
Elmsley, Sarah. *Jane Austen's Philosophy of the Virtues.* New York: Palgrave Macmillan, 2005.
Erdt, Terrence. *Jonathan Edwards: Art and the Sense of the Heart.* Amherst: University of Massachusetts Press, 1980.
Eslinger, Richard L. *Narrative and Imagination: Preaching the Worlds That Shape Us.* Minneapolis: Fortress Press, 1995.
Eveson, Philip H. *The Book of Origins: Genesis Simply Explained.* Darlington: Evangelical Press, 2001.
Ezell, Margaret, "Bunyan's Women, Women's Bunyan." *Trauma and Transformation: The Political Progress of John Bunyan.* Ed. Vera J. Camden. Stanford: Stanford University Press, 2008. 63-80.
Farley, Edward. *Faith and Beauty: A Theological Aesthetic.* Aldershot: Ashgate, 2001.
Faye, Deirdre Le, Ed. *Jane Austen's Letters: New Edition.* Oxford: Oxford University Press, 1995.
Ferguson, Everett. *Backgrounds of Early Christianity.* Grand Rapids: Eerdmans, 1987.
Ferguson, Sinclair. *Mastering the Old Testament: Daniel.* Ed. Lloyd J. Ogilvie. Dallas: Word Publishing, 1988.
Ferretter, Luke. "The Power and the Glory: The Aesthetics of the Hebrew Bible." *Literature and Theology* 18.2 (2004): 123-38.
—. *Towards a Christian Literary Theory.* London: Palgrave Macmillan, 2003.
Fischer, Kathleen R. *The Inner Rainbow: The Imagination in the Christian Life.* New York: Paulist Press, 1983.
Fish, Stanley. "Progress in the Pilgrim's Progress." *Self-Consuming Artifacts: The Experience of Seventeenth-Century Literature.* Berkeley: University of California Press, 1972. 224-64.
Forbes, Cheryl. *Imagination: Embracing a Theology of Wonder.* Portland: Multnomah Press, 1986.
Frame, John. "Images of God." *Doctrine of God.* Philadelphia: Presbyterian and Reformed Publishing, 2002. 362-86.
Franklin, J. Jeffrey. "The Merging of Spiritualities: Jane Eyre as Missionary of Love." *Nineteenth-Century Literature* 49.4 (1995): 456-82.
Furey, Constance. *Erasmus, Contarini, and the Religious Republic of Letters.* Cambridge: Cambridge University Press, 2006.
Gadamer, Hans Georg. *Truth and Method.* 1965. 2nd ed. London: Sheed and Ward, 1975.
Gaskell, Elizabeth. *The Life of Charlotte Brontë.* 1857. London: Penguin, 1997.
Gaut, Berys. *Art, Emotion and Ethics.* Oxford: Oxford University Press, 2007.
Gay, Penny. *Jane Austen and the Theatre.* Cambridge: Cambridge University Press, 2002.
Giffin, Michael. *Jane Austen and Religion: Salvation and Society in Georgian England.* New York: Palgrave Macmillan, 2002.

Gilbert, Sandra M. and Susan Gubar. "A Dialogue of Self and Soul: Plain Jane's Progress." *The Madwoman in the Attic: The Woman Writer and the Nineteenth-Century Literary Imagination.* New Haven: Yale University Press, 1979. 336-71.
Gilmour, Robert. *Samuel Rutherford: A Study Biographical and Somewhat Critical, in the History of the Scottish Covenant.* Edinburgh: Oliphant, Anderson & Ferrier, 1904.
Gitterman, Debra. "'Making Out' Jane Eyre." *English Literary History* 74.3 (2007): 557-81.
Glen, Heather. *Charlotte Brontë: The Imagination in History.* Cambridge: Cambridge University Press, 2002.
—. "Introduction." *New Casebooks: Jane Eyre.* Ed. Heather Glen. New York: St. Martin's Press, 1997. 1-33.
Glyer, Diana. *The Company They Keep: C. S. Lewis and J. R. R. Tolkien as Writers in Community.* Kent, Ohio: Kent State University Press, 2007.
Goldberg, S. L. *Agents and Lives: Moral Thinking in Literature.* Cambridge: Cambridge University Press, 1993.
Greaves, Richard. *Glimpses of Glory: John Bunyan and English Dissent.* Stanford: Stanford University Press, 2002.
Green, Garrett. *Imagining God: Theology and the Religious Imagination.* Grand Rapids: William B. Eerdmans, 1989.
—. *Theology, Hermeneutics, and Imagination: The Crisis of Interpretation at the End of Modernity.* Cambridge: Cambridge University Press, 2000.
Gribble, Jennifer. "Jane Eyre's Imagination." *Nineteenth-Century Fiction* 23.3 (1968): 279-93.
Guin, Ursula Le. "The Ones Who Walk Away from Omelas." *The Wind's Twelve Quarters.* New York: Harper & Row, 1975.
Haggis, J. "Ironies of Emancipation: Changing Configurations of 'Women's Work' in the 'Mission of Sisterhood' to Indian Women." *Feminist Review* 65.1 (2000): 108-26.
Haines, Simon. "Deepening the Self: The Language of Ethics and the Language of Literature." *Renegotiating Ethics in Literature, Philosophy, and Theory.* Eds. Richard Freadman, Jane Adamson and David Parker. Cambridge: Cambridge University Press, 1998. 21-38.
Hart, Ray L. *Unfinished Man and the Imagination: Toward an Ontology and a Rhetoric of Revelation.* New York: Herder and Herder, 1968.
Hart, Trevor. "Imagination and Responsible Reading." *Renewing Biblical Interpretation.* Eds. Colin Greene, Craig Bartholomew and Karl Moller. Vol. 1. Carlisle: Paternoster Press, 2000. 307-34.
—. "Imagination for the Kingdom of God? Hope, Promise, and the Transformative Power of an Imagined Future." *God Will Be All in All: The Eschatology of Jurgen Moltmann.* Ed. Richard Bauckham. Edinburgh: T & T Clark, 1999. 49-76.
—. "Introduction." *Faithful Performances: Enacting Christian Tradition.* Eds. Trevor A. Hart and Steven R. Guthrie. Aldershot: Ashgate, 2007. 1-9.
—. "The Sense of an Ending: Finitude and the Authentic Performance of Life."

Faithful Performances: Enacting Christian Tradition. Eds. Trevor A. Hart and Steven R. Guthrie. Aldershot: Ashgate, 2007. 167-86.

—. "Tolkien, Creation and Creativity." *Tree of Tales: Tolkien, Literature, and Theology.* Eds. Trevor Hart and Ivan Khovacs. Waco: Baylor University Press, 2007. 39-53.

Hass, Andrew. "Seeing Through a Glass Face to Face." *Believing in the Text: Essays from the Centre for the Study of Literature, Theology and the Arts, University of Glasgow.* Eds. David Jasper, George Newlands and Darlene Bird. Oxford: Peter Lang, 2004. 57-73.

Havely, Cecily Palser. "Troubles With Men." *The English Review* 17.2 (2006): 21-23.

Hayes, Richard B., *The Conversion of the Imagination: Paul as Interpreter of Israel's Scripture.* Cambridge: Eerdmans, 2005.

Heilman, Robert B. "Charlotte Brontë, Reason, and the Moon." *Nineteenth-Century Fiction* 14.4 (1960): 283-302.

Hein, Rolland. *Christian Mythmakers: C. S. Lewis, Madeleine L'Engle, J. R. R. Tolkien, George Macdonald, G. K. Chesterton, Charles Williams, John Bunyan, Walter Wangerin, Robert Siegel, and Hannah Hurnard.* Chicago: Cornerstone Press, 1998.

Heinemann, Margaret. *Puritanism and Theatre: Thomas Middleton and Opposition Drama Under the Early Stuarts.* Cambridge: Cambridge University Press, 1980.

Homans, Margaret. "Dreaming of Children: Literalisation in *Jane Eyre.*" *New Casebooks: Jane Eyre.* Ed. Heather Glen. New York: St. Martin's Press, 1997. 130-46.

Hooper, Walter. *C. S. Lewis: A Companion and Guide.* San Francisco: Harper, 1996.

Hopkins, Gerard Manley. *The Poems of Gerard Manley Hopkins.* 1918. 4th ed. London: Oxford University Press, 1967.

Hoyle, Lydia Huffman. "Nineteenth-Century Single Women and Motivation for Mission." *International Bulletin of Missionary Research* 20.2 (1996): 58-63.

Hughes, R. Kent. *Disciplines of Grace: God's Ten Words for a Vital Spiritual Life.* Wheaton: Crossway Books, 1993.

Innes, A. T. "Samuel Rutherfurd." *Studies in Scottish History, Chiefly Biographical.* London, 1892. 3-60.

Ishida, Tomoo. *History and Historical Writing in Ancient Israel.* Studies in Biblical Historiography. Leiden: Brill, 1999.

Jacobs, Alan. "George Eliot: Good Without God." *First Things* 102 April (2000): 50-3.

—. *A Theology of Reading: The Hermeneutics of Love.* Oxford: Westview Press, 2001.

—. *What Became of Wystan: Change and Continuity in Auden's Poetry.* Fayetteville: University of Arkansas Press, 1998.

Jasper, David. *The New Testament and the Literary Imagination.* London: Macmillan, 1987.

Jay, Elisabeth. *The Religion of the Heart: Anglican Evangelicalism and the Nineteenth-Century Novel*. Oxford: Clarendon Press, 1979.

Jeffrey, David Lyle. *People of the Book: Christian Identity and Literary Culture*. Grand Rapids: Eerdmans, 1996.

Jenkins, Ruth. *Reclaiming Myths of Power: Women Writers and the Victorian Spiritual Crisis*. Lewisburg: Bucknell University Press, 1995.

Johnson, B. A. "Falling into Allegory: The "Apology" to the Pilgrim's Progress and Bunyan's Scriptural Methodology." *Bunyan in Our Time*. Ed. R. G. Collmer. Kent: Kent State University Press, 1989. 113-37.

Johnson, Galen K. "Glimpses of Glory: John Bunyan and English Dissent." *Christianity and Literature* 52.4 (2003): 577-61.

Johnson, Luke Timothy. "Imagining the World Scripture Imagines." *Theology and Scriptural Imagination*. Eds. L. Gregory Jones and James J. Buckley. Oxford: Blackwell, 1998. 3-18.

Johnson, Mark. *The Body in the Mind: The Bodily Basis of Meaning, Imagination, and Reason*. Chicago: University of Chicago Press, 1987.

Joshua, Essaka. "'Almost My Hope of Heaven': Idolatry and Messianic Symbolism in Charlotte Brontë's *Jane Eyre*." *Philological Quarterly* 81.1 (2002): 81-107.

Kaufman, Geoffrey. *The Theological Imagination: Constructing the Concept of God*. Philadelphia: Westminster Press, 1981.

Kearney, Richard. *Poetics of Imagining: Modern to Post-Modern*. 1991. New ed. Edinburgh: Edinburgh University Press, 1998.

—. *The Wake of Imagination: Ideas of Creativity in Western Culture*. London: Hutchinson, 1988.

Kermode, Frank. *The Sense of an Ending: Studies in the Theory of Fiction*. New York: Oxford University Press, 1967.

Kilby, Clyde S. *The Christian World of C. S. Lewis*. Grand Rapids: Eerdmans, 1964.

Kittel, Gerhard, Geoffrey Bromiley, Eds. *Theological Dictionary of the New Testament*. Vol. 3. Grand Rapids: Eerdmans, 1965.

Koppel, Gene. *The Religious Dimension of Jane Austen's Novels*. London: UMI Research Press, 1988.

Lakoff, George, and Mark Johnson. *Metaphors We Live By*. Chicago: University of Chicago Press, 1980.

Langan, Janine. "The Christian Imagination." *The Christian Imagination*. Ed. Leland Ryken. Colorado Springs: Shaw, 2002. 63-80.

Laverty, Megan. *Iris Murdoch's Ethics: A Consideration of her Romantic Vision*. London: Continuum, 2007.

Lewis, C. S. *Allegory of Love: A Study in Medieval Tradition*. Oxford: Oxford University Press, 1936.

—. "Bluspels and Flalansferes." *Rehabilitations and Other Essays*. London: Oxford University Press, 1939. 135-58.

—. "Christianity and Culture." *C. S. Lewis: Essay Collection and Other Short Pieces*. Ed. L. Walmsley. London: HarperCollins, 2000. 71-92.

—. "Christianity and Literature." *C. S. Lewis: Essay Collection and Other Short Pieces.* Ed. Lesley Walmsley. London: Harper Collins, 2000. 411-20.
—. *An Experiment in Criticism.* Cambridge: Cambridge University Press, 1961.
—. *The Four Loves.* London: Fontana Books, 1963.
—, Ed. *George Macdonald: An Anthology.* London: Geoffrey Bles, 1946.
—. *Mere Christianity.* Glasgow: Fontana Books, 1952.
—. "Myth Became Fact." *C. S. Lewis: Essay Collection and Other Short Pieces.* Ed. L. Walmsley. London: HarperCollins, 2000. 138-42.
—. "A Note on Jane Austen." *Selected Literary Essays by C. S. Lewis.* Ed. Walter Hooper. Cambridge: Cambridge University Press, 1969. 175-86.
—. "The Pilgrim's Regress." *C. S. Lewis: Selected Books.* London: HarperCollins, 2002. 1-221.
—. *Surprised by Joy: The Shape of My Early Life.* Glasgow: HarperCollins, 1955.
—. *Till We Have Faces.* San Diego: Harcourt, 1956.
—. "Transposition." *C. S. Lewis: Essay Collection and Other Short Pieces.* Ed. L. Walmsley. London: HarperCollins, 2000. 267-78.
—. "The Vision of John Bunyan." *Selected Literary Essays.* Ed. Walter Hooper. Cambridge: Cambridge University Press, 1969. 146-53.
—. "The Weight of Glory." *C. S. Lewis: Essay Collection and Other Short Pieces.* Ed. L. Walmsley. London: HarperCollins, 2000. 96-106.
Lewis, W. H., Ed. *Letters of C. S. Lewis.* New York: Harcourt Brace Jovanovich, 1966.
Lilley, Philip W. "Samuel Rutherford, 1600-1661." *Transactions of the Hawick Archaeological Society,* 1935. 11-15.
Loades, David Brown and Ann, Eds. *Christ: The Sacramental Word.* London: SPCK, 1996.
Loane, Marcus. "Samuel Rutherford: The Saint of the Covenant." *Makers of Religious Freedom in the Seventeenth Century.* London: SCM, 1960. 57-102.
Lombardi, Elena. *The Syntax of Desire: Language and Love in Augustine, the Modistae, Dante.* Toronto: University of Toronto Press, 2007.
Longman III, Tremper. *Song of Songs.* Grand Rapids: Eerdmans, 2001.
Lundin, Roger. *The Culture of Interpretation: Christian Faith and the Postmodern World.* Grand Rapids: Eerdmans, 1993.
—, Ed. *Disciplining Hermeneutics: Interpretation in Christian Perspective.* Leicester: Apollos, 1997.
—. "Skipping the History: The Question of Art as Sacrament." *Image: A Journal of the Arts* 35 (2002): 83-91.
Lutzker, Emily. "Ethics of the Sublime in Postmodern Culture." 1997. <http://www.egs.edu/mediaphi/Vol2/Sublime.html> 26 August 2008.
Luxon, T. H. *Literal Figures: Puritan Allegory and the Reformation Crisis in Representation.* Chicago: University of Chicago Press, 1995.
Lynch, Beth. *John Bunyan and the Language of Conviction.* Cambridge: D. S.

Brewer, 2004.
Lyons, J. D. "Descartes and Modern Imagination." *Philosophy and Literature* 23.2 (1999): 302-12.
Lyotard, Jean-François. *Lessons on the Analytic of the Sublime*. Trans. E. Rottenberg. Stanford: Stanford University Press, 1994.
—. *The Postmodern Condition: A Report on Knowledge*. Trans. G. Bennington and B. Massumi. Manchester: Manchester University Press, 1984.
MacDonald, George. "The Imagination: Its Function and Culture." *A Dish of Orts*. 1907. 2-36.
Machar, A. M. "A Scottish Mystic." *The Andover Review* 6 (1996): 379-95.
Machosky, Brenda. "Trope and Truth in *The Pilgrim's Progress*." *Studies in English Literature, 1500-1900* 47.1 (2007): 179-99.
MacIntyre, Alasdair. *After Virtue: A Study in Moral Theory*. Notre Dame: University of Notre Dame Press, 1981.
Martz, Louis. *The Poetry of Meditation: A Study in English Religious Literature of the Seventeenth Century*. New Haven: Yale University Press, Revised Edition, 1962.
Mathes, Valerie Sherer. "Nineteenth Century Women and Reform: The Women's National Indian Association." *The American Indian Quarterly* 14.1 (1990): 1-18.
Matter, E. Ann. *The Voice of My Beloved: The Song of Songs in Western Medieval Christianity*. Philadelphia: University of Pennsylvania Press, 1990.
McGinn, Bernard. "The Language of Inner Experience in Christian Mysticism." *Spiritus: A Journal of Christian Spirituality* 1.2 (2001): 156-71.
McGinn, Colin. *Mindsight: Image, Dream, Meaning*. Cambridge, Mass.: Harvard University Press, 2005.
McInnis, Jeff. *Shadows and Chivalry: C. S. Lewis and George MacDonald on Suffering, Evil, and Goodness*. Paternoster: Milton Keynes, 2007.
McIntyre, John. *Faith, Theology and Imagination*. Edinburgh: Handsel Press, 1987.
—. *On the Love of God*. London: Collins, 1962.
McQuilkin, Robertson. *Introduction to Biblical Ethics*. Wheaton: Tyndale, 1995.
Meier, Hans H. "Love, Law and Lucre: Images in Rutherfurd's Letters." *Historical and Editorial Essays in Medieval and Early Modern English for Johan Gerritsen*. Eds. H. Wirtjes and M.-J Arn. Groningen, 1985. 77-96.
Meyer, Susan. "Colonialism and the Figurative Strategy of *Jane Eyre*." *New Casebooks: Jane Eyre*. Ed. Heather Glen. New York: St. Martin's Press, 1997. 92-129.
Michie, Elsie. B. "Introduction." *Charlottë Bronte's Jane Eyre: A Casebook*. Oxford: Oxford University Press, 2006. 3-21.
Midgley, Clare. "Female Emancipation in an Imperial Frame: English Women and the Campaign against Sati (Widow-Burning) in India, 1813-30."

Women's History Review 9.1 (2000).
Mills, Kevin. *Justifying Language: Paul and Contemporary Literary Theory.* New York: St. Martin's Press, 1995.
Mithen, S. "The Evolution of Imagination: An Archaeological Perspective." *SubStance* 30.1 and 2 (2001): 28-54.
Moltmann, Jurgen. "Hope and Reality: Contradiction and Correspondence." *God Will Be All in All: The Eschatology of Jurgen Moltmann.* Ed. Richard Bauckham. Edinburgh: T & T Clark, 1999. 77-85.
Mott, Stephen. *Biblical Ethics and Social Change.* Oxford: Oxford University Press, 1982.
Mouw, Richard J. *The God Who Commands: A Study in Divine Command Ethics.* Notre Dame: University of Notre Dame Press, 1990.
—. *He Shines in All That's Fair: Culture and Common Grace.* Grand Rapids: Eerdmans, 2000.
Murphy, Francesca Aran. *Christ the Form of Beauty: A Study in Literature and Theology.* Edinburgh: T&T Clark, 1995.
Murray, John. *Calvin on Scripture and Divine Sovereignty.* Philadelphia: Presbyterian and Reformed Publishing, 1960.
—. *Principles of Conduct: Aspects of Biblical Ethics.* Grand Rapids: Eerdmans, 1957.
Newey, Vincent, Ed. *The Pilgrim's Progress: Critical and Historical Views.* Liverpool: Liverpool University Press, 1980.
Nissen, Johannes. "Bible and Ethics: Moral Formation and Analogical Imagination." *Theology and Literature: Rethinking Reader Responsibility.* Eds. Gaye Williams Ortiz and Clara A. B. Joseph. Houndmills: Palgrave Macmillan, 2006. 81-100.
Nussbaum, Martha. *Love's Knowledge: Essays on Philosophy and Literature.* Oxford: Oxford University Press, 1990.
Packer, J. I. *Honouring the Written Word of God: The Collected Shorter Writings of J. I. Packer, Volume 3.* Carlisle: Paternoster Press, 1999.
Palmer, Frank. *Literature and Moral Understanding: A Philosophical Essay on Ethics, Aesthetics, Education, and Culture.* Oxford: Oxford University Press, 1992.
Paris, Bernard J. "George Eliot's Religion of Humanity." *George Eliot: A Collection of Critical Essays.* Ed. George R. Creeger. Englewood: Prentice Hall, 1970.
Parker, David. "Introduction: The Turn to Ethics in the 1990s." *Renegotiating Ethics in Literature, Philosophy, and Theory.* Eds. Richard Freadman Jane Adamson and David Parker. Cambridge: Cambridge University Press, 1998. 1-17.
Pater, Walter. *The Renaissance: Studies in Art and Poetry.* Ed. Adam Phillips. Oxford: Oxford University Press, 1986.
Peterson, Eugene. *Subversive Spirituality.* Grand Rapids: Eerdmans, 1994.
Pettit, Norman. *The Heart Prepared: Grace and Conversion in Puritan Spiritual Life.* New Haven: Yale University Press, 1966.
—. *The Heart Renewed: Assurance of Salvation in New England Spiritual Life.*

Lampeter: The Edward Mellen Press, 2004.
Philip, Adam. "The Golden Book of Love." *The Devotional Literature of Scotland*. London: James Clark & Co, 1920. 116-25.
Pinnock, Clark H. *The Scriptural Principle*. San Francisco: Harper & Row, 1984.
Polhemus, Robert M. *Erotic Faith: Being in Love from Jane Austen to D. H. Lawrence*. Chicago: University of Chicago Press, 1990.
Politi, Jina. "*Jane Eyre* Class-Ified." *New Casebooks: Jane Eyre*. Ed. Heather Glen. New York: St. Martin's Press, 1997. 78-91.
Pratt, Richard L. *Designed for Dignity: What God Has Made It Possible for You to Be*. Phillipsburg: Presbyterian & Reformed Publishing, 1993.
Price, Martin. *Forms of Life: Character and Moral Imagination in the Novel*. New Haven: Yale University Press, 1983.
Prickett, Stephen. *Words and the Word: Language, Poetics and Biblical Interpretation*. Cambridge: Cambridge University Press, 1986.
Pyle, Forest. "A Novel Sympathy: the Imagination of Community in George Eliot." *Novel* 27.1 (1993): 5-23.
Rae, Scott B. *Moral Choices: An Introduction to Ethics*. Grand Rapids: Zondervan, 2000.
Rai, Amit S. "The Black Spectre of Sympathy: The "Occult" Relation in *Jane Eyre*." *Literature Interpretation Theory* 14.3 (2003): 243-68.
Rendell, Kingsley G. *Samuel Rutherford: A New Biography of the Man and His Ministry*. Fearn: Christian Focus, 2003.
Ricoeur, Paul. "The Bible and the Imagination." *The Bible as a Document of the University*. Chicago: Scholars Press, 1995. 49-75.
—. "Biblical Time." *Figuring the Sacred: Religion, Narrative, and Imagination*. Minneapolis: Fortress Press, 1995. 167-80.
—. "Creativity in Language: Word, Polysemy, Metaphor." *Philosophy Today* 17 (1973): 97-111.
—. *Interpretation Theory: Discourse and the Surplus of Meaning*. Fort Worth: Texas Christian University Press, 1976.
—. "Naming God." *Figuring the Sacred: Religion, Narrative, and Imagination*. Minneapolis: Fortress Press, 1995. 217-35.
Robert, Dana. "Evangelist or Homemaker? Mission Strategies of Early Nineteenth-Century Missionary Wives in Burma and Hawaii." *International Bulletin of Missionary Research* 17.1 (1993): 4-10.
Roberts, Maurice. "Samuel Rutherford: The Comings and Goings of the Heavenly Bridegroom." *The Trials of Puritanism: papers read at the 1993 Westminster Conference*, 1993. 119-34.
Robinson, Edward. *The Language of Mystery*. London: SCM Press, 1987.
Rookmaaker, H. R. *The Creative Gift: Essays on Art and the Christian Life*. Westchester, Illinois: Cornerstone Books, 1981.
Rosner, Brian S. *Paul, Scripture, and Ethics*. Grand Rapids: Baker Books, 1994.
Ross, J. M. "Post-Reformation Spirituality 3: Samuel Rutherford." *The Month*. July (1975): 207-11.

Ruderman, Anne Crippen. *The Pleasures of Virtue: Political Thought in the Novels of Jane Austen.* London: Rowmand and Littlefield, 1995.
Ryken, Leland, Ed. *The Christian Imagination.* Colorado Springs: Shaw Books, 2002.
—. *The Liberated Imagination: Thinking Christianly About the Arts.* Colorado Springs: Shaw Books, 1989.
—. "Literature in Christian Perspective." *God and Culture: Essays in Honor of Carl F. H. Henry.* Eds. J. D. Woodbridge and D. A. Carson. Grand Rapids: William B. Eerdmans, 1993. 215-34.
—. *Triumphs of the Imagination: Literature in Christian Perspective.* Downers Grove: InterVarsity Press, 1979.
—. *Worldly Saints: The Puritans as They Really Were.* Grand Rapids: Zondervan, 1986.
Ryle, J. C. *Old Paths: Being Plain Statements on Some of the Weightier Matters of Christianity.* Cambridge: James Clark & Co. 1972.
Sayers, Dorothy L. *The Mind of the Maker.* London: Methuen, 1941.
Schad, John. *Queer Fish: Christian Unreason from Darwin to Derrida.* Brighton: Sussex Academic Press, 2004.
Schaeffer, Francis A. *Art & the Bible : Two Essays.* Downers Grove, Ill: InterVarsity Press, 1973.
Schakel, Peter J. *Imagination and the Arts in C. S. Lewis: Journeying to Narnia and Other Worlds.* Columbia: University of Missouri Press, 2003.
—. *Reason and Imagination in C. S. Lewis: A Study of 'Till We Have Faces'.* Grand Rapids: Eerdmans, 1984.
Shakespeare, William. *A Midsummer Night's Dream.* New York: Airmont Publishing, 1965.
Schoenfeldt, Michael C. *Bodies and Selves in Early Modern England: Physiology and Inwardness in Spenser, Shakespeare, Herbert, and Milton.* Cambridge: Cambridge University Press, 1999.
Seerveld, Calvin. *Bearing Fresh Olive Leaves: Alternative Steps in Understanding Art.* Toronto: Tuppence Press, 2000.
Sharrock, Roger. *John Bunyan: The Pilgrim's Progress.* London: Edward Arnold, 1966.
Sheldrake, Philip F. "Christian Spirituality as a Way of Living Publicly: A Dialectic of the Mystical and Prophetic." *Spiritus: A Journal of Christian Spirituality* 3.1 (2003): 19-37.
Sherry, Patrick. *Spirit and Beauty: An Introduction to Theological Aesthetics.* Oxford: Clarendon Press, 1992.
Sherry, Patrick. *Spirit and Beauty: An Introduction to Theological Aesthetics.* 2nd ed. London: SCM Press, 2002.
Sherry, Patrick. *Images of Redemption: Art, Literature and Salvation.* London: T&T Clark, 2003.
Showalter, Elaine. *A Literature of Their Own: British Women Novelists from Brontë to Lessing.* Expanded ed. Princeton: Princeton University Press, 1999.
Sidney, Philip. *Defence of Poesie.* London: Ponsonby, 1595.

Sim, Stuart. *Negotiations with Paradox: Narrative Practice and Narrative Form in Bunyan and Defoe*. Savage: Barnes & Noble, 1990.
Simpson, Richard. *North British Review* 52 (1870): 129-52.
Smith, C. Ryder. *The Biblical Doctrine of Man*. London: Epworth Press, 1951.
Stachniewski, John. *The Persecutory Imagination: English Puritanism and the Literature of Religious Despair*. Oxford: Clarendon Press, 1991.
Steiner, George. *Real Presences: Is There Anything in What We Say?* London: Faber and Faber, 1989.
Thiselton, Anthony. *Interpreting God and the Postmodern Self*. Edinburgh: T & T Clark, 1995.
Thomas, Ronald. "*The Advertisement* of Jane Eyre." *Charlottë Bronte's Jane Eyre: A Casebook*. Ed. Elsie B. Michie. Oxford: Oxford University Press, 2006. 47-77
Thormählen, Marianne. *The Brontës and Religion*. Cambridge: Cambridge University Press, 1999.
Til, Cornelius Van. *The Protestant Doctrine of Scripture*. Phildalephia: den Dulk Christian Foundation, 1967.
Tkacz, Catherine Brown. "The Bible in *Jane Eyre*." *Christianity and Literature* 44.1 (1994): 3-27.
Tolkien, J. R. R. "On Fairy-Stories." *Tree and Leaf; Smith of Wootton Major; the Homecoming of Boerhnoth*. London: Allen & Unwin, 1975. 11-79.
Turner, Denys. *The Darkness of God: Negativity in Christian Mysticism*. Cambridge: Cambridge University Press, 1995.
Vanhoozer, Kevin J. *Biblical Narrative in the Philosophy of Paul Ricoeur: A Study in Hermeneutics and Theology*. Cambridge: Cambridge University Press, 1990.
—. *The Drama of Doctrine: A Canonical-Linguistic Approach to Christian Theology*. Louisville: Westminster John Knox, 2005.
—. *First Theology: God, Scripture and Hermeneutics*. Downers Grove: InterVarsity Press, 2002.
—. *Is There a Meaning in This Text? The Bible, the Reader and the Morality of Literary Knowledge*. Leicester: Apollos, 1998.
—. "The World Well Staged? Theology, Culture and Hermeneutics." *God and Culture: Essays in Honor of Carl F. H. Henry*. Ed. J. D. Woodbridge. Grand Rapids: William B. Eerdmans, 1993. 1-30.
Vejvoda, K. "Idolatry and *Jane Eyre*." *Victorian Literature and Culture* 31.1 (2003): 241-61.
Veith, Jr. Gene Edward, *State of the Arts: From Bezalel to Mapplethorpe*. Wheaton, Illinois: Crossway Books, 1991.
Wallace, Mark I. "Introduction." *Figuring the Sacred: Religion, Narrative, and Imagination*. Minneapolis: Fortress Press, 1995.
Walton, Heather. *Literature, Theology and Feminism*. Manchester: Manchester University Press, 2007.
Warfield, B. B. *The Inspiration and Authority of the Bible*. Philadelphia: Presbyterian and Reformed Publishing, 1948.
Warfield, Benjamin. "Imitating the Incarnation." *The Savior of the World*.

1916. Edinburgh, 1991. 245-70.
Warnock, M. *Imagination*. London: Faber & Faber, 1976.
Weeks, Noel. *Gateway to the Old Testament*. Edinburgh: Banner of Truth Trust, 1995.
Wesley, John. "Spiritual Idolatry." <http://wesley.nnu.edu/JohnWesley/078> 30 August 2008. Copyright 1993-2007 by the Wesley Center for Applied Theology.
Wheeler, Michael. "Religion." *Jane Austen in Context*. Ed. Janet Todd. Cambridge: Cambridge University Press, 2005. 406-14.
White, William Luther. *The Image of Man in C. S. Lewis*. Nashville: Abingdon Press, 1969.
Whyte, A. *Samuel Rutherford and Some of His Correspondents*. Edinburgh, 1894.
Wielenberg, Eric. J. *God and the Reach of Reason: C. S. Lewis, David Hume, and Bertrand Russell*. Cambridge: Cambridge University Press, 2008.
Wilder, Amos. *Theopoetic: Theology and the Religious Imagination*. Philadelphia: Fortress Press, 1976.
Williams, Carolyn. "Closing the Book: The Intertextual End of *Jane Eyre*." *New Casebooks: Jane Eyre*. Ed. Heather Glen. New York: St Martin's Press, 1997. 227-55.
Wolfe, Jesse. "Jane Austen and the Sin of Pride." *Renascence* 51.2 (1999): 110-31.
Wolterstoff, Nicholas. "A Response to Trevor Hart." *Renewing Biblical Interpretation*. Eds. Colin Greene, Craig Bartholomew and Karl Moller. Vol. 1. Carlisle: Paternoster Press, 2000. 335-41.
Woolf, Virginia. "Jane Austen." *The Essays of Virginia Woolf*. Ed. Andrew McNeillie. Vol. 4. London: Hogarth, 1986.
—. *A Room of One's Own*. 1929. Ed. Hermione Lee. London, 1991.
Wordsworth, William. "The Tables Turned." *Wordsworth: Poetical Works*. Ed. T. Hutchinson. Oxford: Oxford University Press, 1973. 377.
Ziegler, Mervin Lee. "Imagination as a Rhetorical Factor in the Works of C. S. Lewis." PhD Thesis. University of Florida, 1973.

Websites

Blue Letter Bible
<http//www.blueletterbible.org/>
Thayer and Smith's Greek Lexicon
<http://www.studylight.org/lex/grk/>

Index

Abrams, M. H. 2, 3, 20.
Adam 51, 52, 130.
Aesthetics: Biblical 60-71, 81-94; Christian 21; Crucified 67, 93, 101, 201-202; Evangelical 63.
Alter, R.: 112, 114-116, 125, 132, 138, 199, 208; *The Art of Biblical Narrative* 113.
Alliston, A. 128.
Ames, W. 61.
Apollo 67.
Apuleius: *The Golden Ass* 178.
Aristotle: 121, 128; and wisdom 108.
Arnold, M. 2, 16, 108, 112.
Auden, W. H. 100.
Auerbach, E. 113.
Augustine: 10, 96, 133, 144, 165, 180, 185; and hermeneutics 94, 101; *On Christian Doctrine* 9.
Austen, J.: 5, 23, 24, 105, 122, 123; *Letters* 112; *Mansfield Park* 118; and practical Aristotelianism 123; *Pride and Prejudice* 30, 107, 112, 125-140.
Austin, M. 64.
Avis, P. 12, 13, 15, 16, 22, 49, 80; *God and the Creative Imagination* 14.
Babel 53.
Bakhtin, M. 19, 101, 102, 103, 106, 121.
Barfield, O. 173.
Barth, K. 8.
Barthes, R. 105, 207.
Basil the Great 122.
Bauckham, R. 165-167, 179.
Baurain, B. 191.
Bausch, J. 204.
Bavinck, H. 29.
Baxter, R. 61-62, 97.
Beaty, J. 146, 147.
Beauty 25, 26, 66-70, 85-86.
Begbie, J. 22, 43, 55.
Belsey, C. 126.
Bernard of Clairvaux 83, 93.

Bezalel 25, 54, 55.
Bible 1, 5, 6, 7, 12, 15, 16, 17-18, 24, 32-36, 44, 45-49, 71, 73-74; and artistry 62; and ethics 111; and plotline 46, 53.
Blake, W. 56.
Bonar, A. 82.
Booth, W. 121.
Branch, L. 62.
Bray, J. 127.
Brontë, C.: 5, 24; *Jane Eyre* 30, 71, 141-168, 209; and Romanticism 142-143, 158-159, 161, 163, 165, 167.
Brontë, P. 143.
Brown, D.: *Christ* 16.
Bruce, F. F. 8.
Bryant, D. 12, 13, 14, 22, 42.
Bunyan, J.: 5, 23, 72, 146, 180; and Dissent 64, 71; and Freudian interpretation 65; *Grace Abounding* 65, 68; *The Holy War* 65; *The Pilgrim's Progress* 29, 59-71, 72, 75, 79, 84, 162, 207; and women 64.
Burke, E. 28.
Busbie, Lady 91.
Butler, M. 62.
Cain 53.
Caleb 82.
Calling 55, 152-154, 156, 158, 163.
Calvin, J.: 7, 91, 94, 105, 109, 139, 148, 208; *Institutes of the Christian Religion* 6, 95; *suavitas* 96.
Calvinism 5, 28, 70, 85, 88, 110, 154.
Card, M. 63.
Carmichael, A. 158.
Carson, D.A.: *The Gagging of God* 10.
Cecil, R. 90.
Characters 116-119.
Church Fathers 6.
Clowney, E. P. 25, 66.
Coffey, J. 88, 104.
Coleridge, S. T. 2, 13, 14, 41, 65, 161, 187.

Cooke, M. A. 158.
Coulson, J.: *Religion and Imagination* 15.
Creation 16, 20, 22, 50-52, 53, 67, 77, 78, 160, 175, 205, 206-207.
Cross 32.
Crowther, P. 107.
Cunningham, V. 8, 9.
Dale, P. A. 154, 164.
Daley, K. 26.
Dante 123.
David 35, 194, 204, 205.
Davies, M. 64.
Dearborn, K. 19, 99.
Deconstructionism 8, 9, 17.
Denham, A. E. 110.
Derrida, J. 9, 17, 178.
Donaldson, M. 185.
Dooyeweerd, H. 29.
Dunan-Page, A. 64.
Dyrness, W. 59.
Edwards, J.: 32, 66, 85-86, 94, 96, 98, 100, 104, 106; and imagination 97, 99.
Edwards, M. 52, 79, 130.
Edwards, S. 97.
Elijah 42.
Eliot, G.: 2; moral sympathy 23-24.
Eliot, T. S. 15.
Emsley, S. 112, 122, 126.
Enlightenment 4, 13, 22, 165.
Erdt, T. 96.
Eschatology 48, 53, 164, 165-168, 169, 177, 179, 185, 210.
Eslinger, R. 44, 193, 195-200, 203.
Eucharist 16, 43, 105, 199, 208.
Evangelicalism 5, 11, 23, 112, 141-144, 155, 161, 163.
Eve 51, 52.
Ezell, M. 64.
Fairy-stories 76, 78, 178.
Fall 52, 77, 203.
Farley, E. 26.
Fergus, J. 137.
Ferguson, S. 198.
Ferretter, L. 9, 66, 160.
Fischer, K.: 12, 13, 16, 22; *The Hidden Rainbow* 14.
Forbes, C. 22.
Foucault, M. 105.

Frye, N. 72.
Furey, C. 95.
Gadamer, H. G.: 12, 21, 108, 197, 200; and prejudice 112, 122, 188.
Gaut, B. 107, 119.
Gay, P. 126.
Genre 44, 47, 73-74, 171, 197.
Gettelman, D. 141.
Giffin, M. 131, 132.
Gilbert, S.: 157; *The Madwoman in the Attic* 145.
Glen, H. 162-163, 164.
Glyer, D. 21, 76.
Goldberg, S. L. 107, 108.
Golden Rule 10, 148.
Greaves, R. 59.
Green, G.: 22, 29, 37, 39, 42; *Imagining God* 13.
Gribble, J.: "Jane Eyre's Imagination" 158-159.
Gubar, S.: 157; *The Madwoman in the Attic* 145.
Haas, A. W. 203.
Hamilton, B. 92.
Hamilton, J. 93.
Hardy, T. 2.
Hart, R. L. 142.
Hart, T. 17, 21, 165-167, 179, 191.
Havely, C. P. 149.
Hayes, R. B. 10.
Heart 31, 33-40, 41, 96, 142, 205-206.
Higher Criticism 2, 3.
Hobbesianism 110.
Hopkins, G. M. 202.
Hoyle, L. H. 154.
Hume, D. 41.
Iconoclasm 60.
Idolatry 14, 141-142, 144-156, 209.
Image of God 25, 50-51, 56, 59, 76, 77, 95-96, 109, 139, 154, 207.
Imagination: 1, 26, 31, 34, 193; and creativity 19, 36, 41, 54, 56, 60, 71-79, 171, 206; definition 32-45; and desire 142-143, 161, 164, 189; evil uses 12, 54, 59, 99, 115, 172, 209; faculty psychology 40; and faith 22-23, 31, 43, 49-50, 80-81, 169, 209; Hebraic 33; and the Holy Spirit 19, 97, 146, 157-

158, 205; and hope 48-49, 143, 158, 167-168, 169, 190-191, 202, 203, 209; and make-believe 118; and meditation 83; moral 24, 107, 110, 112, 113-140; and originality 56-57; postmodern 165-166; and *praxis* 60, 132, 200; realistic 42, 80, 94, 137; relational 101, 202; and sympathy 23; and synthesis 22; and truth 56-57, 59, 176-177, 183-184, 186-187, 200; and typology 47; verbal 115-116, 199; visual/verbal 193-203, 206.
Incarnation 14, 16, 23, 43, 46, 75, 100, 103, 106, 116, 172, 175, 176, 183, 184, 200, 208.
Inklings 76.
Inspiration: 19; and creativity 50-57; and the Holy Spirit 17, 18, 20, 54.
Interpretation: biblical 31, 84; historical-critical method 44; and the Holy Spirit 6-7; Puritan 60.
Intertextuality 73-74, 76.
Ishida, T. 179.
Jacobs, A.: 94, 102, 106, 112, 120-122, 128, 133, 137; *A Theology of Reading* 101.
Jasper, D.: 3, 13, 16, 19, 72; *The New Testament and the Literary Imagination* 15, 17.
Jenkins, R. 23.
John 15, 195.
Johnson, G. 65.
Joshua 82.
Joshua, E. 141, 147, 156, 164.
Jubah 54.
Kafka, F. 178.
Kant, I. 41, 42, 119.
Kaufman, G.: 13; *The Theological Imagination* 12.
Kearney, R. 29, 33, 36.
Keeble, N. 59.
Kenmure, Lady 92, 98.
Kenmure, Viscount 92.
Kermode, F. 178.
Kenosis 101-104, 122.
Koppel, G. 137.
Kuhn, T. 13.
Kuyper, A. 29.

Leavis, F. R. 112.
Le Guin, U. 189.
Lewis, C. S.: 5, 21, 30, 48, 56, 77, 105, 122, 129, 133, 139, 197, 209, 210; "Bluspels and Flanlansferes" 172; "The Chronicles of Narnia" 186; *The Four Loves* 185; "Myth Become Fact" 75, 78; myth, metaphor and Joy 169, 172-192; *Perelandra* 186; *The Pilgrim's Regress* 175, 176, 184; *Surprised By Joy* 177, 188; *Till We Have Faces* 60, 169-70, 178-192; "Transposition" 173, 175; "The Weight of Glory" 177.
Loades, A.: *Christ* 16.
Locke, J. 96.
Longfellow, H. W.: *The Saga of King Olaf* 189.
Lowth, R. 48.
Loyola, I. 91.
Lundin, R.: 4, 5, 20, 21, 55; *Disciplining Hermeneutics* 10.
Lutzker, E. 27.
Lynch, B. 65.
Lyotard, J-F. 4; and the postmodern sublime 27-28.
MacDonald, G. 19, 49, 51, 99, 140.
Machosky, B. 66.
MacIntyre, A. 112, 122, 123, 128.
Marriage 130-132, 156.
Martyn, H. 155.
Martz, L. 83.
Marx, K. 167.
Marxism 9.
McInnis, J. 181.
McIntyre, J.: 22, 29, 31, 41, 42, 43, 44, 49, 80, 94, 104, 147; *Faith, Theology and Imagination* 19.
McWard, R.: *Joshua Redivivus* 82.
Meier, H. H. 82, 89, 91-92.
Metanarrative 28, 31, 45-47, 162.
Miles, M. 197.
Millar, J. H. 87.
Mills, K. 10, 201, 202, 203.
Missionary 152.
Moltmann, J. 67, 167, 188, 200.
Moral Law (or Decalogue) 109, 110, 111, 139, 142.
Moses 54.

Mouw, R. 28, 109, 110, 122, 125, 139.
Murdoch, I. 43, 46, 120-121, 128.
Murphy, F. A.: *Christ the Form of Beauty* 25.
Murray, J. 8.
Mysticism 83, 101.
Naming 51-52.
Narrative 45, 72-73, 112, 113-125, 196, 199.
Nathan 194, 204, 205.
Newman, H. 14.
Niebuhr, R. 21.
Nietzsche, F.: 23, 208; *Twilight of the Gods* 24.
Nissen, J. 10.
Nussbaum, M. 108, 120, 121, 126, 129, 138.
Nussey, E. 148.
Nuttall, A. D. 138.
Oholiab 25, 54, 55.
Otto, R. 184.
Palmer, F. 112, 116-121, 138, 140, 209.
Paris, B. J. 23.
Parker, D. 107.
Pascal, B. 52, 53.
Pater, W.: 27; *The Renaissance* 26.
Paul 45, 55, 56, 134, 144, 147, 193, 194, 197, 198, 199, 200, 201, 202, 203, 210.
Pentecost 173.
Performance 11.
Peterson, E. 106.
Pettit, N. 96.
Polhemus, R. M. 145.
Polyani, M. 22.
Postmodernism 4.
Poststructuralism 9.
Potter, B. 189.
Price, M. 107, 117.
Prickett, S. 2, 3, 4, 8, 16, 17, 19, 72, 105.
Psychoanalysis 9, 160.
Puritans: 60, 70, 96; and aesthetics 98; and the Bible 61; and Covenanters 82, 88, 89; and imagination 99; typology 62.
Pyle, F. 23.
Redemption 67, 169.
Reformation 6.
Reformed theology 80, 94, 95, 101, 104, 105, 108, 208.

Rembrandt 203.
Resurrection 14, 48, 200.
Ricoeur, P.: 13, 19, 29, 31, 60, 71, 72, 76, 79, 118, 174, 176, 178, 191, 196, 207, 208, 210; and metaphor 169-172, 195, 197, 200; and poetic discourse 74-75, 78, 170-172; *The Rule of Metaphor* 170.
Romantic Comedy 129-130.
Romanticism: 4, 13, 21, 26; and aesthetics 18; and imagination 141-142, 144, 157; and original genius 21, 25; and the poet 20, 56.
Rookmaaker, H. 28.
Ruderman, A. C. 123, 130.
Ruskin, J. 26.
Rutherford, S.: 5, 23, 95, 97, 100, 105, 106; *Letters of Samuel Rutherford* 29, 80-94, 98, 99, 101, 103, 104, 208; *Lex Rex* 81; and women 91.
Ryken, L. 28, 56, 103.
Ryle, G. 122.
Salvation 32.
Sapir-Whorf hypothesis 3.
Sartre, J-P. 41, 42.
Sayers, D.: 21, 51; *The Mind of the Maker* 20.
Schad, J. 9.
Schaeffer, F. 28.
Schakel, P.: on C. S. Lewis's use of imagination 187-188.
Shakespeare, W.: *Much Ado About Nothing* 121.
Seerveld, C. 28.
Sermon on the Mount 111, 122, 139.
Seth 53.
Shaftesbury, Lord 122.
Sheldrake, P. F. 95.
Shelley, P. B. 56.
Sherry, P. 20, 32, 86, 93.
Showalter, E. 157.
Sidney, P.: *Defence of Poesie* 56, 71.
Simpson, R. 129.
Stuart, S. 65.
Solomon 35.
Steiner, G.: 22, 115; *Real Presences* 17.
Stockhausen, K. 28.
Strachniewski, J.: 64; *Jane Eyre* 71;

Manichean teleology 65.
Therapy 5.
Thielicke, H. 11.
Thiselton, A. C. 14, 48, 112, 123-124.
Thomas, R. 146.
Thormählen, M. 143, 147, 155.
Tillich, P. 67.
Tkacz, C. 147.
Tolkien, J. R. R.: 29, 60, 77, 79; recovery 78; and sub-creation 21, 76.
Trinity 20.
Tubal-Cain 54.
Turner, D. 96.
Van Til, C. 8.
Vanhoozer, K. J. 9, 10, 14, 16, 17, 19, 28, 44, 76, 78, 94, 105, 106, 199, 208.
Vejvoda, K. 141, 147.
Venn, H. 156.
Walton, H.: and feminist theology 145.
Warfield, B.: 101; *The Inspiration and Authority of the Bible* 7.
Warnock, M. 29, 31, 117, 197, 198.
Weeks, N. 179.

Weil, S. 140.
Wesley, J.: "Spiritual Idolatry" 151.
Westminster Assembly 82, 88.
Wheeler, M. 112.
White, A. 1198.
Whitehead, A. 14.
Wielenberg, E. J. 173.
Wilde, O. 27.
Wilder, A.: 13, 22; *Theopoetic* 12.
Williams, C. 160.
Wittgenstein, L.: 41, 42; *Gestalt* theory 13; language games 117.
Wolfe, J. 107, 128, 129.
Wolterstorff, N. 17.
Woolf, V.: *A Room of One's Own* 157.
Wordsworth, W. 14, 26, 41, 159.
Wright, N. T. 72.
Wright, T. R. 3.
Ziegler, M. L. 181.
Zillah 54.
Zwingli, U. 105.